Technology Supported Learning and Teaching:
A Staff Perspective

John O'Donoghue, University of Wolverhampton, UK

Information Science Publishing

Hershey • London • Melbourne • Singapore

Acquisitions Editor:	Michelle Potter
Development Editor:	Kristin Roth
Senior Managing Editor:	Amanda Appicello
Managing Editor:	Jennifer Neidig
Copy Editor:	Amanda O'Brien
Typesetter:	Jessie Weik
Cover Design:	Lisa Tosheff
Printed at:	Integrated Book Technology

Published in the United States of America by
Information Science Publishing (an imprint of Idea Group Inc.)
701 E. Chocolate Avenue
Hershey PA 17033
Tel: 717-533-8845
Fax: 717-533-8661
E-mail: cust@idea-group.com
Web site: http://www.idea-group.com

and in the United Kingdom by
Information Science Publishing (an imprint of Idea Group Inc.)
3 Henrietta Street
Covent Garden
London WC2E 8LU
Tel: 44 20 7240 0856
Fax: 44 20 7379 0609
Web site: http://www.eurospanonline.com

Library of Congress Cataloging-in-Publication Data

Technology supported learning and teaching : a staff perspective / John
    O'Donoghue, Editor.
      p. cm.
      Summary: "This book enumerates the difficulties in implementing
    technology within the educational curriculum in the context of institutional
    policy and procedures"--Provided by publisher.
      Includes bibliographical references and index.
      ISBN 1-59140-962-4 (hardcover) -- ISBN 1-59140-963-2 (softcover)
    -- ISBN 1-59140-964-0 (ebook)
      1. Educational technology. 2. Computer-assisted instruction. 3. Learning.
    I. O'Donoghue, John., 1954-   .
    LB1028.3.T39745 2006
    371.33--dc22
                                                            2006003558

British Cataloguing in Publication Data
A Cataloguing in Publication record for this book is available from the British Library.

All work contributed to this book is new, previously-unpublished material. The views expressed in this book are those of the authors, but not necessarily of the publisher.

Dedication

This book is dedicated to Erika, my beloved mum, whose health is unfortunately beyond the help of technology.

I also wish to dedicate this book to my wife, Carole, and my children, Hannah and Alice, for their patience and forbearance. They do have a lot to contend with.

Technology Supported Learning and Teaching: A Staff Perspective

Table of Contents

Section II: Pedagogical Issues

Preface

The physical environment in which teaching and learning occurs is being replaced with an electronic classroom, but the process of teaching is very much the same. In the second phase, however, we will begin to use technology in new ways, to advance beyond what was possible in the classroom. (Downes, 2004)[1]

Successful use of appropriate innovative technologies by staff and students in education is not a mystical or ethereal goal. Real innovation is often driven by the passionate few, frequently developed in their own time and enthused by a real desire to make a difference to the learning of their students. This motivation is not unique, unusual, or perhaps unexpected. However, the real problem is in "mainstreaming" this innovatory practice or activity.

Technology has been used in education for some years now, yet it still appears not to be making any significant difference to areas of learning which students are exposed to, or the way in which we teach. For example, we still have serried ranks of often hundreds of students in lecture theatres, and we still assess their learning by sitting them in examination halls and asking them to regurgitate memorised information, rather than to apply knowledge.

Academics in the main are not anti-technology. They frequently use the computer to write, analyse, present, and communicate with colleagues and students. So why is it that it is considered sufficient to put online what works off-line and expect the same responses and acceptance from the learner? We would not expect to learn a practical activity solely online, would we? If I want to learn something about nature, I have to experience it. Simply transferring class-based notes into an online repository or virtual learning environment is insufficient if we are to equip our citizens of the 21st century to be able to evaluate, problem solve, criticise, and ultimately create new knowledge.

I will qualify this by suggesting that some of my colleagues feel that they have developed e-learning based courses by "allowing" students to submit assignments by e-mail. We can all identify with colleagues who now put their PowerPoint files online and "advise" students that the formal lecture is no longer required. If this is all there is to this e-learning phenomena, then there is very little to get excited about. It will have changed very little of what we do as educators and, in fact, in some cases, we have regressed into learner disengagement.

The barriers to the use of technology within education are often blamed on the more tangible assets (i.e., communication links, limited hardware, inappropriate software, etc.). This is understandable, but equally easily addressed. The "real" and more difficult issues are with the culture, nature, motivation, and resistance to change within institutions, establishments, and infrastructures and the staff within them.

The content of this book highlights the many areas in which practitioners are attempting to implement learning technologies and reflects themes of current topical interest. The book has three main sections: Infrastructural and Cultural Issues, Pedagogical Issues, and Technological Issues. The first section on infrastructure will consider aspects related to the major infrastructural, cultural, and organisational changes required, if innovation is going to effect any change in the institutional regime. It will focus on the role of the student and the tutor in the learning process. The section on pedagogical issues will present descriptions of the different ways in which practitioners have attempted to use learning technologies and give personal examples which illustrate both the potential and dangers of learning technologies. The section on technological issues will present descriptions of the "tools" that practitioners are using, outline their strengths and weaknesses, and highlight issues that need to be considered when planning to implement new learning technologies. The "tools" covered will include Web-based tools such as virtual learning environments and computer-mediated communication, as well as non Web-based tools such as videoconferencing

While the chapters are located within a section, the nature of technological use cannot be so compartmentalised, so many of the studies and topics reported here cut across many boundaries, infrastructural and cultural, pedagogic and technological. The key issues that will be highlighted and discussed include widening access and participation, student-centred and collaborative learning, and the changing role of the tutor/pupil/student.

Chapter Descriptions

This book consists of 19 chapters, written by 37 authors, loosely grouped into three sections as follows.

Chapter I

This chapter introduces the issues, implications, and cultural upheavals posed for the staff in higher education by the advance of technology. It does so from the standpoint of someone who has been an innovative university teacher, but who is now retired and mainly serves as a grassroots teacher. It summarises the challenges he has been encountering recently, and concludes with questions which he hopes will feature in much imminent, and needed, action research.

Section I: Infrastructural and Cultural Issues

Chapter II

This chapter provides an overview of issues lecturers said they faced when using a virtual learning environment (VLE), such as WebCT or Blackboard, to support their face-to-face teaching. It draws on data collected for doctoral research that explored the reasons lecturers gave for their use of a VLE, the teaching approach supported, and the factors affecting this use. It concentrates on the latter and as such contributes to an under-researched area by reporting the subjective views of academics who have adopted information and communications technology (ICT) to support their teaching.

Chapter III

This chapter describes drivers which have influenced the adoption of e-learning within the UK HE sector and resulted in the increasing adoption of VLEs within institutions. It identifies a range of issues at the institutional and individual academic staff levels which need to be considered and addressed when designing and implementing a VLE within an HE institution. The authors draw on their personal experience in supporting a diverse range of academic staff to integrate e-learning and VLEs within their academic practice, and their experience in implementing VLEs in a range of institutions to develop a series of guidelines and lessons for institutions to consider.

Chapter IV

This chapter details research into the use of asynchronous computer conferencing (ACC) within a campus-based higher education (HE) environment. First, it will highlight some of the issues impacting implementation of the pedagogy. The findings are summarised from a piece of action research that was conducted over a period of five years with final-year undergraduates studying ethics/professional issues in computing. The main objective of this research was to investigate and subsequently develop Salmon's (2000) five-stage strategy for implementing ACC. Finally, the chapter will not only develop the Salmon (2000) model but will also challenge the necessity for e-moderating online discussions within a campus-based HE environment.

Chapter V

This chapter reports a study conducted in 2004 at The Chinese University of Hong Kong (CUHK) aimed at obtaining a much clearer picture about the use of e-learning at the university so as to develop new strategic directions on a firm evidence base. Multiple sources of data were collected, including: site logs, experts' review of selected active Web sites, and interviews with 26 teachers. The data illustrate that e-learning at CUHK is still largely in the "innovators" and "early adopters" stages (Rogers, 2003). There lies a "chasm" ahead inhibiting moving further into the "mainstream" area. The analysis of the data revealed that what the teachers *want* from the technology, what they actually *do*, and what they can have access to for *support* are not totally aligned. The focus of the chapter is on how to improve this alignment so as to bridge the chasm.

Chapter VI

This chapter discusses the provision of continuing professional development (CPD) for allied healthcare professionals (AHPs) through e-learning. External pressures are increasing on AHPs to engage with CPD on a regular basis to improve the quality of care services and facilitate changes in working practice. E-learning has the potential to reach this group of diverse learners and integrate learning into their work schedule at a time and place convenient for them and their employers: eCPD. Ultimately the findings suggest that the solutions provided meet the needs of this specific group of learners and are potentially transferable for all e-learners.

Section II: Pedagogical Issues

Chapter VII

This chapter examines staff perceptions of information and learning technology (ILT) in the learning and skills sector in the UK. It is divided into two sections dealing in turn with pedagogic and cultural issues. The section on pedagogical issues explores the use of the VLE/intranet as an alternative teaching method, and asks why these modes of learning are comparatively rare in the learning and skills sector. This section is also concerned with perceptions of the impact of ILT on students' retention and attainment and explores the concept of variable use and variable impact by level and subject area. The cultural and infrastructure issues explored in the second section relate to staff development and training opportunities (such as the number and type of courses on offer) the additional help requested and the barriers to further uptake.

Chapter VIII

The authors discuss key findings from three focus group discussions held with practitioners in a higher education institution about their experiences of using learning technologies to support student learning. Focus groups were organised in March 2004 to further explore staff responses to a 2003 campus-wide survey, which gave a general overview of learning technology use among teaching staff. The chapter examines the key issues that staff raised during the focus group discussions, including the barriers to and implications of introducing and implementing learning technologies into different subject disciplines within a research-led institution. The question of whether or not the use of learning technologies enhances, or has the potential to enhance, the teaching and learning experience, and the lessons that staff have learnt from this use are also discussed.

Chapter IX

Professional development for academic staff in e-learning is currently a priority for higher education institutions in the Republic of Ireland, as lecturers experience increasing demands to incorporate e-learning into their teaching practice. This chapter reports on the design and implementation of a blended module in e-learning for the continuous professional development of such lecturers. In it the co-authors (who designed and developed the module) discuss the effectiveness of exposing lecturers as online students in order to experience first-hand the advantages and disadvantages of e-learning. It argues that a constructivist, collaborative interaction can provide the scaffolding for lecturers' future journeys into e-learning and into constructivist practices within their own teaching. Important outcomes were achieved in terms of influencing lecturers' thinking and approaches to both their own and to their students' learning.

Chapter X

This chapter reports on an investigation into the institution-wide use of a virtual learning environment (VLE) in a UK University. The aim was to collect information on staff use of the VLE from the student perspective. It was used to evaluate, and reformulate, current e-learning strategic initiatives aimed at enhancing the VLE-based student experience. Three aspects were investigated. These were: (i) the amount, mode, and location of the use of the VLE; (ii) respondents' perceptions of the nature and value of their teachers' VLE support; and (iii) respondents' preferred uses of VLE-based learning. Analysis shows a predominantly information transmission mode of VLE use, with only some use of active learning. Respondents requested more VLE-based formative assessment opportunities. The chapter concludes with five considerations for strategic development of blended e-learning and with three for staff using VLEs.

Chapter XI

This chapter describes the experiences of the authors as lecturers in the development of a new approach to teaching large groups of first-year undergraduate students in psychology. Online material, with a strong emphasis on active engagement, is used to introduce students to the content before undertaking a more detailed reading of the key theoretical and research issues in the textbook. With this introduction to the material, lectures function as a "Review and Discussion" session rather than a didactic monologue. Outcomes of the mixed method suggest no adverse effects on student performance and staff and students evaluate the new approach favourably. The mixed model approach to teaching large groups is one that might be adapted for a range of disciplines and content.

Chapter XII

In this chapter, the authors contend that the encouragement of reflective writing within professional learning programmes is not new. They suggest that electronic technologies, however, afford exciting opportunities to develop this practice to support participative and collaborative learning beyond barriers of time and place. This chapter explores the value of asynchronous dialogue in creating and sustaining communities of practice, with particular emphasis on the role of the e-mentor.

Chapter XIII

This chapter provides a case study of a postgraduate course focused on network-based learning, which from its original design was based on constructivist learning principles. Over time, this course has evolved to incorporate increasing use of learning technology — particularly synchronous and asynchronous communication tools. This evolution has led to a reappraisal and less emphasis on face-to-face class meetings. The course has also increased its student base through distance and offshore offerings. These shifts have translated into changes in the way the course is resourced in both human and infrastructure terms.

Chapter XIV

The authors present research results and advice on the role of the online instructor in relation to a particular example of technology supported learning and teaching — the use of asynchronous discussion forums. Pedagogical issues and studies discussed are based on six years of designing, coordinating, and teaching into Swinburne Astronomy Online (SAO), an online international program. Implementation issues associated with the use of asynchronous forums and the induction of instructors are discussed, as well as the role of the online instructor as a "guide on the side." As an example of issues involved in maintaining a constructive online learning environment, strategies are shared which are used to accommodate students with varying degrees of prior learning.

Section III: Technological Issues

Chapter XV

This chapter discusses the design, technical development, delivery, and evaluation of two online learning activities in environmental geography. A "blended" approach was adopted in order to best integrate the new materials within the existing unit. The primary aim of these online activities was to provide students with opportunities to develop and demonstrate valuable practical skills, while increasing their understanding of environmental management. A purpose-built system was created in order to overcome initial technological challenges. The online activities have already been delivered successfully to a large number of students over two academic years. Evaluation and staff reflection highlight the benefits and limitations of the new activities and the chapter concludes with recommendations for others wishing to adopt a similar approach.

Chapter XVI

This chapter examines the implementation of two learning management systems (LMS) in a university environment. Within the context of a case study and from the perspective of academic users, there is a review of the technological and organizational challenges that arise. There is an in-depth analysis of the implementation in terms of what went well and what should be done differently (i.e., lessons learned). Along with the macro-environmental factors that influence the global e-learning space, the related pedagogical issues, learning models, and technological toolsets are also explored. The authors hope that the experiences chronicled in the case study may act as a lesson to others contemplating such a project of the many technical and organizational issues that need to be addressed, with an emphasis on understanding the importance of the viewpoint of academic users.

Chapter XVII

Synchronous computer conferencing, or "chat," is an effective and versatile tool of online learning, providing users with opportunities for real-time communication. Chat can be used for a variety of educational purposes, including academic seminars, student tutorials, recruitment interviews, and student presentations. In this chapter, the authors argue that through practice, in a socially open learning environment, chat is a focused learning activity, providing a forum where identities emerge and activity is at its greatest. They demonstrate the diverse and growing uses of chat through reference to examples from the chat archives of online distance courses at the University of the Arts London.

Chapter XVIII

This chapter describes the development of software for teaching music and music technology at the University of Huddersfield in three projects spanning the last 12 years. The importance of engaging music students with sound itself and the potential of technology to facilitate this is a key feature of all three projects. The value of developing software that is adaptable and extensible is explained. The lessons that have been learnt in the development of these projects are described, and the chapter ends with a provocative vision for the future.

Chapter XIX

Streamed video is being increasingly introduced into higher education, allowing remote students to participate synchronously or asynchronously. This chapter reports the outcomes arising from three uses of asynchronously streamed video in undergraduate psychology modules. Student feedback and estimation of the impact of using streamed video on examination performance were obtained. The feedback was sufficiently positive and, with reservations, the impact on examination performance was sufficiently apparent for it to be concluded that streamed video offers tangible benefits for the student learning experience and may improve learning performance. Tutors have a flexible, accessible, and productive means of incorporating moving images into learning resources and institutions may need less teaching accommodation.

Conclusion

Computers, technology, and the Internet are a valuable resource, enriching the educational resources we provide already. The key is providing appropriate environments and then reinforcing the experiences with concrete activities. It is important that e-learning be recognised as a supplement to the personal interaction provided by lecturers, teachers, parents, and peers, not a replacement.

Technology provides opportunities never before available — such as remote global communication and file sharing, collaboration and exploration, simulation, and active independent individualised learning. Yet school, college, and university departments are in danger of sabotaging — through incomplete and, in some cases, detrimental implementation plans — the power of technology to transform the teaching and learning process.

The 19 chapters in this book were selected from a large number of submissions. They cover vastly different subjects, group sizes, and institutional types — music to geography, whole class to individual delivery and engagement, large universities to small departments. They are driven by the passion of the staff involved to "make a difference," not by simply using technology, but by applying technology in an innovative way to enhance, enrich, and extend the learning in which our students are involved.

The book presents case studies, research findings, developments, and interventions which will provide guidelines and benchmarks with which the reader will be able to see how, why, and where their own implementation of e-learning and technology-supported learning is either struggling or "not making a difference."

My fervent hope is that this book will make a difference to the many classrooms of computers and technology which increasing pervade and saturate our educational institutions and the lack of "real" or meaningful learner engagement provided by this intrusion.

Endnote

[1]   Downes, S. (2004). From classrooms to learning environments: A midrange projection of e-learning technologies. *College Quarterly, 7*(3).

Acknowledgments

I would like to thank Mehdi Khosrow-Pour the Senior Academic and Technology Editor at IGP for affording me the opportunity to edit this book. It has reinforced my concerns for the intransigence of educational communities to change. Equally, it has reassured me that change is possible, driven by the passion, enthusiasm, and excitement of an increasing band of innovators; 37 of them present their findings here in 19 chapters. I thank them all, however, particular thanks to John Cowan, who is "old" enough to have seen more change, innovation, and deliberation than I. His introductory piece is both illuminating and quizzical. His original title of "Putting New Wines in an Old Bottle" is most adroit.

I also thank all the referees who provided constructive and comprehensive reviews of all the chapters. They work anonymously in the background, but their tireless effort is much appreciated.

Many thanks to the team at Idea Group Publishing, in particularly Michele Rossi and Kristin Roth, who have answered my queries, provided advice, guidance, and support, and patiently tolerated my inability to always keep to the schedule.

Finally, I must again thank all the authors for the excellent contributions. They have shared their work, failures, and successes. E-mail is wonderful and this publication would not have been possible without it. The disadvantage of such a medium is that it does not provide me with the personal opportunity to thank you all for contributing to a book which will hopefully enlighten, support, and encourage colleagues to venture into the technology-supported learning and teaching arena.

John O'Donoghue

Chapter I

Introduction

John Cowan, Napier University, Edinburgh, UK

Abstract

This chapter introduces the issues, implications, and cultural upheavals posed for the staff in higher education by the advance of technology. It does so from the standpoint of someone who has been an innovative and researching university teacher, but who is now retired and mainly serves as a grassroots teacher. It summarises the challenges he has encountered recently, and concludes with some questions which he hopes will feature in much imminent and needed action research.

Our Context

I find it difficult to assemble my own overall impression of the educational context in which the new technologies are undoubtedly being applied on a wide scale, at this point in time. On the one hand, since reviewing the stimulating book edited by Bonk and King (1998), I have encountered or read of many teachers who have epitomised a vision of what *can* be done, and clearly in many places has already *been* achieved, to harness the potential of learner-centred technologies. Recent and forthcoming papers in this field (BJET, 2004, 2005) discuss such sophisticated issues as learner positioning in learning networks, structuring online discussions for meaningful discourse, the use of neural networks to study learning styles as revealed by browsing behaviour, and the desirable characteristics of pedagogical agents as learning companions (PALs) provided from within the software. Heady stuff.

Yet, on the other hand, the devastating worldwide review edited by Carr-Chellman (2005) reports stark contrasts between the rhetoric and the reality. It highlights the ever-increasing gulf between the have's and the have-not's as far as learning technologies are concerned. It emphasises the not always educationally desirable results of the political and economic pressures which are so often thwarting democratic aspirations to ensure equivalence of access and opportunity. It implies that the driving forces which impel change can often lead to education of questionable worth and quality.

My own, admittedly restricted and personal, experience has taken me recently to UK universities where a small minority of specialist academics are doing wonderful things with the new learning technologies. The remainder, and not by any means even *all* of the remainder, are satisfied if they can only put the PowerPoint sequences from their lectures up on their institution's intranet. I encounter a few students who are enjoying deep and fulfilling learning supported splendidly by the new technologies, but for many, e-learning is a misnomer, for what it offers them, at best, is e-reading. The printing workload is simply being transferred from the institutions' print units to the (relatively expensive and slow) printers linked up to the PCs for student use. And the assessment of all of this, sadly, may merely feature regurgitation of what is available on the intranet.

I am confused. What is the overall situation, and where are we heading?

Author's Background

I am an elderly, part-time university teacher. I was appointed to lecture in a university more than 40 years ago, at a time when we wrote in chalk on blackboards and when an overhead projector was either a rarity or a luxury. I moved happily through the transition into individualised resource-based learning, using tape-slide and other pre-recorded instruction. I coped with the advent and impact of word-processing, and then of e-mail, for communications with learners. I mastered the then new challenges posed by telephone conference calls and PowerPoint; and I have even taken on with enthusiasm the facilitation of learning within a virtual learning environment (VLE), with its discussion boards and chat rooms. Nowadays, in consequence, I often work with learners whom I never meet and with whom I may not even speak on the telephone. The role of urgent m-learning, using the mobile telephone in the workplace while a student is in the midst of a placement, is the next challenge apparently emerging for me.

It was as one with great experience of putting newer and newer wines into an older and older bottle, that I hoped to be able to present and represent just such an opening perspective, from the grassroots — without in so doing, I hope, being too pedestrian, or sounding too much like a grumpy old man. To that end, and to introduce the contributions of more profound and experienced writers than I, I shall concentrate here upon my personal experiences of the past few years. I hope that this may facilitate analytical reflection on the part of you, the reader, in identifying the challenges and possibilities which this cultural upheaval has unearthed for all of us in higher education.

My Message in Brief

The new technologies have made noteworthy demands on my students and me for three different reasons:

- They offer my students and me the possibility of working toward valuable higher level learning outcomes, which were mainly outwith the scope of the higher education in which I was educated and in which I began to teach.

- They, therefore, call upon me to work in ways which are radically different from those which served me well in the past.

- The rapidity of change and development almost compel my colleagues and me to become action researchers of our own practices and of their outcomes, with consequent benefit to all concerned.

I shall try to expand upon each of these points briefly, drawing upon personal examples which, I am afraid, are almost all I have to offer in support of what I assert. This, then, will be a personal viewpoint — which I invite readers to test out against their own experiences and to amplify in their reading and assimilation of the chapters which follow.

The Major Challenges

Changed Goals

Higher education today is radically different from the educational world I entered more than 40 years ago. One of the many reasons is the advent of information communication technology (ICT) in the workplace. Our students do not need to learn to do much of what was in the curricula 40 years ago — because computers now do that in their place. The old syllabuses, with their heavy emphasis on knowing, understanding, and applying, are out of date. The new demand is for students to concentrate upon the higher levels of learning in the cognitive domain, and elsewhere. For this they need to have, and to continue to develop, sophisticated abilities in problem-solving, making judgements, searching, analysing, thinking critically, and collaborating with others. In this radically changed context, the teacher can no longer be simply a lecturer or instructor, someone who passes on knowledge and advice about "how to do it." The first major challenge is that the teacher must learn to be, above all, a facilitator, moderator, tutor (at times), and even a fellow-learner.

Autonomous Learning

Back in the 1970s, many of us were to discover quickly that partial autonomy, which the Nuffield Project team and others somewhat misleadingly and optimistically called "Independence in Learning", was leading quickly to new possibilities and challenges for learners and their teachers (Hewton, 1981). Individualised learning meant that the learners could work at their own choice of pace, sometimes faster than their peers, sometimes slower and more considered. It meant that teachers could offer learners different routes to achieve the chosen objectives, as learning outcomes were called in these days. It even meant that we could go further, and engage learners in deciding *what* they should study, as well as *how* they should study. In all of this, however, students depended upon resources assembled for them by teachers, or on limited library stocks — limited in breadth, limited in availability. Nevertheless, flexibility brought the next major challenge. This centres upon the new learning skills which are to be exercised in the cognitive domain; for they have now come overtly onto the agenda for teachers and learners, and must feature in *our* teaching, *their* learning, and *our* assessment — for they are skills of real use and importance in lifelong learning.

Worldwide Resources

With the growth in widespread access to the Web and the advent of materials based upon CD-ROM, the number of available sources mushroomed. Thus, the list of learning skills to be developed was extended by the need to ensure effective and personally cost-effective use of time in searching, sifting, judging, and sometimes in discarding without reading. The works of Homer could be scanned for metaphors involving domestic and wild animals in minutes, rather than days, making certain types of demanding and trailblazing undergraduate project enquiry feasible for the first time. Problem-based learning could utilise a much wider range of sources then ever before, and so learners could derive more and more from truly open-ended problem-solving and consequent learning. Students increasingly concentrated on what *they* had chosen as worthwhile to study, usually with intrinsic motivation. The result for many learners has been much deeper and wider ranging learning than we would ever have contemplated hitherto. The next major challenge, then, is that the technologies offer us incredible potential to deepen learning — and we must exploit that potential to the fullest.

Unintended Learning Outcomes

In recent years, I have taken, tongue in cheek, to mildly deploring the commitment to lists of intended learning outcomes in programme specifications which have been formulated according to the UK's Quality Assurance Agency template. In suitable conversations I tend to mention, with examples, that several of my students have recently achieved learning outcomes which are in accordance with my module aims and teaching objectives — but were not listed as "*intended* learning outcomes." I have made a plea for us to recognise the attainment of *unintended* learning outcomes, provided they are in accordance with our declared goals. Every time I have mentioned this, I have found that about half the teachers in the group will nod or voice agreement, and some will immediately quote examples of unintended learning outcomes achieved by one or more of their own students. These were outcomes which they, the teachers, valued, but for which they had not planned, and so they could not reward them within formal assessment. The major challenge here is to do justice to valuable but unintended learning outcomes, which emerge when learning is flexible and learner-directed.

Changes in Teaching

These, then, have been some of the "issues, implications, and cultural upheavals" which have brought challenges for me — and, I suspect, for many others. Using a different metaphor, they have called on this old dog to learn and practice new tricks — in a VLE and elsewhere. Over these 40 years, I have repeatedly had to learn to teach in a totally different way, with totally different aims in mind for my students. I am now facilitating, moderating, nurturing the reflective practitioner, nudging learners into their zone of proximal development or ZPD (Wertsch, 1985) — aye, and all of that in these days of ever-increasing numbers and wider access. I have had to learn almost devious ways of carefully structuring, with good intent, the interactions between learners and tutors, and between learners and learners, within the low level of resource allocated to tutor-led activity. In addition to these radical changes in what is still called "teaching," I have equally had to find valid and reliable ways of assessing higher level abilities All of these, I submit, represent major challenges for all university teachers, and not just for me.

Minor Challenges

In the passing, there also have been minor challenges upon which I will dwell in this section. It might fairly be argued that most of these feature already for all good teachers in higher education, and that the advice to myself which I have drawn from my experiences simply encapsulates the principles of good teaching, whatever the medium. So be it. I merely submit that I, and many others like me, had perhaps escaped the full challenge of these detailed demands, until they became starkly apparent in the VLE.

The minor challenges which I have encountered in the VLE have often concerned relatively detailed points, where getting it wrong could have created greater difficulties than I would have experienced in face-to-face teaching. With that in mind, I offer my experiences frankly and to prompt your own recall of minor challenges which you have already encountered in this setting.

The First Contact

Working in the VLE, I have had strong feedback from undergraduates, postgraduates, and staff setting out on continuing professional development (CPD) activity, telling me that the first contact between us was extremely important to them — because they had been apprehensive or uncertain, and it had removed that apprehension or uncertainty. I take the point that this was very important to them, and even to those who had had two years of experience of totally online study. I do not know what it is that I have done so far which has created an initially positive reaction. I wish I *did* know, since it clearly matters to virtual learners.

Advice: Take great care over the first contact and try to find out what can make it effective for learners.

The Tasks

In face-to-face teaching, when I declared a task, I was there to field immediate questions; I could read bewilderment and explain further; I could see action resulting from a misunderstanding and take steps to correct it. In the VLE, even if I am available, the option to contact me is seldom taken up immediately. By the time one student has done so, the group will already have formed their own impressions of an unreasonable demand which made them angry, an apparent ambiguity which irritated them immensely, or a suspicion which soon became embedded.

Advice: Ensure tasks are utterly clear, uncluttered by confusing extras, and precisely convey your intention.

Feedback, Feedforward, and Collegial Suggestions

I take feedback to be an explanation of judgements made in assessment — explaining that "This was sound, because …" or that "That was weak, because …" I take feedforward to be constructive suggestions about how the learner can improve next time, without brain surgery or working any harder. I take collegial suggestions to be the sharing of ideas, methods, or information which have worked for me and might spark off something useful for a student.

When commenting on electronically submitted writings by students reporting their critical thinking, I have found that learners can have great difficulty in distinguishing between different types of comment from me and their purposes, as well as in responding to them appropriately. Consequently, I use different formats nowadays to convey these different purposes. I put my facilitative comments in footnotes. If these comments are tutorial in nature, as when I am trying, for example, to improve the student's use of the reflective process, I take care to flag this by including such a phrase as "Many people find it helpful to ..." I put my (judgemental) feedback on a proforma, where I explain the making of my judgement. I put my feedforward in my electronic cover note, the first message from me which is encountered when I am returning the work. If I have collegial suggestions to offer, such as to commend a book which I have found especially helpful, I usually mention this in an e-mail, sent a day or so later.

I have undertaken formative evaluations about a third of the way through a module where I have been differentiating types of comments in this way. I have been told by the students that they were aware of the differences in types and purposes of comments, signalled by the way they are presented and separated; and that they found this helpful or even valuable.

Advice: Signal types of tutor comment distinctly and do not neglect feedforward

Asynchronous Communication

If a student asks me a question in person, then I will usually answer immediately, with the normal tendency in conversation which is to repeat yourself in slightly different words. If a student asks me a question in the VLE, I can consider my answer, certainly read it before I post it, and maybe revise it. It will be more succinct, hence, I hope more easily assimilated than if I were talking, face-to-face. The same, of course, is true of students' responses to me and of student-to-student conversations in the VLE. When the form of communication lets us pause, even for the brief hiatus which occurs even while assembling a brief contribution in a chat room, it behoves us all to think, consider, formulate, and then confirm our meaning before posting our response.

Advice: Exploit asynchronous communication for its strengths in being specific.

File Handling and Records

In face-to-face situations, the ingathering and receipting of folders (with their standard cover sheets consistently completed) was a fairly straightforward business. In the VLE, getting students to label files as requested, and even merely to use university e-mail facilities rather than their own, has proved a tough task, whatever instructions or requests I table at the outset. I learn, from colleagues in other institutions, that they have had the same problem, which is admittedly minor, but can be irritating and extremely time-wasting.

Advice: Try to make sure that you get file naming and e-mail addresses as you require, from the outset; but build in ways to correct departures from this if they arise.

Different Writing Styles in Different Contexts

In the VLE, it has been a real surprise to me in the past year (2003-2004) to see different wordings and sentence structures used by the same students, in the same company, when they are in discussion boards, e-mails, chat rooms, and reflective journalling. It was clear to many of them what medium they should choose to use and when they wanted (needed?) to transact business with each other and perhaps with me. It might sometimes be a discussion board, a chat room, an e-mail, or a phone call. They chose for reasons which they could explain: "The chat room is for transacting business and allocating tasks; it can be brisk and businesslike, and any misunderstanding will emerge quickly and we can put it right by e-mail. The discussion board, as its name rightly implies, is for carefully considered discussion. We need to get it right there, so our sentences are well thought through, and we will go back to them." It has been common for many of my students to use txt-message abbreviations in e-mails, and in chat rooms, but not on discussion boards.

Advice: Possibly expect rapid change here — including the use of txt-ing to have mushroomed by the time you read this.

Plagiarism and Cheating

Unacknowledged quotations have always been a problem. Nowadays, whole essays can be checked against "Google" and found, almost complete, on the Internet. Cheating is a burgeoning industry, And in some quarters, a distinct form of cheating, which is the sub-contracting of writing to someone else, is by no means unusual. We have to use all the means at our disposal to identify such cheating — and, surely, to do more than that, by anticipating and excluding it. Surely, one pedagogically sound way to tackle the problem of plagiarism is to move, as the healthcare professions have already done, toward assessment tasks which are more individualised and do not lend themselves to downloading from the Web.

Advice: We need to devise and use assessment tasks which thwart plagiarism, rather than those whose responses impel us to detect any plagiarism.

Time Management

Plans for personal and professional development often reveal, especially at the first-year level, the needs which are high in the learners' lists of priority. Apart from the frequently expressed desires to lose weight and to eliminate overdrafts, one common aim is a concern to improve in time management. It is clear from the plans which evolve from such aims that the writers envisage that, if only they could be systematic, then they would manage to complete all that they judge is expected of them. If they can be helped to see that it is as important and effective to *prioritise* as it is to *manage* time commitments, to delete aspirations rather than re-order them, then they are likely to emerge less stressed, and with more achieved to good effect. The notion that perhaps some commitments need to be pushed off the end of the table is initially strange, and counter to expectations. However, students can come to see the transferability of the lesson learnt, and approach more than Web searches and literature surveys with the intention to distinguish "need to know" from "nice to know," and especially from "don't need to bother."

Advice: Link prioritising to time management and emphasise its relevance.

Minor Challenges Lead to the "So What?" Question

I have shown here the minor challenges which have emerged for me as I have attempted to harness the potential of the new technologies for learning and teaching. Perhaps these have not been challenges for you; perhaps you have met other, even more radical issues. Whatever the case, I submit that the need is for each of us to address the "So what?" question, and ask ourselves what we shall do next and to good effect, in the face of such challenges. For me, the answer seems to entail a fairly substantial commitment to action research, with my students.

Action Research: To Good Effect?

While I am still teaching in this rapidly changing situation, with so many novel features and responses to them, I have a demanding agenda of questions for which I require answers. Time restraints and lack of resources will not permit me to engage in full, generalisable educational research into these questions, nor to await the findings, should others find it possible to carry out such enquiries. Therefore, it is imperative for me, and I suspect for others like me, to engage in action research, probably and preferably in conjunction with our students, using sound methods to ascertain the nature of the learning and of the learning experience in this new setting. Only then can we confidently respond creatively to the findings which emerge.

Just as I have shown minor challenges in a personal way, as examples rather than comprehensive coverage, so I pose here seven questions of importance to me and my current students, without claiming they are the most important questions for the sector at this time. I also outline the methods which my colleagues, my students, and I will use; I hope, to find answers relating to *our* teaching of *our* subject with *our* students in the VLE at the present time.

Question 1: How (well) do my students navigate and select priorities within the VLE we have created for them and what is their learning experience in consequence?

I know, having checked from data, that my students who eagerly use links in the early days of their studies on our course can often completely forget what they learnt at that time. They can even forget that there *is* a link which points to such information, and may sincerely protest that it has never been made available to them!

From studies I have carried out in the past on computer-assisted learning in mathematics, economics, and languages, I also know that some of the most successful learners can reach a high achievement level by following what those who designed the materials have regarded with astonishment as bizarre and potentially disastrous approaches.

Further, I have found in my studies that there are factors which strongly influence choice and use of material, and which matter significantly to learners, without having been anticipated or appreciated by those who designed the materials.

I see no reason to expect only predictable learning and behaviour in the current and flexible VLEs within which I support learning. I need, perhaps, to commission some genuine learners to provide talk-aloud protocols, which we can analyse together, and whose findings we can test out with a larger sample. Without this information, I have little basis on which to review or refine my present approach to supporting the learning which I value.

Question 2: How deeply, or shallowly, do lurkers learn?

The term and the concept of the "lurker" have regrettably negative connotations. Recently, working in two different discussion board settings with undergraduate and postgraduate participants, I have noted that a majority of the participants have simply lurked. Yet these lurkers have logged on frequently, and have remained logged on for appreciable periods, perhaps for what they regarded as a good purpose. So I need to set out to learn what this lurking experience entails — and yields.

I should arrange for volunteer lurkers to be prepared for a short (anonymous) interview, in which they are asked to report the most significant learning during their lurking period, and to try to pinpoint what led to that learning. This is a style of interview which proved fruitful for me in the Open University, while we were trying to identify good and significant practice in telephone conference calls. With large numbers involved, of course, I would summarise the findings from a small and articulate (but not necessarily representative) pilot sample. I would then test the findings out on a larger group, in Likert-style questionnaires which feature quotes and seek responses from "Strongly Agree" to "Strongly Disagree," with the option of open-ended comment in conclusions.

I need to know what this apparently passive experience does for lurkers, in terms of the learning outcomes I have in mind for my discussion activities, or the other learning outcomes which matter to the learners. Without that knowledge, I cannot exploit the potential of lurking for them, nor can I review the usefulness of the parts of the VLE which they may access.

Question 3: What **triggers** comments from me on student contributions in the VLE, how do (and should) I decide the content and form of my comments, and what impact do they have on learners and learning?

Over the years, and before venturing into a VLE, I have carefully analysed the triggers in student work which led me to make some sort of response, usually in the form of a comment or question worthy of consideration. I have tried to classify my interjections and the triggers which prompted them and have found some sort of pattern — a finding repeated when I have analysed my comments in the VLE and the triggers which prompted them.

In distance learning situations, a colleague and I have used Kelly's Repertory Grid (Kelly, 1965) to assist learners to classify our comments and their responses to them, and so to inform us which types of comments they have found most useful and why. That information has significantly influenced our formulation and use of comments outwith the VLE. I need to follow through the same process, now, in the VLE — so that my commenting will be useful and crafted with informed understanding of how it may be received.

Question 4: What new skills are demanded of the learner in the VLE, and how can I facilitate their development?

Learners nowadays need to be able to plan, execute, and monitor searches; they need to judge the soundness of what their searches unearth; they need to discuss, plan, agree, and decide in groups in the VLE, without the benefit of body language or intonation, and they need to learn further, from successes and failures in communication and empathy while so doing. No doubt other abilities could be added. The shopping list of needs emerges fairly readily if learners keep reflective learning journals which concentrate on the process mastery demanded of them. It is more difficult to determine what kinds of interaction and effort from teachers like me, in the VLE, can most effectively nudge learners into their ZPDs, to be the best that they can be in these respects.

Individual efforts to build jointly, tutor and student, on generalisations formulated in reflective learning journals and to actively experiment together to bring about development — effectively — have worked well for me, and for my students in the recent past. But they are far from cost-effective.

I need to analyse the students' journals from the past few years and identify general advice to myself and to my next students, with such learning needs in mind in respect of transferable capabilities. I need to seek cost-effective ways of arranging for socio-constructivist interactions between students which prompt to good effect, while being less dependent on commitment of my time.

Question 5: What is the difference between contact in the VLE with someone known face-to-face and with a purely virtual contact?

I do not, for the moment, seek to engage with the contrast between blended and purely online learning. Rather, am I concerned to ask, of the work of tutorial teams of more than one tutor, what are the advantages and disadvantages when one tutor, say, is met by learners purely in the VLE? This question has arisen for me because for some years I taught mainly in the VLE, but with initial and occasional face-to-face contact. Then, on one course, I was restricted to virtual contacts — although face-to-face encounters still occurred for the students' groups, but not with me. My strong impression was that the purely virtual relationship was more focussed on the business in hand in our relationship, more searching and rigorous, yet at the same time one in which deeper and more meaningful tutor/student relationships developed. Post hoc contact with these students tends to strengthen that suspicion.

When my knowledge of a student, and their knowledge of me, is purely restricted to what we have keyed to each other in the context of their learning activity, does that indeed lead to a different type of relationship and interaction — and to more worthwhile outcomes? I judge this question important, but, for the moment, do not know how to seek answers without engaging in social engineering which I would find unacceptable.

Question 6: Why is trust important to learners in the VLE and what engenders it?

I have saved my most baffling question until the end. Over the years, I have sought feedback from learners on what I do for and with them. Usually this feedback has been positive, directly helpful, or both. For my work in the VLE, I use the same format — Likert-scale questions plus open-ended questions. Since I began to tutor students whom I never meet, I have been struck by the number who have chosen to tell me that they trust me. Naturally, I am glad that this is so. I also hope that the learners whom I met face-to-face trusted me as well, but it is only with virtual contacts that this point has been declared.

I have asked respondents what it is that they trust me to do, and they simply reply "I just trust you." I have asked what they trust me *not* to do with the same response. I have asked what it is that I do which leads them to trust me. They cannot answer this question. I cannot see any way to pursue this issue, other than by setting up focus groups, facilitated by a colleague, in which this group of questions will be further probed.

To be trusted as a virtual tutor is important to me, as a devotee of Carl Rogers, just as it is clearly important to these learners to be able to trust their tutor (Rogers, 1961). I need to find out what I am doing successfully, and how, so that I do not lose it from my practice.

The Final Challenge

As an ordinary grassroots teacher, nowadays, I do not have sufficient time or resources to seek out the answers to all of these vital questions. I suspect that the same will be true for most readers of this book. Even the best I can manage in the way of action research, with my students, in my own settings, can only tackle a part of this agenda. The greatest challenge for each of us, of course, is not so much that our attempts at action research will only discover part of what we need to know, rather it is that any findings we obtain, the lessons we learn from them, and the decisions we base upon them may well be somewhat out of date even before we have been able to respond adequately. I noted, for example, that as I edited the final version of a chapter I had first drafted only six months earlier, I was conscious that my experience and thinking and insights had all moved on significantly and that there was much more that I would have wished to add. And so this book is particularly timely, since the contributions which it contains may prompt us all to ask, and to answer in good time, more pertinent questions than we could generate on our own.

References

Bonk, C.J., & King, K.S. (Eds.). (1998). *Electronic collaborators*. Mahwah, NJ: Lawrence Erlbaum Associates.

British Journal of Educational Technology, 35(6) and *36*(1), complete issues.

Carr-Chellman, A.A. (Ed.). (2005). *Global perspectives on eLearning: Rhetoric and reality*. Thousand Oaks; London; New Delhi: Sage Publications.

Hewton, E. (1981). Looking for a change: An analysis of the findings of the Nuffield Group for Research and Innovation in Higher Education. *British Journal of Educational Technology, 12*(3), 180-97.

Kelly, G.A. (1955). *The psychology of personal constructs*. New York: Norton.

QAA. Web site for the Quality Assurance Agency. Available online at www.qaa.ac.uk/

Rogers, C. (1961). *On becoming a person*. Boston: Houghton Mifflin.

Wertsch, J.V. (1985). *Vygotsky and the social formation of mind*. Cambridge, MA; London: Harvard University Press.

Section I:

Infrastructural and Cultural Issues

Chapter II

What Lecturers Say Helps and Hinders Their Use of a Virtual Learning Environment to Support Face-to-Face Teaching

Sue Morón-García, Loughborough University, UK

Abstract

The purpose of this chapter is to provide an overview of issues lecturers said they faced when using a virtual learning environment (VLE), such as WebCT or Blackboard, to support their face-to-face teaching. It draws on data collected for doctoral research that explored the reasons lecturers gave for their use of a VLE, the teaching approach supported, and the factors affecting this use. It concentrates on the latter and as such contributes to an under-researched area by reporting the subjective views of academics who have adopted information and communications technology (ICT) to support their teaching. Four sets of issues were identified: student, technical, pedagogic, and institutional. These are summarised and discussed with reference to comments made by interviewees, and the implications for different audiences are outlined.

Introduction

This chapter describes and discusses the issues that lecturers said helped and hindered their use of a virtual learning environment (VLE) to support face-to-face teaching. Lecturers, the generally accepted term for academic teaching staff in UK universities, were the focus of this research because they are responsible for selecting (within institutional limits) and setting up the learning environment for the students. If they are unable to demonstrate its purpose or motivate students to use a VLE, then any potential advantage to use will be lost.

E-learning is reported as "a stalled revolution" (Zemsky & Massy, 2004), despite the increased take up of VLEs. Lecturer attitudes are considered part of the problem, because, it is said, they refuse to change how they teach (op. cit.). However, it is too easy to blame lack of progress simply on lecturers' attitudes, indeed the lecturers interviewed for this research were found to be more student-focused than teacher-focused in their approach to teaching (Morón-García, 2004), willing to innovate and to review their teaching style. What needs to be challenged are the overly optimistic claims made for educational technology that ignore the "organisational, social, and personal considerations at play in a given educational setting" (Kearsley, 1998, p. 50).

The importance of looking at the "educational environment" is something highlighted by Britain and Liber (2004), similarly the subjective views of academics who have adopted information and communications technology (ICT) to support their teaching has been recognised as an under-researched area (McShane, 2004). Although problematic for some, these views are important in helping us understand the impact of structures and processes and help to explain why lecturers still find it difficult to change their practice and embed technology use in their teaching and their students' learning. Furthermore, they provide a missing part of the VLE picture: The 2003 UK VLE survey (Browne & Jenkins, 2003) was only able to report on the institutional perspective.

The following section explains the context of the research and describes the methods used and the lecturers interviewed. Four sets of issues were identified (student, technical, pedagogic, and institutional) and are described and discussed in the subsequent section. Analysis of the data demonstrated the complexity and variety of factors affecting lecturers' adoption and use of a VLE, even among those who could be characterised as open and willing to innovate and to reflect on their practice. The interrelationship of the issues identified is shown in the final part of that section; the factors identified have clear implications for the adoption of ICT tools, such as VLEs, within the tertiary sector, suggesting that the level of support is far from adequate and that there needs to be more thought and transparency around the purpose and suitability of ICT adoption, both from an institutional and individual lecturer perspective.

Research Context

This research focuses on VLEs, as a specific example of ICT, because of their increased uptake in UK higher education (Browne & Jenkins, 2003; Jenkins, Browne, Armitage, 2001). A VLE "... uses Web and Internet-based technology to create a learning environment where interaction and collaboration can take place in the virtual world of Web and Internet-based applications. The tools provided aid the teacher(s) in controlling and tailoring the virtual environment for use by their students, who are able to interact with, contribute to and move through the content. The main difference between a VLE and other computer-based learning or computer-supported learning environments is the possibility of communication and collaboration with peers and teachers within the same virtual environment that holds the content. Content may include the results of collaboration and student contributions, not only course materials. The tools used include synchronous and asynchronous computer mediated communication software and those that enable the delivery of course materials online" (adapted from Morón-García, 2001).

The data described and discussed here formed part of an investigation into the use of VLEs in UK higher education. The aim was to examine claims that the Web and Internet-based technology (on which VLEs are based) can and will lead to a student-centred model of education. According to Collis (1996), the creation of student-centred learning environments is one of the reasons to use Web and Internet-based technology. Other researchers argue that this technology will cause the teacher to adopt the facilitator role needed in the student-centred model of education (Westera, 1999), accentuating the "student as worker and teacher as coach paradigms" (Wegner, Holloway, & Garton, 1999, p. 6).

These claims are allied to the belief that the availability of this technology should lead to the adoption of a "new" student-centred paradigm or pedagogy, described as a change from the passive absorption of information to active discovery and the creation of knowledge (Barr & Tagg, 1995) and be used to change the learning experience (Alexander, 1995). They also seem to have given rise to a perception that VLEs can enhance teaching and learning- the main management reason given for VLE adoption in the UK VLE surveys (Browne & Jenkins, 2003; Jenkins et al., 2001). I interpreted enhancement as the adoption of student-centred approaches to teaching and learning because of the association with improving student learning; research has shown a correlation between higher quality learning outcomes and deep approaches to learning (Marton & Saljo, 1997) and between a deep approach to learning and a student-focused approach to teaching (Trigwell, Prosser, & Waterhouse, 1999).

However, "...the reality of change presents the teacher with new challenges..." (Thorpe, 1999, p. 40) and the context of use is important because while "[t]eachers may have a certain degree of autonomy, [...] basically they have to work within the framework and structures dictated by the institution (which in turn has to operate within nationally dictated policies and resourcing limitations)" (Biggs, 1994).

The connection between context and teaching approach adopted has been shown by other researchers (Prosser & Trigwell, 1997; Trigwell, Prosser, Martin, & Ramsden, 1998). Prosser and Trigwell (1997) found that lecturers who felt that they had more control over their teaching (what is taught and how) were more likely to adopt student-focused approaches. These approaches were affected detrimentally if the class size was thought to be too large, student diversity too great, and workload too heavy.

Issues identified from the literature (e.g., Barnard, 1999; Fraser, 1997; Johannasen & Eide, 2000; Somekh, 1998) and previous research (Morón-García, 2000) were used to create a series of questions and prompts to investigate contextual issues that might impact on VLE use. These were revised following a pilot study interviewing 12 lecturers across four higher education institutions (HEIs – two post-1992 and two pre-1992). The aim was to explore:

- the impact and effectiveness of technical training and support (the effect of lecturer ICT comfort levels and the availability of technical support);

- the effect of the environment of use (the impact of institutional or departmental ICT ethos);

- the availability and focus of any advice and support (whether this was perceived as adequate and whether there was an emphasis on technology or pedagogy that affected lecturer perceptions and use);

- the effect of the context of use (whether lecturers had any concerns about the suitability of use with respect to types of students and courses and the way in which student attitudes to changes in teaching methods and their expectations affected use);

- the applicability of the VLE provided (lecturers' perceptions about VLE functionality and usability).

Interviewees were encouraged to identify improvements in the system or its environment of use and to comment further about their own experience, at the end of the interview.

Data Collection

Thirty-one humanities and social science lecturers from 10 HEIs (six post-1992, including one college of higher education, and four pre-1992) in the UK were interviewed, individually and face-to-face, about their VLE use. Based on pilot study findings, I thought I was more likely to find a VLE being used as a tool to support learning within this category of lecturer, rather than learning about or how to use the technology as an end itself. While it could be argued that this limits the applicability of the findings to other disciplines, I believe it highlights the issues that inhibit those who are most likely to use the added-value tools in a VLE (those for collaboration and communication, as defined) because they come from more discursive disciplines. Therefore, if they find it difficult to engage with these tools because of contextual factors, it follows that other disciplines may also find it problematic.

The intention was to obtain an even spread of interviewees from the two main types of HEI (pre- and post-1992) and of users of a range of VLEs. However, as found by the UK VLE survey (Jenkins et al., 2001), use was more widespread in post-1992 universities (see

Table 1. Type of HEIs represented in the study and lecturer numbers

Type of HEI	Number of HEIs	Number of lecturers
Pre-1992	4	9
Post-1992	6	22
Totals	10	31

Table 2. VLEs in use at universities (one university had two VLEs available)

Type of VLE	Number of universities
WebCT	5
Blackboard	3
COSE	1
Learning Space	1
Learnwise	1

Table 3. Subjects taught and number of lecturers

Subject	Numbers	Subject	Numbers
History	5	Anthropology	1
English	4	Art History	1
Business studies	3	Cultural studies	1
Information science	3	Drama	1
Sociology	3	Economics	1
Communication studies	2	Geography / research methods	1
Law	2	Politics	1
Religious studies	2	Total	31

Table 1) and more institutions had adopted WebCT (see Table 2). Table 3 shows the range of subject areas represented and the number of interviewees teaching those subjects.

Interviewees explained that a variety of interrelated issues impacted on their ability to use a VLE. Thematic analysis of full interview transcripts (aided by the use of QSR qualitative analysis software, formerly Nudist) resulted in the classification of data into four sets of issues (student, technical, pedagogic, and institutional). These issues describe the factors lecturers perceived as influencing their VLE use; they are outlined in the next section.

Factors Affecting VLE Use

The following subsections discuss the issues that lecturers described as being of concern to them and are summarised in Tables 4 to 7. The final subsection illustrates the interrelatedness of these issues.

Table 4. Factors affecting VLE use and classified as student issues

Student issues	Interviewee perceptions of elements of concern to students and factors that they thought impacted on effective student use of a VLE. These were based on their observations of actual student use and any problem students encountered; together with feedback received (both informal and formal).
• Skills	⇒ Student ICT literacy levels, the need for ongoing ICT training and support, orientation sessions and the impact on subject contact time (affected by the fact that colleagues do not use a VLE so students forget how).
	⇒ A need to instil sensible working practices such as frequent saving and proper storage of work, remembering to check for course e-mail and how to cope with different software versions at home and on campus.
• Access	⇒ Overcoming physical barriers to use such as the lack of provision for disabilities, registration problems, numbers of open access computers available on campus, software availability in different locations.
	⇒ Expense such as the printing of online materials, PC ownership and Internet costs.
• Attitude	⇒ Coping with the 'does it count?' mentality and the use of assessment to motivate student usage of a VLE.
	⇒ Overcoming a perception that VLE use would lead to attendance problems and aiming to prevent this.
	⇒ Dealing with resistance to changes in the way they are taught as they are expected to become more active and take more responsibility for their learning.

Interviewees indicated that more ICT training and support was needed for students, they were concerned about the inadequate and voluntary nature of most induction sessions which meant many students missed out and put an increasing burden on them to provide this support. The resulting tension between providing ICT training and teaching subject content suggests a need to build familiarisation sessions into subject content in order to afford an opportunity to try things out. Drop-in sessions and workshops provided centrally, as well as printed help guides, were cited as useful. The move, in some institutions, to offering an ICT skills certificate (often online) as a credited part of undergraduate and some graduate programmes is a positive move. With respect to VLE use in particular, it was suggested that greater use by colleagues would aid student familiarity, making it the norm, and help to change attitudes.

Problems with access had the potential to frustrate and discourage students.,While network stability and speed of access have improved greatly, thanks to more investment in server capacity and network connections, initial problems had encouraged interviewees to examine their use of a VLE (e.g., use of a discussion forum to structure a wider debate around course themes rather than to support groupwork with campus-based students, because they were found to subvert lecturer intentions by meeting up in the learning centre to input comments). Problems caused by registration and passwords were combated through orientation sessions to ensure all students were issued with pass-words, knew how to "log on," and could access the VLE.

In order to reduce access problems when using large online databases or to reduce the costs associated with having to access course handbooks online, some institutions and lecturers provided CD-ROMs containing the relevant materials for students to take away. Thought is needed about what students should be expected to pay for and how a VLE is used, for example, whether course documents are provided for all with the VLE being used as back-up for lost copies or with only online documents being available. Complaints about printing costs had prompted interviewees to think about the type of material that was suitable for placing within a VLE and to reflect on actual use, for example, less use of a VLE for holding content and more guidance to enable students to find information as well as formative assessment. Necessary content was provided in non-HTML format (e.g., Adobe .pdf) to facilitate downloading and printing. It was notable that students were not encouraged to create their own version of content by using the notepad tool available within some VLEs and on all Windows computers (from within the Accessories menu). This would have enabled the cutting and pasting and annotating of HTML content and is something that could be explored.

Interviewees were concerned about the impact of problems encountered by students on their evaluation scores, and what they perceived as the unfairness of being held responsible for technical and registration problems that were out of their control. They reported that students were reacting against both the technology (which may be unfamiliar, especially to those who are returning to education) and against having to adopt a new way of working (from having to access lecture handouts or content information that was formerly distributed at face-to-face sessions to completing an online task before attending a face-to-face session). Of course, some student antipathy or reluctance could be attributed to lecturers not being sure how to make best use of the tools or not making it clear to students why they are being asked to use a VLE in a particular way, identifying purposeful use was another lecturer concern.

A perception, and a reality in two cases, that VLE use could lead to greater absenteeism was combated by various strategies including re-versioning lecturer handouts and making students turn up to class to get solutions to and feedback on problems set and worked through online as well as linking use to assessment. Concerns about student motivation and a need to encourage them to change the way they worked led to interviewees incorporating assessment into VLE use. This highlighted a tension between a reason given for much VLE use (to facilitate access to a wider variety of resources and ideas and to encourage students to "go wider" than conventionally possible) and student reluctance to do things that "don't count." Lecturers reported that students perceived worthwhile tasks as those that were assessed, however, some interviewees resisted because of different skill levels and where it was not possible to guarantee equality of access. This suggests a wider need to rethink how we "measure" learning and evaluate progress and convey this to students.

A further problem was the student perception that learning supported by VLE use was "hard work" and "difficult" and increased the amount of work students thought they had to do. One reason for this may be that using a VLE involved more active learning, that is, students had to work to find out information that they expected to acquire in lectures and complete activities designed by their lecturers. Another may be to do with information overload: By providing access to a greater variety of resources, students may feel they have to view or absorb all of these, instead of making a selection. Once again this indicates a need to make it clear to students what is expected.

Technical Issues

Comfort level and experience with ICT affected an interviewee's VLE use and was identified by them as a potential barrier for colleagues. Learning how to use and set up a new system, no matter how user-friendly, takes time. Finding this time, along with the time to revise and review courses already created, was a commonly voiced need. It was identified as a particular problem for part-time staff as they rarely had the time to become familiar with new systems and had wider implications for innovation attempts. Changes in the VLE or the version used necessitated re-learning and the re-creation or re-entering of materials which was a source of further anxiety and in some cases inhibited further development. This underlined the need for these new pressures on lecturers to be taken into account and provision for adequate support and training to be considered.

The provision of training and orientation sessions for lecturers who wanted to use a VLE was varied. It depended on the focus of the institutional strategy aimed at getting lecturers involved with VLE use and what was possible to achieve with the resources and staff available. For example, one university used school-based teaching fellows to support VLE use, while another used online learning fellowships (including time away from teaching) as catalysts; two provided online training via the VLE to build up the number of users and one provided individual help, although there was some doubt that this level of support would continue. Two faculties at one university shared one faculty support officer.

Interviewees had undertaken different levels of training depending on what was available, what they thought they needed, and what they had the time to do, although the majority were self-taught users of the VLE. There was no overall consensus about the best way to provide training, as this would depend on a user's approach to learning, as well as their attitude toward and experience of ICT. Thus, some interviewees described themselves as competent, self-taught users who preferred to learn by experience and by trying out software while others would have preferred to be introduced to new technology before trying it out for themselves; they resented the time it took to work out how to use a VLE on their own.

Table 5. Factors affecting VLE use and classified as technical issues

Technical issues	The technical issues interviewees spoke about related to their personal skills, technological and contextual factors relating to VLE use, such as usability and the availability of training.
• Skills	⇒ Technophobia & the "comfort factor", affected by previous experience, the need for training.
	⇒ Time to become familiar with the technology.
• Usability and functionality	⇒ "Clunkiness" - linear structure, too many menus -, the look of the interface, inflexible names and labels, interoperability with other systems.
	⇒ Quick and easy registration and amendments (institutional need to examine processes), the 'closed' community (logging on).
• Environment	⇒ System stability and registration, being able to gain reliable access to the VLE (a stable network and good technical support).
	⇒ Technical support, technical staff level of understanding and system expertise (relative to users).
	⇒ Training (focus on pedagogy or technology), dealing with upgrades.

While VLE use is supposed to remove the need for higher level technical skills, several interviewees had found an understanding of HTML useful so that content could be edited and displayed even when there might be problems with accessing the VLE, suggesting that there may be a role for wider knowledge. Complaints about the unreliability and awkwardness of VLE use seemed to be predominantly from those interviewees who had tried to use a VLE for more than its ability to hold and display content, those who had tried to integrate the use of other features into their VLE "site"; features such as the discussion forum or the quiz tool to set up a series of multiple-choice questions and the generation of usage reports.

The "closed community" aspect of VLEs, the ability to restrict access to those registered on a course or module, was considered both a benefit and a barrier. It afforded an element of privacy, especially where students were sharing personal views or there were copyright issues, and the possibility of creating a sense of community among users. However, one interviewee felt that this had a negative impact on recruitment possibilities compared to a shared network drive that was accessible to all subject students and therefore usable for publicity purposes. Others pointed out that this demonstrated the importance of deciding what material should be for internal and external consumption. It was also felt that the "closed" community of a VLE contradicted some of the claimed benefits of online learning, such as access to a wider community. It had proved a barrier to collaboration with other institutions in at least one case, while making visitor access difficult in two cases and hindered collaboration across year groups.

Additional concerns included the level of technical support available and the way in which help was accessed. Interviewees were generally happy with the level of technical support they had received when beginning to use a VLE; it was typically individual or workshop-based because of the need to think through the pedagogy of use. However, they wondered how more users would fare. The technical support available was usually via a help desk, and in some cases interviewees found that they knew more about the VLE system than the technical staff supporting it or were learning about it at the same time as those staff. One interviewee thought this situation was unlikely to change because of a lack of institutional commitment to properly fund support posts.

Speed of response was important and the adoption of a call centre methodology to sort out technical problems was criticised as not being responsive or specific enough and necessitating much repetition. It had been subverted by some interviewees so that they could get immediate help, though this again leads to questions about the way support may work if and when there are more users. Further difficulties were caused when it was not clear who provided support or if it was necessary to deal with different bodies (IT services/staff development/learning centre) when seeking help. There was no overall consensus about the best location for support services (centrally or at faculty level), perhaps this indicates the need for some sort of hybrid.

It was difficult to separate the desire for pedagogic advice from the need for technical familiarisation sessions because learning how to use the technology meant thinking about the teaching, and its application. The highest praise was reserved for support people who allowed interviewees to explore use, providing suggestions and solutions as required, and who were able to understand the teaching strategies interviewees aimed to support. One interviewee lamented the lack of any way to build on and share what he had created and would have welcomed some sort of review and suggestions for improvement from experienced staff.

There was evidence that these early adopters did subsequently supplement institutional support by taking on a support role for colleagues. This happened formally, in that they were appointed to teaching and learning roles within their departments, often with a focus on the use of ICT, or informally, by way of dissemination events or by being someone people approached when first thinking about VLE use. However, this also led to resentment if early adopters felt their colleagues were using them so that they did not need to learn how to do something.

Institutional Issues

Interviewees had concerns about the effect of VLE use on their workload and were worried about management intentions in promoting VLE use. Furthermore, they suggested that for them to overcome some of the problems they had to deal with (like student attitudes, skill levels, and changing the way they taught), VLE use had to become the norm. This could only happen if colleagues were willing and able to contribute, if the use of ICT was accepted as a teaching tool, and the institutional culture supported teaching innovation. Access problems could be resolved by investing in better infrastructure and equipment (which contrary to popular belief is still an issue for many) and improving the interoperability of systems and processes such as registration.

Although universities appeared to be reluctant to make VLE use mandatory, they had devised a number of incentives and strategies to encourage use. It was noticeable that about a third of those interviewed had received extra help to develop VLE use (as distinct from taking part in training courses or receiving one-to-one planning support). This help had been provided both internally and externally and included monies to pay for better equipment or time off for the planning of VLE-supported courses as well as technical help. Three interviewees had been involved with external projects that funded teaching innovation with a focus on ICT use, two had received external monies to cover the cost of development, and a further two won some funding to develop students as independent learners for which they intended to use a VLE.

This extra help was an important catalyst in the development of VLE use among lecturers who already had an interest in developing their teaching and the use of ICT. However, it did not fully compensate them for the amount of effort expended nor did it explain how other less motivated colleagues were to be engaged. The type of help received suggested issues that institutions needed to address in order to facilitate VLE use: time to prepare, the provision of support staff to help design and input content, and monies to cover development costs. Interviewees complained that management did not have a realistic understanding of the impact of VLE use on working practices in terms of staff time needed and, for one academic in particular, health and safety issues related to constant keyboard use (arising in that case with developing a course under time pressure).

The existence of an institutional strategy was considered important, although this did not mean interviewees wanted standardisation. There was criticism from within institutions where interviewees felt that VLE use lacked direction or that adequate support and

Table 6. Factors affecting VLE use and classified as institutional issues

Institutional issues	Issues interviewees spoke about that needed to be dealt with at an institutional or departmental level and that would need to be tackled for VLE use to become the norm.
• Managerial support	⇒ Positive attitude to ICT i.e. support for change, the provision of money and resources including development incentives, such as time off to plan use and responsibility posts ⇒ Concerns about the appropriateness of compulsion and job security, the use of a VLE to alleviate an increase in student numbers ⇒ Policy issues in respect of the status or use of Web sites and VLE 'modules'
• Culture and ethos	⇒ Colleague ICT skills and use, the existence of a "Community of practice" ⇒ Support for teaching innovation and technology use – conflict between teaching and research

training was not provided. The experience of interviewees at one university was particularly illustrative of the effect of a lack of support. They felt let down by the removal (due to cost cutting) of a central department supporting their use of the VLE stating that this had seriously impeded progress. They had all used the staff within this department to help plan, design, and implement online learning, something identified by interviewees at other institutions as being important and necessary. It fueled fears that interviewees had about possible institutional intentions, for example, the replacement of full-time members of staff with part-time lecturers and online materials, and explained some reluctance to consider a change in the structure of teaching time to remove some face-to-face contact.

Management willingness to provide adequate resources was another issue. One interviewee explained that being able to demonstrate the module helped student comfort level, while another found use of a VLE went up after a familiarisation session. However, this was dependent upon gaining access to a lecture room equipped with a data projector and a screen and having access to specially equipped computer labs, something that was not always possible. In institutions where there were difficulties accessing equipment, lecturer ability to demonstrate VLE use and to support students adequately or to move away from the idea that a VLE is something separate to what happens in the classroom, rather than an embedded support tool that enhances the teaching and learning, was questionable. There was also evidence that some early adopters were subsidising development out of their own pocket: paying for broadband access at home and buying Web authoring software.

Interviewees claimed to spend a great deal of time dealing with registration problems which were said to have a number of causes: layers of bureaucracy arising from a centralised and unresponsive registration system that inhibited the ability to edit, amend, or update registrations and a lack of adequate administrative support where departments or lecturers were expected to input registration details themselves. This indicated a need to find a compromise between centralisation and lecturer control over registration. In one university, a "rapid fix system" had been put in place. This gave students an element of control to register themselves and get in touch with someone (other than their lecturer) quickly, if they have trouble. This solution was in line with a desire to encourage students to take more responsibility for their own learning.

The culture and ethos of an institution, school, or department, with regard to technology use and teaching innovation affected what interviewees felt able to do. While interviewees said that they learnt a lot from colleagues, valuing any opportunities to share good practice and pick up ideas, they were also irritated by those who were reluctant to use a VLE or electronic resources and those who dismissed VLE users as "technophiles" (implying unquestioning adoption of the technology). This could leave them feeling isolated and impacted on student use.

Interviewees said it was easier for them to make use of a VLE and electronic resources if students met them elsewhere, so that use was considered the norm. Interviewees identified a need to promote a culture of use and the sharing of ideas and problems encountered, so VLE use can become self-supporting through a community of practice. Events arranged to share good practice were important as a way of examining the benefits of VLE use. The prevalent culture in some universities made innovation and the sharing of good practice very difficult. For example, research-led universities did not always give credit for teaching innovation, and interviewees thought colleagues might be reluctant to open up their teaching to examination or to change their practice. Where there was no central body co-ordinating VLE use, sharing strategies was problematic.

Interviewees thought that one of the reasons colleagues did not use a VLE was because they did not have the requisite IT skills or confidence and that some were fearful of admitting they did not know how to do something, especially if they had a reputation to keep up. Although attempts to improve the skills and practice of new lecturers had been put in place in many institutions, there was concern that lecturers later in their careers seemed to have been forgotten and that this would have an impact on use. It was recognised that some people may feel technology use was not relevant to them. However, interviewees felt let down and used if colleagues were quite willing to use them as support people rather than learning how to do something themselves or if colleagues did not take up the opportunities offered. Interviewees thought some institutional cultures did not help this aspect, as work with ICT was not valued; therefore, it had the potential to become an extra burden for those who took it on board.

Pedagogic Issues

VLE use was still exploratory and evolving and will be for some time by all accounts. It was affected by the practical problems identified in earlier sections of this chapter: access, reliability, student feedback, and an understanding of what was possible, practical, and suitable in the time available. Interviewees thought that while a VLE could be a useful tool and provided a vehicle to support student learning it was important not to think that it was a way of solving problems such as increased marking loads. It was also necessary to tailor use to specific situations and recognise that not all tools would be needed for all courses. The most obvious, straightforward, and popular use of a VLE was to display materials, provide links to other resources, and act as an "electronic filing cabinet." This model had been encouraged to some extent by institutional mandates to place course guides and resources for particular course levels within the VLE by a certain date, giving rise to a certain inertia to develop use in some cases.

Although interviewees did not agree on which were the most appropriate students to begin use with, they wanted leeway to decide best use. Some questioned the wisdom of starting with first-year students because they may not have the necessary technical skills and, in the case of discussion lists, students may not be confident enough about subject matter to participate; it was thought that they needed to be inducted into the ways of the discipline first and obtain some background knowledge. Others thought that there would be less resistance to VLE use if students began during their first year. When creating a course online, interviewees found it was necessary to be responsive to the needs of different types of students, providing more structure for first-year students, while master's students were willing and able to respond to a more discursive style of teaching.

While there was evidence of interviewees exploring the use of different tools within a VLE, there was actually little reported use of elements such as the integrated communications tools (synchronous, chat, and asynchronous, e-mail, and discussion forums). This may have been because of a desire to keep face-to-face interaction or because of a misunderstanding about the type of communication supported. One interviewee thought using discussion tools meant getting students to sit down all at the same time; the prospective complications of this prospect filled her with horror. A typical use of a discussion forum was to provide a frequently asked question area to reduce office hours, avoid the repetitive answering of the same questions, and facilitate peer support.

Interviewees pointed out that use has to be focused, structured, and seen to have purpose by the students, something which also had to be borne in mind when preparing materials that were, in effect, going to be on display. Additional pressures included adopting what was for some a new way of working, having to prepare well in advance, and, in one university, submitting to greater levels of quality control as well as learning new pedagogic skills such as how to moderate online interactions. There was concern about the amount of time it took to prepare and maintain materials as well as to administer online courses; interviewees thought that those encouraging VLE use had little idea of the work involved.

Interviewees in receipt of online learning fellowships at one university, which included time off teaching and individual support, were instructed to reciprocate by reducing their

Table 7. Factors affecting VLE use and classified as pedagogic issues

Pedagogic issues	Pedagogic issues classified any difficulties interviewees said they encountered when attempting to apply a VLE to their teaching and concerns they had when working out how, when and where to use a VLE most effectively, as well as any needs this generated.
• Identifying purposeful use	⇒ The suitability or practicality of computer mediated communication for face-to-face classes, the use of a VLE within a face-to-face classroom (workshop format, access to resources) ⇒ Understanding what is possible and being able to apply it
• New way of working	⇒ Visibility, preparation, revision and updating of materials, time to prepare, creating different student expectations ⇒ More rigorous validation procedures, focus of support staff, time to support discussion groups
• Changing how you teach	⇒ The need to think through what you do, time to implement and support changes

contact time through VLE use. However, problems were associated with the assumption that moving teaching and materials online reduces staff time. Where teaching had moved online, interviewees reported this changed their role to more of a "guide on the side" and had led to increased expectations requiring lecturers to be always present, to make sure resources were available immediately, and generally to provide a constant supply of authored materials and information. This was thought to be unrealistic. It also contradicted one of the expected benefits of VLE use, to make students take more responsibility for their own learning, and it highlighted the need to set boundaries and to create guidelines for response time.

Other interviewees considering reducing contact time were inhibited by the expected teaching structures in their institutions; this is something that needs to be reviewed if institutions are serious about changing the type of teaching and learning that goes on, that is, moving away from the traditional lecture plus seminar and tutorial model and encouraging the use of active learning. Interviewees were keen to emphasise that, although the use of a VLE may change the teaching strategies adopted, this did not mean that there was no place for face-to-face teaching. Indeed, many lecturers stressed that they could only see a VLE as being valuable alongside face-to-face teaching for a number of reasons, not the least of which was student expectation.

There was little evidence of the team planning and preparation that might help with this extra load; one lecturer planning and implementing use was the norm. Although one interviewee found the preparation of online materials released her from the time pressures associated with preparing hard copy, this was unusual and more often found to be an additional task for those who were still obliged to prepare hard copy because of institutional expectations. Another area of concern was the effect that the extra work resulting from VLE use may have on other areas of their job, particularly, in respect to the impact on time available for research. It could be argued that the two areas could be combined to satisfy requirements, but this may not be compatible with lecturer research interests or with institutional priorities. Interviewees in pre-1992 HEIs, in particular, felt that work with a VLE was not valued and that teaching innovation was valued less than subject area research.

The Interrelationship of the Issues Identified

This chapter provides an overview of issues that interviewees said helped or hindered their use of a VLE. There were four main interrelated issues, expressed as four categories: student, technical, institutional, and pedagogic. The relationships between the categories are shown in Figure 1 which also illustrates that student, technical, and institutional issues impact upon pedagogic matters and will affect the way in which a VLE is used, aside from the demonstrable problems lecturers have in deciding how best to use a VLE to support their teaching and their students' learning.

The interviewees, who could be characterised as cautious enthusiasts, keen to try out new ways of teaching and supporting their students, had benefited from incentive strategies employed by their institutions, and as "innovators" or "early adopters" (Zemsky & Massy, 2004) thought they were well supported. They described evolving use. Nevertheless, the issues highlighted (concerns about institutional intentions and the effect of VLE use on their students as well as the impact of wider adoption on the support services) indicate a need for a greater level of resources and thought about teaching structures if adoption is to move beyond this first group of users. The issues identified would equally apply to the adoption of other forms of information and communications technology, such as mobile devices.

Conclusion

What is surprising is not the type of issues lecturers still have to deal with when trying to use the ICT on offer, in this case VLEs, but the fact that adoption takes place in such a hit and miss way. Although it is recognised that VLE adoption has the potential to change and improve the way teaching and learning takes place (through its association with the enhancement of teaching and learning), development and innovation appear to be taking place in a very ad hoc and individual way. This may suit the first stages of use but does not bode well for sustainability (witness the comments about needing a community of use) and encouraging non-users. There is a reluctance to dictate how a VLE should be used because of ideas of academic autonomy and concern about too much standardisation; as a consequence, it is difficult for lecturers to know how to make effective use of a VLE and where to target that use.

Figure 1. The relationship between "needs and concerns" categories

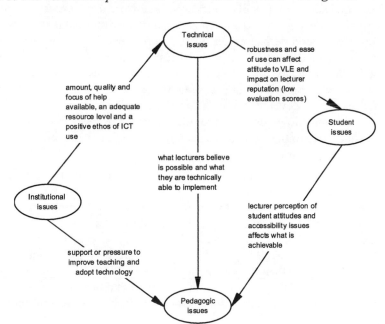

The issues outlined indicate a need for a greater level of resources if adoption is to move beyond the first group of innovators and early adopters as well as thought about the type of teaching structures supported. Institutions have to be clear why they want to encourage the use of VLEs because different aims call for different uses and solutions:

- just a delivery mechanism (some HEIs are moving into distance education, especially in specialist areas)

- flexible learning (different demands on staff and infrastructure and changes in the structure and organisation of face-to-face teaching)

- the enhancement of teaching and learning (added bells and whistles or a change in the teaching approach adopted, that is, more student-centred, and if so how will students be supported to take more responsibility for their own learning and how will academics be helped to adopt new models of teaching?)

There is a tension between the institutional motivations and those of individual departments and academics, illustrated by some of the comments recorded. An institution will want to see a return on its infrastructure investment in terms of student satisfaction, usage statistics, and better learning outcomes, while lecturers may just want to find ways of supporting their teaching in the face of increasing student numbers and decreasing resources. Some interviewees felt that VLE use enabled them to compensate for a diminution in the service (typically a reduction in contact time) they were able to offer students.

Implications

The issues identified have a number of implications for different audiences. Clearly, there are resource implications that need to be considered by institutional managers, not the least to ensure that everyone has access to the same version of standard software. Decisions need to be made about the type of VLE use to be encouraged and supported and what impact this may have on current structures, schedules, and workload (something highlighted by current literature, e.g., Garrison & Kanuka, 2004). The use of incentives such as time to develop and adapt courses as well as responsibility posts have proved effective to encourage use and provide a core of users who can disseminate practice. The adherence to the lecture, plus seminar model, has proved restrictive for some trying to change their practice.

Staff developers need to consider the best way to develop the IT literacy of staff while encouraging them to explore different models of teaching and learning. The type and focus of staff development and support is a major theme in recent literature on lecturer use of Web and Internet-based technology, underlining issues raised by this research. The need to develop lecturer IT skills is recognised by Haynes et al. (2004), while Kent described the importance of having an institutional strategy that informs what is considered effective use and then supports its application (2003). Grant (2004), McShane (2004), and Errington (2004) highlighted the importance of taking into account lecturers' perspectives on professional development, their role concept and teaching choices, and what they believe is possible, in trying to understand why lecturers became involved in innovation and how best to begin supporting them.

Lecturers who are themselves contemplating VLE adoption should find out what support and time is available to them in developing or adapting their courses and seek examples of "good practice" within their institutions or elsewhere. The Learning and Teaching Support Network (LTSN) subject centres would be a good starting point (now part of the Higher Education Academy), as would the recently published set of case studies from HEFCE in association with JISC (2004). They need to decide what they want to do with the technology and not underestimate the amount of time it takes to create online materials or to re-version traditional face-to-face courses.

References

Alexander, S. (1995). *Teaching and learning on the World Wide Web*. Last updated November 5, 1996. Retrieved September 30, 2004, from http://ausweb.scu.edu.au/aw95/education2/alexander/

Barnard, J. (1999). *Factors affecting the use of computer assisted learning by further education biology teachers*. Unpublished Ph.D. thesis. Open University, Milton Keynes, UK.

Barr, R.B., & Tagg, J. (1995). From teaching to learning — A new paradigm for undergraduate education. *Change, 27*(6), 12-25.

Biggs, J. (1994). Student learning research and theory — Where do we currently stand? In G. Gibbs (Ed.), *Improving student learning — theory and practice*. Oxford: Oxford Centre for Staff Development.

Britain, S., & Liber, O. (2004). *A framework for the pedagogical evaluation of virtual learning environments*. Retrieved January 25, 2005, from www.jisc.ac.uk/uploaded_documents/VLE%20Full%20Report%2006.doc

Browne, T., & Jenkins, M. (2003). *VLE surveys: A longitudinal perspective between March 2001 and March 2003 for higher education in the United Kingdom*. Retrieved September 30, 2004, from www.ucisa.ac.uk/groups/tlig/vle/vle2003.pdf

Collis, B. (1996). *Tele-learning in a digital world*. London: Thomson Computer Press.

Errington, E. (2004). The impact of teacher beliefs on flexible learning innovation: Some practices and possibilities for academic developers. *Innovations in Education and Teaching International, 41*(1), 39-47.

Fraser, M. (1997). Dearing & it: Some reflections. *Computers & Texts*. Retrieved September 30, 2004, from http://info.ox.ac.uk/ctitext/publish/comtxt/ct15/fraser.html

Garrison, D.R., & Kanuka, H. (2004). Blended learning: Uncovering its transformative potential in higher education. *The Internet and Higher Education, 7*(2), 95-105.

Grant, M.M. (2004). Learning to teach with the Web: Factors influencing teacher education faculty. *The Internet and Higher Education, 7*(4), 329-341.

Haynes, P., Ip, K., Saintas, P., Stanier, S., Palmer, H., Thomas, N., et al. (2004). Responding to technological change: IT skills and the academic teaching profession. *Active Learning in Higher Education, 5*(2), 152-165.

HEFCE. (2004). *Effective practice with e-learning: A good practice guide in designing for learning.*Retrieved July 2005, from www.jisc.ac.uk/index.cfm?name=elp_practice

Jenkins, M., Browne, T., & Armitage, S. (2001). Management and implementation of virtual learning environments: A UCISA funded survey. Retrieved September 30, 2004, from www.ucisa.ac.uk/groups/tlig/vle/VLEsurvey.pdf

Johannasen, T., & Eide, E.M. (2000). The role of the teacher in the age of technology: Will the role change with use of information- and communication technology in education? *European Journal of Open and Distance Learning.*

Kearsley, G. (1998). Educational technology: A critique. *Educational Technology, 38*(2), 47-51.

Kent, T. (2003). Supporting staff using WebCT at the University of Birmingham. *Electronic Journal of eLearning, 1*(1), 1-9.

Marton, F., & Saljo, R. (1997). Approaches to learning. In F. Marton, D. Hounsell, & N. Entwistle (Eds.), *The experience of learning* (pp. 39-58). Edinburgh: Scottish Academic Press.

McShane, K. (2004). Integrating face-to-face and online teaching: Academics' role concept and teaching choices. *Teaching in Higher Education, 9*(1), 3-16.

Morón-García, S. (2000). *Real learning in a virtual environment? The Wolverhampton online learning framework (WOLF).* Unpublished master's project, University of Wolverhampton, Wolverhampton, UK.

Morón-García, S. (2001, September 26-27). Are virtual learning environments being used to facilitate and support student-centred learning in higher education? In B. Zayas & C. Gama (Eds.), *5th human centred technology postgraduate workshop — Information technologies and knowledge construction: Bringing together the best of two worlds* (pp. 9-11). Brighton, UK: University of Sussex.

Morón-García, S. (2004). *Understanding lecturers' use of virtual learning environments to support face-to-face teaching in UK higher education.* Unpublished doctoral thesis in Educational Technology, Open University, Milton Keynes.

Prosser, M., & Trigwell, K. (1997). Relations between perceptions of the teachng environment and approaches to teaching. *British Journal of Educational Psychology, 67*(1), 25-35.

Somekh, B. (1998). Supporting information and communication technology innovations in higher education. *Journal of Information Technology for Teacher Education, 7*(1).

Thorpe, M. (1999). New technology and pedagogical challenges. *Lifelong Learning in Europe, 4*(1), 40-46.

Trigwell, K., Prosser, M., Martin, E., & Ramsden, P. (1998). Improving student learning through a focus on the teaching context. In C. Rust (Ed.), *Proceedings of the 1997 5th International Symposium on Improving Student Learning: Improving Stu-*

dents as Learners (pp. 97-103). Oxford: Oxford Centre for Staff and Learning Development.

Trigwell, K., Prosser, M., & Waterhouse, F. (1999). Relations between teachers' approaches to teaching and students' approaches to learning. *Higher Education, 37*, 57-70.

Wegner, S.B., Holloway, K.C., & Garton, E.M. (1999). The effects of Internet-based instruction on student learning. Retrieved September 30, 2004, from www.aln.org/publications/jaln/v3n2/v3n2_wegner.asp

Westera, W. (1999). Paradoxes in open, networked learning environments: Toward a paradigm shift. *Educational Technology, 39*(1), 17-23.

Zemsky, R., & Massy, W.F. (2004). Thwarted innovation: What happened to e-learning and why. Retrieved July 25, 2004, from www.irhe.upenn.edu/Docs/Jun2004/ThwartedInnovation.pdf

Chapter III

Academic Experiences of Using VLEs:
Overarching Lessons for Preparing and Supporting Staff

Barbara Newland, Bournemouth University, UK

Martin Jenkins, University of Gloucestershire, UK

Neil Ringan, University of Bolton, UK

Abstract

This chapter describes the drivers which have influenced the adoption of e-learning within the UK HE sector and consequently resulted in the increasing adoption of VLEs within institutions. It identifies a range of issues at the institutional and individual academic staff levels which need to be considered and addressed when designing and implementing a VLE within an HE institution. The authors draw on their personal experience in supporting a diverse range of academic staff to integrate e-learning and VLEs within their academic practice and their experience in implementing VLEs in a range of institutions to develop a series of guidelines and lessons for institutions to consider. Evidence from a range of case studies undertaken by the authors is utilised to provide examples from academic practice, which illustrate how effective implementation of these guidelines and lessons can enhance the student learning experience and support the role of academic staff within the HE sector.

Introduction

The introduction of virtual learning environments (VLEs), which have seen steady and consistent growth in the UK, (Armitage, Browne, & Jenkins, 2001; Browne & Jenkins, 2003) has been a significant factor in the recent development of e-learning. Both the Department for Education and Skills (DfES) and the Higher Education Funding Council for England (HEFCE) published e-learning strategies in March 2005, indicative of the importance placed on this area. While recognising the potential, the HEFCE strategy also notes that "institutions are still struggling to 'normalise' e-learning as part of higher education processes" (HEFCE, 2005b). While there is now extensive use of information and communication technologies (ICT) in higher education, its impact on the curriculum is limited; mainly supplementing face-to-face delivery (Collis & van der Wende, 2002; Bell et al., 2002; Browne & Jenkins, 2003). In a recent study, Bricheno, Higgison, and Weedon (2004) note that there is "little change to the teacher role, or of a move towards student centred learning."

However, examples of innovative practice in the use of VLEs to support learning do exist. Such evidence is available through case studies developed by the Learning Environments and Pedagogy (LEAP) project (LEAP, 2005) and from the Association for Learning Technology (ALT) study tours to Australia (Boezerooy, 2002) and the Netherlands (Roberts & Riachi, 2004). These studies have highlighted a range of issues for students, staff, and institutions, focusing on the educational application of VLEs, staff development, student support, and change management.

This chapter explores the increasing adoption of VLEs from an academic staff perspective, discussing the experiences of the authors and evidence from the research literature in preparing and supporting staff to work within this new paradigm. The chapter is divided into three sections. The first explores the range of drivers for increasing adoption of VLEs. This is followed by a section which identifies issues associated with the implementation of VLEs from the perspectives of institutions, academic staff, and students. Finally, a series of lessons are discussed which need to be considered at the institutional or individual level in relation to staff support if the increasing adoption of VLEs is to significantly enhance the student learning experience.

Drivers for Change in the Use of VLEs

The increase in the adoption of VLEs within the higher education (HE) sector has been the result of a number of "top-down" and "bottom-up" approaches at the national, institutional, and individual levels. A range of drivers can be identified which have contributed to this growth and which impact on the ways in which staff require to be supported in the use of e-learning.

Wider Higher Education Environment

Government and other national body initiatives have changed the perception of e-learning as its adoption has become more prevalent. This has been clearly illustrated in the UK, with the shift from the distance online delivery vision of the early 1990s to the almost universal focus on a blended approach, combining a range of online and face-to-face provision, evident in responses to the HEFCE e-learning strategy consultation (HEFCE, 2004). This view was also reinforced in early 2005 with the demise of the UK e-University (UkeU), primarily due to the lack of students wishing to enroll in online distance learning programmes (HEFCE, 2005c). Funding remaining within the UKeU has subsequently been disbursed to individual institutions to embed e-learning in support of the HEFCE strategy, thus allowing local approaches to be developed (HEFCE, 2005a).

Evidence of this shift in the view of e-learning, from fully distance to blended, is also apparent from the Universities and Colleges Information Systems Association (UCISA) VLE Surveys conducted in 2001 and 2003 (Armitage, Browne, & Jenkins, 2001; Browne & Jenkins, 2003). In 2001, the main reasons given for VLE use were enhancing teaching and learning, efficiency, distance learning, and flexibility. Two years later the key drivers were increasingly viewed as the enhancement of teaching and learning and flexibility, but no longer distance learning. With increasing participation rates in higher education and a subsequent increase in the diversity of students entering HE, the focus in many institutions is now on retaining existing students. The use of e-learning is thus increasingly focused on how it can support this agenda rather than on developing new distant markets.

Institutional Environment

The institutional perspective on the use of VLEs is influenced by the need of institutions to consider their position in the wider education market. External agendas drive the "You can't not do it" syndrome identified by Collis and Moonen (2001), and have encouraged the development of the use of VLEs (Browne & Jenkins, 2003). In the UK, the HEFCE e-learning strategy emphasises the institutional embedding of e-learning, stating:

Over the past few years, education has been affected by rapid developments in the use of ICT. It is timely to consider the need to support the sector further in taking best advantage of these developments, as it moves to:

- *meet the greater diversity of student needs;*

- *increase flexibility of provision;*

- *enhance the capacity for integrating study with work and leisure through work-based and home-based learning; and*

- *develop approaches to individualised support for planning and recording achievements.*

While individual institutions may view one or more of these factors as the principal driver for embedding e-learning and adopting a VLE, it is often unclear how staff are supported in operationalising such a vision.

Academic Staff

From the individual staff perspective, there are different drivers for using VLEs which are influenced by the individual's understanding of teaching, their preferred teaching methods, and their subject discipline. One of the main reasons that many staff use a VLE is to enhance their teaching (Newland et al., 2004). They also want to decrease their administrative load so that they have more time to spend on their research or teaching. The drivers will also change over time as the use of VLEs moves from the early adopters and enthusiasts to the "majority" of academics.

There is a tension (Bricheno, Higgison, & Weedon, 2004) between the use of e-learning to sustain a mass higher education system and the desire to shift toward a more innovative learning and teaching culture. This can create a potential conflict between institutional and individual drivers for the use of VLEs, and consequently the ways in which their implementation is supported.

Students

There is a continuing drive for greater participation in HE, and technology is increasingly viewed as an enabling factor in this dynamic. However, increasing participation rates have resulted in wider student diversity in terms of academic background, age, ICT skills, and personal commitments such as family, work, and care. To address the increasing number and diversity of students, there has been an increase in the flexibility of awards which are offered, ranging from foundation degrees to more work-based and franchised awards. Many of these rely on technology to support learners and to deliver programme content through a VLE to meet the specific requirements of the student population and of potential employers.

Many prospective and current students, in particular those entering directly from school, have an increasing sophistication in their expectations of the level of resources and support delivered electronically due to their experience of using the Internet at school and socially. With the introduction of student tuition fees within the UK, there is an increasing view of the student as a customer who comes with a range of expectations and requirements. As a result, e-learning has become an integral, if supplementary, part of many students' learning experience (Browne & Jenkins, 2003).

At present, the use of VLEs within a subject area varies from use by a sole academic to an entire department. Evidence from student evaluations and surveys shows that use of VLEs is generally seen as a positive aspect which they wish to see developed further (Newland et al., 2004). Student pressure on academic staff to adopt e-learning can thus be a significant driver for change. Initially, students are appreciative of the use of e-learning in any aspect of their studies, but as increasing numbers of staff adopt VLEs to support their teaching, students will have higher expectations of the quality and nature of its use.

Issues

The increasing adoption of e-learning and VLEs in response to the drivers outlined has resulted in a number of issues emerging which require to be considered when developing an implementation or support strategy. These issues can be considered at the institutional, academic staff, and student levels.

Institutional Environment

Rationale for Adoption

For the adoption and implementation of e-learning to successfully enhance the student learning experience, it is vital that institutions have a clear vision of how and why it is deploying e-learning. This does not mean having a "one size fits all" approach to its implementation, but rather creating an institutional framework which encourages developments by individual academic staff. Unfortunately, many institutions have adopted e-learning as a result of the "You can't not do it" syndrome (Collis & Moonen, 2001) in response to a range of perceived drivers resulting in confusion for individual staff as to what is expected and required of them.

As an example, Lisewski (2004, p. 183) discusses how setting an institutional target of utilising the VLE to provide a "Web presence" for every module can lead to a wide variety of interpretations. As a consequence, this can lead to a lack of engagement, if it is interpreted that limited action is required, or fear and trepidation if the expectation is seen as too high. Trowler and Knight (2002) (in Lisewski, 2004) state that a university needs to recognise that learning technology developments will bring a range of outcomes and that "learning quality might be better encouraged by encouraging a diversity of innovations" (p. 185). It is important for the university position on e-learning to be phrased in terms that can be identified within the local culture where it can be interpreted against local practice. In situations where the institutional policy differs from local practice, the role of the "educational developer" is important to mediate the processes.

Lack of clarity of the institutional role of e-learning is also increasingly likely to result in its use solely to supplement face-to-face teaching without adding any value to the learning process (van der Klink & Jochems, 2003). VLEs can provide the context of delivery which enables students to achieve the maximum benefit from their study. This is vital as, in the words of Laurillard (2001), "the most stunning educational materials ever developed will fail to teach if the context of delivery fails." The role of the VLE is particularly relevant in providing the teaching context and the learning activities during the presage and process phase of the 3P model (Biggs, 2003).

Holistic Approaches to E-Learning

Successful implementation of e-learning requires a holistic approach (Jochems, Prosser, & Waterhouse, 2003, p. 5) with institutions addressing pedagogical, technical, and organisational factors.

If one of these three factors is seen to "lead" the development of e-learning without due consideration of the other two, then the chances of success are reduced. Such an approach requires collaborative working and innovation in practice within institutions which in turn requires a complete change of culture to ensure that a broad range of stakeholders is involved in designing and developing approaches to implementation and support. Existing processes within an institution must be scrutinised and changed to support effectively these new approaches.

Taking such a holistic approach also ensures that artificial barriers are reduced. E-learning should be seen as an integral part of the business of HE rather than something special. Consequently all of the systems and processes which support learning and teaching should therefore recognise e-learning and be supportive to its further development. Yet, it is often the case that institutions require additional quality assurance processes for e-learning. This creates a developmental burden that does not compare with more traditional forms of delivery. The consequence is that this adds to the perception of e-learning as being differentiated from other forms of learning and teaching and being more time intensive.

Embedding and Sustaining E-Learning Developments

Collis and Moonen (2001) developed a model for the institutional adoption of flexible learning, describing the factors which affect the initiation and implementation of technology innovations using the "4Es":

- Environment (institutional): vision, support, and actual level of use within the institution and readiness for change.

- Education effectiveness (perceived): likelihood of benefit.

- Ease of use.

- Engagement (personal): self-confidence, interest in new technologies.

The 4Es identified vary in significance at different times in the implementation and support cycle. During the initiation stage, the work of enthusiasts and early adopters predominates. Many early VLE developments have been localised project developments funded through short-term activities initiated by enthusiasts (Browne & Jenkins, 2003). However, such an approach is not sustainable and does not lead to long-term embedding or the raising of skills capacity and expertise within the institution (ELTI, 2003).

To effectively move through the implementation stages of e-learning requires support to ensure that the "majority" of staff understand and embrace the potential of e-learning. This change in the nature of the staff engaged requires a move from more abstract to more practical concerns, reflecting the shift that Gynn and Acker (2001) identified as they moved beyond early adopters in their staff development provision. The majority of potential users of the VLE are unlikely to have high "engagement" vectors as identified by Collis and Moonen (2001). Consequently, there is a need to ensure that e-learning staff development provision blends technical skills with the pedagogic understanding of how and where the technologies can be effectively implemented to enhance student learning.

Senior Management Support

The support of senior managers is often cited as a key factor in the successful embedding of e-learning (Newland & Ringan, 2002). The DfES e-learning strategy has reinforced this importance but also identified how a lack of understanding of the issues can act as a barrier to developments. "Leaders were uncertain about ICT's benefits, so it was not often linked to institutional strategies" (DfES, 2005, p. 34).

This has meant that business processes are generally not aligned with the needs of staff utilising e-learning, reinforcing the requirement for e-learning to be seen in a more holistic way (Jochems et al., 2003). Senior managers with responsibility for other key areas of activity such as registry are not aware of the significance to them, or indeed how their sphere of influence impacts on e-learning developments.

Academic Staff

The issues associated with academic staff adoption of VLEs and e-learning in general can be correlated with the more widespread model of innovation growth as defined by Rogers (1995) and Robinson (2001). Within the context of this study, the most significant issues affecting academic staff adoption relate to their understanding of the role of e-learning within their own context and how they are supported in its implementation.

Benefits

For staff to adopt VLEs, they need to see that there will be a benefit in so doing as defined in Rogers' (1995) factor of relative advantage. Potential benefits can be seen in different ways, including improving the learning experience for students, but a common theme from studies is the impact on staff time and the need for recognition (Jenkins & Oates, 2005).

Academic staff have competing demands on their time including teaching, research, administration, and income generation. However, it is still the case that in the majority of institutions, recognition and promotion is linked to research activity rather than innovative teaching developments. The UCISA survey (Browne & Jenkins, 2003) highlighted that career progression is not perceived as being a reward for VLE development. However, there is the potential for VLEs to decrease the time spent on administrative or routine teaching activities, thus freeing time to undertake research and scholarly activity.

Values and Beliefs

Prosser and Trigwell (1999) developed a model illustrating how teachers approach each learning situation and how they perceive and act within that situation. This model encapsulates how the teacher's response will be influenced by their prior experiences (or lack of) with new methods, and also how the environment they are working within and their perceived needs of students will influence their choice of teaching approach.

The majority of current academics have not studied using a VLE nor seen how e-learning can be effectively utilised to support a range of teaching situations. Their experiences, and consequently their values, are thus predominantly those of the face-to-face paradigm. Increasing drivers at the institutional and student level are encouraging staff to increase adoption of e-learning, but often without effective underpinning pedagogic or technical skills support. The consequence of this is that in many cases there is simply a transfer of existing teaching and learning situations and values from the face-to-face to online contexts. This is reinforced by Alexander and Boud (2001) who state: "the potential of technology for improving learning is being lost because it too often replicates the limiting didactic practices it was intended to replace."

It is essential that staff are enabled to revise the entire learning and teaching paradigm to ensure that delivery through a VLE is appropriately designed and supported. There has been much research comparing traditional delivery with new technologies; many of these studies have shown no significant difference in effectiveness (No Significant Difference, 2005). Bates and Poole (2003) argue that the reason for this lack of differentiation is a result of the technology being used to deliver the same traditional approaches, rather than supporting a continuum of e-learning, from the use of presentation software to fully online distance delivery.

Skills and Staff Development

The initial adoption and growth in the use of VLEs was fueled by enthusiasts who were happy to experiment and more likely to accept problems and occasional setbacks as part of the development process. With institutions implementing VLEs across the curriculum and adoption of technology moving beyond the early adopters to the "majority", it is vital that a stable, easy-to-use platform is provided.

Technical, operational, and administrative difficulties which are perceived as being part of the VLE can rapidly affect staff perceptions of the technology. Therefore, it is essential that staff are supported in developing the full range of skills in the technical utilisation of the VLE as well as effective pedagogic implementation of e-learning. A base level of ICT skills should be considered as a prerequisite for any member of academic staff.

Time

The issue of time is arguably the most frequently cited factor affecting the further development of VLE use (Browne & Jenkins, 2003). The difficulties that staff have in finding the time, amongst other competing demands, to develop their use of VLEs is limiting. This factor tends to reinforce small-scale developments which supplement face-to-face delivery, thus encouraging an evolutionary approach. Wider institutional adoption of e-learning requires redevelopment and redesign of existing courses and represents a significant time investment. Therefore, new course developments provide the most accessible opportunities for significant change, with existing provision continuing to adapt through evolutionary change.

Garrison and Anderson (2003) argue that it is important for institutions to "incubate" new learning technology developments alongside traditional delivery, thus allowing the institution to develop the expertise and be ready to exploit opportunities as they arise. To enable this, staff would need to be allowed time for exploration and development, in competition with other demands. This issue needs to be recognised by management as evidenced in other research: "Learning technology innovations must be recognised alongside other competing agendas and that the 'notion of lack of space' principally in terms of time may not be acknowledged by senior management" (Lisewski, 2004, p. 182).

Visibility and Dissemination

The visibility of new developments is an important part of the change process. Rogers (1995) noted that the establishment of a social network for the exchange of ideas and experiences was a key factor: "The heart of the diffusion process is the modelling and imitation by potential adopters of the near-peers' experiences who have previously adopted a new idea" (p. 304).

There have been many projects in HE (e.g., LEAP, Subject Centres) to collect examples/case studies of practice and disseminate these. These have had only a limited impact, in part due to the other "barriers" such as time. There is also an apparent unwillingness to share resources and ideas from other institutions and across disciplines.

Students

Students with an increasingly broad range of experience, knowledge, and skills are being encouraged through widening participation strategies to study in HE resulting in a range of issues for staff.

For many students, conventional delivery methods are no longer appropriate as they work full- or part-time as "learner-earners" or "earner-learners" and/or have family commitments. They wish to take full advantage of the flexibility of e-learning in attendance and delivery modes, challenging staff perceptions of attendance. Students of different ages have different attitudes toward using technology (Tapscott, 1998). Learners who have grown up in a world in which computers are part of life like to multi-task and are used to continuous communication through texting, phone calls, e-mail, and instant information via the Internet (Oblinger, 2003). These students expect a range of Web-based learning facilities, including resources, assessment, and communication tools to support their studies.

A more flexible approach to learning is also facilitated by increased student ownership of PCs including laptops with widespread wireless access to the Internet. This portability has implications for where, when, and how students are able to study. They are no longer restricted to using PCs supplied to encourage individual work in computer classrooms and libraries, but instead can easily participate in group work, either face-to face or virtually.

Overarching Lessons to Prepare and Support Staff

Evidence from the personal experience of the authors in supporting the implementation of VLEs and from their participation in the LEAP project in the UK and the ALT study tours to Australia and the Netherlands can help to identify mechanisms to prepare and support staff and so address the issues highlighted in the previous section. The LEAP project was formed by the Learning and Teaching Support Network (LTSN) Generic Centre in 2002. Initially, 14 case studies were commissioned from a group of experienced learning technologists who had already been through the phases of selection and implementation of VLEs and had moved into a phase of effective usage within their institutions (LEAP, 2005). The case studies have a pedagogical focus and provide evidence in practice on the use of VLEs in learning and teaching. In 2005, follow-up studies were undertaken to identify any changes to the key conclusions from the original case studies.

Senior Management Support

Evidence shows the need for policies on the use of VLEs within the curriculum to be an integral part of departmental and institutional e-learning strategies (Newland & Ringan, 2002). De Boer and Collis (2005) state that "instructors should work within an institutional environment that is encouraging them to try new ideas in responding to the needs of their students, and on the other hand the institutional environment should be able to respond quickly to the needs and questions of instructors." Bricheno, Higgison, and Weedon (2004) report that network learning has had the greatest impact in institutions that have combined both a top-down management and bottom-up approach to developments. The balance is important; local developments encourage ownership and appropriate management provides a direction for developments.

An example of an institution that has provided such an approach is Deakin University in Australia, which has a long history of e-learning developments built on distance learning programmes. By the late 1990s, the university had reached a position of varied e-learning across the institution with FirstClass, TopClass, WebCT, and Blackboard all being used across the university (Boezerooy, 2002). A strategic decision was therefore taken to consolidate its online learning through "Deakin Online" which took three years to plan, being fully implemented in 2002. The planning integrated the university's Teaching, Learning, and Management Plan along with strategic policy, including integration of systems and rationalising to one VLE. This strategy provides Deakin with a baseline for a commonality/minimum of provision, however, control of teaching and learning and how the VLE is used remains with the faculties. Therefore, this approach combines a management steer with local control (and ownership) of deployment.

Holistic Approaches to E-Learning

E-learning and the VLE need to be considered as a "whole" and not just an assembly of parts to provide the context of delivery. The departmental strategy can provide the overview of existing use of the VLE as well as a vision for its future in relation to institutional strategies. There are variations in both how the leadership by heads of department and course coordinators is experienced by lecturers and in academic leaders' own conceptions of how they support teaching. A focus on collaborative, supportive, and purposeful leadership for teaching is associated with a culture of strong teamwork and student-focused approaches (Martin, Trigwell, Prosser, & Ramsden, 2002; Ramsden, Prosser, Martin, & Trigwell, 2003).

The need for departmental strategies in the use of VLEs is illustrated at the University of Durham. The initial use of discussion boards in the Law Department generated a high level of intelligent debate, and often students were willing to provide answers for other students. However, the follow-up study 2 years later found the use of discussion boards had increased throughout the department and resulted in a decrease of quality of their use by students. Therefore, it has been necessary to develop a departmental policy on their use (LEAP Case Study 13, 2005).

Professionalisation of Teaching

It has been highlighted earlier how a lack of awareness and understanding of the potential for e-learning is an important factor in slowing development and adoption of VLEs. Similarly, the teaching approaches of staff will be based on their own experiences as a student and the culture of their discipline and institution. The move toward professionalisation of teaching in the UK does mean that new academic staff are now increasingly likely to undertake a Higher Education Academy (HEA) accredited post-graduate teaching certificate programme. Many of these programmes include an element on e-learning and provide staff with the opportunity to experience a VLE from the student perspective. This experience may bring about change within departments and there is a perception of this change mechanism operating already in some institutions. A university-wide evaluation of VLE use at the University of Gloucestershire found such evidence, with senior managers expecting that change would come with new staff rather than through a centrally imposed strategy (Jenkins & Oates, 2005).

Academic Staff: Ownership of Change

The role of the individual in developing the use of learning technology is significant. Early developments are often led by local champions, formal and informal. Yet these individuals often have as significant a negative impact as a positive one; the evangelical role that they take up is as likely to dissuade as persuade (Jenkins & Oates, 2005). It is important for individual academics to have ownership of change.

Bricheno, Higgison, and Weedon (2004) report that the attitudes of staff are "critical to the success of networked learning", in terms of engaging staff and enabling institutions to change cultures. They link this to the issue of ownership and the importance of ensuring that individual staff feel "empowered" to develop e-learning. This is illustrated by experience from the Netherlands where it is widely recognised that flexibility in staff development support is required (Roberts & Riachi, 2004). For example, the University of Twente offers a mixed economy model. The central unit offers a comprehensive central support programme, but some faculties choose not to use this support and instead provide their own local support. As a consequence individual academics have ownership of the developments. The VLE was seen as a tool to support learning and teaching and the staff picked the appropriate starting point for themselves and have moved along this continuum at a pace they can control.

The University of Gloucestershire provides an illustration of how attitudes of staff, through their commitment to a VLE development can create additional pressures and demands to ensure the overall quality of the student experience. While staff may be convinced of the design and delivery of e-learning, they may have reservations of its impact on traditional modes of delivery and increased workloads. It is such issues that need to be managed as part of changing cultures (LEAP Case Study, 20).

Academic Staff: Development and Skills

Educational developers and learning technologists have an important role in providing the link between different communities. In particular, they can play an important role in "translating" ideas so they can be transferred and accepted from one community to another (Armitage, 2004). They can enable the effective inter-linking of support for e-learning from the wider HE environment with institutional policy and also relate institutional policy to faculty practice, which can inform the development of departmental and institutional strategies. This helps academics to cope with the complexity of information and keep up-to-date with new developments.

A good example is the creation of the sophisticated support structure of HELO managers at the Hanzehogeschool, Groningen in the Netherlands (Roberts & Riachi, 2004, p. 14). Within the framework of an institutional flexible learning environment, they have created a central support structure complemented by local managers in each department, who provide both technological and pedagogical support. The staff in these roles are given time and have a facilitative role, including sharing information with staff in the same roles in other schools. They have found that this approach has encouraged local ownership and encouraged growth.

Academic staff development must recognise a hierarchy of needs involving ICT skills and pedagogy. Many of the LEAP case studies show that the development of new skills, such as e-moderating, are necessary to support the use of online discussions (LEAP Case Studies 3, 6, 7, 8, 9, & 11, 2005). Recognition of potential skills required in advance of the delivery and planning of staff development should be an important part of course design and validation process. However, Oliver and Dempster (2003) in Lisewski (2004, p. 183) note that in the "complexity of supporting e-learning, no single model of staff development may be able to engage all staff."

Individual's Rationale for Adoption

Most academics start by using the VLE as a repository for documents (the so-called "document dump" mentality), as this is an easy option (Collis & Messing, 2001). However, this provision of documents online can have positive benefits and can enable the development of an inclusive curriculum which supports all students (Doyle & Robson, 2002). Disabled students find access to documents prior to lectures particularly helpful as otherwise they have the problems of taking notes and may have to rely on their peers. Using another student's notes imposes secondary learning on them as the student has to interact with materials which have undergone interpretation by someone else who will have a different perception of the learning (Newland, Pavey, & Boyd, 2005). Academics are often concerned that students will not attend lectures if lecture notes are available online. However, research has found that only 1% of students stop attending lectures for this reason (Newland, 2003).

Many academics do not move beyond this "document dumping" stage, but others become "repeat offenders" who, having started with the very basic use, begin to explore discussion boards or think about quizzes (JISC, 2004). Therefore, it is very effective to encourage staff to use the easiest features first as they may become more deeply involved in the further use of VLEs. Evidence from the University of Huddersfield has shown how a combination of student pressure to increase the use of VLEs beyond their use as a simple document repository, coupled with increasing interest and skills development by academic staff in the ways in which VLEs could be employed, resulted in some extremely innovative approaches to supporting learning within the clinical area (LEAP Case Study 2).

Case studies from the LEAP project illustrate how VLEs have been implemented from this simple starting point, for providing access to information and other means. These have included making notes available for students (LEAP Case Studies 4 & 6, 2005), so making these resources permanently available and allowing students advance access. Similarly, for a teacher training qualification there was a need to provide an audit of basic knowledge and the VLE was used, initially, solely for this purpose (LEAP Case Study 1, 2005). Another example, in Health and Social Care Education at Bournemouth University, shows how the gradual introduction of e-learning activities contributed to the success of the blended learning approach. It helped the academic find the time for its development and to encourage and support students to adjust to the new approach (LEAP Case Study 19, 2005)

Link with Subject Specialism

In preparing staff to use a VLE, it is important that they are shown an "open door" which enables them to choose their route rather than trying to force them to adopt an approach or a tool which is of less relevance for them. The individual academic works within the context of their subject, and each discipline will vary in its pedagogical approach so there is no "one size fits all" for the adoption of e-learning. For example, arts subjects are more likely to use online discussions than quizzes which tend to be more widely utilised in medicine, science, and engineering. For example, students taking self assessment quizzes in Primary Science Education at the University of Gloucestershire felt that it was good to be able to test and monitor their knowledge and understanding as the course developed (LEAP Case Study 1, 2005).

Visibility of Initiatives and Dissemination

The LEAP follow-up studies found that in most cases the valuable experience of using a VLE was not disseminated within the department. It was often seen as belonging to an individual and would end if the academic stopped teaching the course and was perceived as too great an innovation for others to explore in their teaching. Therefore, more support is required to increase awareness and implement change (LEAP, 2005). However, the outcomes of the case studies were more widely disseminated externally across the subject community.

The University of Gloucestershire provides an example of how dissemination of existing practice has been used to engage new academic staff and promote new uses. A skills-based module using a VLE was developed and demonstrated by presentation. Building on this showcase, similar successful developments such as this case study were spawned (LEAP Case Study 20, 2005).

Conclusion

Preparing and supporting staff in the use of VLEs requires a holistic approach which enables staff to adopt approaches consonant with their subject discipline and needs of their students, but which also integrate with institutional vision and strategies. Staff also need to be supported in the development of both technical and pedagogic skills to ensure that their implementation of VLEs truly enhances the student learning experience. The organisational, technical, and pedagogical factors surrounding e-learning need to be considered (Jochems et al., 2003) and an appropriate balance achieved.

Without this holistic approach the impact of the use of VLEs will be diminished as barriers reduce the potential engagement of staff in learning technologies and prevent students experiencing the flexibility which e-learning undoubtedly affords.

The change process, however, has to be evolutionary since many of the drivers and issues identified in this chapter relate to culture change within and across institutions. To effectively embed this change requires a combination of top-down managed support within a defined framework and bottom-up, academic-led implementation allowing flexibility of adoption to address local needs.

In the majority of institutions, it is not yet possible to claim that significant changes in practice are embedded, however, we have illustrated in this chapter how institutions have sought to effect change and embed the use of VLEs. A wide diversity of approaches has been adopted, but all are underpinned by a desire to encourage and support staff in the effective adoption of these innovative new tools.

References

Alexander, S., & Boud, D. (2001). Teaching and learning online. In B. Stephenson (Ed.), *Learners still learn from experience when online*. London: Kogan Page.

Armitage, S. (2004, April). *Learning technologists: Split personality or community of practice?* Symposium presentation at Networked Learning Conference, Lancaster University.

Armitage, S., Browne, T., & Jenkins, M. (2001). *Management and implementation of virtual learning environments: A UCISA funded survey*. UCISA. Retrieved August 26, 2005, from www.ucisa.ac.uk/groups/tlig/vle/index_html

Bates, A.W., & Poole, G. (2003). *Effective teaching with technology in higher education: Foundations for success*. San Francisco: Jossey-Bass

Bell, M., et al. (2002). *Universities online: A survey of online education and services in Australia*. Commonwealth Department of Education Science and Training, Higher Education Group. Available online at www.dest.gov.au/sectors/higher_education/publications_resources/indexes/by_series/documents/02_a_pdf.htm

Biggs, J. (2003). *Teaching for quality learning at university* (2nd ed). Open University Press.

Boezerooy, P. (Ed.) (2002). *Keeping up with our neighbours: ICT developments in Australian higher education*. Oxford: ALT/SURF

Bricheno, P., Higgison, C., & Weedon, E. (2004). *The impact of networked learning on education institutions*. Final Report of the JISC INLEI Project. UHI Millennium Institute, University of Bradford and Scottish Further Education Unit.

Browne, T., & Jenkins, M. (2003). V*LE surveys: A longitudinal perspective between March 2001 and March 2003 for Higher Education in the United Kingdom*. Retrieved August 26, 2005, from www.ucisa.ac.uk/groups/tlig/vle/index_html

Collis, B., & Messing, (2001). Usage, attitudes and workload implications for a Web-based learning environment. *ALT-J, 9*(1).

Collis, B., & Moonen, J. (2001). *Flexible learning in a digital world: Experiences and expectations*. London: Kogan Page.

Collis, B., & van der Wende, M. (2002). *Models of technology and change: An interna-tional comparative study on the future of ICT in higher education.* Centre for Higher Education Policy Studies. Retrieved August 26, 2005, from www.utwente.nl/ cheps/documenten/ictrapport.pdf

de Boer, W., & Collis, B. (2005). Becoming more systematic about flexible learning: Beyond time and distance. *ALT-J, 13*(1).

Department for Education and Skills (2005). *Harnessing technology: Transforming learning and children's services.* London: DfES. Retrieved August 26, 2005, from www.dfes.gov.uk/publications/e-strategy

Doyle, C., & Robson, K. (2002). *Accessible curricula: Good practice for all.* UWIC Press.

ELTI (2003*). Embedding learning technologies institutionally.* JISC. Retrieved August 26, 2005, from www.jisc.ac.uk/index.cfm?name=project_elti

Garrison, D.R., & Anderson, T. (2003). *E-learning in the 21ˢᵗ century: A framework for research and practice.* London: Routledge Falmer.

Gynn, C., & Acker, S.R. (2001). *Faculty development for the late adopters: Innovation for the reluctant.* Discussion paper prepared for WebCT Conference 2001. Re-trieved August 26, 2005, from www.webct.com/2001/viewpage?name =2001_discussion_abstracts

Higher Education Funding Council for England (2004). *HEFCE e-learning strategy consultation.* Retrieved August 26, 2005, from www.hefce.ac.uk/pubs/circlets/ 2004/cl09_04/

Higher Education Funding Council for England (2005a). *HEFCE circular letter on allocations of funding to support e-learning.* Retrieved August 26, 2005, from www.hefce.ac.uk/pubs/circlets/2005/cl05_05/

Higher Education Funding Council for England (2005b). *HEFCE strategy for e-learning.* Retrieved August 26, 2005, from www.hefce.ac.uk/pubs/hefce/2005/05_12/

Higher Education Funding Council for England (2005c). *The e-University project: Lessons learnt by HEFCE.* Retrieved August 26, 2005, from www.hefce.ac.uk/ learning/tinits/euniv/lessons.doc

Jenkins, M., & Oates, L. (2005, February). Evolution and change: *A university wide evaluation of WebCT use.* Paper presented at the WebCT European Users Confer-ence, Barcelona.

JISC (2004). *Effective practice with e-learning: A good practice guide in designing for learning.* Bristol: JISC

Jochems, W., van Merrienboer, J., & Koper, R. (2003). *Integrated e-learning: Implica-tions for pedagogy, technology and organization.* London: Routledge Falmer.

Laurillard, D. (2001). *Rethinking university teaching: A framework for the effective use of learning technologies* (2nd ed). London: Routledge Falmer.

Learning Environments and Pedagogy (LEAP) (2005). Retrieved August 26, 2005, from www.heacademy.ac.uk/leap.htm

Lisewski, B. (2004). Implementing a learning technology strategy: Top-down strategy meets bottom-up culture. *ALT-J Research in Learning Technology, 12*(2), 175-188.

Martin, E., Trigwell, K., Prosser, M., & Ramsden, P. (2002). Variation in the experience of leadership of teaching in higher education. *Studies in Higher Education.*

Newland, B. (2003). Evaluating the impact of a VLE on learning and teaching. *Proceedings of EDMEDIA World Conference on Educational Multimedia*, Hypermedia and Telecommunications, USA.

Newland, B., Newton, A., Pavey, J., Murray, M., & Boardman, K. (2004). *VLE Longitudinal Report*. DUO (Durham University Online) 2001-2003, Bournemouth University.

Newland, B., Pavey, J., & Boyd, V. (2005). Influencing inclusive practice: The role of VLEs, Improving student learning: Diversity and inclusivity. *12th Improving Student Learning Symposium Proceedings*, UK.

Newland, B., & Ringan, N. (2002). *A guide for heads of departments*. LTSN Generic Centre e-Learning, Series No. 2.

No Significant Difference Web site (2005). Retrieved August 26, 2005, from www.nosignificantdifference.org/

Oblinger, D. (2003). Boomers, gen-xers and millennials, Understanding the new students. *Educause Review.*

Oliver, M., & Dempster, J. (2003). Embedding e-learning practices. In R. Blackwell & P. Backmore (Eds.), *Towards strategic staff development in higher education.* Buckingham: SRHE/Open University Press.

Prosser, M., & Trigwell, K. (1999). *Understanding learning and teaching: The experience in higher education.* Buckingham: SRHE and Open University Press.

Ramsden, P., Prosser, M., Martin, E., & Trigwell, K. (2003). University teachers' experiences of academic leadership and their approach to teaching. *British Journal of Educational Psychology.*

Roberts, G., & Riachi, R. (Eds.). (2003). *Making connections: British perspectives on learning technology developments in Netherlands higher education.* Oxford: Association for Learning Technology.

Robinson, B. (2001). Innovation in open and distance learning: Some lessons from experience and research. In F. Lockwood & A. Gooley(Eds.), *Innovation in open and distance learning: Successful development of online and Web-based learning.* London: Kogan Page.

Rogers, E.D. (1995). *Diffusion of innovations* (4th ed). New York: The Free Press.

Tapscott, P. (1998). *Growing up digital: The rise of the net generation.* New York: McGraw Hill.

Trowler, P.R., & Knight, P.T. (2002). Exploring the implementation gap: Theory and practices in change interventions. In P.R. Trowler (Ed.), *Higher education policy and institutional change.* Buckingham: SRHE/Open University Press.

Van der Klink, M., & Jochems, W. (2003). Management and organization of integrated e-learning. In W. Jochems, J. van Merrienboer, & R. Koper. *Integrated e-learning: Implications for pedagogy, technology and organization* (pp. 151-163). London: Routledge Falmer.

Chapter IV

Using Asynchronous Computer Conferencing to Support Learning and Teaching in a Campus-Based HE Context:
Beyond E-Moderating

Pat Jefferies, De Montfort University, UK

Roy Seden, University of Derby, UK

Abstract

This chapter details research into the use of asynchronous computer conferencing (ACC) within a campus-based higher education (HE) environment. Drawing from the literature, the chapter will firstly highlight some of the issues impacting implementation. It will then go on to outline some of the findings from a piece of action research that was conducted over a period of five years with final-year undergraduates studying ethics/professional issues in computing. The main objective of this research was to investigate and subsequently develop Salmon's (2000) five-stage strategy for implementing ACC. Finally, the chapter will not only develop the Salmon (2000) model but will also challenge the necessity for e-moderating online discussions within a campus-based HE environment. As such, it will give practitioners a greater understanding of how the learner, the learning task, and a particular technology (ACC) interact within a campus-based HE context and will provide guidelines for developing best practice.

Introduction

This chapter details research into the development of network-based learning environments within a campus-based higher education (HE) context. That a need for such research exists has been well documented in the literature because, as Ragan (1999) notes, the use of technology within education has, in many respects outstripped the development of theory on which to base such utilization. The focus for this particular research was, therefore, to develop a distributed, blended learning pedagogy for using asynchronous computer conferencing (ACC), as a particular technology, to support the learning experience of campus-based undergraduate students.

Drawing from the literature, the chapter will firstly highlight some of the issues to be addressed when implementing ACC to support teaching and learning. It will then go on to outline some of the findings from a piece of action research that was conducted over a period of five years with final-year computing undergraduates studying computer ethics/professional issues in computing. Such students were based on campus, but in several of the fieldwork studies undertaken, they were in geographically dispersed universities (e.g., UK, Ireland, Denmark, USA). The main objectives of the chapter will be to investigate and subsequently challenge the strategy proposed by Salmon (2000) for e-moderating online discussions. It will also investigate and develop Salmon's (2000) five-stage model (Access & Motivation, Online Socialisation, Information Exchange, Knowledge Construction, and Development) in order to give practitioners a greater understanding of how the learner, the learning task, and a particular technology (ACC) interact within a campus-based HE context. This will be achieved by: a) providing a summary of findings from seven fieldwork studies; b) providing a pedagogically sound foundation to underpin and justify the design of a "mixed mode"/blended approach for enhancing the learning experience of the campus-based undergraduate; and c) providing recommendations and guidelines to support a blended learning approach to module design.

Background

The concerns that led to this research were initially related to the way technology has largely been implemented within the UK campus-based HE context. For example, the literature identified that there were various drivers for change that have subsequently impacted implementation:

- Rapid expansion of networking capabilities (Mason, 1998)
- Improved access to the technology through increased provision and functionality (Brittain & Liber, 1999)
- Professional uncertainty and differing academic orientations towards learning development (Currier, Brown, & Ekmekioglu, 2001; Annand, 1997; Land, 2000)
- Political "push" provided by government initiatives to encourage e-commerce, technology use in education, and the like (JISC, 1996; NCIHE, 1997)
- Implementation and integration difficulties — institutional readiness (Twigg, 1999)
- Technological "pull" provided by the ever-increasing expectations to use the growing functionality provided by the Internet for supporting education (JISC, 1996; NCIHE, 1997)
- Limitations of understanding regarding the impact of technology on the learning experience (Lipponen, 2002; Phipps & Merisotis, 1999)

There was, however, an added perception that the various political and technological drivers, some of which were identified, have exacerbated the gap between technology and pedagogy. As Wintlev-Jensen (2000) notes, there is "a growing concern amongst pedagogists regarding the widening gap between educational theories and existing learning environments, the development of which is driven mainly by technological advances rather than educational objectives" (p. 4).

Thus, "being swept forward by the constant waves of technological innovation is simply not a satisfactory solution to the fundamental problems facing educators and teachers today" (Wintlev-Jensen, 2000, p. 4). Rather, it is "necessary to stand back and re-examine the relevance of current mainstream activities in the light of new thinking" (Wintlev-Jensen, 2000, p. 4). With the advent of networked technologies, such new thinking now ought to be based on a distributed, blended learning pedagogy.

The challenge for technologists and educators in a campus-based HE context is, however, highly complex in developing such a blended learning approach — they not only need to take into account the variety of drivers that are prompting implementation but also the multitude of issues related to the impact of using these new technologies in a way that protects both the integrity of degree awards as well as the learning experience in general. As Kellner (1999) notes, "a technological revolution" is going on. "It will have massive effects, and it is of utmost importance to us concerning how we will actually use the new technologies — or whether they and the forces that control them will themselves use us in their projects" (p. 202).

Academic staff, therefore, regardless of the "technological pull" or "political push," need both a pragmatic and educational justification for using particular media to support the learning experience — thus "the social infrastructure is primary to the technical infra-structure" (Lipponen, 2002, p. 6) and pedagogical issues need to be overtly addressed if effective integration of the technology within course design and delivery is to be achieved. Strategies or models for integration, suitable for use in a campus-based HE environment, therefore need to be developed in order to guide practice.

With specific regard to the use of computer conferencing to support learning and teaching within a UK campus-based HE context, it soon became clear, from available literature reviewed, that there were no real models available at the start of this particular piece of research to guide practice except for the one proposed by Salmon (2000). This particular five-stage model was, however, based on research with distance, largely postgraduate students studying with the Open University and one of the primary features is, of course, the use of "e-moderating" to scaffold the learning experience within the conferencing environment. While this might be felt necessary, indeed unavoidable, in a predominantly distance-learning context, this may not, however, be a sufficient or necessary condition in scaffolding the use of computer conferencing within a campus-based, blended learning approach. Tutors undertaking the role of an "e-moderator" (Salmon, 2000) do, in fact, perpetuate models of learning that may not be appropriate in supporting adult learning within a campus-based HE context. For example, if the tutor acts as e-moderator, the opportunities for students to take greater responsibility for learning may be diminished. As Jacques (1995) notes, "The teacher who is an incurable helper, in satisfying one of his or her basic needs, may fail to develop the student's capacity for self-growth into greater autonomy and responsibility" (p. 17). Similarly, Burge (1996) suggests that, in the case of the adult learner, learning styles may be influenced by social perceptions as they may need to become "self-responsible" in the new learning environments. This essentially means changing the traditional roles of teacher and learner and concepts of power relations in order for them to achieve this.

However, upon further examination, the Salmon (2000) model also appeared to lack both a preparation and post-evaluation phase that it was felt would be necessary for implementation within a campus-based undergraduate context. Therefore, in order to develop and test alternative models within the campus-based environment, this particular research was conducted with the aim of subsequently providing implementation guidelines aimed at improving practice.

A Pedagogical Basis for Networked Learning

Any review of the literature will reveal that many pedagogical approaches are likely to be based on either the acquisition or transmission models of learning. So, in order to provide a framework for this particular investigation, the three models of learning that Koschmann (1994) proposes (Acquisition, Participation, and Transaction) were applied to the Leidner and Jarvenpaa (1995) model (Figure 1). Such framework then illustrated the potential pedagogic justification for using networking technologies to facilitate the whole range of learning approaches, but particularly that of collaboration:

a.   Instructor interacting with the Peer group, or

b.   Peer Group interaction (Social Constructivism, Socioculturalism).

In addition, the rationale for using computer conferencing, in particular, can be underpinned not only by the theoretical models of learning (transaction/participatory) but also by the fact that researchers have already identified the positive effects of social

Figure 1. Dimensions of learning mapped to technological tools

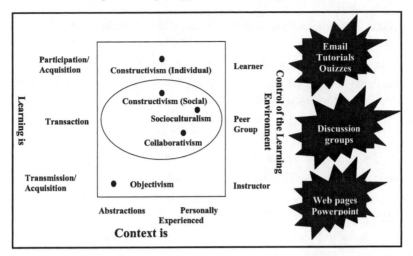

interaction during learning. Collaboration with other students has been shown to stimulate activity, make learning more realistic, and to stimulate motivation (see Lehtinen, Hakkarainen, Lipponen, Rahikainen, & Muukkonen, 1999, for a review). It is also suggested that learning might be further enhanced if collaboration can take place within a wider context across different locations and cultures (Campos, Laferrière, & Harasim, 2000) and that dialogue is an important aspect of a rich learning experience, particularly in complex, discursive domains (Jeong & Chi, 1997) where any dialogue produced remains available to students for reflection over long periods of time. Research has, for example, suggested that "learning can occur not only through participation in dialogue but also through observing others participating in it" (Stenning, McKendree, Lee, & Cox, 1999, p. 1).

However, the problem domain being faced by those wishing to implement computer-supported collaborative learning (CSCL) in HE institutions has, it seems, two dimensions — there is the logical dimension (relating to the educational process, subject specific issues, and the technological issues) and the cultural dimension (relating to the organizational issues, the political issues, and issues arising from the wider social context). While there has been much research and debate into the pedagogy of using ICT in HE that addresses the issues relating to the logical dimension of the problem, there has been much less work on the impact of the issues in the cultural dimension. These equate to measures of the institutions attitude or Institutional Readiness Criteria (Twigg, 1999). Irrespective of the technology used, therefore, these will be the criteria for successful implementation and sustainable development of CSCL which means that an integrated approach to learning, together with identification of the stakeholders in the political, social, and organizational dimensions, needs to be undertaken. For example, the current project-based approach, where systems are developed outside the cultural framework within which they will be used, appears to lead to failure (e.g., the BEATL project (Winter, 2001)).

Further review of the literature has then suggested that there are several factors within both the logical and cultural dimension that influence CSCL and these include:

- the role of the tutor (Mitchell, 2001; Jacques, 1995)
- institutional factors (Becher & Trowler, 1989, 2001) and orientations toward academic development (Land, 2000)
- group dynamics (Banet & Hayden, 1977)
- the teaching strategies used to prompt or support learning (Stiles, 2002; Grout, 2002; Booth, Bowie, Jordan, & Rippen, 2000)
- the design and characteristics of VLEs (Shih, 1998)
- the learning context and individual learning styles (Knowles, 1978; Conner & Hodgins, 2000)
- staff/student attitudes toward assessment (Boud, 2002; Rust, 2002; Norton, Tilley, Newstead, & Franklyn-Stokes, 2001)

This chapter will now go on to outline how such findings have subsequently underpinned development of a "mixed mode" or "blended" (teacher-mediated and technology-mediated) approach to learning with specific regard to the use of ACC within a virtual learning environment (VLE) for CSCL as an emerging paradigm of educational technology (Lipponen, 2002).

Fieldwork Studies

All seven of the fieldwork studies undertaken involved final-year, campus-based, undergraduates studying selected modules within the computing/information systems discipline. In terms of evaluation a number of instruments were variously used.

- Student/staff feedback via questionnaires, interviews – Fieldwork Studies 1-7
- Monitoring/observation of message posting – Fieldwork Studies 1-7
- Usage statistics/computer-generated reports – Fieldwork Studies 1-7
- Learning outcomes (e.g., learning as product) – Fieldwork Studies 1-7
- Process measurements
    - Transaction Analysis (Freeman, 1978, 1979) – Fieldwork Studies 2-7
    - Community of Inquiry Model (Garrison, Anderson, & Archer, 2001) – Fieldwork Studies 5-7

The main ideology underpinning all of these fieldwork studies comprised a social constructivist (Vygotsky, 1978), blended learning approach to learning and teaching within a campus-based HE context. As such, the approach emphasised "the active, constructive nature of the knowledge acquisition process wherein the learner is not a passive recipient of information but an active and constructive interpreter of meanings." (Vosniadou, 1994, p. 13).

In order to test the potential identified within the literature for using computer conferencing to facilitate greater student autonomy, the particular implementation was, therefore, originally perceived to be embodied in Brittain and Liber's (1999) adaptation of Stafford Beer's (1981) Viable Systems Model illustrated in Figure 2.

Within this model, the students are perceived of as a self-organising community of learners composed of multiple zones of proximal development. There was, therefore, to be no "omniscient teacher, but instead there were participants with different degrees and areas of expertise" (Pfister, Wessner, Holmer, & Steinmetz, 1999, p. 1).

Thus, while adopting the traditional role of "sage on the stage" (Guzdiel & Weingarten, 1995) within the traditional lecture setting, the tutor would also be required to act as facilitator within the virtual (ACC) environment (reflective of the more liberal, divergent approaches to learning).

Subsequent evaluation of adopting this approach within the first fieldwork study (using the Basic Support for Collaborative Working (BSCW) application), however, revealed that, although students were using the conferencing environment to share ideas, the discussions proved to be somewhat anarchic. Questionnaires and discussions with both the tutor and students revealed that the reasons underpinning these findings were primarily related to the lack of sufficient focus within the particular module being studied (Innovative Trends in Information Systems) coupled with the perceived lack of students' critical evaluation skills.

Figure 2. Adaptation of the viable systems model (Brittain & Liber, 1999)

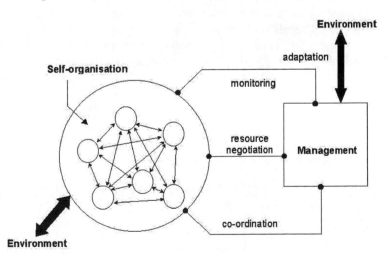

These findings then indicated that tutor moderation was probably required in order to provide the necessary scaffolding or structure for discussions (see Jefferies & Constable, 2000, for further details). This perceived need for tutor moderation was then further supported by a number of researchers (Ragan, 1999; Beaudin, 1999; Salmon, 2000), all of whom suggested that the role of the instructor was key to organising interaction. However, another somewhat unexpected factor was that, despite all of the students being experienced computer users, some of them had been very daunted by the prospect of using this very "visible" and "permanent" form of communication. Mason (1998) has also noted that this might be an issue with ACC.

Reflection on all of these findings meant that in the second fieldwork study (using WebCT as the platform), a more focused, discursive module that supported development of critical analysis was chosen (Computing & Ethics) and tutor moderation was implemented. Students were then told what the tutor expectations were (in terms of expected professional approach and impact on assessment) and were generally encouraged to experiment. Such explanation of expectations and encouragement then became a feature of all subsequent fieldwork studies.

As a consequence of tutor moderation in Fieldwork Study 2, however, the message posting evidenced by the students showed a significant decline in terms of quantity in comparison with what had occurred previously (see Table 1 for a comparison).

Furthermore, when transaction analysis (Freeman 1978, 1979) was applied to the discussions, it became clear that threads were either terminated following tutor intervention or that a "star" pattern of communication was evidenced between the tutor and students (see Figure 3).

Similar findings to these have also been reported by Marris (1965) and Veerman, Andriessen, and Kanselaar, (1999) who note that their "observations have shown that tutors challenging and countering their students immediately ends any discussion" (p. 11). Changes in the particular technology used between the first two fieldwork studies did not however seem to affect findings.

Therefore, in Fieldwork Study 3, the same module (Computing & Ethics) and the same technology (WebCT) were to be the subject of investigation in order to test out the impact of returning to a policy of having no tutor intervention within the same module and technological context. The rationale for reverting to this approach was that "research has documented, over and over, when participants make the learning their own, when they get to talk about it their way, without being manipulated and controlled, learning increases" (Jensen, 1996, p. 174). A further variable (of including students who were

Table 1. Comparison of messages posted with and without tutor moderation

	Fieldwork Study 1	Fieldwork Study 2
Total number of students	56	32
Total number of messages	1007	49
Tutor intervention	No	Yes

studying the same module across two geographically dispersed campuses) was, however, introduced at this stage in order to make use of ACC a more "authentic" form of communication for the students in that they were facilitated by the technology to share ideas across geographically dispersed, campus-based groups within the same institution.

Within this fieldwork study, the message postings increased significantly — of the 103 students studying the module, 694 messages were posted — an average of approximately seven messages per student. This was clearly a significant improvement on statistics evidenced from the previous fieldwork study. It was also noted that the quality of the student's messages significantly improved as they became more confident with the medium — they were clearly evidencing a great deal of thoughtful engagement with the module outside of normal contact times. As the role of the tutors within this fieldwork study was one of "monitoring" rather than "moderating" the discussions a number of topics raised by the students were then followed up in the face-to-face (F2F) contact sessions in order to provide further encouragement for them to use the online facility. Equally, some topic discussions were initially set up in the F2F sessions and continued online. This was particularly important in supporting the integration of the different forms of communication (online and off-line). Transaction analysis subsequently revealed that online communication was now more evenly spread amongst the students even though some were clearly posting more messages than others (see Figure 4).

Figure 3. The "star" network pattern of transaction (Freeman, 1978, 1979)

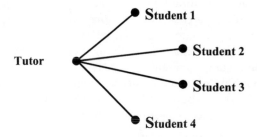

Figure 4. Transaction analysis of a discussion thread without tutor intervention

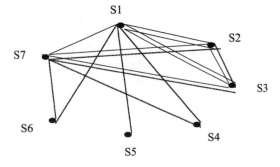

Another interesting factor was that there was a 92% pass rate for the module within this fieldwork study (without tutor intervention) as opposed to a 75% pass rate in Fieldwork Study 2 (with tutor intervention).

In Fieldwork Study 4, however, when all 61 students were based on a single campus, it was subsequently found that, while there was still no tutor moderation, the average number and quality of messages posted declined. Although part-time students reported that the discussion boards were useful in supporting their studies, clearly most of the students preferred to communicate, quite naturally, on a F2F basis.

Thus, as the fieldwork studies developed, it was realized that the discussion forum needed to be "authentic" for the students as well as being more clearly structured and integrated with the F2F contact sessions. For example, if the structuring was not being done through moderation by the tutor, then it needed to be done through the tasks imposed and/or through some form of assessment. Furthermore, the discussion forums would need to be more rigorously evaluated in some way to determine whether or not "deep" rather than "surface" learning was actually occurring.

As a consequence, Fieldwork Studies 5, 6, and 7 were designed around a number of task-oriented structures. This was in addition to introducing an internationally based, cross-institutional dimension. This latter, cross-institutional dimension was introduced to improve student motivation and engagement through giving them even more "authentic" reason for using the conferencing environment.

In addition, in Fieldwork Study 5 (using Blackboard VLE as the platform) and Fieldwork Study 6 (using WebCT VLE as a platform), an assessed group task was introduced whereby students had to collaborate via the discussion board to produce their report. The rationale for introducing this form of assessment was based on the idea that "group learning gives students practice in thinking and explaining; it exposes them to multiple viewpoints, which helps them to make connections among concepts and ideas; it provides opportunities for 'scaffolding'; it often results in students teaching each other" (Jacques, 1995, p. 17). As the students were studying modules concerned with professional issues in computing/computing and ethics, this was particularly important in relation to the desired learning outcomes. For example, students were automatically facilitated, through ACC, in exchanging ethical ideas from different perspectives and cultural backgrounds as they were all based in different universities and countries.

In Fieldwork Study 5, there was some moderation of the discussion board by the tutor, and this resulted in 41 students producing a total of 549 message postings (13 per student). Further evaluation of these discussions was then undertaken using the Cognitive Inquiry Model (Garrison et al., 2001) to identify the different types of message that students were posting ("triggering" (initiating the inquiry), "exploration" (a divergent phase), "integration" (constructing shared meaning), or "resolution" (resolving the issues or problem posed in the first phase)). Results from this indicated that students were clearly engaging in "deep" learning while also adopting different roles within the group activity. Such findings then provided another area for investigation (Grodzinsky, Griffin, & Jefferies, 2002).

However, in Fieldwork Study 6, tutor intervention was not undertaken and the message postings increased significantly — 117 students producing 2,624 message postings (an average of 22 messages per student). This was a significant improvement and again analysis and feedback from tutors and students indicated that they were clearly seeing the value of using the medium and gaining real benefits from engaging with the technology to support their learning. Once again, while the process of setting up the system was slightly different in each environment (Blackboard and WebCT) this change of technology did not seem to have impacted student usage. However, while it was felt that significant improvements had so far been made in integrating and evaluating the use of the conferencing environment in a blended learning approach, it was considered that further improvements could be made by providing even more structure to the conferencing environment.

Thus, in Fieldwork Study 7 (using Blackboard), the students (48 based in different universities in different countries) were initially tasked with determining their perception of their own role within group working through use of the Belbin (1981) Self-Perception Inventory. This inventory then classified students within one of eight identified team roles (chairman, shaper, plant, monitor/evaluator, company worker, resource investigator, team worker, finisher/completer). Results from this were then used to set up eight international groups comprised of six students — two students in each group from each of three different countries involved (see Jefferies, Grodzinsky, & Griffin, 2003, for more details).

The rationale for using the Belbin (1981) Self-Perception Inventory was that it:

- provided tutors with an objective way of grouping the students.

- helped the students focus on the different roles required for effective team working.

- offered the opportunity for cross-matching perceived Belbin types to the different categories of message posting identified through application of the Cognitive Inquiry Model (Garrison et al., 2001).

Once grouped, the students' first task was to socialize via each of the group discussion boards in order to build trust (Jarvenpaa & Leidner, 1998; Salmon, 2000). The students were then required to negotiate, via the discussion boards, in order to develop a strategy aimed at achieving the assessment outcome. Finally, they had to collaboratively develop a group report related to a chosen ethical dilemma. The framework for structuring production of the assessed report was, in fact, largely based upon the "Action Learning Forum" (Hale, 2000) approach to learning.

Within this approach the group defines the questions to be addressed that are related to their chosen case study (e.g., ethical dilemma) scenario. Then, each member of the group individually defines the questions they wish to tackle, therefore, the body of knowledge is accessed on an individual basis. As such, this knowledge will then be integrated with the individual's understanding and further experience. Knowledge may then be accessed and acquired from a range of sources and as such will not be provided in a "programmed" way but will be gained on a just-in-time basis at the place and in the format that the individual prefers. All of this work had, of course, to be done through use of the discussion boards because of the geographically dispersed nature of the students involved in each group.

Findings from this fieldwork study identified that there was a need for clear guidance and rationale to be given to tutors in the initial stages in order to boost confidence regarding their non-moderation role. Both students and tutors also needed to be convinced of both the extrinsic and intrinsic gains they would accrue by use of the technology. It was, therefore encouraging that, despite initial reticence, students did report that they had found the experience of using ACC valuable even though evaluation of their formulated strategies indicated that these had not worked as well as they had expected.

Feedback from 23 out of 48 students involved with this particular fieldwork study further identified that:

- The requirement for students to socialise helped them to overcome their initial reticence towards posting messages.

- Collaboration with students from abroad, together with the setting of a project to address a real-life scenario were valued aspects.

- Using the Belbin (1981) Self-Perception Inventory to objectively group students and focus attention on group dynamics proved to be useful for students in developing their strategies.

- Use of ACC was found to be particularly suited to adult learning styles as students were able to contribute in their own time, place and were facilitated in reflecting on the ideas of others — engaging in "vicarious" learning (Stenning, McKendree, Lee, & Cox, 1999).

- Much reflection on particular difficulties encountered, as well benefits gained, was evidenced in the detailed student comments provided.

Finally, it was noted that the international "virtual" work groups had produced, on average, much better final reports than others that were campus-based only. While this finding undoubtedly might be attributable to a number of factors, it did seem that the use of CSCL through the ACC medium was having a positive impact on student engagement and performance.

Synthesising the findings from all the fieldwork studies undertaken has subsequently identified that the role of the tutor and the teaching strategies they decide to use are likely to be two of the most significant factors in impacting use of ACC. In particular, the issue of deciding whether to "moderate" (Salmon, 2000) or "monitor" the online discussions is "key" as tutor intervention was not only found to affect transaction patterns but also overall module grades (e.g., Fieldwork Study 2). Tutors also need a commitment to integrate use of the technology within module design in an authentic manner. For example, attitudes towards assessment meant that engagement was much improved when geographically dispersed students had to complete an assessed piece of work through the use of the ACC medium itself. Institutional factors and orientations towards academic development also had an impact in terms of availability and support for the use of appropriate technology. However, once implemented, a number of other factors will impact ACC development. For example:

- Group dynamics are likely to impact the number and type of message postings (e.g., Fieldwork Studies 5, 6, and 7)

- The campus-based learning context will mean students are likely, after a short "novelty" phase, to revert to wanting to communicate either F2F (or synchronously through online chat) unless there is some authentic reason for them to use the ACC medium.

It has, therefore, been concluded that the factors that encourage use of ACC are wide-ranging and that good instructional design is essential whether it is online or F2F. Findings from both the literature review and fieldwork studies have, as a consequence, now been used to formulate a pedagogically sound foundation to underpin and justify the design of a "mixed mode" context for supporting learning.

A Pedagogically Sound Foundation to Underpin and Justify the Design of a "Mixed Mode" Context for Supporting Learning

The literature review and fieldwork studies reported here have, it is felt, indicated that the use of ACC, based on a social constructivist model of learning (Vygotsky, 1978) can be pedagogically justified within a campus-based HE context. However, it has also illustrated the fact that "whilst creating new learning environments or learning communities, it is not just a matter of implementing and putting into use new technology but in many cases, also applying simultaneously new practices of learning and instruction" (Lipponen, 2002, p. 6). An iterative prototyping approach towards module design is therefore now proposed in the following stages.

Stage 1 involves analysis, considering pedagogical, ethical, and technological (PET) issues in order to fully inform and justify use of ACC to support module delivery. For example, there will be a need to ask questions such as: "What type of learning is being supported through use of the technology?" "What are the learning outcomes that will be achieved through such usage?" "What is the 'value added' of using the technology?" "What are the privacy, intellectual property rights and access issues (hardware/software availability, SENDA) that will need to be addressed?" "What technology can be used and is it available?" "Can it be supported and how?"

Stage 2 then builds on this initial analysis in order to develop a requirements specification aimed at facilitating the authentic integration of the technology with the F2F contact sessions. For example, the questions to be addressed at this stage will include: "What skills do students have/need to have?" "What incentives are needed to engage students in using the medium?" "What behaviour (in terms of usage) is expected and how can a professional approach be encouraged?" "Do the discussions need to be structured and how will this be best achieved?" "How can the use of ACC be assessed and evaluated? "What strategies need to be developed in order to integrate the conferencing activity into what is happening in the F2F contact sessions?" Having addressed these sorts of questions an integrated approach to module design can then be undertaken.

Stage 3 is then the implementation stage that follows analysis and design. A further extension to the Salmon (2000) model is now proposed for this particular phase (see Figure 5): In the preparation stage, suggested in this new model, tutors will need to ensure that:

Figure 5. A proposed model for implementation

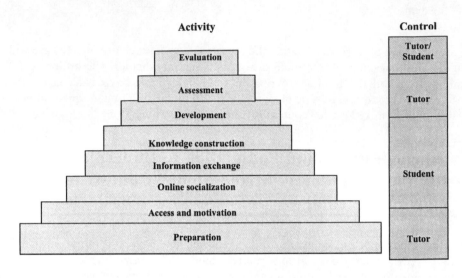

- Students are equipped with the necessary technical skills they require for operating efficiently within the virtual discussion environment.
- Students' critical analysis has been/will be developed.
- Students' organisational and groupwork abilities have been/will be developed.

The tutor will be responsible also at this stage for ensuring that accessibility issues have been addressed as well as providing students with the "rules for engagement" — for example, expectations of the tutor in terms of how the students should use the environment, impact on assessment, advising of tutor monitoring of the conferencing activity, and the like. Encouragement/motivation for the students to engage with using the technology will also form an important part of an introductory session — that is, students will need to appreciate the "value" of using ACC to support their learning experience. Such "value" might include identifying extrinsic rewards such as contribution to overall module assessment, developing work-related skills (through engaging in international communication links), and/or opportunities to transcend the boundaries of the classroom to widen their learning experience. Tutors will also need to set up the groups and provide structure for the discussions through identifying the tasks that students will need to be undertaking — for example, socialisation, production of a strategy, information exchange, knowledge construction, and development of the final report.

During this stage, when students are engaged with using the discussion boards, it is then important that tutors monitor the conferencing activity and overtly relate this to what is happening in the F2F contact sessions in order to stimulate engagement. The tutor(s) involved will then undertake assessment of the final group reports. In the final "evaluation" stage, it is then vital that the impact that ACC has had upon the students' learning experience is evaluated by both staff and students in order to inform future development.

Recommended Guidelines

Based on the literature review and model identified, the following set of guidelines are now proposed:

- Choose an appropriate, focused module that has a discursive nature and supports development of critical analysis.
- In order for ACC to be used to best effect, the approach to module design should be holistic and overtly incorporate usage of the ACC environment (i.e., there needs to be a strong link between module objectives/learning outcomes and the use of the technology).
- Outline both the intrinsic and extrinsic benefits that can be gained from using the conferencing environment (ACC).
- Brief students as to the monitoring that will be undertaken and how they are expected to use ACC.
- Propose introductory exercises for students to undertake so that they can gain confidence in using the environment (e.g., socialisation, strategy formulation).
- Encourage students within the F2F contact sessions to organise themselves and use ACC effectively.
- Facilitate consideration of group roles in strategy development and implementation.
- Encourage further development of critical evaluation and responsibility for learning through adopting a non-moderating role within group discussions.
- Monitor the ACC environment on a regular basis to pick up any issues that can then be addressed in the F2F contact sessions.

Therefore, student and tutor activities would be as shown in Table 2.

Table 2. An outline of student/tutor activity

Student Activity	Tutor Activity
Prepare – group roles	Prepare – resources
Socialize	Motivate
Develop strategy	Set task
Exchange information	Monitor
Knowledge Construction	Blend with F2F
Development	Assess
Evaluate	Evaluate

Future Trends

As educational institutions across the sector are increasingly trying to develop pedagogical strategies for developing a blended learning approach, it is clear that there remains a great deal of scope for further research. For example, other virtual group dynamics related to cohesiveness, culture, group norms, gender, motivation, and stages of development are additional areas that need further research in order to provide a fuller understanding of CSCL environments within a campus-based HE context.

Conclusion

As the literature review revealed, "professional uncertainty is clearly a major problem for institutions to address. For teaching staff, part of this concern is over the issue of pedagogy" (Currier, Brown, & Ekmekioglu 2001, p. 17). How academics approach the new teaching possibilities that emerge is, therefore, important if the learning experience is to be enhanced. Thus, "it is up to each individual to determine how they will live the new technologies and cyberspaces, how they will themselves deploy them, and whether they will ultimately be empowering or disempowering" (Kellner, 1999, p. 202).

Therefore, it is important that tutors do not have their pedagogical approach dictated by the technology. In order to obviate this possibility, tutors need to, as these fieldwork studies have illustrated, focus on education needs and identify what they want to teach rather than on selecting the technology. As Boddy and Tickner (1999) advise "before designing the technological aspects of the learning environments, educators and designers should best begin by analysing the actual activities learners engage in during the course" (p. 39). Furthermore, it has been found that any learning technology that is not perceived as being used for "authentic" reasons and is not properly integrated within module design is unlikely to be well rated and therefore used by the learners.

The proposed recommendations and guidelines outlined here, therefore, contribute towards giving practitioners a greater understanding of how the learner, the learning task, and a particular technology (ACC) interact within a campus-based HE context. The challenge now is for other practitioners to test and refine these guidelines within their own context in order to further develop models of best practice.

References

Annand, D. (1997). Instructor's orientations towards computer-mediated learning environments. *Journal of Distance Education, 12*(1/2), 127-152.

Banet, A.G. Jr., & Hayden, C. (1977). A Tavistock primer. In W. Pfeiffer & J. Jones (Eds.), *Annual handbook for group facilitators.* San Diego: University Associates Inc.

Beaudin, B.P. (1999). Keeping online asynchronous discussions on topic. *Journal of Asynchronous Learning Networks, 3*(2), 1-13. Retrieved May 8, 2000, from www.aln.org/alnweb/journal/Vol3_issue2/beaudin.htm

Becher, T., & Trowler, P.R. (1989, 2001). *Academic tribes and territories* (2nd ed). Open University Press.

Beer, S. (1981). *The brain of the firm* (2nd ed). Chichester: John Wiley.

Belbin, R.M. (1981). *Management teams: Why they succeed or fail.* Oxford: Heinemann.

Boddy, D., & Tickner, S. (1999). Barriers to electronic networking: Technology, student needs or social context? *Active learning, 10,* 39-43. Joyce Martin (Ed.), CTISS Publications, University of Oxford.

Booth, C., Bowie, S., Jordan, J., & Rippen, A. (2000). The use of case method in large and diverse undergraduate business programmes: Problems and issues. *The International Journal of Management Education, 1*(1).

Boud, D. (2002). *Assessment for life.* Lecture made as visiting lecturer. University of Middlesex.

Britain, S., & Liber, O. (1999). *A framework for pedagogical evaluation of virtual learning environments.* JISC Technology Applications Programme, Report No. 41. Retrieved May 8, 2000, from www.jisc.ac.uk/jtap/htm/jtap-041.html

Burge, E.J. (1996). Inside-out thinking about distance teaching: Making sense of reflective practice. *Journal of the American Society for Information Science 47*(11), 843-848.

Campos, M., Laferrière, T., & Harasim, L. (2001). The post-secondary networked classroom: Renewal of teaching practices and social interaction. *Journal of Asynchronous Learning Networks, 5*(2), 36-52.

Conner, M., & Hodgins, W. (2000). *Learning styles.* Retrieved February 24, 2003, from www.learnativity.com/learningstyles.html

Currier, S., Brown, S., & Cuna Ekmekioglu, F. (2001, November). *INSPIRAL – Investigating portals for information resources and learning,* final report. JISC. Retrieved July 10, 2002, from http://inspiral.cdlr.strath.ac.uk/

Freeman, Linton. C. (1978, 1979). Centrality in social networks: Conceptual clarification. *Social Networks, 1,* 215-239.

Garrison, D.R., Anderson, T., & Archer, W. (2001). Critical thinking and computer conferencing: A model and tool to assess cognitive presence. *American Journal of Distance Education.*

Grodzinsky, F., Griffin, J., & Jefferies, P. (2002, November). Reinventing collaborative learning using Blackboard: A Web-based resource, in the teaching of a multi-institutional computer ethics module. In the *Proceedings: ETHICOMP,* Lisbon, Portugal.

Grout, I.A., (2002, April). Overview and development of a test engineering teaching module." In the *Proceedings: 13th EAEEIE Annual Conference on Innovations in Education for Electrical and Information Engineering (EIE),* York.

Guzdial, M., & Weingarten, F.W. (1995). *Setting a computer science research agenda for educational technology* (CRA Report No. 1995). National Science Foundation.

Hale, R.I. (2000). Leading with questions: A new age of action learning through the forum method. *VUJ Journal, 3,* 106-112.

Harasim, L. (2000). *Shift happens: Online collaborative learning as a new paradigm in education.* Keynote Speaker at Fusion 2000, Glasgow, Scotland.

Jacques, D. (1995). *Learning in groups* (2nd ed). Kogan Page.

Jefferies, P., & Constable, I. (2000). Using BSCW in learning & teaching. Educational Technology & Society. *Journal, Special Issue On-line Collaborative Learning Environments, 3*(3).

Jefferies, P., Grodzinsky, F., & Griffin, J. (2003). Advantages and problems in using ICT to support the teaching of a multi-institutional computer ethics course. *Journal of Educational Media, Special Edition on Blended Learning, 28*(2,3).Taylor & Francis.

Jensen, E., (1996). *Brain-based learning.* Del Mar, CA: Turning Point Publishing.

Jeong, H., & Chi, M.T.H. (1997, December 10-14). Construction of shared knowledge during collaborative learning. In R. Hall, N. Miyake, & N. Enyedy (Eds.), *Proceedings of Computer-Supported Collaborative Learning '97* (pp. 124-128), Toronto, Ontario. Ontario Institute for Studies in Education of the University of Toronto. Retrieved October 28, 2003, from www.oise.utoronto.ca/cscl/papers/jeong.pdf

JISC (1996). *Joint Information Systems Committee Five Year strategy 1996-001.* Retrieved August 23, 2001, from www.jisc.ac.uk/pub/strategy.html

Kellner, D. (1999). New technologies: Technocities and the prospects for democratization. In J. Downey & J. McGuigan (Eds.), *Technocities.* Sage Publications.

Knowles, M.S. (1978). *The adult learner: A neglected species.* Houston: Gulf Publishing.

Koschmann, T. (1994). Toward a theory of computer support for collaborative learning. *Journal of the Learning Sciences, 3,* 219-225.

Land, R. (2000). Agency, context and change in academic development. *The International Journal for Academic Development,* Taylor and Francis Ltd. Retrieved July 10, 2002, from www.tandf.co.uk/journals

Lehtinen, E., Hakkarainen, K., Lipponen, L., Rahikainen, M., & Muukkonen, H. (1999). *Computer supported collaborative learning: A review of research and development* (The J.H.G.I.Giesderbs Reports on Education, 10). Netherlands: University of Nijmegen, Department of Educational Sciences.

Leidner, E.D., & Jarvenpaa, S.L. (1995). The use of IT to enhance management school education: A theoretical view. *MIS Quarterly, 19*(3), 265-291.

Lipponen, L. (1999, December 12-15). The challenges for computer supported collaborative learning in elementary and secondary level: Finnish perspectives. In C. Hoadley & J. Roschelle (Eds.), *Proceedings of the Computer Support for Collaborative Learning (CSCL) 1999 Conference,* Stanford University, Palo Alto, CA. Mahwah, NJ: Lawrence Erlbaum Associates. Retrieved May 2, 2002, from www.ciltkn.org/cscl99/A46/A46.HTM

Lipponen, L. (2002). Exploring foundations for computer-supported collaborative learning. In T. Koschmann, R. Hall, & N. Miyake (Eds.), CSCL2: Carrying forward the
conversation. Mahwah, NJ: Lawrence Erlbaum Associates. *Proceedings of the
Computer-supported Collaborative Learning 2002 Conference* (pp. 72-81). Retrieved May 2, 2002, from http://newmedia.colorado.edu/cscl/31.html

Marris, P. (1965). *The experience of higher education.* London: Routledge and Kegan
Paul.

Mason, R. (1998). *Globalising education. Trends and applications.* Routledge, Retrieved
April 15, 2003, from http://iet.open.ac.uk/pp/r.d.mason/globalbook/globaledu.html

Mitchell, D. (2001). *The end of all our exploring; Or if technology is the answer, what
was the question?* Keynote Speech, Alt- C 2001, Edinburgh.

NCIHE (1997). *National Committee of Inquiry into Higher Education: Higher education in the learning society.* Available online at www.leeds.ac.uk/ncihe

Norton, L.S., Tilley, A., Newstead, S.E., & Franklyn-Stokes, A. (2001). The pressure of
assessment in undergraduate courses and their effect on student behaviours.
Assessment and Evaluation in Higher Education, 26(3).

Pfister, H., Wessner, M., Holmer, T., & Steinmetz, R. (1999, December 12-15). Negotiating
about shared knowledge in a cooperative learning environment. In C. Hoadley &
J. Roschelle (Eds.), *Proceedings of the Computer Support for Collaborative
Learning (CSCL) 1999 Conference,* Stanford University, Palo Alto, CA. Mahwah,
NJ: Lawrence Erlbaum Associates.

Phipps, R., & Merisotis, J. (1999). *What's the difference? A review of contemporary
research on the effectiveness of distance learning in higher education.* Washington, DC: The Institute for Higher Education Policy. (Washington, DC, The Institute
for Higher Education Policy). Retrieved October 28, 2003, from www.ihep.com/
Pubs/PDF/Difference.pdf

Ragan, L.C. (1999). Good teaching is good teaching: An emerging set of guiding
principles and practices for the design and development of distance education.
Cause/Effect 22.1. Retrieved August 23, 2001, from www.educause.edu/ir/library/
html/cem9915.html

Rust, C. (2002). The impact of Assessment on student learning. *Active Learning in
Higher Education, 3*(2), 145-148.

Salmon, G. (2000). *E-moderating.* Kogan Page Ltd.

Shih, C-F. (1998). Conceptualizing consumer experience in cyberspace. *European Journal of Marketing, 32*(7/8).

Stenning, K., McKendree, J., Lee, J., & Cox, R. (1999, December 12-15). Vicarious learning
from educational dialogue. In C. Hoadley & J. Roschelle (Eds.), *Proceedings of the
Computer Support for Collaborative Learning (CSCL) 1999 Conference,* Stanford
University, Palo Alto CA. Mahwah, NJ: Lawrence Erlbaum Associates. Retrieved
December 12, 2001, from http://kn.cilt.org/csc199/A43/A43.HTM

Stiles, M.J. (2002, September 10-11). *Strategic and pedagogic requirements for virtual
learning in the context of widening participation.* Paper for At the Interface --
Virtual Learning and Higher Education Conference, Mansfield College, University

of Oxford. Retrieved February 5, 2002, from www.inter-disciplinary.net/Stiles%20Paper.pdf

Twigg, C.A. (1999). *Improving learning and reducing costs: Redesigning large-enrolment courses.* Troy, NY: The Pew Learning and Technology Program, Rensselaar Polytechnic Institute.

Veerman, A.L., Andriessen, J.E.B., & Kanselaar, G. (1999, December 12-15). Collaborative learning through computer-mediated argumentation. In C. Hoadley & J. Roschelle (Eds.), *Proceedings of the Computer Support for Collaborative Learning (CSCL) 1999 Conference,* Stanford University, Palo Alto, CA. Mahwah, NJ: Lawrence Erlbaum Associates. Retrieved March 5, 2001, from http//kn.cilt.org/cscl99/A77/A77.HTM

Vosniadou, S. (1994). From cognitive theory to educational technology. In S. Vosniadou, E. De Corte, & H. Mandl (Eds.), *Technology-based learning environments* (pp. 11-18). Berlin: Springer-Verlag.

Vygotsky, L.S. (1978). *Mind in society: The development of higher psychological processes.* Cambridge, MA: Harvard University Press.

Winter, J. (2001). *BEATL/93 Final Summary Project Report.* Retrieved November 26, 2003, from www.uwe.ac.uk/fbe/beatl/summary_report.pdf

Wintlev-Jensen (2000, June 6). *Issues for further discussion* (European Commission Chair), Workshop on Future European RTD Agenda for Advanced Learning Environments, Report Version 1.1. Retrieved October 29, 2003, from www.proacte.com/downloads/nextsteps.doc

Chapter V

Improving E-Learning Support and Infrastructure:
An Evidence-Based Approach

Carmel McNaught, The Chinese University of Hong Kong, China

Paul Lam, The Chinese University of Hong Kong, China

Christina Keing, The Chinese University of Hong Kong, China

Kin Fai Cheng, The Chinese University of Hong Kong, China

Abstract

This chapter reports a study conducted in 2004 at The Chinese University of Hong Kong (CUHK) aimed at obtaining a much clearer picture about the use of e-learning at the university so as to develop new strategic directions on a firm evidence base. Multiple sources of data were collected, including: site logs, experts' review of selected active Web sites, and interviews with 26 teachers. The data illustrate that e-learning at CUHK is still largely in the "innovators" and "early adopters" stages (Rogers, 2003). There lies a "chasm" ahead inhibiting moving further into the "mainstream" area. The analysis of the data revealed that what the teachers want from the technology, what they actually do, and what they can have access to for support are not totally aligned. The focus of the chapter is on how to improve this alignment so as to bridge the chasm. The study has been successful in eliciting university support for changes to the e-learning support system.

Background

There is a growing worldwide trend in the use of Web technology for the support of learning and teaching in universities. While e-learning can mean any use of computer technology to support learning, in the context of this chapter, we are referring to materials and activities involving Web-based environments. The emphasis of this chapter is on institutional decision-making about e-learning support; however, it is relevant to set the scene by briefly commenting on why e-learning strategies are believed to have the potential to enhance student learning environments. [These comments are based on pedagogical considerations and not on technical matters of connectivity such as access to networked computers with sufficient bandwidth. In Hong Kong, the technical infrastructure is largely reliable and the vast majority of students have good access.]

Interactivity and Engagement

One key aspect of e-learning design is interactivity — how students interact with learning materials, with the teacher and with peer learners (Swan, 2003). Broadly, interactivity can be thought of as interactions with either the content which might be text, audio visual resources, graphics and static visual representations, scenarios, simulations, and/or quizzes; or with people via asynchronous online communication (threaded discussions/newsgroups) and/or synchronous communication (chat) (Kearsley, 2000). Interactivity is thought to enhance learning because feedback and reflections effectively help the construction of meaning and give structure to knowledge and information (Taylor & Maor, 2000; O'Connor, 1998).

Other writers emphasize the social aspects of Web-assisted learning. Both Laurillard (2001) and Wenger (1998) discussed how "communities of practice" can emerge through the use of Web technology. In these communities, learners can pursue shared enterprises through discussion and collaboration in a highly active form of learning. Similarly, Preece (2000) suggested that the Web has allowed learners to form into "online communities" that enable ongoing interactions in an "anytime, anywhere" format that can support the development of autonomy in learners.

One of the purposes of this study was to see to what extent the views of teachers at The Chinese University of Hong Kong (CUHK) echo the enthusiasm about the potential of e-learning that can be found in the literature.

Evaluation of E-Learning Designs

There is a growing literature on how educationally effective various e-learning designs and projects are. Some studies have focused on the potential of generic learning designs; for example, a recent Australian project (Learning designs, 2003; Hedberg, Wills, Oliver, Harper, & Agostinho, 2002) identified 52 technology-based learning design exemplars of which 28 were selected for evaluation. An international evaluation team of 64 members studied these 28 cases, using two evaluators for each learning design exemplar. The results of the evaluation phase assisted the project team to select a number of exemplars suitable for redevelopment in a more generic form. The project concluded that the following learning designs have high potential for facilitating learning, and the project Web site provides suggestions and examples about how to use these designs success-fully: collaborative activities, a focus on conceptual or procedure development, problem-based learning, the use of practical projects or case studies, and role-play. In this study, we will look to see what designs are used by CUHK teachers.

Many reported evaluation studies are done by teachers or teacher-designer teams reporting on specific e-learning projects in which they have been involved. This type of evaluation can be generally described as action research studies and the reports provide rich descriptions of what works well in particular contexts (e.g., McPherson, 2004; Levy, 2003). Reading across these accounts tends to strongly confirm the principles of interactivity and engagement. There are several useful edited collections (e.g., Eisenstadt & Vincent, 1998, and, indeed, this volume) that look across several individual studies so as to provide more generalisable principles.

Evaluation data about e-learning is occasionally provided by an "evaluation service" such as that provided by the e3-learning (enrich, extend, evaluate learning) project in Hong Kong. Project staff work with teachers to design, develop, and evaluate educa-tional Web sites. As this project has been involved with over 100 Web sites, a more systematic meta-analysis across projects is possible (McNaught & Lam, 2005). In this study, we attempt to look across the online courses of several CUHK teachers so as to provide insights that will assist future planning for e-learning support at CUHK.

Evaluation of E-Learning at Institutional Level

However, in addition to studies on individual course e-learning experiences, it is increasingly clear that institutional policy relating to e-learning is an essential factor in maximizing the potential benefits of Web-enhanced teaching and learning.

McNaught, Phillips, Rossiter, and Winn (2000), in an Australia-wide study involving 25 universities in all states of Australia, found that the issues surrounding the adoption of e-learning at universities are complex, and no single factor will result in adoption. Instead, there is a range of policy, culture, and support factors that need to be addressed. Several universal factors in relation to widespread use of e-learning were identified:

- coherence of policy across all levels of institutional operations and clear specific policies which impact on e-learning within the institution;

- clear intellectual property policy, particularly with respect to the role of copyright in emerging online environments;

- strong leadership and institutional culture;

- support for staff issues and attitudes: namely, professional development and training, staff recognition and rewards, and motivation for individuals to use e-learning;

- specific resourcing issues related to funding for maintenance or updating of e-learning materials and approaches, staff time release, and support staff.

In deciding how technology should be used in any university, e-learning policy makers need to decide how the technology should be used, and the deliberations should be on the basis of educational needs rather technological fixes. The case of RMIT University in Australia is often cited in Australia as a university that invested heavily in techno-logical systems that failed with far-reaching consequences (McNaught, 2005). As the first author was witness to the RMIT saga, there is a clear commitment to decision-making at CUHK being based on an understanding of the nature of the learning designs being used in the programmes and courses here at CUHK, and on the perceived needs of teachers.

Current Context of E-Learning @ CUHK

In Hong Kong, there are eight government-funded higher education institutions (University Grants Committee, 2005), each with a distinctive character. None of the Hong Kong universities are large; all have undergraduate populations of less than 15,000 students, most of whom are full-time students, straight from an education in local Hong Kong schools. The Hong Kong undergraduate population is thus quite homogeneous — much more so than in many other countries. The Chinese University of Hong Kong (CUHK) is an essentially collegial university. There are three research-intensive universities in Hong Kong, with CUHK being the one with the strongest Chinese cultural ethos.

The combination of the maintenance of Chinese cultural values with an active outreach to the world is an intriguing challenge. Much of the work in understanding East-West distinctions (e.g., Bond, 1991; Nisbet, 2003) involves looking at how value hierarchies and priorities for action differ across cultural boundaries. For example, the primacy of family and respect for elders and associated groups norms in Chinese culture have implications for students' perceptions of Western curricula and classroom behaviour (McNaught, 2003a). However, the differences between Chinese and Western universities are not the focus of this chapter. It will suffice to comment that these differences are subtle. Our research evidence (Kember et al., in press) is that there are few differences globally between teachers' conceptions of what constitutes good teaching; however, the enactment of educational principles may well need somewhat different strategies, in that conflict in groupwork is not acceptable to Chinese students (McNaught et al., 2005). While the West views talkative students as being praiseworthy, active and talkative students in many Chinese classrooms are deemed to be showing off (Schoenhals, 1994). E-learning may allow students to bring up their concerns and ideas in a less "intimidating" but more student-centred environment, and this could well be a very good supplement to classrooms in a Chinese context. The same need to avoid public conflict can be seen at institutional level in the value system that guides the policy decision-making process. One reason why this study was carried out was to establish what we, as e-learning support staff, already knew and to present it as a formal written report. It is not that Western universities do not work from an evidence base, but there are subtle differences in the negotiation strategies that occur in the two contexts. As De Freitas and Oliver (2005) emphasized, the fact that policy is not value free and is heavily reliant on the value system of those who develop it is pertinent.

Five years have passed since CUHK first introduced e-learning at an institutional level. As will be described later in the chapter, a steady and significant growth in the user base and application areas has been recorded. During 2004, a study was carried out at CUHK with two main purposes in mind: to enable us to have a much clearer picture about the current e-learning situation at the university, and thus be able to develop new strategic directions on a firm evidence base. The two academic units involved in this study were the Centre for Learning Enhancement And Research (CLEAR) and the Information Technology Services Centre (ITSC). CLEAR is a small education development unit offering a range of teaching and learning services across the university. Evaluation research is an integral part of CLEAR's role. ITSC provides systems hosting and maintenance, and technical support to teachers and students at the university.

CUHK is a devolved university, with significant decision-making occurring at department and faculty levels. The e-learning system reflects the diversity of this devolved culture. Centrally, two main platforms are supported — WebCT and a home-grown platform, CUForum (CUHK, Web-based Teaching and Learning Project, 2002). The main difference between WebCT and CUForum is that CUForum does not support online quizzes. At present, both are supported because of the significant number of WebCT users; as CUForum is further developed it may become the only platform. There is support provided for other Web-based teaching, including a real-time virtual classroom (iClass) and on-demand lectures. However, the majority of CUHK teachers who use ITSC's services use only WebCT or CUForum. In addition, there are a large number of educational Web sites hosted on faculty or departmental servers. A more corporate university might have a "cleaner" e-learning infrastructure; however, it is important that the devolved nature of the university be understood and taken into account. Any forced migrations or mandatory tools just would not be accepted here.

Methodology of This Study and Quantitative Data

The study (eL@CU) was composed of three phases. A number of methods were used to collect data so as to: (1) understand the general use of the Web technology in teaching and learning across the university as a whole; (2) understand more about e-learning processes by inspecting selected active course Web sites; and (3) get a deeper understanding of e-learning from the teachers' points of view by interviewing a group of selected teachers who have been actively engaged in e-learning. Our evaluation design is summarized in Figure 1; the data collected for the study are listed in the boxes at the bottom of Figure 1.

Figure 1. Evaluation design for the eL@CU study

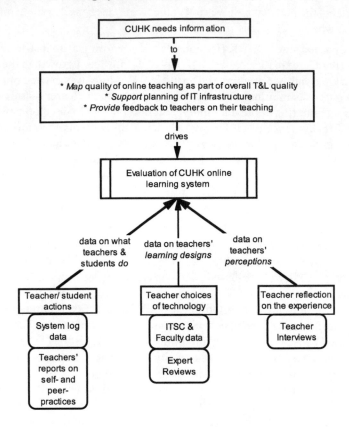

Phase 1 of the Study: General Use Over the University

In this first phase of the study, multiple sources of data were used to reveal the current status of e-learning at the university. The data sources about the abundance and nature of the educational Web sites at the university were:

- the system log records of the two learning management platforms WebCT and CUForum;

- the feedback received from a university-wide e-mail survey conducted in the beginning of May 2004;

- the information obtained informally from colleagues in the university's seven faculties concerning the use of the Web by teachers in their faculties; and

- a description of a number of Web sites not hosted by ITSC, shortlisted by going through information contained in departmental Web sites; from data provided by the Faculty of Engineering, the largest user of such sites (216 in the 2003-2004 year); and by checking the validity of a self-reporting course Web site list which has been developed during the past three years ago (CUHK WBT Links, 2003-2004).

Figure 2. Web functions in the Web sites hosted in WebCT and CUForum

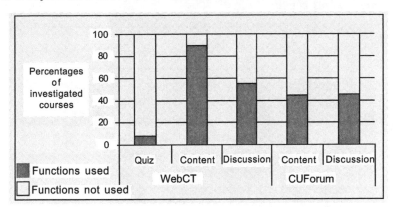

During the 2003-2004 academic year, there were 877 WebCT sites serving 1,113 courses (some teachers use the same WebCT site to teach several courses), 708 forum sites in the home-grown CUForum platform, and 291 course sites on non-ITSC-supported servers based in departments and faculties. In 2003-2004, WebCT and CUForum attained an average annual growth rate of 30% and 23%, respectively, in the number of courses and forums hosted. Site log records also showed that 70% of the entire student population were WebCT or CUForum users. Within a short period of time, the growth in the number of students will approach saturation; however, the intensity of e-learning use also needs to be considered and is continuing to rise. At present, during semester time, there are more than 4,000 accesses to course Web sites each day, and this is about two and a half times the number two years ago.

However, despite this increasing trend in e-learning use, e-learning is far from a popular teaching and learning strategy at the university. Among the 4,637 (undergraduate and postgraduate) courses offered at CUHK in the 2003-2004 year where the enrolments were greater than 10 students, only about 45% had a supplementary online course site. So, while most students have some online experience, this is usually not in all the courses they study. This percentage shows that e-learning at CUHK is still largely in the "innovators" and "early adopters" stages of Rogers' (2003) phases of technology take-up; we cannot comfortably claim that e-learning is a "mainstream" trend. The "chasm" (Moore, 1991) between the early adoption and mainstream use is one we now need to bridge.

Generally speaking, as shown in Figure 2, content provision and discussion are the most widely used functions, and quizzes are rarely used. To what extent, the content is "static" or "interactive" could not be determined at this overall level. This was one of the reasons we looked at a number of individual sites, as will be described later.

Regarding the discussion function, the records show that there were 10 courses that had more than 1,000 discussion messages. However, most of the forums in general were not very active; Figure 3 indicates that most of the forums in courses in both the WebCT and CUForum platforms have less than three postings. CUHK is a relatively small university

Figure 3. Number of postings made by students in WebCT and CUForum forums (counts are for whole courses running in 2003-2004)

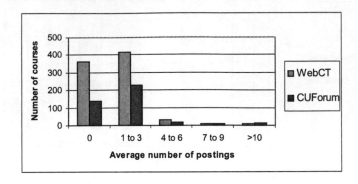

and all undergraduate, and most postgraduate, courses have strong face-to-face components. Therefore, it is not surprising that online communication is not used to a great extent. However, we consider that this very low level represents some lost opportunities for students to articulate and explore ideas in a reflective manner and to practice written communication skills in both English and Chinese.

Usage of non-core functions like "assignment drop-box" and "online quizzes" has been growing, but in 2003-2004, they were still rarely utilized. For example, less than 10% of the WebCT course site owners made use of the quiz function (Figure 2). Most Hong Kong universities are still exam-oriented with the focus of assessment being of a summative nature with formal tests and examinations. The importance of formative assessment for learning is not as strong as in the UK or Australia. This is one possible explanation for the lack of interest in online quizzes. The other is that at a research-intensive university such as CUHK, there are few rewards for activities such as writing and Web-mounting quizzes, an activity that can be time-consuming.

Phase 2 of the Study: Evaluation of Selected Active Sites

Broadly, the Web enables communication and also provides access to information and tasks. Across these two broad areas there are four main teaching and learning functions that the Web usually enables (McNaught, 2002). These are:

1. **Discussion/ communication:** The use of forums is the primary form.

2. **Assessment and feedback to learners:** Here quizzes and peer review activities can be used.

3. **Study management and skills support:** In this grouping is a range of "static" information and resources, including lecture notes.

4. **Content enrichment:** In this grouping, the resources are intended to be more interactive or task-oriented.

Table 1. Categories used in examining active Web sites and the experts' ratings

		No. inst.[1]	High (3)	Med. (2)	Low (1)	Wt. mean [2]
A. Communication						
Asynchronous	1. Forum	13	2	3	8	1.5
Synchronous (can be reviewed when the exchanges are archived)	2. Chat-room	0*				
	3. Graphic-enabled Chat	0				
	4. eLecturing	0				
	5. Video-Conferencing	0				
B. Assessment & feedback to learners						
	6. Quizzes	7	6	0	1	2.7
	7. Online feedback of assignments	3	0	1	2	1.3
	8. Peer review	1	1	0	0	3.0
C. Study management & skills support						
	9. Course information	24	8	6	10	1.9
	10. Teacher's information	11	5	1	5	2.0
	11. Lecture notes and/or PPTs	27	21	3	3	2.7
	12. Lab notes/ Lab handbooks/ Tutorial questions/	9	7	2	0	2.8
	13. Learning skills (tips, links, inventories)	0				
D. Content enrichment						
	14. Online learning resources	3	1	2	0	2.3
	15. Past papers and assignments	5	3	1	1	2.4
	16. Glossary	3	3	0	0	3.0
	17. FAQ on content	0				
	18. Cases and scenarios	1	1	0	0	3.0
	19. Students' work/ presentations as resources	3	3	0	0	3.0
	20. Role-related games	1	0	1	0	2.0
	21. Tools	1	0	1	0	2.0
	22. Student websites	0				

* The zero entries have still been included because we do have cases at CUHK where these Web functions are used, though not in this sample of 30 sites. [1] Number of instances [2] Weighted mean

In order to select "active" WebCT, CUForum, or "non-ITSC" Web sites, we used a rough quantitative measure. Essentially, we looked at the logs in order to find courses with active use of the main four teaching and learning functions described. In this way, a set of 30 "active" sites was selected. These were examined by the first three authors who, together, have developed a rich set of technical and educational experience in advising and assisting teachers in learning enhancement through e-learning. They reviewed these course-related Web sites at the university in three expert-review meetings. These sites were classified using a "matrix"; each Web site was listed as "high," "medium," or "low" on a refined list of 22 Web functions, which were an elaboration of the four main functions mentioned. Table 1 shows the number of cases where each of the functions were found to be in use and how the "experts" rated them according to both the quality and quantity of the materials presented. For example, a "high" rating on a forum was given when there were several postings per student and the quality of the postings was substantive. This involved, of course, looking at the forum statistics and reading through the postings. A "low" forum had few postings, mostly about procedural matters such as due dates and so forth. The ratings were done by an iterative process, which was time-consuming and intensive, as most processes involving qualitative judgements are. The final rankings were independently confirmed by the fourth author.

The functions in order of popularity were content related to study management (71 instances), content enrichment (17 instances), discussion forums (13 instances), and feedback to learners (11 instances). This is a content-focused picture. It is heartening that while the number of cases listed under "content enrichment" is low at 17, it does, however, indicate that more than half of these active e-teachers had designed and developed opportunities for learners to interact and work with online content resources.

If we compare our list with the learning designs mentioned in the background section (Learning designs, 2003; Hedberg et al., 2002), we can see that some, but not the majority, of our CUHK active teachers use the Web to carry out the following learning designs:

• **Collaborative activities:** The two "high" forums are examples here.
• **Focus on conceptual or procedure development:** Examples are the six "high" quizzes, the one "high" peer review, and the several "high" examples in "study management and skills support" and "content enrichment."
• **Problem-based learning:** Sadly, there are zero in this sample.
• **Use of practical projects or case studies:** There is one "high" example.
• **Role-play:** There is one "medium" example.

Of course, this is not to say that these learning designs are not used by other teachers in this group, and across the university, in paper-based and face-to-face forms. Indeed, we know that this occurs. However, currently, there is little use of the Web to support these learning designs. It is another "chasm" we feel needs to be bridged.

Phase 3 of the Study: Experiences of Selected Active E-Teachers

Twenty-six teachers who were actively engaged in e-learning were interviewed about their stories of using the Web and their reflections on their experiences. They were either the site owners of the selected sites described or were selected based on responses made to a university-wide teacher e-mail survey in May 2004 which revealed several enthusiastic and committed e-teachers. The teachers were interviewed from July to September 2004 in the third phase of the study. The group of 26 teachers included representatives from all of the seven faculties at CUHK (arts, business administration, education, engineering, medicine, science, and social science). The sample is not a representative sample of CUHK teachers. We were not trying to find out why some teachers are not interested in e-learning. The purpose of these interviews was to find out the perspectives and priorities of teachers who are already engaged in e-learning. How can future e-learning support services improve the better course Web sites so that they become effective exemplars for others? It has been our experience in the past that working with keen teachers who become models for their peers is more effective than trying to persuade reluctant teachers to set up a course Web site (McNaught, 2003b; Inglis, Ling, & Joosten, 2002, chapter 8). In other words, we are focusing on our more experienced e-teachers in considering how best to cross the chasm toward mainstream use of e-learning at CUHK.

During the interviews, several areas of interests were discussed. Questions asked included:

Q1: What was the rationale behind your setting up this Web site? Or using the resources you have selected for your course?

Q2: What was the story of how you used the site (how, what, when, etc.)?

Q3: Were the original purposes of using the Web achieved? How do you know?

Q4: What do you feel about the experience of teaching online (i.e., workload, changes in teaching methods, strengths and weaknesses)?

Q5: What is your next plan for using the Web in teaching (if any)?

The interviews were each about an hour long. They were recorded and a summary of each interview was made the same day as the interview and approved by the teachers. Most of the interviews were conducted in Cantonese. Direct quotes are not given in the discussion, as the time involved in producing accurate translations did not seem to be warranted in this study.

The Current E-Learning Situation at CUHK: The Qualitative Focus

The more quantitative data from phases 1 and 2 were already described to some extent previously, alongside the description of how the data were extracted. The third phase of the study (interviews with 26 teachers) was especially revealing about current e-learning needs at the university. The summary reports from all 26 interviews were then analyzed by classifying the teachers' comments into three groups:

- What teachers generally *want* from e-learning (teachers' needs). Why do teachers use learning technologies? What do they hope to achieve?

- What teachers actually *do* toward achieving their "wants" (teachers' practices). What is actually on their course Web sites? What are the tasks they set students to do online?

- What resources teachers have as *support* (teachers' context). What financial support do they have for building or obtaining content resources? What technical help do they have access to?

Any individual point made by a teacher was recorded as one count in the frequencies reported. The resulting pattern of responses was examined in order to suggest some clear strategic directions.

Teachers' Needs: What They *Want*

One of the key question sets asked in the teacher interviews was "What was the rationale behind your setting up this Web site? Or using the resources you have selected for your course?" The teachers' replies were multifaceted and yet could be grouped into two main themes — "teaching efficiency" and "learning enhancement."

Teaching efficiency is not a surprising finding in that the use of the Web to assist with large class management, giving out announcements, arranging logistics for activities, distributing notes, course material and information, is quite common with these teachers. For example, a teacher from the English Language Teaching Unit said that the Web could ease her marking load by the use of the automatically generated online quiz scores produced by WebCT. A computer science and engineering teacher said that the Web could let him disseminate a higher quality of information more easily.

It is pleasing that learning enhancement was the other main objective that the teachers clearly wanted to achieve through the Web. This was mentioned as frequently as teaching efficiency, each 21 times (Table 2). Student learning was expected to be enhanced in various ways, such as: introducing flexible learning so that students with different backgrounds and learning styles could engage in online learning at varied times and places; and improving students' motivation. For example, a teacher from management said that accessibility and flexibility particularly benefited the part-time MBA students.

Some hoped that their interactive Web materials would provide better explanations of different concepts; some were hoping for enhanced cognitive skills such as problem-solving; and some wanted students to engage in meaningful online discussions to enhance their capacity for critical thinking. A psychology teacher, for example, regarded the Web forum as a place for idea exchange and sharing about a number of different perspectives.

While teachers spoke about wanting to support their students' learning, they did not do this from any theoretical standpoint. For example, the language of constructivism is just not part of the vocabulary of CUHK teachers. Course outlines here are still often described in terms of lists of content topics, and, while there is an increasing focus on the development of intellectual and communicative capabilities, teachers still largely think of learning in terms of becoming knowledgeable about the concepts and processes of particular disciplines.

Table 2. Main themes of what the 26 teachers want

Themes	Mentioned by no. of teachers
Teaching efficiency	*21*
Notes and course material distribution	10
Announcements	7
Large class management	6
Better logistics of activities	4
Handle enquiry about course	2
Course information data record	2
Learning enhancement	*21*
Student-student communication on content	10
Flexible learning (time, place, learner background, learning styles)	9
Visual impact for clearer explanation	6
Transfer of skills and knowledge (cases)	4
Deep motivation to learning	3
Teacher-student communication on content	3
Deep strategies to learning	2
Self-directed learning	2
Others	*2*
Funding obtained	2

Teachers' Practice: What Teachers *Do*

What the teachers said about what actually happened on their course Web sites on the whole seemed to fall short of effectively achieving what they *want* described above. Teachers were asked what Web functions were actually used in their teaching. Each teacher mentioned one or more functions used. Their mentioned Web functions were compiled together. Two rounds of classification and categorization were worked out and five main categories of Web functions resulted:

- **Content delivery:** uploading files — mentioned 25 times.

- **Communication:** the use of forums for communication and interaction among class members — mentioned 19 times.

- **Assignment and grading management:** the use of the virtual learning environment as a platform for assignment distribution, assignment submission and assignment grading distribution — mentioned 11 times.

- **Information dissemination:** the dissemination of course-related information to students — mentioned nine times.

- **Engagement:** the allocation of some marks for online participation — mentioned six times.

The main way the teachers used the content delivery function was to put up notes and PowerPoint slides (15 of the 26 cases). The next common use was for content on the Web as course and reading materials (13 of the 26 cases). Multimedia and interactive learning resources were comparatively rare (three cases); these few teachers included many videos and animations in their course sites to provide visual support for students' learning and understanding of the course topics. For this small minority of teachers, the Web was clearly more than a convenient storage house for easy distribution of course materials to students.

Most communications were done through online forums and the design was simple: mostly teacher-student communication about course and course content, and some student-student communication concerning discussion topics assigned by the teachers. However, some more sophisticated online activities were mentioned by a few teachers, such as "online debates" and peer-review activities. As noted, the teachers interviewed were the more experienced teachers in e-learning. If we look again at the overall CUHK picture, we can see that participation in most of the forums in the sites was low, with students, on average, posting one to three messages (Figure 3).

During the interview, teachers were invited to talk about their feelings about their success or failure in achieving what they wanted in using the Web in their teaching. More positive feelings than negative feelings were mentioned (46 versus 29). However, these related to the learning enhancement area, and to matters such as students' enjoyment; there are more negative comments than positive comments in the teaching efficiency area. Table 3 is a summary of these feelings. The comments received concerning the teaching efficiency theme are mixed: for example, 10 felt positive about workload, while 10 felt

Table 3. Successes and failures mentioned by the 26 teachers

Areas of success or failure	Mentioned as success	Mentioned as failure
Teaching efficiency		
1. Workload	10	10
2. Technology-induced benefits/ problems	4	8
3. Time-saving	2	3
4. Easy material distribution	2	0
5. Class management	1	1
6. Efficiency	1	0
7. Getting copyright clearance	0	2
Learning enhancement		
8. Allowance of new teaching strategies	9	0
9. Communication	2	0
10. Learning impact	2	1
11. Flexibility	1	0
Others		
12. Enjoyment	11	0
13. Support gained	1	3
14. Recognition	0	1
Totals	**46**	**29**

negative; four mentioned technical benefits, while eight mentioned technical problems; and two mentioned that e-learning actually saved time, while the other three said the opposite. Teachers mentioned that putting materials online raises the concern of violating copyright laws. They also were concerned about dealing with plagiarism problems as the use of the Web as an information source is increasing. Especially in an English-as-second-language environment, the "temptation" to plagiarize is high.

The teachers seemed to be more positive about using the Web for learning enhancement. As shown in Table 3, a few teachers mentioned the success of the Web in gaining "flexibility," "efficiency," "learning impact," "communication," and "allowance of new teaching strategies." A teacher from sports science and physical education said that he had used the Web in his courses for several years, and he had the impression that the students scored higher in their skill-related assessments. An experienced teacher of Japanese studies said that some students had attained better language skills than he originally expected.

The teachers, however, also remarked that these impressions of success or failure are the result of mostly subjective and non-systematic observations on each teacher's part, usually by talking to one or few of the students. For example, one teacher realized the students in his science course had benefited from the animations that showed molecular motions. Another teacher talked about his students in his architecture class enjoying three-dimensional visual impacts from computer graphics. Few systematic evaluations on the effect of e-learning on students' learning have been carried out at CUHK. To date, these teachers had been putting effort into designing and developing Web materials and activities, but not into evaluating their effectiveness. So, while they wanted learning enhancement as much as teaching efficiency, they had only anecdotal evidence about how successful they were in this regard.

Teachers' Context: What Teachers Have for *Support*

The teachers told us that most of them (11 out of the 26) rely on their teaching or research assistants (mostly postgraduate students) to build and maintain the Web sites for them. Some technical services are available in some departments, but this is by no means ubiquitous. Some teachers were fortunate to receive CDG or other funding so they could develop their courses in one condensed time period. However, most of them said they no longer have resources for further development and even have difficulties in maintaining their course sites.

Teachers generally felt that support from their departments and from their peers was insufficient. They would like departments to have a clearer policy about encouraging and supporting e-learning. Also, teachers felt disappointed that their effort on building a Web site was not recognized by their peers and their department heads. The university does have "innovative pedagogy" as a criterion for promotion, but, at this research-intensive university, research grants and publications still hold sway. A teacher from management said that though she was a pioneer of e-learning five years ago, she did not use the Web extensively now because the workload was too heavy.

A Diagrammatic Summary and Interpretation of the CUHK Teachers' Perceptions

The situation at CUHK is illustrated in Figure 4. We have used this diagrammatic form to try to get an overview of the multiple factors operating in our own situation. The size of ellipses is not to scale but the purpose of the diagram is to show relationships and positioning. *W* represents what the teachers *want*. *S* is the set of e-learning-related services teachers have for *support*. *D* is what the teachers at the end actually *do* as we explained previously. It is an interpretative diagram that we then use to see what needs to change in the CUHK context in order for better alignment to occur. We have found this form of visual "mapping" to be a useful strategy in supporting decision-making.

In Figure 4a, *area a represents what the teachers want to achieve but in the end fail to realize, probably because of lack of support*. This area includes technical difficulties (e.g., complex material development), time issues (e.g., getting assistance to quickly and easily build and maintain the Web sites), educational advice on design and evaluation, and recognition and departmental support. There is an *area b where teachers still manage to work out something on their own without much support from the institution*. This area includes: spending time and effort on preparing materials; maintaining personal servers; and doing limited evaluations. *Area c includes the needs of the teachers that they cannot currently realize*; instead they relegate them into their future plans. Materials with more interactivity and richer coverage are examples. *In area d are the needs realized with institution's support. Area e includes existing services that seem to be neglected*, at least by the 26 teachers interviewed. These services include the assignment drop-box function, online quizzes, multimedia possibilities, and videoconferencing.

Figure 4b has an additional *area P to represent the other learning and teaching possibilities that the Web can support, but which are now not actively supported at our university*. Teachers may not be aware of this "potentials" territory. One example is mobile technology; while there are a number of mobile projects in Hong Kong (e.g., Csete, Wong, & Vogel, 2004), this is not a feature of e-learning support at CUHK. *P* is portrayed

Figure 4. What teachers want, do, and have as support (see text for key)

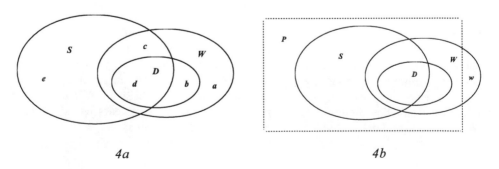

4a   4b

Figure 5. Idealized e-learning situation

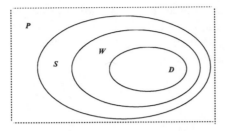

in a dotted line because the margins of the possibilities are not clearly known yet, and indeed the boundaries are constantly shifting. We have also included an *area w that relates to unrealistic requests that some teachers have*; for example, a quest for convenience to the extent that teachers are waived all the workload of building and maintaining the site is not reasonable.

Future Directions for E-Learning at CUHK

The idealized situation of the e-learning situation is portrayed in Figure 5. It is a situation where there is a closer match between the potential of the Web, the support given to the teachers, what the teachers want, and what they do.

Contrasting Figures 4 and 5, there seem to be indications of how the improvement of the whole e-learning situation can be achieved:

- building awareness in teachers about a wider range of strengths, weaknesses, potentials, and strategies of e-learning through professional development (to enlarge the *W* area and shift *W* to fall within *P*);

- provision of concrete commitments and long-term resources to teachers (extension of *S* to cover *W*) to support teachers through all the stages of planning, development, implementation, and post-implementation;

- enabling teachers to design better e-learning environments (extension of *D*);

- researching and evaluating the various e-learning strategies (extension of *W*, *D* and *S* to cover more of *P*). Some examples are Web-enabled cultural interactions between students in different countries, peer and group assessments, self-directed learning, and so forth. We do have a few "pioneering" teachers in these areas who can help to explore the limits of the potential.

In order to do this, changes in the three areas of policy, culture, and support (McNaught et al., 2000) are needed. Policy changes are needed to provide the resources to give more effective support that might produce better exemplars as models. These exemplars can support the process of changing the culture of teaching and learning so that innovation, including in e-learning, is adequately rewarded, but that also requires policy changes , and so the interactions continue.

Final Comment

In this chapter, we have outlined the ways in which we have tried to get a clear picture of e-learning at a highly devolved university. We have tried to articulate the educational value system of our CUHK teachers. We have found some excellent e-teachers and some good examples of e-learning. However, it is clear that e-learning at CUHK is still largely in the "innovators" and "early adopters" stages and we are facing a "chasm" before we can enter the "mainstream" area. This chasm is currently causing an under-utilization of the potential of the Web in supporting teaching and learning. Re-design and extension of our services can provide better matches between what teachers *want* from the technology, what they actually *do*, and what they have access to as *support*; this is critical in overcoming the chasm. A report on this study has been presented to the university who has agreed that this study provides sufficient evidence to justify the establishment of an e-learning centre; through this centre we will be able to provide consultancy support to each department of the university. Without the evidence of the study, we would not have been successful. We are hopeful that this study that has been of value to our own university may be of interest to others.

References

Bond, M.H. (1991). *Beyond the Chinese face: Insights from psychology*. Oxford: Oxford University Press.

The Chinese University of Hong Kong, Web-based Teaching and Learning Project (2002). Retrieved September 14, 2005, from www.cuhk.edu.hk/wbt

The Chinese University of Hong Kong. (2003-2004). *Web-based teaching links*. Retrieved September 14, 2005, from http://www.cuhk.edu.hk/wbt/wbtlinks/

Csete, J., Wong, Y.H., W. & Vogel, D. (2004, June 21-26). Mobile devices in and out of the classroom. In L. Cantoni & C. McLoughlin (Eds.), *ED-MEDIA 2004* (pp. 4729-4736). *Proceedings of the 16th annual World Conference on Educational Multimedia*, Hypermedia & Telecommunications, Lugano, Switzerland. Norfolk, VA: Association for the Advancement of Computers in Education.

De Freitas, S., & Oliver, M. (2005). Does e-learning policy drive change in higher education? A case study relating models of organisational change to e-learning implementation. *Journal of Higher Education Policy and Management, 27*(1), 81-96.

e3Learning (enrich, extend, evaluate learning) project. Retrieved September 14, 2005, from http://e3learning.edc.polyu.edu.hk/

Eisenstadt, M., & Vincent, T. (Eds.) (1998). *The knowledge Web: Learning and collaborating on the net.* London: Kogan Page.

Hedberg, J., Wills, S., Oliver, R., Harper, B., & Agostinho, S. (2002, June 24-29). Developing evaluation frameworks for assessing quality ICT-based learning in higher education. In P. Barker & S. Rebelsky (Eds.), *ED-MEDIA 2002* (pp. 729-735). *Proceedings of the 14ᵗʰ annual World Conference on Educational Multimedia, Hypermedia & Telecommunications*, Denver, CO. Norfolk, VA: Association for the Advancement of Computers in Education.

Inglis, A., Ling, P., & Joosten, V. (2002). *Delivering digitally: Managing the transition to the knowledge media.* London: Kogan Page.

Kearsley, G. (2000). *Online education: Learning and teaching in cyber-space.* Belmont, CA: Wadsworth/Thomson Learning.

Kember, D., Ma, R., McNaught, C., & 18 exemplary teachers (in press). *Excellent university teaching.* Hong Kong: Chinese University Press.

Laurillard, D. (2001). *Rethinking university teaching: A framework for the effective use of educational technology* (2nd ed.). London: Routledge.

Learning designs (2003). Retrieved September 14, 2005, from www.learningdesigns.uow.edu.au/index.html

Levy, P. (2003). A methodological framework for practice-based research in networked learning. *Instructional Science, 31*, 787-109.

McNaught, C. (2002). Adopting technology should mean adapting it to meet learning needs. *On The Horizon, 10*(4), 14-18.

McNaught, C. (2003a). Supporting the global eTeacher. *International Journal of Training and Development, 7*(4), 1-16.

McNaught, C. (2003b). The effectiveness of an institution-wide mentoring program for improving online teaching and learning. *Journal of Computing in Higher Education. 15*(1), 27-45.

McNaught, C. (2005). Integrating teaching and learning principles with IT infrastructure and policy. In K. Fraser (Ed.), *Education development and leadership in higher education. Developing an effective institutional strategy* (pp. 108-128). London: Routledge Falmer.

McNaught, C., & Lam, P. (2005). Building an evaluation culture and evidence base for e-learning in three Hong Kong universities. *British Journal of Educational Technology, 36*(4), 599-614.

McNaught, C., Lau, W.M., Lam, P., Hui, M.Y.Y., & Au, P.C.T. (2005). The dilemma of case-based teaching and learning in science in Hong Kong: Students need it, want it, but may not value it. *International Journal of Science Education, 27*(9), 1017-1036.

McNaught, C., Phillips, P., Rossiter, D., & Winn, J. (2000). *Developing a framework for a usable and useful inventory of computer-facilitated learning and support materials in Australian universities*. Evaluations and Investigations Program report 99/11. Canberra: Higher Education Division Department of Employment, Education, Training and Youth Affairs. Retrieved September 14, 2005, from www.dest.gov.au/highered/eippubs1999.htm

McPherson, M. (2004). *Developing innovation in online learning: An action research framework*. London: Routledge Falmer.

Moore, G.A. (1991). *Crossing the chasm*. New York: Harper Business Essentials.

Nisbet, R.E. (2003). *The geography of thought*. New York: The Free Press.

O'Connor, M.C. (1998). Can we trace the efficacy of social constructivism? *Review of Educational Research, 23*, 25-71.

Preece, J. (2000). *Online communities: Designing usability, supporting sociability*. Chichester: Wiley.

Rogers, E.M. (2003). *Diffusion of innovations* (5th ed). New York: Free Press.

Schoenhals, M. (1994). Encouraging talk in Chinese classrooms. *Anthropology & Education Quarterly, 25*(4), 399-412.

Swan, K. (2003). Learning effectiveness: What the research tells us. In J. Bourne & J.C. Moore (Eds.), *Elements of quality online education* (vol. 4). Olin and Babson Colleges: Sloan Center for Online Education.

Taylor, P., & Maor, D. (2000). Assessing the efficacy of online teaching with the Constructivist On-Line Learning Environment Survey. *Teaching and Learning Forum 2000*. Retrieved September 14, 2005, from http://lsn.curtin.edu.au/tlf/tlf2000/taylor.html

University Grants Committee (2005). www.ugc.edu.hk/eng/ugc/site/fund_inst.htm

Wenger, E. (1998). *Communities of practice: Learning, meaning, and identity*. Cambridge: Cambridge University Press.

Chapter VI

Developing E-Learning Provision for Healthcare Professionals' Continuing Professional Development

Susi Peacock, Queen Margaret University College, UK

Gloria Maria Dunlop, Queen Margaret University College, UK

Abstract

This chapter discusses the provision of continuing professional development (CPD) for allied healthcare professionals (AHPs) through e-learning. External pressures are increasing on AHPs to engage with CPD on a regular basis to improve the quality of care services and facilitate changes in working practice. E-learning has the potential to reach this group of diverse learners and integrate learning into their work schedule at a time and place convenient for them and their employers: eCPD. We provide a practical reflection grounded in the experience of practitioners and students who have been involved in our deployment of eCPD over the last three years. The issues that have arisen from this initiative will be familiar to many of those who have been involved in the deployment of e-learning in our sector. Ultimately, we hope that the solutions we have provided to meet the needs of this specific group of learners will address those for all e-learners. In addition, we believe that it will support the process of embedding ("normalising") e-learning across an institution.

Background

Allied healthcare professions (AHPs), such as physiotherapists, occupational thera-pists, and radiographers, need to engage with CPD on a regular basis in order to practice legally in the UK (DOH, 1999, 2000). In addition, evidence of CPD must be submitted to the UK regulatory body for AHPs, the Health Professions Council (HPC). Key publica-tions such as "Working Together- Learning Together" (DOH, 2001) have also impacted on requirements for CPD. This particular publication, for example, focussed on the role of CPD to improve patient care and to expand National Health Service (NHS) career opportunities through the development of a lifelong learning culture. Following on from this publication, the Department of Health, working with the Workforce Development Agency, has identified mechanisms that would best support NHS staff in England to develop learning for post-registration as part of the NHS modernisation agenda (DOH, 2004a). At the same time, Agenda for Change (DOH, 2004b) directly links salary with evidence of CPD, and lifelong learning activities are providing another driver for CPD. Furthermore, compliance with European working hours' legislation has resulted in renegotiated working conditions for doctors and consultants (DOH, 2004c). This has led to new roles for AHPs, nurses, and care workers, which places a further demand for the attainment of new knowledge and skills through CPD.

The Joint Information Systems Committee (JISC, 2003) and the Higher Education Funding Council for England (HEFCE, 2005) state that e-learning offers specific benefits for employers and employees over traditional institutionally based programmes. For ex-ample, employees are able to update their skills and knowledge without the loss of time associated with traditional institutionally based teaching and to improve the balance of their work/life responsibilities. In the case of healthcare professionals who are coping with increasing pressures to change working practices with a limited workforce while maintaining a demanding workload, they are now less able than ever to leave the workplace to physically attend an educational institution for CPD (Oblinger & Hawkins, 2005). As one health professional stated: "I like online learning. This is because I do not have to request a duty-off from my workplace for attending classes. It is very difficult to apply for a study day as our wards are short of manpower these days" (Sit, Chung, Chow, & Wong, 2005, p.144). For academic institutions, eCPD programmes have the potential to reach out to this new group of learners as well as augmenting the institution's relationships with NHS partners in the workplace.

The Case Study

Queen Margaret University College (QMUC) in Scotland has a broad portfolio of CPD opportunities for healthcare professionals which are offered at various academic levels, from SCQF level 9 (Scottish Credit and Qualification Framework, 2003) to master's level (SCQF level 11). These include: understanding clinical effectiveness; research and critical appraisal; facilitation of practice-based learning; and introduction to health economics. The learning units range from non-accredited short episodes of learning to accredited half and full modules. Over the last three years, our tutors have been providing eCPD for AHPs using our virtual learning environment (VLE): WebCT. Reflection on current practice to inform and shape future developments is now timely. To support this, we have collected staff and student feedback through interviews and module evaluation forms.

The Tutor Experience

Feedback gathered from tutors who were involved in the development of a certificate programme for carers highlights many of the issues raised by all of our tutors involved in the development of eCPD programmes. This programme, consisting of 12 modules, involving a team of five tutors, had originally been developed for face-to-face delivery. However, external funding was provided to develop a blended approach to learning with minimal face-to-face contact and student support being offered through paper-based study guides and online discussions. Our CPD curriculum development manager, who supported the tutors moving to the online environment, found this a difficult process because:

Some [tutors] were not convinced of this approach to learning and were unclear why it was being used; others although wanting to embrace e-learning were uncertain of its benefits for this particular group of learners. One tutor was enthusiastic and had a clear understanding of how e-learning should and could be used based on studying a module about network technologies.

She also described the difficulty that tutors had in designing for a more blended approach than a traditional face-to-face, 12 week module delivery. Half-way through the development, she realised that often there had been neither module redesign nor consideration about how the different delivery formats would blend within the module and between the modules. A number of short meetings ensued with each tutor as material was being produced to discuss integration and relevance of material; this resulted, as she explained, in materials being re-edited and modules being re-designed "on the hoof":

In my view, the lack of pre-planning resulted in the modules becoming too complex, too crowded, and too demanding for online delivery, for both the learner and the tutor. A substantial rethink was required on how to deliver the information. In addition, other tutors focused on developing text based materials rather than on planning student activities within the online environment; there was too little consideration of the role of the online discussion tool. Everyone was so busy tidying up lecture notes to be presented for online access.

In starting to reflect on the experiences gained from this initiative, we also talked to the tutors involved:

While the development of WebCT-based material is an attractive challenge, difficulties have been evident. These include the lack of appropriate time allocated for the task and an unrealistic expectation of the education organisation resulting in the absence of a clear structure and plan for the development of the programme.

Another tutor, more experienced in e-learning, offered a different perspective:

I think it is good that our students are being given this opportunity. So many of them have little IT experience and get others to type reports and interact with the computer. It will provide confidence and support to those who cannot travel to classes. A great initiative.

The Student Perspective

Positive feedback gathered from our eCPD students focuses on the convenience and flexibility of studying at a distance and at a time and place that is convenient for them. AHP students are not able to accommodate a fixed timetable for face-to-face learning, which therefore makes distance learning very attractive. Furthermore, the accessibility of the e-facility allows learners to feel less isolated as they can easily communicate with other learners and tutors through online discussions accessed either from the workplace or from home. Certainly, an issue that seems to influence whether to e-learn is the lack of IT provision within the NHS. A number of AHPs have reported limited access to computers in the workplace and time for CPD study is not ring fenced. However, these issues are gradually being addressed, for example, more computers are being made available for clinical staff, and the need for allocated study time is being recognised.

Support Staff Feedback

Our evaluation also included feedback from support staff, for instance, we discussed the matriculation process of our eCPD students. The first online experience an eCPD learner will have with an institution will be at the enquiry and enrolment stage; this function is usually provided by the registry at our institution. However, there is a critical difference between our eCPD students who are and are not undertaking a credit-rated programme. Those students who only require verification of successful completion of a programme of study can be registered using a small Excel spreadsheet maintained by one individual working alone outside the registry. This has advantages as the member of staff responsible for the process explains:

I am able to respond to an electronic enquiry immediately, sending information with an application form. Once the form is returned, registration with access to the e-learning programme can be completed within one day which includes sending the relevant access details electronically to the CPD learner.

She contrasts this with the matriculation process of a student undertaking an eCPD programme which awards academic credit. The student has to be enrolled through the central student database; this involves the completion of several application forms which need to be passed between registry and the applicant. This often extends the enrolment process by two weeks and has meant that:

Some learners have not been able to enrol on a programme or have enrolled late. For our eCPD health professionals, juggling work and family commitments, this application process for eCPD accredited programmes does not introduce the applicant to a flexible, user-friendly, speedy, and easily accessible learning experience.

Feedback from support staff in information services focuses on access issues for our students when using their facilities from outside the institution, for instance, Web mail. Although many of our students are experienced computer users, support staff state that some of the students' problems when accessing services are caused by their reluctance to read manuals. As a consequence, support staff are trying to cope with frustrated, time-poor students who want "the computer problem" solved immediately rather than being prepared to take joint ownership of the problem and working with the service to resolve the issue, for example, by carefully reading the documentation provided.

Issues

Many of the issues raised in the feedback (see summary in Tables 1, 2, and 3) will be familiar to those supporting the embedding of e-learning in any institution, in any subject area, and are well-documented in learning technology research. From the tutor perspective, we have found, particularly, that there is a lack of understanding about the potential of a VLE (especially online discussions) in the learning experience and how online delivery links to face-to-face delivery. This is exacerbated by the tutors' lack of IT skills, time to dedicate to learn about, plan, and redesign modules in the VLE (often due to competing demands in their working lives) and critical reflection on what happens in the face-to-face learning environment.

Clearly, our eCPD students prefer the online environment because of its flexibility which helps them to juggle their various commitments while enabling them to study. However, the move to learning online raises their expectations of the type and level of support offered by the educational provider which is exacerbated by the time constraints characteristic of this group of learners. The result is that our support services are dealing with students who have moved into a different mode of learning where there are no longer set boundaries and timings. Consequently, the students expect that everything required to support their learning will be instantly and constantly available: a 24/7 approach to support and access to the online environment (Frand, 2000).

The Way Forward

To address the issues raised through the evaluation, we have focused on staff development in workshops and accredited programmes (online and face-to-face) and tutor support. Our support departments are also exploring innovative approaches to meeting the needs of these students. It is hoped that these initiatives will also support the embedding of e-learning across the institution.

Staff Development and Multi-Layered Tutor Support

Surprisingly, across the sector, only a limited number of staff has received any training in using an institution's VLE (SHEFC, 2005) and that training is typically only available for academic staff. Like most institutions, we offer workshops and raising-awareness events on the use of a VLE for blended and distance learning. However, we have found that an accredited master's module run over a semester can offer tutors, academic-related and administrative staff, protected time in a safe environment to explore and reflect upon the role of technology in learning and teaching. Initially, run over a semester with three face-to-face meetings, due to staff pressure, it is now completely online with one optional group face-to-face meeting.

The module provides as many online opportunities as possible as the tutor reflects:

Most staff have experience of being taught in the traditional format of lecture and seminar in their undergraduate studies. Few have experience of being in a student-led learning environment and fewer of that 'environment' being online. To me, the online discussions are the most important part of the module. At first, they allow staff to take the role of the online learner: working in groups online, discussing with an external expert with whom they have never met, and then finally experiencing being the e-tutor. We have much lively and heated debate about the difference between e-mail and online discussions, e-moderation, and the role of the e-tutor.

Practical and theoretical approaches are combined with staff critiquing pedagogic models of technologies (JISCinfoNet, 2005) and then applying them to the development of a module in a VLE. There is a specific focus on the student perspective, as the tutor of the module reflects:

When I am working with tutors involved in eCPD we think about providing a module that is as flexible as possible to help their students balance work and personal commitments. We also consider student confidence in using IT in learning: a few of our CPD students feel ill-prepared to use technology in their learning. So we consider how to introduce eCPD learners to the online learning environment.

Module feedback indicates that by the end of the module, staff understand the importance of having a model of learning and teaching underpinning their plans for e-learning. They have moved away from seeing themselves as the only content provider for a module (with students having a significant role in this) and have started to re-design their modules. In addition, they have a greater awareness of online discussions and their role as an e-tutor.

To sustain the impetus provided through workshops and accredited programmes, we provide tutors with just-in-time support. A central support unit offers phone, e-mail, and face-to-face support at a time convenient for tutors. Support is also offered by experienced e-tutors, for instance, champions within a subject area can be extremely helpful in encouraging e-learning. In addition, academic-related staff have developed a taste for supporting e-learning and have been provided with training from the central support unit in order to undertake this role. They are often physically located nearer to tutors than central support staff and are keen to handle first-line support issues, such as uploading files into the VLE while passing on more complex pedagogical or institutional-related issues to the central unit (Peacock, Adamson, Mckenzie, & Williams, 2004).

An example of this multi-layered approach to support has been trialled in the development of an eCPD programme for facilitators in the clinical setting. Based on several face-to-face CPD programmes, this eCPD programme provides a multi-professional learning experience for healthcare professionals regardless of their geographical location. The programme has reduced teaching time commitments and provided a more coherent approach across subject areas. Initially, the tutor involved in the development of the programme had been provided with some central support regarding e-learning. Further ongoing, just-in-time support was offered by an e-learning champion, who had attended the accredited module in network technologies and had subject-specific knowledge. This support took the form of an extended discussion on re-thinking module delivery to accommodate the specific needs of the AHP adult learners. The champion describes the process:

We began by deciding on the learning outcomes — 'What did we want the learners to achieve at the end of this programme?' This was followed by a step-by-step plan of how we proposed to guide the learners to achieve these outcomes online which included how and when the programme content could be accessed and used. We discussed which learning resources would be provided on the programme, where they would be located, and how we would guide the learners to these resources. Finally, we debated how we could ensure that the learners would be guided and supported in achieving the final assessment. Adequate time for preparation and reflection was essential.

The e-champion also played a vital role in the planning and support of the online discussions. Drawing on her own experience of using our VLE (especially that from the accredited module), the e-champion encouraged the tutor to think about linking the online discussions to appropriate sections of the module and organising these discussions around specific topics at relevant times. Online group discussions in which learners could exchange concepts and experiences with each other rather than looking to the tutor for the right answer were also planned. Toward the end of the first iteration of the module, the tutor stated:

Having had a number of years of experience delivering this material face-to-face I was struck by the challenge of this learning environment. Changing the style of delivery to suit this user-friendly flexible environment really made me think about the content and its format. I feel the flexibility of this learning environment is one of its key strengths — students can work at their own pace, can go back over materials as many times as they need to and, as with our module, can allow them to fit their studies around other commitments. I have really enjoyed this development and have gained great satisfaction in seeing it all come together.

The tutor is now delivering the second iteration of this module, finding her online voice, and mentoring another tutor who will in turn deliver the module whilst mentoring another tutor.

The Role of the Support Departments

Our support services are exploring how they can respond to the needs of our eCPD students. Discussions are currently underway with our registry to implement a speedier enrolment process for eCPD learners. Already this has included reducing the number of forms required for eCPD learners and funding has recently been made available to implement electronic processes from the first point of contact with our institution.

Good quality library services are another way of reaching out to our eCPD learners, making them feel less isolated and more part of the educational institution (Bye, 1999). Our library has implemented a number of initiatives including linking with the provision of e-resources, in the NHS for example, the NHS E-Library. Subject librarians have also participated in online discussions with our eCPD learners:

The main advantage to a VLE, from my point of view, is that you are, virtually, sitting in the classroom. Not only can you follow what the students are doing, which gives the much needed context that is missing in traditional reference enquiries, but you can also hear about problems firsthand and leap in and offer suggestions, often where students may not recognise that their query is a traditional, 'library' enquiry. Paradoxically, this sitting in on the tutorials and eavesdropping in the "café" has meant that I feel a lot closer to these students than I do to many of the students who walk physically into the library (Quotation from subject librarian).

With regard to IT, our Helpdesk (e-mail and phone) is available for longer hours and during the weekend and has started to develop a set of frequently asked questions (FAQs) for our students. We are also investigating more imaginative solutions, such as the one currently being trialled in an initiative at the LSE (London School of Economics): "The Round the Sun Helpdesk." This is collaboration between Macquarie and Newcastle

Universities in Australia, the University of Colorado in the United States, and the LSE whereby a remote e-mail helpdesk service has been developed to address the demand for out-of-hours IT support for learners. By exploiting the time difference between the cities, it has been possible to extend a computing advisory service to students during times when local services are closed. The service is in operation 24 hours a day during weekdays, and each partner institution takes responsibility for a six-hour shift. The institution currently on shift monitors the generic IT support mailboxes of the other partners and deals with incoming queries.

Discussion

A critical element in the success of our eCPD initiative will be appropriate, timely, and multi-layered support for tutors. Feedback from our tutors shows that they need to know why and how to adapt their traditional approaches to learning and teaching when working in the online environment (Haigh, 2004). This will involve them thinking about the

Table 1. Summary of issues relating to use of a VLE by tutors

SUMMARY OF ISSUES RAISED THROUGH THE EVALUATION WHICH IMPEDE TUTOR ENGAGEMENT WITH A VLE	
Lack of understanding about the potential role of a VLE	Our feedback shows that because tutors do not fully appreciate the potential role of a VLE, they are initially tempted to use it in its simplest form: an electronic filing cabinet that provides learners easy access to documents, for example, copies of PowerPoints (Williams, 2002; Sigala, 2002). This results in a focus on tutor-development of resources (which is usually unsustainable) and the under-utilisation of those applications in a VLE which will reach out to our eCPD students: communication and collaboration.
Lack of understanding about online discussions and the emoderator role	Emoderation is a completely new educational skill for many of our tutors which is demonstrated in their use (or lack of use) of online discussions. For example, a few tutors have assumed that they will have to answer every response in online discussions and consequently will check the online area, almost daily, resulting in too much teacher presence. There is often anxiety about the number of postings and these concerns are exacerbated if they find that there are 'lurkers' within their group. Alternatively, some tutors have assumed that they have a very limited role in the online discussions and suppose that because there is somewhere for students to 'chat' online they will do so. The result has been that many tutors have shied away from using such a communication tool in their use of a VLE and, at best, used it as an administrative notice board.
Lack of IT skills	Many tutors, especially those in non-scientific subject areas, have poor IT skills including email and file management. This provides another barrier to moving online and leads to a 'toe in the water' approach to deploying a VLE.
Lack of reflection on the face-to-face learning experience	Tutors often do not consider what they 'do' in the face-to-face learning environment and then whether and how it can or cannot be transferred into the online environment to meet the needs of their students. For example, tutors' limited use of online discussions often reflects that they have not deconstructed what they 'do' when facilitating face-to-face discussions.
Lack of time	Research, teaching and administrative commitments often mean that staff have insufficient time to attend training events, reflect on the learning and teaching process and call upon central support to help whilst designing modules in a VLE.

Table 2. Summary of student-related issues

SUMMARY OF STUDENT-RELATED ISSUES RAISED THROUGH EVALUATION	
Lack of time and flexibility	Time-poor, eCPD students cannot accommodate a fixed timetable of face-to-face learning. Lack of large chunks of free time to commit to learning is often a problem whereas providing access to online learning at times convenient for each learner is more manageable.
Attitudes to online discussion	Online discussions provide a welcome communication channel for our eCPD students. It provides them with opportunities to exchange ideas and feel part of a community. They like the nature of asynchronous discussion which allows them to think and to reflect mirroring other work in the health sciences (Lockyer et al., 1999; Connor, 2003).
Need for quick and efficient administrative procedures	CPD students usually have a specific timeframe applied by their professional body to complete their studies. Also many of our eCPD students are also seeking funding, support and protected time for study, which means they need a rapid response to requests, for example, enrolment. Otherwise, students may have to postpone studies to a later programme, which may have serious implications, for example, eligibility to practice.
Limited access to computers	Feedback from our eCPD students shows that access to a computer cannot always be assumed and research indicates that this can be a key barrier for learners (Crook, 2002; Williams, 2001; McGorry, 2002). In the health arena access to computers in the workplace may be restricted because of limited resourcing: the more reliable computers will be used for more urgent requirements, for example, prescribing and those few computers available may not be connected to the Internet for security reasons. The result is that most of our eCPD students are accessing the online environment in the evening and during the weekend, often from home and usually competing for access to the family computer.

learning process in the face-to-face environment. They will then need to be prepared to radically rethink how to conduct themselves in their new teaching role (Broad, 2004) especially when e-moderating (Twomey, 2004). The trial involving the tutor supported by the e-champion was successful because the support offered ensured that the tutor had been involved since the inception of the module, accepted ownership of the e-module and acknowledged the relevance of e-learning delivery. In addition, the module was designed from the beginning for e-learning with a focus on providing a supportive learning environment for which the students were well-prepared (Aspden, Helm, & Thorpe, 2003; Howland & Moore, 2002). Also, there was a strong focus on active learning rather than content development. The support continued throughout the first iteration of the module while the tutor found her e-voice. The tutor's development has now led to a cascading of skills throughout the subject area with limited central support.

To meet the requirements of our eCPD students, we need our support departments to work together in a partnership with tutors. At QMUC, over the last few years, we have held a Learning Technology Roundtable based on the methodology developed in the United States by the Teaching, Learning and Technology Group (TLTG). This is a group drawn from across an institution to support the large-scale deployment of learning technologies (Kemp & Peacock, 2003). Our roundtable consists of library, registry, staff developers, and technical staff. At our roundtable, we are able to raise issues encountered by our eCPD learners and work together to find practical solutions. For example,

Table 3. Support-related issues

SUMMARY OF ISSUES RAISED BY SUPPORT DEPARTMENTS	
Coping with student expectations	As stated in Table 2, our students like e-learning because it is accessible and often instantaneous; this raises student expectations that the administration and support services of our institution will function in a similar way. Our eCPD students expect support departments such as Information Services to support their 'Martini' approach to learning (any time, any place, anywhere) and to ensure that: "more comprehensive methods of technical support are available should the system fail during the evenings or weekend" (Chelin, 2004, p. 4). For Information Services this impacts on both technical and front-line support staff especially when students have the expectation that their access issues are the sole responsibility of Information Services.
24/7 access to online resources	Our eCPD students are excited by the possibility of accessing a wide range of information; thus eCPD programmes for health professionals will often link to e-databases and e-journals from our collections and those provided by their employer. For students, one of the features of online learning they find most valuable is remote access to library facilities (Pelletier (2002), Urquhart *et al* (2004)). For the Library this will mean that students will no longer physically visit the library premises but will expect most, if not all materials, to be readily available electronically.

tutors have been able to explain to registry staff about the pressures on AHPs to undertake CPD and the need for a speedy enrolment process. In turn, registry has been able to discuss the legal requirements in the matriculation process especially for Higher Education Statistics Agency (HESA), and then we have used the group to find a way forward. This group also provides a forum for "thinking out of the box" and discussing initiatives like those implemented at LSE.

Underpinning these developments is the need for institutional commitment to the delivery of eCPD for healthcare professionals. For us, this has been through the provision of adequate and timely funding, appropriate and inter-related strategies, such as learning and teaching and information services (e.g., QELTA, 2004), championing of e-learning projects and rewarding learning innovation. Furthermore, institutional incentives and human resource policies like those suggested by HEFCE (2005) and SHEFCE (2005) could ensure that tutors are rewarded and seen to be rewarded for their commitment to e-learning.

Conclusion

Over the next 10 years, the growth in demand for CPD for health professionals will undoubtedly increase. By offering eCPD programmes, institutions may reach a potential new market of diverse learners as well as have the opportunity to augment their existing relationships with workplace partners. In this chapter, we have identified a number of issues, gathered through our evaluation over three years (familiar to those already involved in the embedding of e-learning) which can impede an institution's ability to provide such programmes. We have offered some examples of good practice to help other institutions in setting up similar e-initiatives. Most critical is targeted, sustained, multi-layered support for tutors to help them cope when moving to the online environment. Furthermore, support departments need to be actively involved in meeting the needs of this specific group of e-learners. With institutional support and joined-up thinking, it is possible to address the issues raised in this chapter. In addition, by addressing these issues, there are considerable advantages for the educational institution including the normalisation of e-learning as well as demonstrating a return on investment (HEFCE, 2005). However, such changes cannot be implemented quickly and require a long-term approach which is enmeshed in an institution's strategies especially if they are to be sustainable and scaleable.

Acknowledgments

The authors would like to thank the tutors, students, and staff who have kindly offered their experiences in eCPD and the guidance provided by Dr. Kate Morss, Dr. Isobel Davidson, Mark Toole, Valerie McKeown, and Susie Bealsey.

References

Aspden, L., Helm, P., & Thorpe, L. (2003, September 1-12). *Research proceedings: Capturing learners' experiences with e-learning: preliminary findings.* Communities of practice. 10th International Conference. ALT-C 2003, Sheffield.

Broad, M., Matthews M., & McDonald, A. (2004). Accounting education through an online-supported virtual learning environment. *Active Learning in Higher Education: The Institute for Learning and Teaching in Higher Education, 5,* 135-151.

Bye, D. (1999). Distance learners and the Internet: Needs and issues. *Vine, 113,* 26-31.

Chelin, J. (2004). *Virtual learning environments—Overview and issues for institutional managers,* SCONUL newsletter. Retrieved August 11, 2005, from www.sconul.ac.uk/pubs_stats/newsletter/28/

Crook, C. (2002). The campus experience of networked learning. In C. Steeples & C. Jones (Eds.), *Networked learning: Perspectives and issues* (pp. 293-308). London: Springer.

Connor, C. (2003). Virtual learning and inter-professional education: Developing computer-mediated communication for learning about collaboration innovations. *Education and Teaching International, 40*(4), 341-347.

Department of Health (1999). *Continuing professional development quality in the new NHS.* Department of Health. London: Government Printing Office.

Department of Health (2000). *Meeting the challenge: A strategy for the allied health professions.* Department of Health. London: Government Printing Office.

Department of Health (2001). *Working together—Learning together. A framework for lifelong learning for the NHS.* Department of Health. London: Government Printing Office.

Department of Health (2004a). *Learning for delivery making connections between post qualifying learning/continuing professional development and service planning.* Department of Health. London: Government Printing Office.

Department of Health (2004b) *Agenda for change.* Department of Health. London: Government Printing Office.

Department of Health (2004c). *A compendium of solutions to implementing the working time directive for doctors in training from August 2004.* Retrieved August 11, 2005, from www.dh.gov.uk/PublicationsAndStatistics/Publications/PublicationsPolicyAndGuidance/PublicationsPolicyAndGuidanceArticle/fs/en?CONTENT_ID=4082634&chk=%2B9s8AE

Frand, J. (2000). The information-age mindset. *EDUCAUSE,* September/October, 14-24.

Haigh, J. (2004). Information technology in health professional education: Why it matters. *Nurse Education Today, 24,* 547-552.

Higher Education Funding Council for England, Joint Information Systems Committee, Higher Education Academy. (2005). *HEFCE strategy for e-learning.* London: HEFCE.

Howland, J.L., & Moore, J.L. (2002). Student perceptions as distance learners in Internet-based courses. *Distance Education, 23*(2), 183-195.

JISC infoNet. (2005). *Effective use of virtual learning environments InfoKit.* Retrieved August 11, 2005 from www.jiscinfonet.ac.uk/InfoKits/effective-use-of-VLEs

Joint Information Services Committee (2003). *Supporting eLearning in the Workplace: From practice to policy.* JISC.

Kemp, C., & Peacock, S. (2003) Roundtables. An approach for implementing and supporting learning technologies through collaborative change management in tertiary education. *Perspectives, 7*(4), 98-104.

Lockyer, L., Patterson, J., & Harper, B. (1999). Measuring effectiveness of health education in a Web-based learning environment: A preliminary report. *Higher Education Research and Development, 18*(2), 233-246.

McGorry, S.Y. (2002). Online, but on target? Internet-based MBA courses: A case study. *The Internet and Higher Education, 5*(2), 167-175.

Oblinger, D., & Hawkins, B. (2005). The myth about e-learning. *EDUCAUSE*, July/August 14-25.

Peacock, S., Adamson, S., McKenzie, J., & Williams, K. (2004). Engaging staff and students in the development and deployment of a departmental Web site: A review. *Focus in Health Professional Education, 6*(2).

Pelletier, D. (2002). *How prepared are graduate nurses to embrace the information technology revolution in Australian university teaching?* OJNI. Retrieved August 11, 2005, from www.eaa-knowledge.com/ojni/

QELTA (2004). *The strategy for quality enhancement of learning, teaching and assessment QMUC*. Retrieved August 11, 2005, from www.qmuc.ac.uk/quality/core/qe/

Salmon, G. (2000). *E-Moderating: The key to teaching and learning online*. London: Kogan Page.

Scottish Credit & Qualifications Framework (2003). *An introduction to the Scottish Credit and Qualifications Framework* (2nd ed.). Scottish Credit and Qualifications Framework.

Scottish Higher Education Funding Council (2005). *e-learning: Higher education training needs analysis*. Scottish Higher Education Funding Council.

Sigala, M. (2002). The evolution of Internet pedagogy: Benefits for tourism and hospitality education. *The Journal of Hospitality, Leisure, Sport and Tourism Education, 1*(2), 22-45.

Sit, J.W.H., Chung, J.W.Y., Chow, M.C.M., & Wong, T.K.S. (2005). Experiences of online learning: Students' perspective. *Nurse Education Today, 25*, 140-147.

Twomey, A. (2004). Web-based teaching in nursing: Lessons from the literature. *Nurse Education Today, 24*, 452-458.

Urquhart, C., Spink, S., Thomas, R., Yeoman, A., Turner, J., & Durbin, J. (2004, September 1-12). Research proceedings: Evaluating the development of virtual learning environments in higher and further education. Blue skies and pragmatism: learning technologies for the last decade. *11th International Conference. ALT-C 2004*, Exeter, 157-169.

Williams, P. (2001). Learning area network: Information dissemination and online discussion in an education environment: The Capabil-IT-y project. *Aslib Proceedings, 53*.

Williams, P. (2002). The learning Web: the development, implementation and evaluation of Internet-based undergraduate materials for the teaching of key skills. *Active learning in higher education, the institute for learning and teaching in higher education, 3*, 40-53.

Section II:

Pedagogical Issues

Chapter VII

Staff Perspectives on ILT:
Findings from a National Evaluation of the Learning and Skills Sector

Colin McCaig, Sheffield Hallam University, UK

Maria Smith, Sheffield Hallam University, UK

Abstract

This chapter examines staff perceptions of information and learning technology (ILT) in the UK learning and skills sector. It is divided into two sections dealing in turn with pedagogic and cultural issues. The section on pedagogical issues explores the use of the VLE/intranet as an alternative teaching method, and asks why these modes of learning are comparatively rare in the learning and skills sector. This section is also concerned with perceptions of the impact of ILT on students' retention and attainment and explores the concept of variable use and variable impact by level and subject area. The cultural and infrastructure issues explored in the second section relate to staff development and training opportunities (such as the number and type of courses offered), the additional help requested, and the barriers to further uptake.

Introduction

This chapter sets out some of the findings from a two year evaluation of the impact of ILT investment on the learning and skills sector colleges in the UK on behalf of the National Learning Network (NLN)[1]. The NLN evaluation final report *The Developing Impact of ILT*[2] found that the majority of staff in further education and adult continuing education colleges were enthusiastic about the use of technology for teaching and learning, but that there was under-utilisation of the potential of technology. This chapter takes a broader and more contextualised look at some of the NLN data with the emphasis on the perspectives of teaching and support staff in the sector.

Background

The UK lifelong learning sector is quite diverse in nature, and includes: predominantly academic colleges (known as Sixth Form Colleges); general further education colleges offering a mix of academic and vocational qualifications and which can be either urban, multi-sited colleges of over 20,000 students, or small rural colleges; and colleges that are specifically vocationally inclined, such as land-based agricultural colleges. In addition, some FE colleges (FECs) and the adult and continuing education (ACE) colleges offer non-accredited short courses and leisure courses. There also are a number of specialist colleges for the education of disabled or visually impaired students, although none of these were included in this research.

When we look at the educational levels and age ranges that are generally taught in the sector, the picture is even more complex. Traditionally, the main business of this sector was to provide post-compulsory qualifications such as A levels for higher education or labour market entry, and higher national certificates and diplomas (HNCs and HNDs) and other vocational qualifications directly relevant to industry. FE is still involved with this provision, categorised as Level 3 (A levels) and Level 4 (HNCs and HNDs), although the majority of the studies undertaken in FE are at foundation and Levels 1 and 2. FE colleges also deliver approximately 13% of all higher education (Level 4) courses in England and Wales (Hyland & Merrill, 2003). Almost two-thirds (58.3%) of studies undertaken at FE colleges are at Levels 1 and 2, and only 21.7% of FE students are taking the A level route into higher education between the ages of 16 and 18 (although a high proportion undertake these at academic sixth form colleges). This is reflected by analysis of the age of students: Only 19.5% of students are 18 or below, while 72.3% are aged between 19 and 59 (Learning and Skills Council, 2003b).

The National Learning Network

The NLN was a *de-facto* funding agency established by the UK government in 1999 to disburse invested in ILT with the aim of bringing the infrastructure of learning and skills sector colleges (FECs and ACE colleges) into line with the traditionally better funded schools' sector and higher education. The first phase of the NLN programme oversaw the investment of £156 million between 1999 and 2002, which is reported to have stimulated the investment of approximately another £500 million by the colleges themselves (NLN, 2002). The second phase of the NLN (2003-2004) was intended to transform the nature of teaching and learning in the sector through a concentration on four key areas: infrastructure; content; staff development; and management and funding. The evaluation of NLN Phase II was carried out by the authors, in conjunction with the Learning Technologies Team at the Learning and Skills Development Agency (LSDA). The aim of the evaluation was to ascertain the impact that the NLN investment had made on the teaching and learning that goes on in these colleges. Data was gathered from a representative sample of eight sector case study colleges[3] and from two national ILT users' surveys (of staff and learners) carried out during 2003 and 2004. For the purposes of this chapter, only a selection of the findings from the staff survey and comments recorded in interviews and in focus groups of staff are used. The full findings can be found in the final evaluation report.

The Developing Impact of ILT[4]

The data provide an insight into the perspectives of staff in the learning and skills sector in relation to the use of the VLE/intranet, the barriers that had to be overcome when utilising ILT, and the types of staff development activity that they undertook in order to use new technology. This chapter also utilises crosstabulation analysis to explore variations by subject area, level taught at, gender, age, mode of employment, and length of time in post. More individual views are provided by selected extracts from the qualitative interviews and focus group sessions carried out in case study institutions as well as open-ended comments on the survey questionnaires. The chapter locates the findings from this research within the context of other recent research into ILT in the learning and skills sector, and also refers to the relevant literature from schools and higher education (at home and internationally) where appropriate.

Characteristics of the Survey Sample

The survey of staff produced 347 responses from 14 NLN evaluation case study colleges (including the eight colleges in our evaluation) and from individuals at non-ILT related staff development and training events around the country. Respondents worked in a total of 54 different colleges in the learning and skills sector. There was a slight bias toward teaching staff with almost two-thirds of our respondents (62%) being teaching staff (compared to 50% nationally). Some 14% of the sample was made up of technical and library staff support staff (13% nationally) and 17% were administration; the remaining 7% described themselves as management. Initially, the survey was distributed to NLN evaluation case study colleges, which were representative of the sector, but the responses were skewed toward non-teaching staff and ILT enthusiasts. Thereafter, a second, opportunistic sweep of the sector was carried out and surveys were completed by FE staff at national (non-IT related) training events, resulting in a more representative sample of the sector.

A considerable proportion of the sample had either been in their job or working in the same college for several years. More than one-third (37%) of staff respondents had been in their job between six and 14 years, while only 20% had been in the same job less than two years. One-third (38%) had been working at the same college between four and nine years, and again only around 20% had been working at the same college for less than two years.

The majority of staff in the sample (79%) were full-time (much higher than the national figure of 49%); two-thirds (66%) were involved with adult students some of the time; and 19% were involved with distance students some of the time. Almost a third (30%) of teaching staff taught ICT, 15% taught business administration, and 14% taught health, social care, and public services. Looking at the sample by level *mostly taught at*, 45% taught at Level 3, 30% at Level 2, 18% taught at Level 4, 18% at Level 1, and 14% at foundation level. More than half (55%) of all staff were female (60% nationally), 41% were over 45, 35% were aged between 35 and 44, and 23% were under the age of 34. In addition, 73 interviews were carried out with members of staff in case study colleges, and a further 49 staff participated in focus groups sessions.

The Key Issues

This chapter is divided into two sections dealing in turn with pedagogic and cultural issues. The section on pedagogical issues explores the use of the VLE/intranet as an alternative teaching method and asks why these modes of learning are comparatively rare in the learning and skills sector. This section is also concerned with perceptions of the impact of ILT on students' retention and attainment and explores the concept of variable use and variable impact by level and subject area. The cultural and infrastructure issues explored in the second section relate to staff development and training opportunities (such as the number and type of courses on offer), the additional help requested, and the barriers to further uptake.

Pedagogic Issues

Much of the debate about ILT and its effect on staff in the leaning and skills sector revolves around the suggestion (often from governments and technology suppliers) that the new technology holds out the prospect of a new teaching methodology which can deliver better or more cost-effective educational outcomes. This could be manifested in two ways: changing how education is delivered by replacing face-to-face learning with asynchronous learning from pre-recorded materials at the students' own pace and convenience; and using the enhanced graphics and interactivity of the new technology and the resource pool of the Internet to engage students who are otherwise disengaged by traditional sessions taught using "chalk and talk" methods supported by textbooks. So, is there evidence here for a new pedagogy, or is technology largely being used to support and enhance traditional teaching? We present evidence on the use of VLEs and distance learning and then go on to examine staff perspectives' of the impact on learning outcomes.

Figure 1.

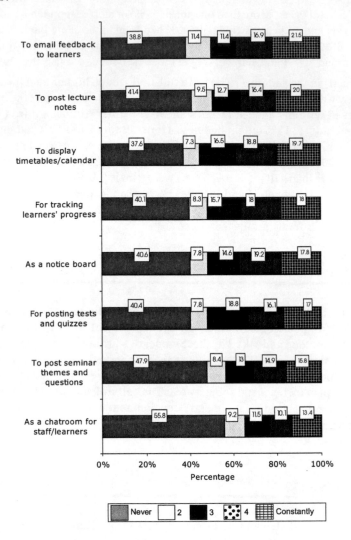

Virtual Learning Environments

Use of the VLE/intranet was defined (in the staff survey questionnaire) in terms of the reported use of a list of functions: to e-mail feedback to students; to post lecture notes; to display timetables/calendars; for tracking students' progress; as a notice board; for posting tests and quizzes; to post seminar themes and questions; and as a chatroom for staff and students. Overall, our survey found staff use of the VLE was very low in the learning and skills sector. Indeed, of all the VLE functions, only e-mail feedback to

Figure 2.

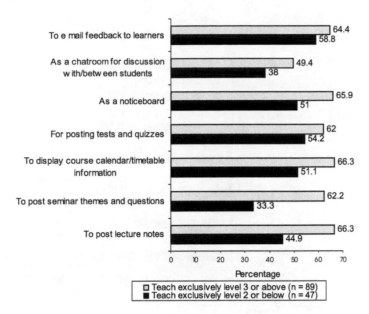

students and posting class notes were reportedly used constantly by 20% or more of the teaching staff (Figure 1). However, around one-third of respondents often or constantly used all elements of the VLE (with the exception of the chatroom function, which would have been disabled in some colleges). In each case, however, the percentage of staff respondents who reported never using the VLE was higher than those who reported frequent use.

The Becta survey of 2003 found that almost all FE colleges use a network of some kind, 59% of which are VLEs (Davies, 2003). However, it is clear from our research that VLE use is a marginal activity in the colleges. In some of the case study institutions staff reported that the existence of the VLE was "not common knowledge" across the institution, and often this was because not all areas of the college were equally connected. At one college, a technician stated "if the VLE was common knowledge it wouldn't be big enough to support [demand for] it." This is reflective of the general literature on VLE use: A recent OFSTED review of focussed 16-19 provision in sixth form centres also reported that "there is very little use of college intranets and virtual learning environments" (OFSTED, 2004), therefore, potential for such networks to allow students to engage in independent learning was not being developed. In the adult and continuing education sector, a recent report found that use of VLEs was even rarer than among FE colleges, with only 4.5% of the sector colleges using them (NIACE, 2004, p. 26).

There were some variations between groups of staff and how much the VLE was used. Most relevant was the apparent difference between staff teaching at different levels, with

Figure 3.

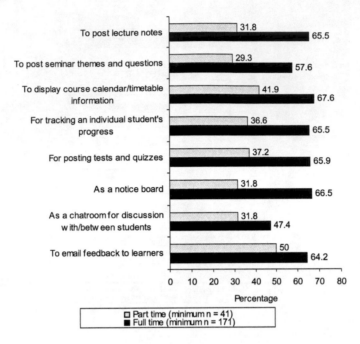

staff who taught at Level 3 or above much more likely to use the VLE than those who taught at Level 2 or below (Figure 2).

It is possible that there may be pedagogic or logistical reasons why Level 3 and above work lends itself more easily to VLE use than lower level work, however, further crosstabulation reveals that other factors are in play. For example, full-time staff were significantly more likely to use all the features of a VLE/intranet than part-time staff (as illustrated in Figure 3), and male staff were also more likely to use the VLE than female staff, although by smaller margins. In addition, staff in post six or more years were more likely to use aspects of the VLE/intranet than those in post up to five years, even though they were less likely to use ILT as a whole. This may be because those in post six or more years were more likely to be teaching at higher levels.

These findings suggest other research questions that were beyond the scope of our evaluation. For example, does use of the VLE/intranet (and ILT use in general) reflect a hierarchy of subjects and levels within the colleges, which are more often taught by full-time senior male staff, and if so, is this justified pedagogically or organisationally? Some of the issues raised here are covered in the following staff development section: for example, the appropriateness of the VLE/intranet for all courses; whether training and development should be compulsory; resistance to the use of the VLE (and other aspects of ILT) among some staff; and whether this is due to time limitations or other factors.

Figure 4.

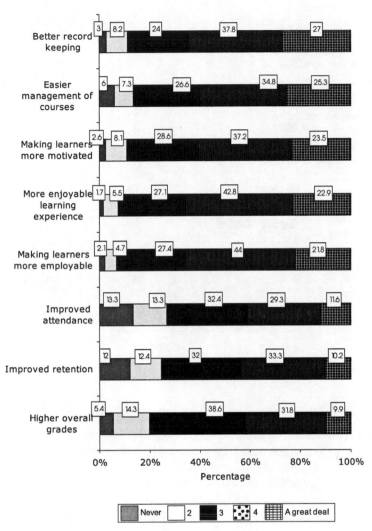

The Impact of ILT on Teaching and Learning

Staff were mixed in their views of ILT's impact on teaching and learning and other aspects of college life. In some ways, they were positive and almost two-thirds of them believed that technology in teaching and learning had had a great deal or a considerable impact on better record keeping. In addition, 60% believed it had led to easier management of courses, and almost two-thirds indicated that in their view, technology would have an impact on making students more employable (Figure 4).

Figure 5.

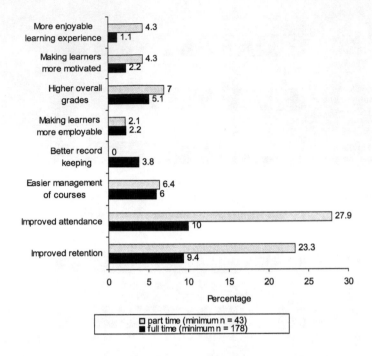

However, staff were more sceptical about the impact on grades, retention, and improved attendance. Less than half of the respondents believed technology had much impact on improved attendance, on higher overall grades, and on improving retention, and less than 10% expected technology to definitely lead to higher grades (Figure 4).

Again, groups of staff differed in their opinions. In particular, part-time staff were much more likely to be sceptical about the impact of ILT on issues such as improved attendance or retention (Figure 5).

Although the quantitative data on the impact of ILT on learner outcomes showed no major differences in attitudes between staff who taught at higher and lower levels, the qualitative data included strongly held beliefs that were typical of our respondents' views in this regard. In particular, many of the staff that we spoke to believed that ILT had a much greater and much more beneficial impact upon those learners who are studying at the lower levels. For example, several staff interviewees discussed how ILT kept students on vocational programmes more interested. One science teacher cited the use of a video clip of a horse's heart beating found on the Internet and uploaded onto the intranet. This helped engage students because they "will stare at a screen but not at a book." When asked directly, many staff also believed that another group to benefit from ILT were those disengaged from education or with communication problems. One who worked with dyslexic students and speakers of other languages thought that "the lower the motivation of the students, the bigger the impact." However, despite this enthusiasm, teaching staff in focus groups and interviews as a whole were sceptical about whether ILT could have a positive impact on learner outcomes, reinforcing the findings from our survey. On the other hand, college managers were generally committed to ILT as they saw it as being linked with retention and the educational marketplace.

Other research in the area of impact on students suggests that there are positive outcomes from the use of ILT, including enhanced confidence, peer support, and motivation (Atwere, 2002; Aldridge et al., 2003; Basic Skills Agency, 2002). The *National Grid for Learning Pathfinders* report, using case studies, also unearthed many examples of positive impact (DfES, 2002b; Powell & Davies, 2002). Atwere (2002) found that students' research and presentation skills were improved, that they enjoyed variety in teaching and learning practice, and reported positive learning experiences and enhanced motivation among the 16 to 18 age group; this was also supported by research for the Ufl (Kambouri, Mellar, Kinsella, & Windsor, 2003).

While this examination of pedagogical issues does not offer much in the way of evidence for the development of radical new teaching methodologies, it is clear that ILT is being used to enhance traditional learning and engage students who would perhaps otherwise have dropped out of further education. VLEs could be used more widely than they are, but the amount of training required is probably a sufficient disincentive even among staff who believe it should become the norm for all courses, as discussed in the following section.

Cultural and Infrastructure Issues

Staff Development Courses Attended by Teaching and Support Staff

The survey of staff inquired about the number and usefulness of courses attended. The findings suggested that one-third of respondents had not attended a single course that improved their technology skills in the last 12 months and another third had attended only one (Figure 6).

Male staff, those who had been in post for under five years, and full-time staff reported attending the most courses, even though female staff, those in post for six or more years, and part-time staff were more likely to report that they needed extra help to develop their confidence with e-learning technology. This suggests that those who would benefit most from training with the technology are least likely to attend the sessions. Research also reports variations by subject level: For example, visual and performing arts and media has a high proportion of part-time staff and also has a low take-up of staff development, while health, social care, and public services teachers are disproportionately female but are more likely to report higher levels of attendance at staff development sessions.

Thus, it appears that inequalities in access to e-learning staff development sessions follow a similar pattern to other structural inequalities in the sector, such as gender, number of years in post, and mode of employment. It also suggests that other variable factors, such as subject area and management attitudes toward e-learning, can equally affect the likelihood of staff receiving such training.

Figure 6.

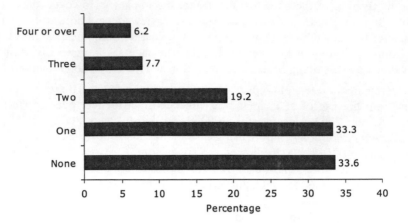

Types of Staff Development Support Requested

The most commonly requested types of help were with network problems and using specific learning software. Help with basic IT problems and help with the VLE were less often requested. Female staff were more likely to request help with basic IT problems, as were staff in post six years or more. Those in post up to five years and part-time staff were more likely to request additional teaching materials training courses, and those in post up to five years were more likely to request bespoke materials design courses.

When asked about the usefulness of various types of additional support, almost two-thirds of respondents indicated that subject-specific help to apply technology in their subject area would be very useful or essential, and a similar proportion indicated that the provision of a repository of materials to use in their own time would be very useful or essential. More than half the staff thought that both courses offered for technology skills development and help in accessing Web-based learning materials would be very useful or essential. Just under half thought general help with technology would be very useful or essential. Part-time, female, and staff in post up to five years were more likely to report that such help was essential across all categories.

Factors Preventing Greater Use of ILT

Staff were asked to indicate which factors dissuaded them from greater use of ILT. The most common response was having the time to prepare materials. Insufficient equipment, ill-equipped rooms, and a lack of support were also common contributory factors to not making greater use of ILT (Figure 7).

The uneven distribution of well-equipped classrooms was cited as a reason for low use of ILT by many staff during interviews and focus groups. In particular, it was reported

Figure 7.

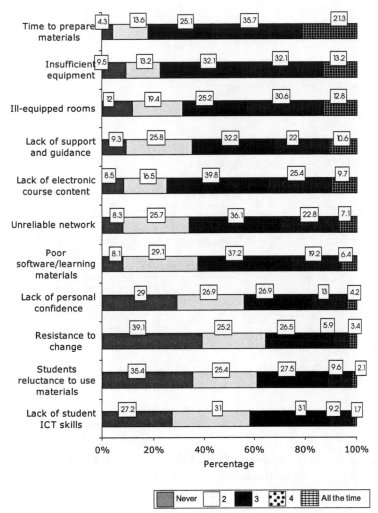

that uneven resource distribution makes it difficult to know what materials to prepare for lessons, and acts as a disincentive if lessons cannot be prepared in full confidence that the room can support the planned lesson. Full-time staff respondents were more likely than part-time to cite lack of time to prepare materials as a factor preventing greater use of ILT. Part-time staff were more likely to cite insufficient equipment, ill-equipped rooms, and a lack of electronic course content. In addition, staff that had been in post for longer periods of time were also more likely to report that there were resource barriers to taking up ILT (Figure 8). This may be due to these staff being older and less "technically minded" than younger staff, or could be merely symptomatic of the fact that staff who have been in post for longer periods of time tend to have a less positive or optimistic outlook than new members of staff.

Figure 8.

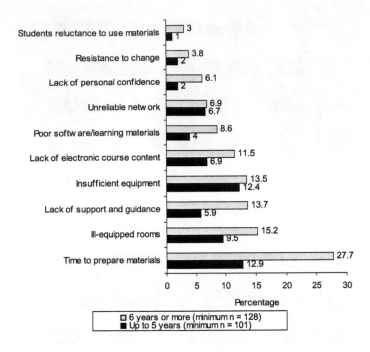

Staff contributions to our interviews and focus groups support the notion that lack of time (or the money to pay for staff remission) is the biggest single factor which leads to the under-utilisation of ILT. The second biggest factor reported was the non-compulsory nature of ILT staff development, which meant that, as one staff development officer said, "only the keen take the time."

Among the factors that impact on the uptake of ILT, the lack of time and/or money is cited by most of the literature, echoing the findings of our research. For example, Rathe (2004) cited the additional workload staff would have to endure, as did the Becta report into the use of managed and virtual learning environments (Becta 2003b, pp. 14-16). LSDA's review of staff development and an HMI report for the Scottish FEFC also identified time as a key factor in the use of VLEs (LSDA 2003b; HMIE, 2001), while another report noted the time effect on the uptake of ILT generally, along with an emphasis on leadership and management training (LSDA 2004, pp. 6, 25).

The DfES report on the Consultation process for *Towards a Unified E-Learning Strategy* found that under-funding was the biggest perceived barrier to further training, but that around one-fifth of respondents thought time and the lack of teachers' IT skills would also be a barrier and called for more incentive schemes such as laptops for FE teachers and the provision of one PC per member of staff (DfES, 2004). LSDA were among the other bodies that identified cost (specifically the cost of good training) and cultural change among staff as significant barriers (LSDA, 2003b, p. 21). There is much literature about the types of training that is thought appropriate and the factors that may impact on the take-up of e-learning among staff. Generally researchers have found a positive relation-ship between the level and amount of training and use of ILT (e.g., Somekh et al., 2004), and much of the literature is concerned with how best to raise the skills of the teaching force. Recent research by the National Information and Learning Technologies Associa-tion found that overall respondents believed that ICT skills were increasing and satisfactory, but that ILT teaching and learning skills were "considered to be much weaker by the large majority of respondents" (Tysoe, 2004).

Conclusion

Pedagogic issues: With regard to the VLE/intranet, overall, our survey found staff usage was very low and the percentage of staff respondents who reported never using the VLE was higher than the frequent use percentages. Cross-tabulation revealed that full-time staff were significantly more likely to use all the features of a VLE/intranet than part-time staff, and that this was replicated by male over female and those in post six years or more over those in post less than five years.

These findings raise several questions for further discussion and research. For example, does use of the VLE/intranet reflect a hierarchy of subjects and levels within the colleges, which are more often taught by full-time senior male staff and, if so, is this justified pedagogically or organisationally? VLE usage is particularly interesting here in relation to male staff in post over six years as it goes against the trend of (total) ILT use which is more prevalent among male staff in post up to five years[5]. As staff in post six or more years are also more likely to be teaching at higher levels, this suggests a link between level and subject hierarchies and access to resources within the college. More broadly, such findings question whether all the elements of ILT are being optimally employed across all teaching levels, and whether there is some level of resistance to the use of ILT among some staff or in some subject areas.

As we have seen, staff held mixed views about the impact of ILT on teaching and learning and other aspects of college life, and this no doubt partly reflects the huge diversity of the sector. Overall, about two-thirds believed that technology would have an impact on employability, but staff were more sceptical about the impact on grades, retention, and improved attendance. These attitudes were explored more fully by interview and focus group sessions with staff, and there was a consensus among attendees that ILT had a larger impact on four (sometimes overlapping) groups: learners studying at lower levels (below Level 3); groups containing a wide ability range; groups containing students with communication problems; and groups containing mature students.

This research does not demonstrate the emergence of a new pedagogy, but it is clear that ILT is being used to enhance traditional learning and has the potential to engage students who perhaps would have otherwise dropped out of education. VLEs could certainly be used more widely than they are, but the amount of resource development time and training required is probably a sufficient disincentive even among staff who believe they should become the norm for all courses.

Cultural issues: As we noted earlier, the second phase of the NLN programme had a specific aim of improving the quantity and quality of ILT staff development activity, and the evaluation sought to explore the relationship between staff development and an increase in the use of ILT in teaching and learning. However, we found that one-third of survey respondents had not received any ILT related training in the preceding 12 months, and another third had attended only one session. Behind the data, this seems to reflect institutional diversity, departmental autonomy, and varying priorities of college managers. Interviews with managers, staff development officers, and teaching staff revealed that, while attending staff development sessions was tied to pay increases in some colleges, this element of compulsion did not require attendance at ILT sessions. In some colleges, staff development activity was devolved to subject departments and was therefore determined partly by the attitude of departmental heads. Even where there was a college-wide staff development programme, the nature of courses on offer, including the prioritisation or not of ILT, was determined by college managers.

Among those who had attended ILT staff development, the survey showed that the most common attendees were male staff, those who had been in post for under five years, and full-time staff, this despite the fact that female staff, those in post for six years or more, and part time staff were more likely to report that they needed extra help to develop their confidence with e-learning technology. This suggests a mismatch between needs and take-up with those who would benefit most from training with the technology the least likely to attend the sessions on offer. Research also reports variations by subject level: for example, visual and performing arts and media has a high proportion of part-time staff and also has a low take-up of staff development, while health, social care, and public services teachers are disproportionately female but are more likely to report higher levels of attendance at staff development sessions.

Thus, it appears that inequalities in access to ILT staff development sessions follow a similar pattern to other structural inequalities in the sector, such as gender, number of years in post, and mode of employment, but also reinforces the notion that that other variable factors, such as departmental autonomy over training provision and management attitudes toward ILT, can equally affect the likelihood of staff receipt of training. The potential impact that ILT, and in particlar the use of the VLE/intranet as a teaching methodology, is therefore prescribed by the reality in the colleges. VLEs are unlikely, in the foreseeable future, to meet the requirements of what is largely a face-to-face learning environment. Other aspect of classroom-based ILT are under-utilised because of a perceived lack of need by staff to invest the time and energy in learning how to make best use of them, even where the resources and infrastructure encourage it. The staff perspectives on ILT use and the prospects for an emerging new pedagogy reported here suggest that staff are yet to be convinced that ILT is a necessary element in all teaching sessions, and that college managers are yet to be convinced that ILT has to be their main priority.

References

Adult Learning Inspectorate (2003). *College and area-wide inspections.* ALI and Ofsted, HMI 1452.

Aldridge, F., Clarke, A., Essom, J., Lindsey, K., Reeve, A., & Scott, J. (2003). *Adult and Community Learning Laptop Initiative Evaluation,* NIACE.

Atwere, D. (2002). *A survey into ILT/ICT skills training in UK further education colleges*

Becta (2003). A review of the research literature on the use of managed learning environments and virtual learning environments in education, and a consideration of the implications for schools in the United Kingdom. *Becta ICT Research Network.* Retrieved June 2004, from www.becta.org.uk/research/reports/vle.cfm

Becta (2004). *A review of the research literature on barriers to the uptake of ICT by teachers.* Becta, June.

Basic Skills Agency (2002). *Getting the most out of ICT in community basic skills programmes.* ACLF, The Basic Skills Agency.

Clarke, A., & Englebright, L. (2003). ICT: The new basic skill. *NIACE.*

Davies, S. (2003, July). *ILT in further education: Laying the foundations for e-learning. A report to the Joint Implementation Group of the National Learning Network.* Becta.

DfES (2002a). *Get on with IT: The Post-16 E-Learning Strategy Task Force Report,* July 2002. Retrived November 2002, from www.dfes.gov.uk/learningstrategyunit

DfES (2002b). NGfL Pathfinders, Final Report on the Roll-out of the NGfL Programme in Ten Pathfinder LEAs. *DfES/BECTA ICT in Schools Research and Evaluation Series no. 11.*

DfES (2002c). *Computers for teachers: An evaluation of Phase 2: Survey of participants.* Report to the DfES by the Institute of Employment Studies. Retrieved March 2003, from www.becta.org.uk/research/reports/cft

DfES (2003a, July). *Towards a unified e-learning strategy: Consultation document.* Crown Copyright.

DfES (2003b). *The big picture: The impact of ICT on attainment, motivation and learning.* Crown Copyright.

DfES (2004a, April). *Progress towards a unified e-learning strategy.* E-Learning Strategy Unit, DfES.

DfES (2004b). *The motivational effect of ICT on pupils.* DfES 2004. Retrieved December 2004, from www.dfes.gov.uk/research/data/uploadfiles/RR523new.pdf

Ferl (2003, February). *Evaluation of the Pilot of the Ferl Practitioners' Programme - Interim Report.* Becta.

HMIE (2001). *Information and communications technology in Scottish further education colleges.* An Aspect Report for SFEFC by HMIE.

Hughes, J., & Attwell, G. (2002, September). *A framework for the evaluation of e-learning.* Paper to the ECER Conference, Lisbon.

Hyland, T., & Merrill, B. (2003). *The changing face of further education. Lifelong learning, inclusion and community values in Further Education.* London: Routledge Farmer.

JISC (2002). *tRISSt Survey 2 Report, The Staff Development Officer's Story: FE/HE perspectives of ICT skills.* Retrieved July 2004, from www.mmu.ac.uk/ioe/trisst/interim.htm

Kambouri, M., Mellar, H., Kinsella, K., & Windsor, V. (2003). *Evaluating the effectiveness of learndirect materials and learner support for learners with skills for life needs: Final report to the Ufl.* Institute of Education, University of London.

Lewis, D., & Goodison, R. (2004). *Enhancing learning with information and communication technology (ICT) in higher education.* DFES Research report RR533.

LSC (2002). *Report of the LSC's Distributed & Electronic Learning Group* (DELG). Learning and Skills Council, Coventry.

LSC (2003a). *National learner satisfaction survey: Highlights from 2002/03.* LSC, Coventry.

LSC (2003b, December). Statistical First Release. ILR/SFR02.

LSDA (2003a). *Computers for FE teachers: Final report.* Learning and Skills Development Agency, London.

LSDA (2003b). *ILT staff development: Some evidence* (unpublished).

LSDA (2003c, June). *The evaluation of information and learning technology.*

LSDA (2004). *LSDA responds: Towards a unified e-learning strategy.* LSDA, London.

Lynch, J. (2003, September 11-13). *Why have computer-based technologies failed to radically transform schooling? Looking for the right question.* Paper presented at the British Educational Research Association Annual Conference, Heriot-Watt University, Edinburgh.

MacKinnon, S. (2003, January-March). The West Virginia story: Technology advances learning and teaching. *TechKnowLogia.* Retrieved July 2003 from www.TechKnowLogia.org

McCaig, C., & Smith, M.J. (2004). *Does ILT investment have an equal impact on all students? Evidence from the United Kingdom's lifelong learning sector.* Paper to the IADIS International Conference e-society, Avila, Spain.

NATFHE (undated). *Online learning: NATFHE survey of academic staff.*

National Audit Office (2001, March 2). *Improving student performance: How English further education colleges can improve student retention and achievement.* Report by the Comptroller and Auditor General HC 276 Session 2000-2001. The Stationary Office, London.

NIACE (2003, December). *Adult and community learning infrastructure survey findings.* Paper for the NLN Evaluation Working Group.

NIACE (2004). Draft research report for the NLN on informing the development of ILT within adult and continuing learning. *NIACE.*

NLN (2002a, October). *Final report to the Evaluation Steering Group and the NLN Programme Board.* Learning and Skills Development Agency and Sheffield Hallam University.

NLN (2002b, October). *It worked here.* Learning and Skills Development Agency and Sheffield Hallam University.

NLN (2004a). *Embedding the NLN materials in the curriculum: Uptake and implementation.* Becta, January-December 2003.

NLN (2004b). *The developing impact of ILT: Final report to the NLN Research and Evaluation Working Group on the impact of information and learning technology.* Learning and Skills Development Agency and Sheffield Hallam University.

Ofsted (2004). *Focused provision 16 to 19: A survey of colleges with sixth form centres.* July 2004, HMI 2277. Retrieved February 2005, fromwww.ofsted.gov.uk/publications/index.cfm?fuseaction=pubs.displayfile&id=3675&type=pdf

Powell, B., & Davies, S. (2002, January). *The state of ICT in Scottish FE colleges.* Becta.

Preston, J., & Hammond, C. (2002). *The wider benefits of further education: Practitioner views.* The Centre for Research on the Wider Benefits of Learning, Institute of Education, London.

Rathe, D. (2004). *An investigation into teachers' perceptions of online learning at an English further education college.* Unpublished thesis. Open University.

Schacter, J. (1999). *The impact of education technology on student achievement: What the most current research has to say.* Milken Exchange on Education Technology, Milken Family Foundation. Retrieved July 2004, from www.mff.org/publications/publications.taf?page=161

Smith, M.J., & McCaig, C. (2004, September). *Technology and social inclusion: Is ILT being used on the right people?* Paper to the ALT-C Conference, Exeter.

Somekh, B., Underwood, J., Convery, A., Dillon, G., Lewin, C., Mavers, D., & Saxon, D. (2004, June). *Evaluation of the DfES ICT test bed project: Summary report.* Centre for ICT, Pedagogy and Learning, Manchester Metropolitan University.

Tysoe, D. (2004). *Report to the NLN Staff Development Working Group on AoC NILTA staff development survey.*

Wenger, E. (1998). *Communities of practice.* Cambridge: Cambridge University Press.

Williams, N. (2003). *Filling the gaps: The impact of ICT/ILT on the Post-16 Sector: A Review of the evidence* (unpublished). A Report to the DfES.

Endnotes

[1]   NLN partners are Becta, DfES, JISC, LSC, LSDA, NIACE, NILTA, and Ukerna. The NLN channelled £156 million into further education colleges between 1999 and 2002 and was extended to incorporate the remainder of the learning and skills sector from 2004 with further funding until at least 2006.

[2]   NLN (2004). *The developing Impact of ILT: Final report to the NLN Research and Evaluation Working Group by the Learning and Skills Development Agency and Sheffield Hallam University on the impact of information and learning technology.* Executive summary, p. 5.

[3]   The colleges were geographically representative of the LSC regions and contained one each from the specialist and ACL sectors, the remainder being a mix of types of college by size and type (i.e., multi-site and single site colleges) and those which were reportedly innovative in their use of ILT.

[4]   NLN (2004b) *The Developing Impact of ILT: Final Report to the NLN Research and Evaluation Working Group on the impact of information and learning technology,* Learning and Skills development Agency and Sheffield Hallam University

[5]   For the full usage statistics see the final report NLN (2004b) *The Developing Impact of ILT: Final Report to the NLN Research and Evaluation Working Group on the impact of information and learning technology,* Learning and Skills Development Agency and Sheffield Hallam University.

Chapter VIII

Drivers and Barriers to the Uptake of Learning Technologies:
Staff Experiences in a Research-Led University

Alison Davies, University of Birmingham, UK

Kelly Smith, University of Birmingham, UK

Abstract

This chapter discusses key findings from three focus group discussions held with practitioners in a higher education institution about their experiences of using learning technologies to support student learning. Focus groups were organised in March 2004 to further explore staff responses to a 2003 campus-wide survey, which gave a general overview of learning technology use among teaching staff. The chapter will examine the key issues that staff raised during the focus group discussions, including the barriers to and implications of introducing and implementing learning technologies into different subject disciplines within a research-led institution. The question of whether or not the use of learning technologies enhances, or has the potential to enhance, the teaching and learning experience is also discussed, as well as the lessons that staff have learnt from this use.

Introduction

Significant social, technological, and economic developments have taken place over the last 20 years that have transformed, and continue to transform, the nature and role of higher education institutions (Robins, 1999; Salmon, 2002). The transition from elite to mass education, changes in the production of knowledge, and developments in information and communications technologies (ICTs) have all had a major impact on staff and students within these institutions, and on their teaching and learning practices.

Learning technologies have an important role to play in realising the Government vision for a higher education system that offers increased "flexibility," "improved standards," and the capacity to remove barriers to participation and achievement (DfES, 2003). An increased use of learning technologies in higher education in recent years indicates that technology can make a positive difference to the learning and teaching experience, particularly in the context of increasing student numbers and a diversifying student population (Davies, Ramsay, Lindfield, & Couperthwaite, 2005a; Armitage & O'Leary, 2003). As Littlejohn (2003) suggests, more and more students are entering higher education with different skills, qualifications, expectations, and needs. Coupled with increased student needs, staff in many institutions are required to be research active and aim for international recognition for their research. Although research can be incorporated into, and inform, good teaching practices, it may be an additional pressure on staff diverting time and resources away from teaching needs.

The University of Birmingham is well-established as a world-class university, teaching and undertaking research in all the major disciplines. There are currently more than 2,500 members of teaching staff supporting over 20,000 full-time equivalent students. It is one of the leading research-led universities in the United Kingdom, being rated the fifth most successful university in the UK for research excellence in the latest (2001) UK Research Assessment Exercise. The University of Birmingham is a member of the Russell Group of 19 major research-intensive universities of the United Kingdom, and of Universitas 21, an elite group of top research universities throughout the world. Furthermore, the aim to enhance student learning through the use of learning technologies is an important part of the University of Birmingham's learning, teaching, and assessment strategy, particularly in relation to student-centred and flexible learning.

As a response to the current context at the University of Birmingham in particular, and across higher education in general, a survey and a series of subsequent focus group discussions were held in 2003-2004 with teaching practitioners at the University of Birmingham to explore their experiences of using learning technologies to support student learning and to inform future practice and strategy.

This chapter will examine findings from focus group discussions conducted in March 2004 to explore staff responses to a campus-wide survey which provided a general overview of learning technology use among teaching staff (Davies & Smith, 2005). It will analyse the key issues that staff raised, including the barriers to, and implications of, introducing and implementing learning technologies into the curriculum. Also discussed are staff views of how the use of technologies for supporting students have enhanced or changed their teaching practices, and the lessons that they have learnt from their experiences. The analysis builds upon prior studies into staff use of learning technologies (e.g., Haywood, 2000; Hanson, 2003) by considering the multiple factors shaping this usage within different subject disciplines within a research-led institution. In doing so, this analysis will provide insights into the different pedagogic considerations and support encouragement and infrastructure issues that may arise in the design, development, and implementation of learning technologies into subject-specific contexts.

Background

A wealth of literature has emerged to investigate the impact and effective use of learning technologies in higher education institutions in response to social, technological, and economic developments. A steady increase in the use of learning technologies in higher education in recent years suggests that computer and Web-based resources such as virtual learning environments (VLEs), network and communication systems, and multimedia materials may provide solutions to some of these issues (Rist & Hewer, 1996). Indeed, studies such as Haywood et al. (2000), Armitage and O'Leary (2003), and Davies et al. (2005b) suggest that technology can make a positive difference to learning and teaching in higher education institutions.

Although learning technologies have been shown to have the potential or ability to enhance the teaching and learning experience, some studies (Govindasamy, 2001; Salmon, 2002; Gorard & Selwyn, 1999) have highlighted issues such as the need for careful consideration of the underlying pedagogy, or how learning technologies are used to support teaching and learning practices. More than a decade ago, Laurillard (1993) stated that there was a focus on particular technologies and how computers might best be used in the educational context, rather than on the best methods of teaching a particular subject and how computers might then be used to enhance this teaching. More recent literature suggests that with the rapid growth and sophistication of learning technologies, this technology-driven perspective is still in evidence (Melling, 2005). It is perhaps not surprising that within the context of increased student numbers, limited teaching space, and pressures to expand access and cut costs, the question of how technology may enhance the learning and teaching experience may take second place to how such technologies may overcome practicalities that staff face.

Mayes and de Freitas (2004) suggest that pedagogic considerations, such as how learning technologies can provide a new way of achieving deeper learning, are not sufficient and must be coupled with a number of pragmatic considerations. They outline eight key issues for effective e-learning implementation: efficiency versus effectiveness; costs; quality assurance; tutor/student ratio; staff development; student support; technical support; and management support. These issues might be seen as interdependent of each other, in that "effectiveness" can depend upon many factors such as the level and availability of technical support and staff development, and the impact that the staff/student ratio can have on costs in delivering this support.

A survey carried out by Haywood et al. (2000) suggests that "costs" in relation to the use of learning technologies include staff time. Their study reveals that one of the main barriers to the uptake of learning technologies in Scottish higher education institutions is the cost in staff time to select, implement, and evaluate the use of technology. Qualitative data from this survey suggested that 50% of respondents had insufficient resources, time, and priority to consider using learning technologies for teaching. Other perceived barriers included lack of infrastructure, software, and training, and a failure by institutions to value teaching-related activities. Beetham (2005) describes the current state of research into e-learning and puts forward a series of questions that still require further investigation. Although it might appear that the barriers mentioned are well understood, one of the questions that Beetham highlights is concerned with constraints to uptake (e.g., time, opportunities for collaboration, reflection and discussions, curriculum constraints, and access to content). This suggests that there is still room for investigation in this area.

The Department for Education and Skills consultation paper entitled "Towards a Unified e-Learning Strategy" (DfES, 2003) lists several weaknesses that need to be addressed to promote e-learning more effectively and suggest the following remedies: provide support to enable educational leaders to lead and manage change processes; allow teachers and researchers more time and support to keep pace with rapid changes in technology; offer training to teachers and lecturers to adopt e-learning; provide incentives such as qualifications, promotion, and access to technology; ensure assessment matches new skills acquired through e-learning; and develop common standards to ensure software is shareable and affordable.

Methodology

A total of 13 members of staff participated in the focus group discussions. Three focus groups were organised according to the three university deaneries: arts and social sciences; life and health sciences; and physical sciences and engineering. Participants were organised in this way to provide the opportunity to compare the key issues and barriers that emerged from different subject disciplines and how these may shape staff use of and attitudes toward learning technologies. Participants held posts as either senior lecturers or lecturers, taught a variety of undergraduate, postgraduate, full-time, and distance learning students, and represented a range of schools and departments at the university. Participants also had a range of experience of working in higher education: some staff had begun working at the university recently, while others had been at the institution for many years.

A structured in-depth interview schedule was developed from the results of a campus-wide survey of learning technology use amongst all teaching staff carried out in October 2003 (see Davies & Smith, 2005). Staff had written their contact details at the end of the survey if they were willing to contribute to the focus group discussions, and were randomly selected from this information. The open-ended structured questions allowed for a range of possible responses and enabled staff to talk at length about their experiences in their own terms. Staff were asked several questions about their use of learning technologies to support students, including what learning technologies they currently used, the benefits of using these technologies, and if there were any problems or barriers that they encountered in using them. Staff were also asked to describe the kind and quality of support they received from the university, and if anything discouraged them from using learning technologies for their teaching-related activities.

The focus group discussions were recorded and transcribed for analysis. A textual analysis was carried out to identify key themes in the data. This process of identifying themes in the data was partly informed by prior survey results (Davies & Smith, 2005) and by our reading of similar recent studies into staff experiences of learning technologies in HE institutions (Haywood et al., 2000; Hanson, 2003).

Findings and Discussion

Three key themes arose from staff discussions about their use of learning technologies for supporting students at the University of Birmingham. These were (1) staff time, (2) pedagogic issues such as the educational benefit of learning technologies and the balance with traditional methods for supporting students, and (3) support and encouragement issues. Staff expressed a range of views about these issues, which were shaped in part by how technology was used in specific ways to support their different subject disciplines.

Time Issues

Staff from all three deaneries suggested that time pressures were among the main barriers that they faced when using or considering using learning technologies to support their students. Staff commented that they had insufficient time to develop as many new materials as they would like because of the time input required in addition to an existing full workload:

I think one of the major problems... is to do with workload... feeling like 'how am I going to manage another initiative, another innovation in my teaching?'... not knowing where that time commitment is going to come from, so I think there's a lot more interest [from staff] than actual follow-through [with learning technologies]. (Lecturer A, Arts and Social Sciences)

This comment from Lecturer A illustrates how staff in the arts and social sciences perceive workloads to be one of the greatest barriers to introducing new learning technologies or "innovations" into their current teaching practices. In particular, staff highlight the time-consuming nature of creating their own resources, suggesting that "to create your own resource is a massive thing" (Lecturer B, Arts and Social Sciences). Similarly, staff in the health and life sciences suggested that introducing innovations into their teaching practices "takes a lot of time to set up." In contrast, staff in physical sciences and engineering did not consider time pressures to be a key barrier to the introduction of new technologies. Staff in this deanery described how readily available dedicated software for students (e.g., MATLAB, Maple, chemical drawing packages) enables them to use existing innovative teaching materials rather than create their own. However, the use of specialist software led these staff to critique the systems in place at the university to support this usage (see the section on Support and Encouragement Issues).

Despite time issues for staff in the arts and social sciences and health and life sciences being a barrier to the uptake of learning technologies, Lecturer A suggests that there is an interest among staff in using such technologies to support their students. They indicate that this usage may increase if they had more time to invest in developing new ways of learning and teaching. This finding is supported by the survey accompanying the focus groups (see Davies & Smith, 2005). The survey results suggested that staff view the potential of learning technologies as "high" or "very high," even though time constraints are considered to be a key barrier to uptake.

Lecturer A also indicates that learning technologies are not the problem per se, but that the process by which *any* new "initiative" — whether technology plays a role in this process or not — is immensely time-consuming for staff. As Gibbs (1996) states, designing "courses and materials, recasting assessment and support systems and adopting new teaching methods... all require new techniques and skills" (p. 20). From a strategic point of view, institutions need to consider how to support staff in implementing e-learning when this is an additional task in the context of someone already making a full-time commitment to teaching.

Schemes have been put in place at the University of Birmingham to buy out existing activities relating to teaching or to provide staff with additional resources such as learning technology support officers within schools. However, the issue for staff is the perceived balance between teaching and research, where research may be considered to be of greater value than teaching.

Training courses are also in place to support staff in the use of WebCT, the institution's chosen managed learning environment. Courses focus on the student experience of using WebCT, construction and management of course content, making use of communication and assessment tools, and using student management tools. Training for general IT skills, e-mail, Web publishing, and QuestionMark Perception (an online assessment tool) is also provided. One-to-one support and advice can be given by a dedicated e-learning team, as well as from IT trainers on request. Staff can also enrol in two modules on "learning to be an e-tutor." The courses cover theories underpinning the use of learning technologies, promoting critical evaluation of e-learning practices, and provide staff with the opportunity to put what they have learned into practice in a supportive environment.

The need for time to learn new skills was voiced by staff during their focus group discussions. Based on their experience of developing course materials more generally, they perceived learning technologies to be very time-consuming to use proficiently if they were unfamiliar with them and suggested that they did not have the time to receive training on how to use such technologies:

Staff are not [generally] familiar with [using technology to support their teaching], they need a lot of help... For example, I didn't find [the VLE] that easy – I did try to transfer my teaching materials into [the VLE], but it's not worth the effort... I haven't got time to struggle with it. (Lecturer B, Life and Health Sciences)

Lecturer B's use of new technologies depends upon a balance between how much effort they believe is required to use learning technologies effectively, as well as how useful these technologies will be in supporting their teaching activities. Their critique of the university's chosen virtual learning environment arises from their experience of, and thus familiarity with, using alternative technologies for similar purposes prior to the implementation of this VLE in 2000. Given the time restraints, this lecturer does not think that it is productive for them to introduce alternative technologies to support students when they can do so with the technologies they are already using.

Staff discussions about time restraints also raised questions over whether or not the use of learning technologies provided them with an efficient and effective means of delivering quality teaching to large numbers of students. A comparison between staff discussions within each deanery suggests that this efficiency and effectiveness is partly dependent upon what technologies staff use in specific contexts and subject areas. As Orill (2002) suggests, careful consideration of the tools, as well as the learning goals and pedagogic approaches, is needed in supporting student interactivity and communication. For example, staff in the School of Mathematics described how computer-aided assessment with immediate feedback enabled large numbers of students to practice problem-solving in mathematics. For staff in the Law Department, Web-based threaded discussion groups provided a useful means of encouraging interactivity amongst large groups of students, whereas a simple discussion group via e-mail was found to be sufficient in the Theology Department, where staff deal with smaller student numbers. In contrast, staff in the School of Economics have found that interactive online quizzes have been more useful than discussion groups where students must "find a right answer" rather than negotiate ideas.

Often, staff suggested that where they provided additional Web-based resources and materials to their teaching-related activities, or replaced some of their lectures with online activities and Web-based learning resources, these approaches were an enhancement and not a substitute for other methods of teaching and learning. For example, staff in the life and health sciences introduced Web-based learning resources but found that students required face-to-face sessions to enable them to use the materials successfully. This increased contact time with students and in some cases increased workloads for staff:

I really haven't saved any time at all, I have increased the time that it takes me [to support students this way]... because I'm not an expert, it takes an immense amount of effort to get anywhere... [also, first-year students] are not very independent learners... so that does mean I have to timetable a session for 380 students in a computer cluster that holds 150! So it means that I have to run the session three times. (Lecturer D, Life and Health Sciences)

Lecturer D highlights how different factors combine their effects to increase workloads and draws attention to three different factors surrounding the issue of time and workload. First, they again suggest that supporting students and developing new materials involves a great deal of effort, and therefore time, because they lack the "expertise" required. Secondly, they draw attention to the learning culture of students when they enter the university. That is, student expectations and learning experiences are shaped by schooling prior to university, meaning that first-year students often need to develop their skills as "independent learners" to enable them to work in their own time without direct instruction from their tutors. Other students are increasingly coming into higher education through non-traditional routes (Littlejohn, 2003) and require different support systems. As a result, Lecturer D feels that timetabled induction sessions are essential to familiarise students with learning technologies and the requirements of online learning. Thirdly, dramatic increases in student numbers mean that their workload increase is compounded as extra introductory sessions are required to provide every student with the opportunity to attend.

Although the focus group discussions suggest that the use of learning technologies significantly impacts upon staff time and workload, this factor alone has not discouraged many staff from using them. As the next section of this chapter will show, staff have experienced significant advantages in using specific technologies within particular contexts to support student learning.

Pedagogic Issues

Staff discussions suggested that there are a number of advantages in using specific learning technologies to support their students. Lecturer E, for example, suggested that having Web-based learning resources instead of lectures enhanced students' factual knowledge, which in turn, improved their exam performance:

Students' factual knowledge in examinations is much better — part of the reason is that they don't have to write things down in lectures and get it wrong while you're lecturing to them. Also, you do talk and you tend to make mistakes, and of course, every student has a copy of that mistake! You've got time with the Web-based material to make sure it's accurate and to fine tune it over the years. (Lecturer E, Life and Health Sciences)

This statement draws attention to how students and staff can both make mistakes in lectures that can affect the accuracy of the information that students subsequently use to prepare for their exams. For Lecturer E, Web-based materials have enabled students to receive accurate factual information that can be "fine tuned" and updated by staff over time.

In further discussion, Lecturer E gave another key advantage of using Web-based materials in that students could "learn at a distance, at their own pace, in their own time." This gave students greater flexibility than traditional methods of teaching and fulfilled the university's aim to encourage "student-centred and flexible learning" (2000). However, Lecturer E went on to provide two key disadvantages with using solely Web-based materials. The first disadvantage was subject-specific and emerged unexpectedly. The Web-based materials introduced students to complex terminology in text format. Students saw the words online, but did not hear the words spoken. As a consequence, students had some difficulty in pronouncing these terms in their end of year presentations.

Recent studies have raised the question of whether or not all traditional classroom activities can be directly applied to online learning activities. Govindasamy (2001) questions whether or not the same pedagogical principles can be applied to online and traditional activities and how adaptable these principles need to be to accommodate rapid changes in technology. Mayes and De Frietas (2004) also suggest that the learning context is complex and the effectiveness of any e-learning approach depends upon whether or not technology "adds value" to the learning experience by enabling students to achieve better learning outcomes. In the case of these students, Web-based materials enabled them to develop their factual knowledge, yet failed to help them develop the required pronunciation skills that would have been possible in a class-based activity. In order to support students fully, and if correct pronunciation is important, then lecturers could either consider using technologies to provide audio information, or provide more traditional learning opportunities to fill the gaps in the student experience. Here, the lecturer had continued to pursue the learning technology route by putting audio snippets of hard to pronounce words online, although this took additional time and effort.

A second disadvantage, identified by Lecturer E, was that using Web-based materials did not always help students to "assimilate" information in a meaningful way. They suggested that while the use of Web-based materials provided students with accurate and detailed information, the presence of these resources did not always encourage or motivate students to read the required information until their examinations:

Students just look at the materials and think 'I can just print that [information] off some time in the future, I don't need to do anything now do I?' — so about a third of the class won't really assimilate the material during term time and you can see that during discussion sessions. (Lecturer E, Life and Health Sciences)

Lecturer E supplemented the Web-based learning with face-to-face seminar discussions where a member of staff was available to provide explanations if required, increasing their contact time with students.

As time went by I supported the Web-based materials with more discussion sessions with students so that they had five two-hour discussion sessions with me. This was getting back to the 12 hours of lectures I gave in the first place, but it works better, even if it's not necessarily saved me a large amount of time. (Lecturer E, Life and Health Sciences)

Although it is tempting to conclude that a deficit in students' ability to assimilate information is a result of the Web-based nature of the learning materials, staff in the Physical Sciences and engineering deanery suggest that such motivational issues are rooted in students' approach to learning more generally:

You can't just sit in a lecture and then go away, then when the end of term comes, look through your notes and say that you are prepared for the exam — you need to learn how to solve problems, you need to practice doing mathematics. (Lecturer F, Physical Sciences and Engineering)

This comment illustrates that one of the difficulties facing staff is motivating students to gain a deeper understanding of the subject, which can be achieved by an ongoing commitment to working through problem-solving exercises. Lecturer F describes how staff teaching mathematics have addressed motivational issues *with* learning technologies, introducing Web-based assessment materials to encourage students to "assimilate" and understand their subject:

If students do exercises in some kind of compulsory setting, like where computer labs are available and they need to do certain assessed tasks, then they do contribute — even if it's just a small amount — and in the end, they'll be very positive... But, if you don't make it assessed, half of them simply do not turn up in the first place, even though they might have liked it when they did it — they simply wouldn't turn up! With computer-aided assessment, they get immediate feedback, but if you look at and compare students' access to questions that are and are not assessed, only a small percentage of students bother going to the unassessed questions. The sad reality of life is that unless you assess it, the bulk of students will not engage with it! (Lecturer F, Physical Sciences and Engineering)

Here, Lecturer F uses computer-aided exercises and assessment to encourage students to understand their subject as fully as possible by giving them immediate feedback to their answers, with information on what mistakes they have made in their calculations and why they may have made them. However, despite the benefits of this immediate feedback, students seem motivated primarily by the assessed and compulsory aspects of their course. Students are often motivated more by achieving course goals to get their degree than by gaining a deeper understanding of the mathematical principles that are taught to them. This is supported by work by McKinney (2005) and Boud, Cohen, and Sampson (1999), who suggest that students focus too much on grades and not enough on learning. Covington and Müeller (2001) argue that the focus on assessment arises from a school system dominated by a system of rewards that focuses on extrinsic motivators such as grades and "gold stars"; grades are recognised as a credible index of overall success and failure in school by students, parents, and by those judging performance after school. Thus, student attitudes and approaches to learning have been shaped over time by their educational and familial experiences, leading them to emphasise achieving the highest grades possible rather than increasing their knowledge or undertaking study as a personal challenge.

Canaan (2003) suggests that students are motivated primarily by their interest in earning rewards for their academic efforts as these are viewed as a kind of currency that can be used in the employment market after completing their studies. However, she also states that students can become interested in developing knowledge in their subject during the degree process and can be encouraged to develop a dedicated approach to learning for its own sake. This is supported by the comments made by Lecturer F — students can develop a positive attitude to deeper learning if they actively participate in assessed classroom activities, particularly if the tasks themselves follow good pedagogical practice.

In addition to assessing tasks and activities to facilitate deeper learning, staff in the arts and social sciences deanery suggest that learning technologies, such as the institutional VLE, can provide useful tracking facilities that enable them to monitor students' work outside the classroom, thereby encouraging student engagement. Again, like the use of assessment to encourage students to engage with their subject area, such monitoring practices have been necessary for some staff to ensure that students understand and participate in the learning process as fully as possible. For example, one member of staff notes that:

You can demand that [students] read something you posted up before they turn up [to lectures] and then you can concentrate on the practical element or get them to reflect on that material [in lectures] in a more productive discussion. You can track them, so you know if they've done the work or not. (Lecturer G, Arts and Social Sciences)

Here, learning technologies are used to provide a tracking system that seems to encourage students to meet weekly course requirements. While this system of tracking cannot tell staff if students have read as well as accessed the materials, Lecturer G has found that student discussions have become more "productive" since the introduction of these technologies. Preparation before lectures means that students are able to develop a more reflective approach during lecture time. Furthermore, access to online texts and materials alleviates resource problems such as providing sufficient hard copies of textbooks for students to prepare for their lectures.

As might be expected in a research-led institution, some staff require an evidence base and are yet to be convinced of the advantages that such learning technologies could offer them and their students. These staff questioned the "educational worth" of making lecture notes available online, for example. As one member of staff noted:

I think there's a feeling of a proof of educational worth — I go to all this effort of putting up all this information [online], I might as well just spend one hour doing the lecture I've just given for the last 20 years — what's the difference? It's all very nice and the kids think it's fun, but am I actually learning it any better? There's a feeling of 'lets do e-learning for the sake of e-learning,' just because you can put it up on the Web. (Lecturer H, Life and Health Sciences)

Lecturer H also raises the question of whether or not online material offers the same quality of information that an experienced lecturer can provide in a traditional lecture format. In a similar way, another member of staff questioned the benefit of using technologies such as animated PowerPoint slides in lectures:

I find the students are getting audio-visual overload. They're getting too much flashy stuff in, and they're actually missing the main points of the lecture. (Lecturer I, Life and Health Sciences)

Lecturer I expanded on this comment to suggest that *how* as well as *what* technologies are used to present lecture content is crucial in engaging students with the subject. While student participation and interaction in the traditional lecture/seminar is limited (Pavey & Garland, 2004), Lecturer I suggests that students engage more with the content if bullet points are presented on slides, rather than the entire lecture. This method of presentation encourages students to listen more and make their own notes, rather than writing word for word anything that the lecturer puts on the screen.

In summary, staff comments show how their attitudes toward and use of learning technologies to support students are primarily pedagogy-driven rather than technology-driven. Staff are interested in the educational worth of using learning technologies and consider the costs and benefits of using learning technologies to enhance students' factual knowledge and encourage a student-centred approach to learning. Before implementing a new mode of teaching, such as using a learning technology, staff query whether it can really improve student learning, or merely provide a new method of delivery.

Support and Encouragement Issues

Support Issues

The type and quality of technical support received by staff is also a significant factor in shaping the use of learning technologies. Haywood et al. (2000) suggest that a "lack of reliable and adequate infrastructure, including technical support" is a key barrier to the uptake of learning technologies.

In the focus group discussions reported here, staff drew attention to the different kinds or layers of support that they believe are necessary to develop and implement e-learning initiatives. They suggested that general technical, administrative, and specialist "in house" support are all required to enable them to use learning technologies effectively. However, even with general technical support in place to maintain lecture room equipment, such as video beam projectors or Internet access, staff noted that limited time to deal with any technical problems has a significant impact on their teaching.

There was the issue about teaching rooms, gaining access to stuff easily… and trying to sort these things out, all of which could take 10 to 15 minutes — well you only have a lecture that effectively, is 40 minutes, 45 at the best of times. These are big losses. Things seem to be getting better though. (Lecturer J, Arts and Social Sciences)

Staff in all three deaneries also described how limited access and time to prepare before a lecture has curtailed the use of technologies within the lecture. For example:

We only have at best 10 minutes before a lecture before you can get into the room, and most of us don't get in because, certainly with the bigger venues, you've got to wait for the students coming out five minutes before the hour — if you're lucky! (Lecturer K, Physical Sciences and Engineering)

As one member of staff stated, these issues can become a "huge dis-incentive to use learning technologies in a class situation" (Lecturer L, Arts and Social Sciences).

In addition to technical support, staff suggest that administrative support is essential to enable staff to explore new learning technologies or develop new materials for supporting students. As Lecturer C explained:

As you build up your student numbers on [the VLE], the traditional sort of administrative model doesn't work any more. You have to have administration and secretarial staff who are trained to handle standard inquiries that come in via e-mail. Instead, we have a tutor or an e-learning development officer handling every little [thing related to the VLE]... which means that they've got no development time for any new projects — they can't do what they are good at! (Lecturer C, Arts and Social Sciences)

Although the production of online materials is time-consuming, administration issues such as limited resources to deal with computer-based inquiries from students or other staff can be even more demanding upon their time. Staff described how they were seen as the "IT person," or how they would make sure they knew a member of academic staff that they could contact within their school to deal specifically with technical inquiries. As a consequence, technically capable members of academic staff experience limited time to develop course materials, explore new learning technologies, or receive training themselves.

In order for academic staff to implement technologies into their courses effectively, administration and secretarial staff are increasingly required to take on roles to deal with standard technical inquiries that traditionally they would not encounter (such as how to register for a VLE course). These additional roles require training and resourcing. Although learning technologies are "increasingly presented as a cost-efficient means of maintaining teaching quality," there are clearly major obstacles to this efficiency (Plewes & Issroff, 2002).

Finally, in addition to technical and administrative support, staff in all three deaneries suggest that specialist "in-house" knowledge is required to maintain specialist software and understand the kinds of resources that staff need to support their teaching practices. For example, staff in the physical sciences and engineering deanery use or would like to use dedicated software such as MATLAB, Maple, or chemical drawing packages. Such software has the potential to enable staff to use existing innovative teaching materials rather than create their own but requires specialist knowledge or support to release this potential.

Encouragement Issues

A review of the teaching and learning infrastructure in UK higher education institutions by Higher Education Funding Council for England (2002) suggests that the infrastructure may have suffered as a consequence of factors such as the Research Assessment Exercise (RAE), which has created competition for resources from research.

Although the RAE was not intended to have any particular impact on teaching, D'Andrea and Gosling (2002) suggest that RAE funding has led to a separation of research from teaching, with research having the "highest status" (see also McNay, 1998). This gradual separation between teaching and research has led to a focus upon research activities, whereby institutions and departments have made time available for active researchers by reallocating some teaching duties to non-research active staff (D'Andrea & Gosling, 2002). Consequently, the discrepancies between the value of research and teaching in higher education institutions have affected staff at individual, departmental, and institutional levels (see also Haywood et al., 2000).

Perhaps not surprisingly for a research-led institution, these discrepancies were highlighted during focus group discussions between staff at the University of Birmingham. In particular, staff suggested that the value of research and teaching within the institution has had a significant impact on their attitudes toward and use of learning technologies to support their teaching-related activities. Like the students that staff seek to motivate and engage, staff revealed that they would be more motivated to consider using learning technologies if they felt that they were given more credit for their teaching-related activities. The following conversation was held in the focus group for the arts and social sciences deanery:

M: The university as a whole doesn't really encourage teaching does it? Unless, it might if it is income-generating.

N: It doesn't reward teaching — people who generate [e-learning materials] will never get thanked.

O: It's a huge incentive to do absolutely flap all preparation for your teaching because you can still get promoted! We get promoted on the basis of research.

M: Well if you're taking 8 or 9 hours per lecture to prepare [new materials], you could be using that time for [research]!

The University of Birmingham does have a system in place for rewarding excellence in learning and teaching as well as in research, management, and administration, however, this dialogue suggests that staff feel that they are rewarded or promoted for research activities rather than those related to teaching. Furthermore, staff suggested that unless their activities can be used to generate income for the university, they did not seem to be encouraged. These factors combine with time issues to discourage staff from using learning technologies for supporting students and, as Lecturer M suggests, to provide greater incentive to use their preparation time for lectures to pursue their research.

The issues that staff have raised surrounding the kind of support and encouragement that they feel they receive at the University of Birmingham are indicative of the wider higher education context in the UK and abroad. The previous sections show that staff are positive about using learning technologies, but some staff have been discouraged by a combination of factors including limitations upon time and access to teaching spaces, increased student numbers, and limited capacity to provide the technical support that staff require at short notice.

Future Trends

The use of learning technologies is considered as a key factor in driving forward the changes that staff and students are experiencing within higher education institutions (MacFarlane, 1998; HEFCE, 2002; Hunter, Clarke, & Shoebridge, 2005). The HEFCE (2005) strategy for e-learning states that learners are bringing new expectations of the power of technology into higher education that will impact further upon teaching practices.

Many institutions are now beginning to respond to the challenges of meeting the demands of increased student numbers and expectations by seeking to develop and implement e-learning strategies. For example, a study by the Joint Information Systems Committee (JISC) in 2003, suggested that 83% of responding institutions were using VLEs at this time. Recent studies (e.g., Hunter, Clarke, & Shoebridge, 2005) suggest that e-learning strategies are evidence of positive attitudes at an institutional level and at the staff/student level. They posit that "some institutions will have over 70% of students accessing online learning content, making VLEs mission critical to the core business of learning and teaching." At the University of Birmingham alone, VLE usage doubled in 2003-2004 and is expected to double again in 2004-2005 (Mortleman, 2004). Studies often use levels of usage as an indictor for increasing and successful uptake of learning technologies to support teaching and learning. However, the monitoring or tracking of student access to online courses and materials does not tell us how this technology is being used, how effective it is in supporting and enhancing the learning and teaching experience, or how the roles of both staff and students may be changing through its use.

If learning technologies are to play an increasingly important role in the support of learning and teaching, then changes in the roles of teacher and learner will also occur (MacFarlane, 1998). Through the use of VLEs and other services, Hunter, Clarke, and Shoebridge (2005) suggest that the "personalization of learning" will take place:

Learners will be able to put together programmes of study specifically tailored to their own learning needs. Learners will have a range of learning opportunities on campus, at home, in the workplace [etc]... enabling them to personalize their own 'e-learning space' and so making the most effective use of the wide range of resources and technologies that are available. (p. 59)

This personalization of learning will therefore bring about changes in the way that learning is supported and managed, although these authors are keen to suggest that while such changes may be seen as a "threat" to many aspects of university life and current teaching practices, "real campuses" and the people within them will remain.

The potential for learning technologies to transform and enhance the learning and teaching experience within higher education institutions has characterised educational commentaries for some time. As Gorard and Selwyn (1999) suggest, with the rise of digital broadcasting, the Internet, and other computerized telecommunications technologies in the latter half of the 20th century, there has been "a rush of excitement" at the possibilities that these technologies offer education (pp. 523-4). Yet, there are many complex factors that have impacted and continue to impact upon actual uptake of such technologies in education. For example, the Universities and Colleges Information Systems Association survey (2003) has shown that in the vast majority of institutions, VLEs are widely recognised as an important component of an institutional strategy, but this is yet poorly matched by delivery (p. 6). Within the context of the "barriers" that are raised in this chapter and elsewhere (Haywood et al., 2000; Plewes & Issroff, 2002), such as lack of time, infrastructure, training, and insufficient value placed on teaching, it is not hard to see why uptake has been, and continues to be, slow and fragmented.

Furthermore, recent studies (e.g., Haywood et al., 2000) have highlighted how culture change in higher education institutions is gradual, making it difficult to see the effects — including the benefits and the weaknesses — of learning technologies at the institutional level. This is partly because "the cyclic nature of academic years result[ing] in changes to courses often [lag] one or two years behind the decision to change" (p 14). Yet, Haywood argues, this gradual change should not be seen as negative: for change to be truly embedded, there needs to be movement on a broad front, engaging significant numbers of staff across these institutions, rather than just a small number of enthusiasts.

We have argued that the focus on research in research-led institutions may have been a deterrent to some staff implementing learning technologies. The need to recognise research in e-learning and the pedagogy of subject teaching has recently been championed by the Department for Education and Skills (2005) who have made recognition of these topics by subject panels a milestone for 2007-2008 under Priority 4 of their "Harnessing Technology" strategy (Priority 4: Provide a good quality ICT training and support package for practitioners). Diana Laurillard, head of the Government's e-learning strategy unit, asked delegates at the Higher Education Academy conference in 2005 to respond to the HEFCE's consultation on the criteria for the 2008 RAE, encouraging subject panels to recognise the importance of teaching and learning online (THES, 2005).

If the call is taken up by RAE subject panels and research into e-learning becomes an accepted topic for subjects outside education, then, within the UK at least, staff may become more positive about implementing learning technologies in research-led institutions. First, staff may be more likely to implement technologies if doing so could add to their research profile, and second, the increase in pedagogic research around learning technologies could provide evidence of "educational worth" and examples of good practice that others could follow.

Conclusion

This chapter has described and discussed comments made by staff at the University of Birmingham in three focus group discussions carried out in 2004. Three main themes were drawn out of the discussion: staff time, pedagogic issues, and support and encouragement issues.

The first, and possibly most important, point is that staff require significant help to overcome unfamiliarity with new methods of teaching which requires an investment of time that some do not feel they are able to make. Time is important for any new initiative whether or not technology is involved, but, for many practitioners, the use of new technologies is outside their current experience and adds an unknowable element to their consideration of benefits and costs.

Second, learning technologies can be used to support students effectively and efficiently. For example, at the simplest level, requiring students to access and read lecture notes and materials online can release face-to-face contact time for more in-depth discussion, potentially leading to deeper learning practices of analysis, synthesis, and evaluation. Learning technologies can also provide flexible learning opportunities based around self-assessment facilities or online discussions.

However, careful consideration needs to be made as to whether a learning technology can add value to student learning or staff teaching practice, and which learning technologies can be used to best match the context and intended outcomes. In many situations, the best model may be to combine technology enhanced learning with more traditional methods (see also Wheeler, Frawley, & Davis, 2000). The decision to deploy learning technologies also should take into account factors such as intrinsic and extrinsic motivations, and processes may need to be developed to engage and encourage student participation. The relationship between intrinsic and extrinsic motivators can be complex. It would appear, however, that embedding extrinsic motivators such as requiring students to access e-learning opportunities through tracking or assessment strategies, can lead to the more intrinsic rewards of learning for learning's own sake and to students feeling involved and taking responsibility for their learning (see also Canaan, 2003).

Finally, support and encouragement issues (Mayes & de Freitas, 2004) can impact on staff uptake and engagement with learning technologies. In particular, institutions need to address aspects of infrastructure relating to access to learning technologies both within traditional learning spaces such as lecture theatres, and virtual learning spaces such as VLEs and other online resources.

Staff time constraints are obviously important, but other support and encouragement issues can also affect uptake. These include the impact of increased student numbers, limited capacity to provide the technical support that staff require at short notice, and reward structures. We suggested that students may need external motivators to stimulate engagement with learning technologies and the same may be argued for staff. Staff need to feel that their time and efforts to implement teaching innovations are supported and valued, particularly where research is seen as being valued above teaching or adminis-tration. This can be done via explicit rewards though procedures such as pay and promotion. Reward systems should be put in place where they currently do not exist, or given higher profile where they do. This has recently been made explicit by HEFCE where one of the measures of success for its e-learning strategy published in March 2005 is as follows:

Staff are supported at all stages to develop appropriate skills in e-learning, and these skills are recognised in their roles and responsibilities and in reward structures. They have access to accreditation for their level of skills and professional practice in linking learning technology with teaching. (HEFCE 2005, p. 9, point g)

It is clear from this chapter that the views and use of learning technologies among staff at the University of Birmingham are not unique, but represent the wider perspectives and experiences of practitioners within higher education institutions across the UK and abroad. The focus group discussions that were held with staff early in 2004 took place within the context of an increasing impetus across campus to engage with learning technologies, and in turn, helped to inform the institution's developing e-learning strategy.

Much has changed since these focus groups were carried out. Developments have included the early adoption of an academic enterprise system, and the formation of communities of practice within academic departments and a nucleus of staff supporting these practices within Information Services, the Learning Development Unit including the e-learning team, and the Centre for Educational Technology and Distance Learning (CETADL). These groups contribute expertise and experience in developing and embed-ding learning technologies across campus and in supporting lecturers wishing to utilise learning technologies for the benefit of learning and teaching. The impact of these changes will be investigated in a further survey and a set of focus groups due to commence April 2005.

Acknowledgments

We would like to thank all University of Birmingham staff who participated in the Learning Technology Survey and focus group discussions in 2003-2004. Our thanks also go to Robert Hunter, Stephen Clarke, and Professor Colin Rickwood for their comments.

References

Armitage, S., & O'Leary, R. (2003). *A guide for learning technologists.* LTSN Generic Centre: E-learning Series no. 4. York: Learning and Teaching Support Network (LTSN).

Beetham, H. (2005). E-learning research: Emerging issues?. *Association for Learning Technology Journal, 13*(1), 81-89.

Boud, D., Cohen, R., & Sampson, J. (1999). Peer learning and assessment. *Assessment and Evaluation in Higher Education, 24,* 413-426.

Canaan, J.E. (2003). *Strategies for engaging students more fully in social theory.* Retrieved May 15, 2005, from www.c-sap.bham.ac.uk/resources/project_reports/admin/extras/16_S_02.pdf

Covington, M.V., & Mueller, K.J. (2001). Intrinsic versus extrinsic motivation: An approach/avoidance reformulation. *Educational Psychology Review, 13*(2), 157-176.

D'Andrea, V., & Gosling, D. (2002). *Promoting research in teaching and learning in higher education: Two case studies of multi-disciplinary pedagogic research.* Retrieved February 2, 2005, from www.tlrp.org/pub/acadpub/Dandrea2000.pdf

Davies, A., Ramsay, J., Lindfield H., & Couperthwaite, J. (2005a). Building learning communities: Foundations for good practice. *British Journal of Educational Technology, 36*(4), 615-627.

Davies, A., Ramsay, J., Lindfield H., & Couperthwaite, J. (2005b). A blended approach to learning: Added value and lessons learnt from student use of computer-based materials for neurological analysis. *British Journal of Educational Technology, 36*(5), 839-850.

Davies, A., & Smith, K. (2005). *Evaluating teaching staff use of learning technologies across the University of Birmingham.* Available online at www.ldu.bham.ac.uk/Learningtechnologysurvey/Staff%20survey%20article%20website.pdf

DfES (2003). *Towards a unified e-learning strategy.* Nottingham: DfES Publications.

DfES (2005). *Harnessing technology: Transforming learning and children's services.* Nottingham: DfES Publications.

Gibbs, G. (1996). Institutional strategies for implementing resource-based learning. In S. Brown & B. Smith (Eds.), *Resource-based learning.* London: Kogan Page.

Gorard, S., & Selwyn, N. (1999). Switching on the learning society? Questioning the role of technology in widening participation in lifelong learning. *Journal of Education Policy, 14*(5), 523-534.

Govindasamy, T. (2002). Successful implementation of e-learning. Pedagogical considerations. *The Internet and Higher Education 4*(3), 287-299.

Hanson, J. (2003). Encouraging lecturers to engage with new technologies in learning and teaching in a vocational university: The role of recognition and reward. *Higher Education Management and Policy, 15*(3), 135-149.

Haywood, J., Anderson, C., Coyle, H., Day, K., Haywood, D., & Macleod, H. (2000). Learning technology in Scottish higher education – A survey of the views of senior managers, academic staff and 'experts.' *Association for Learning Technology Journal, 8*(2), 5-17.

HEFCE (2002). *Teaching and learning infrastructure in higher education.* Retrieved June 13, 2005, from www.planning.ed.ac.uk/SHEFC/HEFCE/JMinfrastructure.pdf

HEFCE (2005). *HEFCE Strategy for e-learning.* Retrieved June 13, 2005, from www.hefce.ac.uk/pubs/hefce/2005/05_12/05_12.doc

Hunter, R., Clarke, S., & Shoebridge, M. (2005). Change management. In M. Melling (Ed.), *Supporting e-learning: A guide for library and information managers.* London: Facet Publishing.

Laurillard, D. (1993). *Rethinking university teaching: A framework for the effective use of educational technology.* London: Routledge.

Littlejohn, A. (2003). Issues in reusing online resources. In A. Littlejohn (Ed.), *Reusing online resources: A sustainable approach to e-learning.* London: Kogan Page.

Lucas, L. (2004). *Linking research and teaching: The significance of research funding and evaluation policies.* Retrieved May 9, 2005, from www.solent.ac.uk/ExternalUP/318/lisa_lucas__paper.doc

Mayes, T., & De Freitas, S., (2004). *JISC e-learning models desk study. Stage 2: Review of e-learning theories, frameworks and models.* Retrieved May 3, 2005, from www.jisc.ac.uk/uploaded_documents/Stage%202%20Learning%20Models%20(Version%201).pdf

McFarlane, A. (1998). Information, knowledge and learning. *Higher Education Quarterly, 52*(1), 77-92.

McKinney, K. (2005). *Encouraging students' intrinsic motivation.* Retrieved March 4, 2005, from www.cat.ilstu.edu/conf/handouts/intrinsicmot.shtml

McNay, I. (1997). The impact of the 1992 RAE in English universities. *Higher Education Review, 29*(2), 34-43.

McNay, I. (1998). The RAE and after: You never know how it will all turn out. *Perspectives, 2*(1), 19-22.

McNay, I. (2003). Assessing the assessment: An analysis of the UK research assessment exercise, 2001, and its outcomes, with special reference to research in education. *Science and Public Policy, 30*(1), 47-54.

Melling, M. (2005). Introduction. In M. Melling (Ed.), *Supporting e-learning. A guide for library and information managers.* London: Facet Publishing.

Mortlemann, J. (2004). *Birmingham University sees surge in e-learning.* Retrieved May 16, 2005, from www.vnunet.com/news/1155818

Orill, C.H. (2002). Supporting online PBL: Design considerations for supporting distributed problem solving. *Distance Education, 23*(1), 41-57.

Pavey, J., & Garland, S.W. (2004). The integration and implementation of a range of 'e-tivities' to enhance students' interaction and learning. *Innovations in Education and Teaching International, 41*(3), 305-315.

Plewes, L., & Issroff, K. (2002). Understanding the development of teaching and learning resources: A review. *Association for Learning Technology Journal, 10*(2), 4-16.

Rist & Hewer (1996). *What is learning technology? Some definitions.* The Learning Technology Dissemination Initiative. Retrieved July 10, 2003, from www.icbl.hw.ac.uk/ltdi/implementing-it/what-def.htm

Robins (1999). *Space, place and the virtual university.* Retrieved October 6, 2003, from http://virtualsociety.sbs.ox.ac.uk/projects/robins.htm

Salmon, G. (2002). *E-Moderating: The key to teaching and learning online.* London: Kogan Page.

THES (2005). *Call for RAE to recognise e-learning.* Retrieved July 28, 2003, from www.thes.co.uk

Universities and Colleges Information Systems Association (2003). *VLE Survey.* Retrieved April 27, 2005, from www.ucisa.ac.uk/groups/tlig/vle/index_html

University of Birmingham (2002). *Learning and teaching strategy.* Retrieved August 4, 2003, from www.ppd.bham.ac.uk/policy/landt.htm

Wheeler, J., Frawley, J., & Davis, J. (2000). e-learning: A Forum perspective. *Forum.* Available online at www.forum.com

Chapter IX

Constructivist E-Learning for Staff Engaged in Continuous Professional Development

Roisin Donnelly, Dublin Institute of Technology, Republic of Ireland

Ciara O'Farrell, Trinity College, Dublin, Republic of Ireland

Abstract

Professional development for academic staff in e-learning is currently a priority for higher education institutions in the Republic of Ireland, as lecturers experience increasing demands to incorporate e-learning into their teaching practice. This chapter reports on the design and implementation of a blended module in e-learning for the continuous professional development of such lecturers. In it the co-authors (who designed and developed the module) discuss the effectiveness of exposing lecturers as online students in order to experience first-hand the advantages and disadvantages of e-learning. It argues that a constructivist, collaborative interaction can provide the scaffolding for lecturers' future journeys into e-learning and into constructivist practices within their own teaching. Although this approach is still in its infancy, important outcomes were achieved in terms of influencing lecturers' thinking and approaches to both their own and to their students' learning.

Introduction

This chapter discusses and reflects on the challenges the authors encountered when designing and developing a blended module on e-learning for lecturers' continuous professional development (CPD). In it, we consider the effectiveness of exposing lecturers as online students in order to experience first-hand the advantages and disadvantages of e-learning, and discuss how a constructivist, collaborative interaction can provide the scaffolding for lecturers' future journeys into e-learning and into constructivist practices within their own teaching.

The blended module designed by the authors is jointly offered by the Learning and Teaching Centre and the Learning Technology Team, located within the School of Lifelong Learning at the Dublin Institute of Technology.[1] The main purpose of the Learning and Teaching Centre is to support the Institution's 1,500 full- and part-time academic staff through provision of ongoing professional development opportunities (including those in e-learning) for all academic staff at individual, department, school, faculty, and institute levels. It aims to enhance the quality of the learning experience for all students.

Higher education institutions worldwide are devoting considerable resources to the development of e-learning and e-teaching. Like their counterparts abroad, academic staff members in our institution are experiencing increasing demands to incorporate e-learning into their teaching practice. As a result, they are required to have a broad range of knowledge and skills to use software and must be able to adapt their skills to a diverse set of classroom situations. The majority of professional development in this area is provided through one-off workshops and training sessions, which are accessed in a central location across disciplines, or in a discipline-based setting (most often by request from a faculty, school, or course team).

One of the main questions staff members have at these technology training events centres on their need to revise the way they teach or design the curriculum because of the influence of technology. As educators, they are acutely conscious of the need to stay current with technology for many reasons. However, like their counterparts in other institutions, they find, by the nature of their varied work responsibilities, that demands such as curriculum development, lesson preparation, student support, staff meetings, and so forth pull them in many directions (Alstete, 2000; Lawler & King, 2000).

As educational developers, our remit in designing an e-learning module was to cultivate an environment where academic staff members could discover new possibilities for learning and teaching through technology. Cognisant of maximizing our participants' effectiveness as educators within an online environment, we needed to show them that producing online learning is far more than simply converting lecture notes to the Web; conversely, we also needed to guide them away from implementing content-high systems that would not engage and aid their students' learning. Thus, the module needed to be both time-efficient and effective where participants would be involved in and challenged by an active learning process. The result was a four week blended module entitled "E-learning in Higher Education: An Engaging Introduction," the first step in a complete professional development program in e-learning.

Rationale

Our rationale originated in a constructivist pedagogy operationalised through an inquiry/exploratory approach and framed within a blended learning environment. Certain studies advocate interaction as a key factor in the e-learning environment and the important role of staff professional development in developing lecturer presence online (Anderson, Rourke, Garrison, & Archer, 2001; Murphy, Smith, Smith, & Stacey, 2001). Research has shown that the online learning and teaching environment can be structured for effective social constructivist learning through an interactive online discussion (Stacey, 2002; Bonk & Cunningham, 1998). The metacognitive, reflective, and social constructivist approach to professional development described in this chapter is a response to the limitations of directive approaches of e-learning within a context of rapid technological change.

Although increasing numbers of learners are working online, few lecturers have themselves learnt this way; therefore, many require professional development in the skills and techniques of facilitating in an online learning environment (Coghlan, 2001). Case studies reviewed endorsed our view that online tutors need to experience online learning as a student before they can effectively support online learners (Kempe, 2001; Salmon, 2000; Ambrose, 2001; Devonshire & Philip, 2001). Consequently, one of our key intentions in designing this program was to highlight the challenges and advantages associated with teaching online by effectively emulating the student experience. Rather than opting for a fully online or fully directive approach for this CPD module, blended learning was chosen for the design. There are a variety of forms of blended learning where e-learning, in its various forms, is combined with more traditional forms of training such as "classroom" training. The blended learning adopted by this module involved primary delivery of the module by WebCT, augmented by a module handbook, and supported on two occasions by half day face-to-face sessions with tutors.

On the one hand, we felt a purely directive approach would have been incongruous to the very idea of an e-learning program. E-learning professional development is essential, but with technology evolving at a rapid rate, directive style training becomes inadequate or out-of-date in a short period of time, normally months, not years. Technology is very diverse and evolves too swiftly for lecturers to be reliant on workshops and seminars (Melczarek, 2000). Online learning can also offer a rich and flexible choice of learning experiences that fit in with one's need, pace, place, aspirations, and learning styles.

On the other hand, we wanted to have some face-to-face contact with our learners/lecturers. Given the independent nature of their work, if lecturers encounter difficulties in their teaching practice, there is often little support available to them. And for those lecturers new to the notion of e-learning, at whom the module was aimed, we felt the notion of some face-to-face guidance would be reassuring.

E-Learning CPD Module Design

At much the same time as we began incubating ideas for this module, we at the Learning and Teaching Centre were approached by the faculty of science to help them develop a curriculum for a master's degree that would utilise e-learning. Experienced users of the World Wide Web, they sought further understanding of how the Internet could be used in teaching. Consequently, we decided to design the module around the requirements of this initial group, but to make it suitably adaptable to the needs of lecturers from any subject area, such as librarians, learning resource centre staff, and/or learning technology support.

The early design and structure of the module were identified through an online needs questionnaire to the 12 perspective science participants. The first section was aimed at collecting background and demographics. The second section asked the respondents to think about their preferred learning styles and motivation for doing the module. The third section asked about their access to appropriate technology. Finally, they were asked about their prior knowledge and practical experience of e-learning in higher education. We then translated these answers into a set of tailored learning outcomes whereby, on completion of the module, participants would be able to:

- Explore the concept of e-learning for their own context.
- Research and critically evaluate electronic resources for their own subject discipline.
- Consider different ways of designing online learning.
- Identify methods of online interaction.
- Evaluate online learning for their own context.

The aims of the module were twofold: first, to introduce to participants the concept and possibilities of e-learning for their own professional context in higher education; second, to enable participants be cognizant of the importance of designing materials and activities to engage their students in learning.

Designed as an accredited module for academic staff as a vehicle for diffusion of professional staff development in e-learning, this module was delivered through WebCT, the institution's VLE of choice. In the past, studies have shown that many academics seem reluctant to adopt Web-supported teaching (Dearn, Fraser, & Ryan, 2002), and research indicates that a number of factors influence levels of adoption. These include inadequate access to staff development and training (Guthrie, 2003), high workload (Scribbens, 2002), lack of time, and lack of adequate recognition and rewards (Alexander & McKenzie, 1998). These factors were all taken into consideration in the design of the module which drew on a framework for designing online learning settings (Oliver & Herrington, 2003) which makes explicit the three interconnecting elements as critical components of the design of e-learning environments: learning tasks, learning supports, and learning resources.

Figure 1 shows the detail of the module design. There were three main components to the Web site: resources, activities, and discussion/reflection (explicit peer and tutor support provided here). On the module home page, there was also a link to module information and module evaluation.

The module was divided up into four sections, one rolled out per week. Each section began with an introduction to the area and an activity to complete over the week. There

Figure 1. A blended model for staff professional development in e-learning

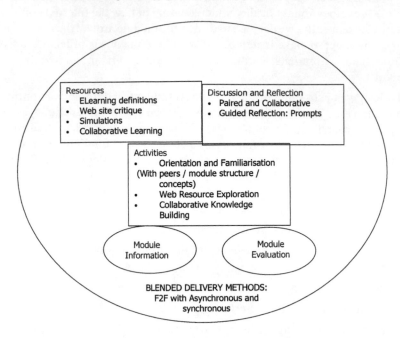

were also a series of reflective questions for participants to consider as each week came to a close. These were for our participants' learning development and were not shared. Due to the highly collaborative nature of the module, the assessment strategy was devised so that participants were assessed on their discussion board participation on a pass or fail basis. The intention at this point was not to assess the quality of their contributions, but rather to strongly encourage them to learn from one another using the asynchronous tools available. As we were working with motivated lecturers, keen to learn as part of their continuous development, timely and comprehensive formative feedback from both peers and the four tutors featured strongly in helping participants reach the learning outcomes.

The 12 participants, who needed no special technical skills other than basic computing skills, received accreditation of one credit and a certificate of completion in return for undertaking to:

- attend the two face-to-face sessions
- log on to the module Web site a minimum of three times per week[2]
- participate in discussion with other participants
- complete the activities for each week
- complete and return the end of module evaluation

Figure 2. Week one activities

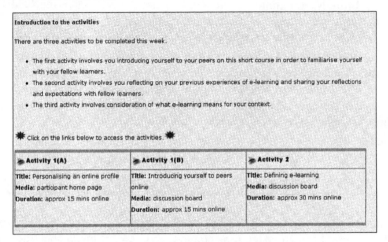

Figure 3. Examples of resources to support activities

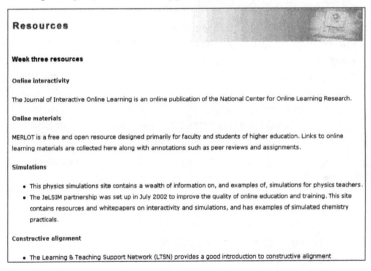

Activities

The activities (Figures 2 and 3 overleaf) were designed to allow participants to actively connect their learning with the potential for their own student learning, to incorporate their learning into practice, and to stimulate new perspectives of teaching with technology.

The small collaborative groups shared with the tutors the perspectives of the group members, sought feedback, and clarified ideas. It was found that learning collaboratively through interaction was achieved by the development of a communal consensus of knowledge, through communicating different perspectives, receiving feedback from other participants and tutors, and discussing ideas, until a final negotiation of understanding was reached within the time set for such activity.

As the participants engaged in this environment and discussed how to use technology in their work, they actively discovered new perspectives and points of application, constructed new ideas, and began to apply their learning to practice. Eventually, a community of practice evolved where, as a group of learners, they began thinking of the next stages of their professional development and planning how they could use it to transform their practice.

Constructivist Framework for Design and Delivery

To orientate lecturers to the online environment, we used a constructivist instructional framework within the blended learning context. Vygotskian social constructivism as an explanatory theory for the effectiveness of e-learning claims that interactive learning, as achieved by the process of communicating online, enables learners to actively construct their own perspectives which they can communicate to a small learning group of peers.

Constructivist theory states that learners construct meaning through self-directed enquiry, guided activity, or community-based co-participation. To apply these theories to an online environment, we were careful to design a module set in a real-world environment that involved social negotiation and mediation, with multiple paths for learners to explore, and with the tutors providing a facilitative rather than directive role. Our intention was to organize a learning environment that would contribute effectively to our participants' individual competencies and learning, within the context of group participation — specifically, within a learning community.

This approach presented numerous challenges. Our first was to convince our participants of the benefits of collaborative learning. One of the values of peer learning is that it exposes learners to multiple points of view, perspectives, and experiences. There was concern, however, that our participants might not wish to collaborate to this extent, that they might be more used to/prefer to work individually, or that they would worry about "sharing" ideas, or being judged by other colleagues.

Thus, each activity was designed to engage learners in peer feedback, and we encouraged learners to participate on discussion boards by e-mailing those who were slow to appear on the first week, or by replying to initial comments ourselves when others were reticent to do so, by using a friendly tone and by always posing further questions in our comments. The focal point of all activities was interpersonal exchange, with individuals talking and reflecting electronically with other individuals. To counter the concern that some participants would only "lurk" (or as we preferred to view it, "browse"), rather than participate in any discussion, we integrated discussion and reflection.[3] Thus, while many of the activities began with information collection, comparison, analysis, and individual reflection, participants were also expected to read the multiple perspectives on any given topic, and review and comment on at least some of them. This shift, essentially from objectivist to constructivist, fostered a connection with peer knowledge and experience, where participants gave and received feedback, reflecting on learning both within their individual contexts and outside of them. The synergizing potential of this strategy encouraged a community of learners who began to seek learning opportunities, applications, and resources together.

The Role of Reflection and Discussion

Esson, Johnson, and Vinson (2002) point to the potential value of reflective approaches which are part of an everyday process of improvement in the natural setting. According to Dobrovolny (2003, p. 36), reflection is an interpretative process that allows learners to "visualise using what they learned by solving a problem or improving something with their new skills; understand the big picture; compare their use of information with how others use the same information; recall a section in the course."

Dialogue and reflection assumed a critical role in our module's activities by facilitating the development of a critical conscience through collective enquiry with peers and tutors. To integrate a strong interpretative process to the learning experience in this module, participants were encouraged to reflect on the critical attributes of concepts and theories, on how they might use the content, how it might fit into a larger framework, and how it might be applied within their individual contexts. As facilitators, we played a role in facilitating reflection by encouraging experiential learning in our activities, and by asking pertinent questions at appropriate times during discussion board conversations. Also, we provided a weekly summary of the main themes covered in the discussion threads, facilitating the sharing of participant's ideas and insights, and highlighting areas for further reflection.

The reflective focus of the module was positively remarked upon by the participants who, during evaluation, gave feedback that they found it "most useful and interesting to think about" what they had done and why they had done it, noting also, "the activities were useful in encouraging reflective thinking about the design and implementation of e-learning resources in general." Reflection helped our learners contextualize the content and, throughout the module, they interpreted many different examples of how e-learning can stimulate the learning experience. With the discussion board being the intellectual hub from which spokes of discussion threads emanated and dispersed, ideas were debated and eventually translated into practice in the initial design of a curriculum for the science master's programme.

Initially, however, participants were unsure of the merits of discussion and were slow to use the discussion board either to present their own ideas or to comment on others. Perhaps this is because most of this particular cohort of participants knew each other on a professional basis, but now encased in an environment where they were considered fellow students, they were reticent to seem critical of another colleague's work, or to be judged themselves. Also, some participants expressed concern at the validity of discussion compared to the straight presentation of facts, an unease that perhaps arose from their scientific background. One participant summed up this feeling up saying, "Discussions were difficult to adjust to. I would have liked more information and less discussion."[5]

Thus, tutors made a conscious decision to lead by example where discussion and reflection was concerned, all the time taking care to remain facilitative and resist falling into an instructional role. As constructivist facilitators, we saw our role as tailoring our teaching strategies to our learners' needs, while encouraging them to maximise interaction. We continued to moderate through facilitative questions to fuel critical thinking, commented and reflected when others were slow to do so, encouraged discussion, and practiced constructive criticism at all times.[6]

By the end of the four weeks, participants were notably more comfortable with the discussion forum and, indeed, this feature was commended positively in feedback. One participant noted that even though the module had initially seemed unstructured because of the discussion format, in retrospect it was well-planned and fully addressed the learning outcomes. Interestingly, the participant who observed that he would have liked "more information and less discussion" went on to note, "However, in hindsight, I probably learnt more the way it was done."

A Learning Community Approach

While one of the advantages of online learning is that it allows learners the flexibility to pace their own learning at their own convenience, a fundamental disadvantage is when learners have to learn alone, separated by time and/or distance. Working with other learners can provide the scaffolding for a journey into learning, affording them the opportunity to learn from alternative perspectives, as well as providing support and encouraging other more social aspects of construction. Interaction with other learners and with facilitators thus not only provides learners with a sense of community, but is fundamental to the tenets of constructivism.

In this module, we wanted to offer participants more than a technologically advanced, faceless, solitary e-learning experience. Our blended learning approach ensured that learners would meet at least twice during the program for half day workshops — once at the beginning and once at the end — and all participants commented favourably on the given mix of face-to-face and blended learning. However, when designing the module, we realized we would need something more than this to maximize learner-learner dialogue collaboration and social negotiation. We thus decided to encourage an online community through the use of asynchronous tools such as e-mail, chatrooms, and, of course, discussion boards.

After a slow start, we found that threaded discussions helped to develop kinship and camaraderie — by the end of the second week, learners were beginning to write more, in a less formal tone, and even exchanged in gentle repartee with each other at one stage. Interestingly, feeling "involved" also became an important factor in feeling successful in the module. Both the learners who dropped out before completing the module (due to time restrictions) expressed that they had fallen behind in the discussions, had lost the sense of community, and as a result were feeling ineffective.[7]

Taking the premise that "communities of practice are groups of people who share a concern, a set of problems, or a passion about a topic, and who deepen their knowledge and expertise in this area by interacting *on an ongoing basis*" (Wenger, Mc Dermott, &

Snyder, 2003), then it remains to be seen whether our approach worked. Certainly for the four-week duration of the module the learners interacted with each other progressively more, sharing opinions, problems, and passions. And, in the final face-to-face session, the group made the unanimous decision to avail of further consultancy and professional development from both our Institute's Learning and Teaching Centre and our Learning Technology Team. Further, rather than working on individual teaching projects, they expressed a strong interest in working together as a community to maximize their experiences, design a curriculum together, and ultimately to create a more valuable learning experience for their students. An impact analysis is scheduled to evaluate the long-term realisation of these ideas, and indeed, the community itself.

As educational developers we cannot control such a community; however, our hope is that this community of practice will have fostered self-directed continuous learning, that members will have continued to engage in reflective dialogue, to receive and provide support to fellow members, and to have stayed connected to new knowledge in education, not just in their content field.

Evaluation Strategy

An integrated evaluation strategy was used in this study, combining analysis of online questionnaires and analysis of transcripts of online discussions with module participants and tutors over the four-week duration of the module. Participants were very positive about most features of the module, especially the opportunity to experience e-learning as a student, the collaborative and reflective nature of the online activities, and the organization of the Web site; however, they requested longer time on the implementation of their own online modules and more time online to complete the activities.

I know the pitfalls of the e-learning process at different levels of student learning and how to strategize e-learning into my courses.

I think it was good to interact with WebCT as would a student; very useful to explore being an e-learner.

I got a lot of useful information regarding how students will learn online, how to design online learning, and how interaction online might work, all which was good.

Future Trends

When academic staff members are given professional development experiences that engage them in discovering educational technology, the stage is set for them to consider principles of instructional design and practice. In this institution, there has been a history of academic staff not adequately accessing currently available opportunities for professional development. This is being addressed by providing a greater variety of opportunities for such development and training and providing a greater variety of local and central activities.

To complement this module on e-learning, exemplars of other activities are specific workshops, refresher courses, sharing of experiences, mentoring from staff who have used Web-supported teaching, and the provision of templates with built-in guidelines for the creation of educationally-sound e-learning content. The programme will continue to focus on subject-specific authentic contexts and resulting workplace practices, as well as sharing the pooling of knowledge and resources among participants. Embedded within will be opportunities for participants to critically reflect on their learning as they progress through the module, and multiple teaching methods will be combined to demonstrate a broad display of the potential of the technology.

In addition, based on the success of this module and on a needs analysis conducted throughout the past academic year, a two year MSc in applied e-learning is currently being designed. This will continue to provide opportunities for online dialogue and reflection amongst participating staff.

Conclusion

This professional development module was designed to help participants learn from experience, to begin to integrate knowledge, and to think reflectively about using e-learning in their teaching practice. It sought to improve both teaching practice and student learning, with participating lecturers seeing the value of e-learning, and embracing it as part of their constructivist practices within their own teaching. Our hope is that their experience of a learner-centred blended learning environment will encourage lecturers to develop more learner-centred delivery models with their own students.

Esson, Johnson, and Vinson (2002) highlight that for too long there has been a focus on "training and development" rather than "professional development." There was ample opportunity within our institution for staff members to learn how to *use* the technology; in this module, we wanted to focus on how to *translate* these new skills into a quality learning experience for students. We believe that effective professional development requires more than skills training; it involves changes in attitude, values, and beliefs that develop confidence for ongoing learning. Constructing knowledge and developing necessary skills to use technology in order to impact learning and teaching does not happen overnight; rather, it becomes the product of a common vision and a set of experiences that prepare educators to embark together on a journey of learning.

References

Alexander, S., & Mckenzie, J. (1998). *An evaluation of information technology projects for university learning.* ACT: Commonwealth of Australia.

Alstete, J. (2000). Post-tenure faculty development: Building a system of faculty improvement and appreciation. ASHE *ERIC Higher Education Report, 27*(4).

Ambrose, L. (2001). *Learning Online Facilitation Online, Moving Online Conference II,* Gold Coast, Australia. Available online at http://flexiblelearning.net.au/leaders/fl_leaders/fl100/lyn_ambrose.htm

Anderson, T., Rourke, L., Garrison, D.R., & Archer, W. (2001). Assessing teaching presence in a computer conferencing context. *Journal of Asynchronous Learning Networks, 5*(2). Available online at www.aln.org/publications/jaln/v5n2/v5n2_anderson.asp

Bonk, C., & Cunningham, D.J. (1998). Searching for constructivist, learner-centred and sociocultural components for collaborative educational learning tools. In C. Bonk & K. King (Eds.), *Electronic collaborators: Learner-centered technologies for literacy, apprenticeship, and discourse.* New York: Erlbaum.

Coghlan, M. (2001). *eModeration— Managing a new language?* Paper presented at NET*Working 2001 Conference. Available online at www.chariot.net.au/~michaelc/nw2001/emo1d_newlang.htm

Dearn, J., Fraser, K., & Ryan, Y. (2002). *Professionalisation of university teaching: A global concern for education development.* Paper presented at the conference: Spheres of Influence: Ventures and Visions in Educational Development. University of Western Australia.

Devonshire, L., & Philip, R. (2001, September 21-24). *Managing innovation and change in flexible times: Reflecting on the role of the educational developer.* Paper presented at the Open and Distance Learning Association of Australia (ODLAA) 15th Biennial Forum, Sydney New South Wales, Australia.

Dobrovolny, J. (2003). *A model for self-paced technology-based training.* Available online at www.learningcircuits.org/2003/oct2003/dobrovolny.htm

Esson, K., Johnson, K., & Vinson, T. (2002). *Inquiry into the provision of public education in NSW.* Sydney: NSW Teachers Federation and Federation of P&C Associations of NSW.

Guthrie, H. (2003) (Ed.) *Online learning: Research findings.* Leabrook SA, Australia: NCVER (National Centre for Vocational Education Research).

Kempe, A. (2001). *Putting the teacher online.* Paper presented at NET*Working 2001 Conference. Available online at http://flexiblelearning.net.au/nw2001/01_attending/papers/4_6Kempe.doc

Lawler, P., & King, K.P. (2000). *Planning for effective faculty development: Using adult learning strategies.* Melbourne: Krieger.

Melczarek, R.J. (2000). *Technology education for teachers: A more self-directed approach.* Paper presented at the ACEC2000. Melbourne: Learning Technologies, Teaching and the Future of Schools.

Murphy, K., Smith, P., & Stacey, E. (2002). *Teaching presence in computer conferencing: lessons from the United States and Australia.* International conference on computers in education (ICCE 2002) proceedings. USA: IEEE Computer Society Press.

Nonnecke, B., & Preece, J. (2003). Silent participants: Getting to know lurkers better. In C. Leug & D. Fisher (Eds.), *From Usenet to CoWebs: Interacting with social information spaces* (pp. 110-132). Springer-Verlag: Amsterdam, Holland.

Oliver, R., & Herrington, J. (2003). Exploring technology-mediated learning from a pedagogical perspective. *Journal of Interactive Learning Environments, 11*(2), 111-126.

Salmon, G. (2000). *E-moderating: The key to teaching and learning online.* London: Kogan Page.

Scribbens, J. (2002). *Innovation through ILT.* Paper presented at the Association of Colleges Annual Conference.

Stacey, E. (2002). *Learning links online: Establishing constructivist and collaborative learning environments.* Paper presented at Untangling the Web: Establishing Learning Links Proceedings. Melbourne: ASET (The Australian Society for Educational Technology.

Wenger, E., McDermott, R., & Snyder, W. (2003). *Cultivating communities of practice.* Harvard: Business School Press.

Endnotes

[1]   A Postgraduate Programme in Third Level Learning and Teaching is also offered through the same school, and a small number of the academic staff who participated on this module had recently graduated from the institutional Postgraduate Certificate.

[2]   We estimated that this would take a minimum of one to three hours weekly. However, participant feedback indicated that it took longer to complete the activities.

[3]   As Nonnecke and Preece argue (2003, p. 122), "lurking" should not be seen as passive but an active involvement in reading and applying strategies to "determine what to read, delete or save"; "Lurking is not free-riding but a form of participation that is both acceptable and beneficial to most online groups." However, we needed to find a balance between personal reflection and participation, and social construction of knowledge in this formatively assessed module. By its nature, the

technology of a discussion board supports interactive communication and reflection; therefore, it was important to infuse this interaction with learning activities that supported good constructivist practice.

[4]   Comment from feedback of cohort members, 2004. All subsequent quoted comments are taken from this cohort.

[5]   In the next iteration of the module, it is planned that there will be less of a focus on discussion and more of an instructional design focus, again using activity-based learning as a framework. Then, participants can avail of creating subject-related materials and gain assistance from instructional technology experts. It is hoped that this will lay the foundation for self-directed instructional design in the future.

[6]   The final result was a level of tutor facilitation that was one of the most consistently favoured aspects of the module in feedback, with participants commending the "prompt and thorough responses," and remarking on the "excellence" of "facilitation and comments on our work." As one participant observed, "It was crucial to see that tutors were reading the posts regularly, and responding where appropriate."

[7]   Both said they would redo the module when they had more time to participate in discussion.

Chapter X

Staff Using an Institution-Wide VLE for Blended E-Learning:
Implications of Student Views

Paul Brett, University of Wolverhampton, UK

Abstract

This chapter reports on an investigation into the institution-wide use of a virtual learning environment (VLE) in a UK University. The aim was to collect information on staff use of the VLE from the student perspective. It was used to evaluate -and reformulate- current e-learning strategic initiatives aimed at enhancing the VLE-based student experience. The chapter examines how staff's use of the VLE is impacting on the student learning experience. Three aspects were investigated: (i) the amount, mode, and location of the use of the VLE; (ii) respondents' perceptions of the nature and value of their teachers' VLE support; and (iii) respondents' preferred uses of VLE-based learning. Analysis shows a predominantly information transmission mode of VLE use, with only some use of active learning. Respondents requested more VLE-based formative assessment opportunities. The chapter concludes with five considerations for strategic development of blended e-learning and with three for staff using VLEs.

Introduction

This chapter reports on the findings from, and discusses the implications of, a study of staff use of an institution's virtual learning environment (VLE). The study was undertaken to evaluate progress made on the institution's e-learning strategy and to inform the future direction of this strategy. The results of this study have implications for both staff involved with designing and implementing e-learning strategies, and also for all staff who are using a VLE in a blended learning context.

The use of e-learning has gained greater prominence recently through international and national policy declarations, initiatives and strategies. The European Union has an e-learning strategy "virtual campuses for all students" (2002). In the UK, the DfES (2005) and HEFEC (2005) both issued e-learning strategies, with HEFCE allocating more than £3 million pounds pro-rata across all English higher education institutions (HEIs) for 2005-2006, to enable development of e-learning strategies. The impact of an institution's e-learning strategy is examined in this chapter.

Background

One of the major digital tools featured in institutional implementation of e-learning in HE are VLEs. These have been on the market since 1998 and current high-profile brands include *WebCT*, *Blackboard*, *LearnWise*, *Moodle*, and *First Class*. VLEs are a Web-based software solution which offers teachers the ability to provide a variety of online learning tasks within the same piece of software. VLEs are being used by the majority of UK HEIs, most adopting a one institution, one VLE approach (JISC, 2003). What have institutions hoped would be among the outcomes of providing VLE-based e-learning? From an institutional perspective, staff use of the VLE has been seen as one way in which universities might meet some of the current challenges posed by mass education, through extending the quantity, quality, and flexibility of learning provision. The JISC study (2002, p. 17) of managed learning environments (of which VLEs form a part) lists the top five reasons for use as: enhancing the quality of teaching and learning; improving access to learning for students off-campus; widening participation/inclusiveness; meeting student expectations; and improving access to learning for part-time students. In addition, Aspden and Helm (2004) propose that VLE use also may assist with the retention of students through the creation of a sense of belonging to a community. VLEs are most commonly used to enhance the learning of those studying in a traditional face-to-face mode. This type of e-learning has been termed blended learning (Thorne, 2002; Jochems, Merrienboer, & Koper, 2003). This study examines staff's use of a VLE in blended learning mode for the purpose of extending the quantity, quality, and the flexibility of student learning.

Research into the Use and Benefits of E-Learning

Advocates of the use of technology as a means of enhancing student learning in higher education (Laurillard, 2002; Collis, 1996) propose that it can and should be used to foster deep approaches to learning (Marton & Säljö, 1997). Key mechanisms to achieve this might be collaborative peer-peer work, carried out through the electronic medium of asynchronous discussion tools (Salmon, 2000) or the exchange of documents and the creation of opportunities for reflection and self-assessment (Boud, 1995). Chickering and Erhmann (1996) set out seven principles of good practice for the use of technology in higher education which, if followed, would encourage students to use deep approaches to learning. (1) Encourages contacts between students and faculty; (2) develops reciprocity and cooperation among students; (3) uses active learning techniques; (4) gives prompt feedback; (5) emphasizes time on task; (6) communicates high expectations; and (7) respects diverse talents and ways of learning. It was hoped that this investigation of staff's use of the VLE would provide evidence of the pursuit of deep approaches to learning and embody these seven principles.

VLE software will typically offer teachers an amalgamation of different tools to support learning (Britain & Liber, 1999; Firdyiwek, 1999). These tools can potentially support individual and group-based learning through: (i) provision of electronic resources to support the content or knowledge base, through written text, different media, and Web links; (ii) opportunities for learners to engage in formative self-assessment through objective tests such as multiple choice questions with feedback; and (iii) enabling collaborative and discursive work between learners, and between learners and teachers through asynchronous discussion boards. Each of these three is seen to have specific learning benefits. The content-focused electronic resources enable staff to provide lecture notes, PowerPoint slides, reference materials, and resources rendered in a variety of media. The electronic medium of a VLE makes these permanently available. The benefits to learning of formative assessment with feedback are well documented, both in and outside of e-learning, for example Boud (1995), Cook (2001), and Black (1998). Researchers such as Charman (1998) have demonstrated improvements in student performance achieved through systematic use of computer-assisted formative assessment. Third, the collaborative asynchronous tools may promote increased communication between staff and students and between students and students. This, when used with the appropriate learning tasks, may promote constructivist learning (Laurillard, 2002; Johnson, 2001; Salmon, 2000; McConnell, 2000). The use of collaborative, discursive tasks, enacted via asynchronous discussion tools, may promote the higher order critical thinking and learning which university education seeks to develop. There is evidence then from such research that institutions' decisions to implement VLEs in order to enhance learning quality are well grounded.

At the level of the programme of study or the module, VLE-based learning can be integrated at any point along a continuum stretching from fully distant learning through to blended learning (blended learning being where VLE-based support supplements face-to-face learning). It is this use which predominates in UK HEIs and is the focus in this study. Although HEIs may have e-learning strategies (Stiles, 2002), they do not usually make the use of the VLE in blended learning a mandatory staff activity. Therefore, the decision as to if, and how, staff choose to use the VLE generally resides with individual teachers and course teams. There is usually access to staff development and technical support should staff wish to use them. The barriers to staff use of e-learning are well documented and include lack of time, deficit of PC skills, and little understanding of the rationale or appropriate pedagogies (e.g., Boys, 2002; McNaught, Kenny, Kennedy, & Lord, 1999). Staff's use of technology has been the main focus of much of the research in this area (Littlejohn & Stefani, 1999; Morón-García, 2000), rather than focusing on the student learning experience. A recent small-scale study by Bangert (2004) of the methodologies used by staff on one master's level Internet-based course did use a student-focused methodology. This found that students felt the course used constructivist methodology. The study reported here uses a similar student-focused methodology, however, it examines a whole institution's blended learning VLE activity.

The Study

The university used in the study is a modern, post 1992 institution with some 22,000 students. It is known for its education of those in the lower socio-economic groups and for achievements in widening participation in HE. The institution has had an e-learning strategy since 1999, which later became one of three strands in the university's learning and teaching strategy. The VLE has been available across the institution for staff to use with their students since 1999. It is an in-house application which is called WOLF. WOLF has all the toolsets found in other VLEs. Although progress in the use of the VLE was slow, as shown by Table 1, by 2004 some 1,950 different modules were using VLE to augment face-to-face learning. The creation of VLE-based module support was not done automatically by the technology. Staff needed to decide to use it and then create an area for their modules in the VLE. Axiomatically, similar increases occurred in the numbers of student users of the VLE.

This grew from 1,237 users in 1999 to 17,300 by the end of the academic year 2004. Clearly, there has been mass buy-in to the use of the VLE by both staff and students. This data provide some evidence to think that the university's e-learning strategic objectives had been achieved.

Aims of This Study

While the quantitative data (Table 1) indicate success in VLE use, more detailed evidence is needed to be able to assess whether the institution's two original strategic objectives have been achieved. There were two groups of research questions (1 and 2), designed to provide insights into the success of the two institutional strategic objectives and one group of questions (3) designed to inform the future direction of the strategy.

Table 1. Numbers of modules in the VLE and numbers of users of the VLE

Year	1999	2000	2001	2002	2003	2004
Number of modules with VLE support	46	132	423	1,191	1,782	1,958
Number of users of the VLE	1,237	2,546	4,321	10,569	15800	17,300

1.   What has been the impact made by staff on their students' learning through use of the VLE? How much use were staff making of the VLE? What number of modules were typically using the VLE to support learning? Related to this, and perhaps more importantly, what was the nature of the learning which staff were providing for students through the VLE? Which of the toolsets were most commonly used by staff and how might they relate to what has been described as the fostering of deep approaches to learning? The final subset of enquiry in this area focused on where the VLE was being used, on the university campus or was it extending the reach of learning into students' worlds outside the institution?

2.   How is staff's use of the VLE perceived to be assisting learning? The study sought to uncover whether perceptions of the VLE-based learning were aligned to deep or surface approaches. Were student experiences of staff pedagogy in the VLE likely to be encouraging deep approaches to learning, as found by Bangert (2004)? Were Chickering and Ehrmann's (1996) seven principles of good practice with technology manifest to VLE users?

3.   The third aspect of the study aimed to gain data to use in the planning of the future e-learning strategy. How would students wish staff to use the VLE to promote their learning in the future? These questions asked what types of VLE-mediated learning students saw as being of most benefit to their learning and how students wished to be engaging with VLE-based learning.

Methods

Data collection was through an anonymous online questionnaire which was available for all the university's students to complete. It was available for three weeks over November and December 2004. All University students were notified of its existence and the necessary URL through an e-mail. There was also a link to the questionnaire from the front page of the VLE. As an incentive to complete the questionnaire, those who did so were offered the chance to enter their e-mail into a draw for one of ten, £10 book tokens.

The questionnaire consisted of 12 questions including both closed and open-ended questions in order to furnish quantitative and qualitative data. Five questions were used to ascertain the extent, nature, and reach of the use of the VLE, as in 1 (Questions 1 to

5). There were five questions aimed at understanding respondents' perceptions of how the VLE was being used for learning, as in 2 (Questions 6 to 10). Finally, there were two questions which asked about respondents' preferences for VLE use, as in 3 (Questions 11 and 12).

Results

This section presents and discusses the data under the headings of the three research areas. The numbers of respondents completing each question declined as they worked their way through the questionnaire, 1,798 responses were received to the first question but only around 1,400 to the last. Of 1,798 responses to the questionnaire, 1,688 reported that they did use the VLE to help with their studies. This is 94.3% of the respondents. The data used are based on the responses of those who used the VLE.

How is Staff Use of the VLE affecting the Amount, Nature, and the Location of Students' Study?

The answers to Question 1 (Table 2) show that the majority of staff are using the VLE. 63% of the respondents reported access to VLE-based support for three or four modules. Responses to Question 2 show the majority of respondents (72%) accessed the VLE three

Table 2. Results from questions 1, 2, 3, and 4

Question No.	Results				
Q1. How many of your current four modules do you use WOLF?	0	1	2	3	4
	2.57%	12.27%	21.78%	20.89%	42.49%
	(n =43)	(n=205)	(n=364)	(n=349)	(n=710)
Q2. How much do you use WOLF (approximately)?	Every day	3 times a week	Once a week	A few times a month	Once a month or less
	30.25%	42.21%	17.87%	7.55%	2.11%
	(n=501)	(n=699)	(n=296)	(n=125)	(n=35)
Q3. How much do you use WOLF on or off campus?	Always on campus	Mostly on campus	50 / 50	Mostly off campus	Always off campus
	13.95%	13.68%	27.98%	31.67%	12.72%
	(n=204)	(n=200)	(n=409)	(n=463)	(n=186)
Q4. Would you like to use WOLF more or less with your modules?	More		Less		Same
	59.7%		2.3%		37.8%
	(n=924)		(n=36)		(n=585)

times a week or more. This indicates that the learning materials or tasks in the VLE are most probably of contemporary relevance. The responses to Question 3 show that the strategy seems to have been successful in extending the reach of module engagement beyond the campus. 43% of uses were reported to be mostly, or always, away from the campus. This was also confirmed by additional data taken from the log of server hits to the VLE, which showed that in 2004 37% of all its use was outside of the times 9 a.m. to 5 a.m. In addition, server hits also showed that 16% of all VLE use was at the weekends. Question 4 shows that VLE use is valued by respondents, with nearly 60% preferring to have more use of the VLE. Table 3 shows the types of staff uses being made of the VLE. The most frequent uses are for module guides, lecture notes, and PowerPoint slides. These are followed by assessment briefs and additional materials. This reaffirms what Stiles and Yorke (2003) depict as simple transfer of "traditional practice" into the VLE. Respondents report around 5% of staff use of the discursive tools, and a similar amount of use of the formative assessments tools. In summary, it appears that the strategic aim of extending the reach and amount of engagement with modules is showing success. However, the fundamental nature of this engagement seems to be information- or content-based, delivered through textual materials, rather than any uses of formative self-assessment or discussion work.

Respondent Perceptions of Staff VLE Use

This second group of questions was designed to elicit respondents' perceptions of the nature and the value of their teachers' VLE support. In particular, were respondents' perceptions of their VLE use aligned to deep approaches to study (Prosser & Trigwell,

Table 3. Responses to the question: What types of use of WOLF are mostly available for you? Please check all that apply.

Table 3 Responses to the question - What types of use of WOLF are mostly available for you? Please check all that apply.		
Type of use	No.	%
Video clips	168	2.58
Discussions on the Forum	329	5.05
PowerPoint slides	1015	15.59
Assessment briefs	748	11.49
Lecture notes	1267	19.46
Module guides	1299	19.95
Additional materials for the module	763	11.72
Web sites	555	8.52
Questions to help you assess your understanding e.g., multiple choice	367	5.64
Total Responses 1510		

Table 4. Responses to the questions about respondents' perceptions of their uses of the VLE

Table 4 Responses to the questions about respondents' perceptions of their uses of the VLE				
Question		.		Total
Q5. Do you think your use of WOLF has helped your success on modules?	Yes	No		
	79.7	20.28		1479
Q6. Has your use of WOLF encouraged you to spend more time on your studies?	Yes	No	Same	
	60.5	1.9	37.5	1408
Q7. Do you think your use of WOLF has encouraged more contact between you and your lecturers?	Yes	No	Same	
	43	24.5	32.4	1358
Q8. Do you think your use of WOLF has encouraged you to work together with your fellow students?	Yes	No		
	41.2	58.7		1322
Q9. Do you think your use of WOLF has helped you to learn from your fellow students?	Yes	No		
	36.5	63.4		1294

1999) and how did they perceive the VLE support to be contributing to their learning? Table 4 shows that nearly 80% of respondents thought that use of the VLE had contributed to their success in modules.

This may be taken to affirm the university's strategic decision to implement the VLE. To examine this further, the frequency-based qualitative analysis of the open-ended responses to the continuation of this question (If so, please tell us how/why?) is shown in Table 5.

It confirms that the majority of staff's VLE use involved information and documents, rather than learning tasks. Learners report that they are using information and documents to improve their engagement with face-to-face sessions, rather than as means to avoid attending. This course content is being used to either prepare for the face-to-face sessions, to aid note-taking, or to check back to see if the users may have missed anything important. This mode of use of such materials is evidenced in the qualitative analysis of those who responded under "Helps my understanding of face-to-face sessions" (n= 239). These responses also contained a total of 636 mentions of the word "lecture." This illustrates how widespread this teaching method is in the university, despite much evidence presented against its efficacy for promoting a deep approach to learning (Bligh, 2000; Gibbs, 1981). However, it does appear that the use of the VLE is assisting learners in their understanding of, and performance in, lectures.

In Question 2 (Table 4), 60% of respondents reported that their use of WOLF had encouraged them to spend more time in studying. This may indicate some success in the original strategic aim of enhancing the quality and effectiveness of learning and teaching, through encouraging more engagement with study. To a lesser extent the 36% of positive responses to the question "Do you think your use of WOLF has encouraged you to work together with your fellow students?" might indicate that Chickering and Erhmann's (1996) principle of reciprocity and cooperation has been in some way facilitated through

Table 5. Qualitative analysis of the open-ended responses to the question: Do you think WOLF has helped your success on modules? If so, please tell us how/why?

Categories of Responses	Nos.	%
Helps my understanding of face to face sessions	239	16
Non-specific comments that WOLF is useful	218	14
Gives basic module information (e.g., notes, module guide)	168	11
Supplies extra module related information	153	10
Supports my note-taking in face to face session/ lecture	107	7
When not been able to attend face to face sessions	102	6.2
Formative assessment opportunities	74	5.9
Ease of access via web	81	5.3
Time management / organisation of study	69	4.5
Increases interaction with my peers	57	3.7
Increased interaction from students to staff	36	2.4
Assessment/Improved exam success	32	2.1

the VLE. Likewise, the 41% positive responses to "Do you think your use of WOLF has helped you to learn from your fellow students?" indicate that at least some peer-peer learning has been fostered through use of the VLE. However, these two figures are in opposition to the 3.7% who reported increased interaction with peers (Table 5) and the 5% who reported use of discussions as a feature of their VLE areas (Table 3). Finally, there is evidence that the VLE has supported a degree of staff to student communication. 43% responded positively to the question "Do you think your use of WOLF has encouraged more contact between you and your lecturers?" following from Chickering and Erhmann's (1996) principle of encouraging contacts between students and faculty. In summary, from the respondents' perspectives the VLE is assisting their learning, enabling them to study more, and encouraging more contact between students and staff.

How Would Respondents Wish Staff to Use the VLE to Promote Their Learning in the Future?

Two sets of data address this issue. Nearly 36% of respondents wished to see more self-assessment work in the VLE (Table 6). Unsurprisingly, given the amount of lecture-related materials already in the VLE and the high importance assigned to these in respondents' perceptions of how the VLE has contributed to their success in modules, lecture notes ranked second. The desire for more of this was indicated by 34% of the respondents. 20% requested video clips of lectures, perhaps signalling that use of a variety of media would be welcome. Even though only 5% of respondents reported any use of discussion tasks in their current VLE, more than 9% would like this tool to be used or used more.

Table 6. Responses to the question: What types of learning materials would you like to see more of in WOLF?

Types of VLE activity	No	%
Discussion tasks to do with my colleagues	119	9.29%
Self-assessment questions e.g., multiple choice questions	461	35.99%
Lecture notes	441	34.43%
Video clips of lectures	260	20.3%
Total Responses	1281	

Further evidence about what the respondents might like to see taking place in the VLE was gathered from the open-ended responses to the Question 12, What changes to WOLF would encourage you to use it more? The most frequent request is for more content, perhaps unsurprising given that this has been the primary use of the VLE. Interestingly the request for more self-assessment opportunities is ranked second, in-line with the 36% figure reported in Table 6. There is evidence that respondents would like staff to use the VLE for more active learning, with the ranking of forum discussions in 6th place and learning tasks as 8th.

Limitations of the Study

At this stage, it is necessary to state some of the limitations of this study. It is a study based in only one university. Only 10% of the total users of the VLE completed the questionnaire. However, the average of 1,600 responses per question did provide a sizeable amount of data. The respondents were also self-selected as they decided themselves to answer the questions. A further limitation was that the number of responses to the questions slowly declined as respondents worked their way through the questionnaire.

Discussion

This section discusses the implications of this data in two distinct areas: (i) for the success of and the direction for the institutional e-learning strategy; and (ii) for staff who use a VLE to supplement their face-to-face teaching.

Implications for the Institution's E-Learning Strategy

Evaluation of Progress on Current Strategy

This study was undertaken to inform on progress with the current e-learning strategy in the three areas embodied in the three research questions. The data suggest the following answers to the three research questions. First, the VLE implementation had been successful in extending the reach and the amount of learning opportunities. In general, the nature of the learning was that of the exchange and consumption of information, with little collaborative work or formative assessment being provided by staff. Second, respondents' perceptions of the value of the VLE mirrored its use, in that it was valued as a lecture note resource. This seemed to be useful because it enhanced the efficacy of the face-to-face learning experiences. Third, respondents appeared to be aware of the potential uses of the VLE to beneficially enhance their learning, requesting more formative assessment and active learning tasks. Overall then, institution-wide implementation of a VLE would seem to have been a useful adjunct to the University's learning provision. These results have informed decision-making on a variety of strategic measures to encourage staff to use the VLE in ways which mirror student wishes and to adopt deep approaches to VLE-based learning which are more closely matched to good practice. These measures — in the use of student feedback, software changes, staff development, and methodologies in use in face-to-face teaching — are now described.

Strategic Change and the Use of Student Feedback

This study reiterates the importance of what Lea, Stephenson, and Troy (2003) advocate, which is that in a learner-centred teaching institution staff need to research learners' attitudes and perceptions of their learning experience. It is our view that we need to use such information to underpin the strategic development of our provision of student learning. The use of the VLE is one aspect of this. This chapter contends that acquiring, analysing, and acting upon information from students is in itself a necessary and essential part of the strategic evaluation and formation processes. In this study, the indications were of a non-alignment between some VLE uses, respondent preferences, and effective pedagogic practice, especially in the area of formative assessment. The evidence of this non-alignment, which was gained from consulting our learners, will be translated into the strategic planning aimed at resolving it. It is now planned to evaluate strategic progress using similar student-provided data on an annual basis. This methodology will now be embedded in the strategic review process, and it is recommended that such research be used in other institutions engaged in strategic reviews.

Strategic Change: Software

To address the minimal staff use of the VLE for active learning and formative assessment and in order to encourage greater use of such tasks, the VLE software is to be re-coded.

The institution is fortunate in that it owns and controls its VLE and is therefore able to do this. The aim of the recoding is twofold. First, it is to make the creation of such formative assessment by staff less complicated and necessitate fewer repetitive mouse clicks. Second, it aims to make staff more aware of the options to use formative assessment tasks and discursive activities each time they add materials to the VLE. This is being done through creating one initial entry screen. This screen offers a three way choice for staff about what they wish to create. These choices are: (i) collaborative activity; (ii) formative assessment; and (iii) content. The most common staff use of the VLE has been to upload documents, which could be done without encountering or considering the discursive tools or the formative assessment options. Staff now creating any learning tasks or materials in the VLE will have these three choices presented to them. From the student perspective this change now means that discursive activities may appear in the same screen area as any notes. The VLE software will also be re-engineered so as to enable staff to divide learning tasks and materials into weekly or topic areas so as to create more coherence to the materials and activities. This ability to be able to initiate such immediate changes to the VLE software so as to enhance staff and student use is one of the benefits of owning and controlling one's own VLE.

Staff Development

Clearly staff have embraced the VLE and most are using it with their students. The data, though, show that it is predominantly used for exchange of materials which are the content for modules. Moreover, respondents wanted more of this, which might indicate that they are being encouraged to adopt surface approaches to their learning. The staff development programme for VLE training is to be changed to add dedicated sessions in the use and benefits of both formative assessment and discussion tasks. These will also be available to staff in a mediated way, through the VLE itself. A further option being offered is intensive staff residential VLE courses, taking place over a period of two days and one night, based away from the University. Likewise, these will focus on use of discussion tasks and formative assessment. The outcomes of these residentials will be both a greater understanding of the pedagogy of the VLE and the supervised creation of VLE learning ready to use with students.

Staff Methodology Outside of the VLE

The final institutional observation which can be made from this data concerns the teaching methodologies being used by staff outside of the VLE context. It is apparent that the lecture is still widely used and recognised as a valid learning and teaching event. It may be that more use, outside of the VLE, could be made of active learning techniques which aim to encourage deeper student approaches to learning. Given that educational researchers generally agree that the lecture is not an overly productive methodology for encouraging deep approaches to learning, institutional staff development needs to be in place to increase understanding and use of a range of more beneficial methodologies for face-to-face sessions. There are plans to incorporate this in all of the Schools' staff development programmes.

Implications for Staff Using VLE-Based Blended Learning

The data also have three major implications for all staff who use, or intend to use, a VLE to support their students' learning. These three are now discussed.

Interplay between Use of the VLE and the Face-to-Face Sessions

The data showed that staff use of the VLE is primarily as a means to convey information, content, and text-based materials. It also showed how VLE users thought this was a valuable aid to their learning. The first implication is that staff need to consider such uses and be aware that students do value materials which relate to face-to-face teaching. These appear to free students from note-taking, allow them to participate more and at a better informed level, and provide some assurance that no essential aspects have been missed. The second implication then is that staff need to think through and plan how best they might use such VLE-based materials to support the face-to-face learning. If, as reported, respondents are accessing and becoming acquainted with materials and information prior to face-to-face sessions, then time could be freed in the face-to-face sessions to engage in learning tasks which use, apply, or develop this knowledge. This type of approach would make face-to-face sessions more active and assist in the development of deeper approaches to learning. It might also enable staff to focus in a more lengthy way on any issues which appear to be problematic for learners.

Extending the Range of VLE Tasks Used

The second implication for staff who use a VLE is that they need to familiarise themselves with and use the full range of the toolsets available. The value and place of formative assessment and its feedback has been well-documented (Boud, 1995; Biggs, 2003), and Cook (2001) demonstrates a correlation between exam performance and amount of computer-aided tests attempted. The data collected here show that this toolset was not frequently used by staff, and yet formative assessment was highly requested by respondents. After appropriate formative assessment questions, and more importantly their feedback, have been written, VLE based self-assessment can be offered without the need for staff marking. Computer-based formative assessments also can be repeated endlessly and serve for exam revision. The discursive tools were also little used, despite the weight of research indicating that asynchronous debate can be extremely useful for developing higher order cognitive skills. Staff then need to consider the range of VLE tools which exist and appropriately deploy a variety of them.

Staff to do the Same Research

This student-focused institution-wide survey has provided data which show how the VLE is being used. It also has shown how the uses of the VLE are seen by respondents as being useful to their learning. It also has highlighted how respondents might prefer that the VLE is used. The implication is that staff might consider using such an anonymous student-centred data collection methodology with their own cohorts. This would provide staff with their own feedback on their VLE uses and on the benefits and needs of individual cohorts. Staff can then use this information to tailor and enhance their VLE-based learning. There are a variety of actions which might possibly be signposted by such data gained at the local level. For example, staff will gain an understanding of the quality of their VLE learning materials and tasks, and can change those not thought useful. They may need to consider how best to use the interplay and overlap between electronic and face-to-face learning in creating opportunities to reach their modules' learning outcomes. They may be informed that the use of a different range and variety toolsets would be valued. Then, staff need to consider how they approach collecting feedback about their VLE offerings. An approach similar to the one used here, but at a micro level, is likely to be informative and useful.

Conclusion

In summary, this chapter has outlined a research study into the institutional use of a VLE. It was undertaken to inform as to the progress on, and to feed into the rearticulation of, the university's e-learning strategy. The data gained from the student-centred study highlighted some of the areas of success in the implementation of blended e-learning. It also revealed some areas in which strategy can be used to promote improved staff practice. Finally, five strategic actions which will arise from the study and three implications for staff using a VLE were described.

References

Aspden, L., & Helm, P. (2004). Making the connection in a blended learning environment. *Educational Media International, Special Issue: Distributed learning Environments, 41*(3), 245-252.

Bangert, A.W. (2004). The seven principles of good practice: A framework for evaluating on-line teaching. *The Internet and Higher Education, 7*(3), 217-232.

Black, P., & Wiliam, D. (1998). Inside the black box: Raising standards through classroom assessment. Retrieved March 24, 2005, from www.pdkintl.org/kappan/kbla9810.htm

Biggs, J. (2003). *Teaching for quality learning at university* (2nd ed). Milton Keynes: Open University Press.

Bligh, D. (2000). *What's the use of lectures?* San Francisco: Jossey-Bass.

Boud, D. (1995). *Enhancing learning through self-assessment.* London: Kogan Page.

Boys, J. (2002). *Managed learning environments, joined up systems and the problems of organisational change.* Retrieved March 24, 2005, from www.jisc.ac.uk/index.cfm?name=mle_related_joined. Bristol: JISC.

Britain, S., & Liber, O. (1999). *A framework for pedagogical evaluation of virtual learning environments.* A report presented to the Joint Information Systems Committee's Technology Applications Programme (JTAP). Retrieved March 24, 2005, from www.leeds.ac.uk/educol/documents/00001237.htm

Charman, D. (1998). Issues and impacts of using computer-based assessments (CBAs) for formative assessment. In S. Brown, P. Race, & J. Bull (Eds), *Computer-assisted assessment* (pp. 85-84). London: Kogan Page.

Chickering, A., & Ehrmann, S. (1996, October 3-6). Implementing the seven principles: Technology as lever. *AAHE Bulletin.* Retrieved March 24, 2005, from www.tltgroup.org/programs/seven.html

Collis, B. (1996). *Tele-learning in a digital world.* London: Thomson Computer Press.

Commission of the European Communities (2002). *eEurope 2005: An information society for all.* COM (2002) 263 final, Brussels, p. 13. Retrieved March 25, 2005, from http://europa.eu.int/information_society/eeurope/2002/news_library/documents/eeurope2005/eeurope2005_en.pdf

Cook, A. (2001). Assessing the use of flexible assessment. *Assessment and Evaluation in Higher Education, 26*(6), 539-549.

Firdyiwek, Y. (1999). Web-based courseware tools: Where is the pedagogy? *Educational Technology, 39*(1), 29-34.

Gibbs, G. (1981). *Twenty terrible reasons for lecturing.* Oxford: Routledge Falmer.

Higher Education Funding Council of England (2005). *HEFCE strategy for eLearning.* Bristol: UK. Retrieved March 27, 2005, from www.hefce.ac.uk/pubs/hefce/2005/05_12/

Johnson, C.M. (2001). Integrated elearning: Implications for pedagogy, technology and organization: A survey of current practice in online communities of practice. *The Internet and Higher Education, 4,* 45-60. Retrieved March 24, 2005, from www.learnloop.org/olc/johnsonOnlineCoP.pdf

Jochems, W., Merrienboer, J., & Koper, R. (Eds.) (2003). *Integrated elearning: Implications for pedagogy, technology and organisation.* London: Routledge Falmer.

Joint Information Systems Committee (2003). *Study of MLE Activity.* Bristol, UK. Retrieved March 28, 2005, from www.jisc.ac.uk/project_mle_activity.html

Laurillard, D. (2002). *Rethinking university teaching: A framework for the effective use of educational technology.* London: Routledge.

Lea, S., Stephenson, D., & Troy, J. (2003). Students' attitudes to student-centred learning: Beyond 'educational bulimia'? *Studies in Higher Education, 28*(3), 321-334.

Littlejohn, A., & Stefani, L. (1999). Effective use of communication and information technology: Bridging the skills gap. *Association for Learning Technology Journal, 7*(2), 66-76.

Marton, F., & Säljö, R. (1997). Approaches to learning. In F. Marton, D. Hounsell, & N.J. Entwistle (Eds.), *The experience of learning: Implications for teaching and studying in higher education* (2nd ed) (pp. 39-58). Edinburgh: Scottish Academic Press.

McConnell, D. (2000). *Implementing computer-supported cooperative learning*. London: Kogan Page.

McNaught, C., Kenny, J., Kennedy, P., & Lord, R. (1999). Developing and evaluating a university-wide online distributed learning system: The experience at RMIT University. *Educational Technology & Society, 2*(4), 70-81.

Morón-García, S. (2000). *Are virtual learning environments being used to facilitate and support student-centred learning in higher education?* Retrieved March 24, 2005, from www.informatics.susx.ac.uk/research/hct/hctw2001/papers/moron-garcia.pdf

Prosser, M., & Trigwell, K. (1999). *Understanding learning and teaching: The experience in higher education*. Milton Keynes: SRHE and Open University Press.

Salmon, G. (2000). *E-moderating*. London: Kogan Page.

Stiles, M., & Yorke, J. (2003, April 8). *Designing and implementing learning technology projects – A planned approach*. EFFECTS/Embedding Learning Technologies Seminar. Retrieved March 24, 2005, from www.staffs.ac.uk/COSE/cosenew/eltfinal.doc

Stiles, M. (2002). Strategic and pedagogic requirements for virtual learning in the context of widening participation. Retrieved March 24, 2005, from www.interdisciplinary.net/Stiles%20Paper.pdf

Thorne, K. (2002). *Blended learning: How to integrate online and traditional learning*. London: Kogan Page.

Trigwell, K., Prosser, M., & Waterhouse, F. (1999). Relations between teachers' approaches to teaching and students' approaches to learning. *Higher Education, 37*(2), 57-70.

Chapter XI

Teaching Large Groups:
Implementation of a Mixed Model

Andrea Chester, RMIT University, Australia

Andrew Francis, RMIT University, Australia

Abstract

This chapter describes the experiences of the authors as lecturers in the development of a new approach to teaching large groups of first-year undergraduate students in psychology. Drawing on constructivist and instructivist approaches, our mixed model incorporates both face-to-face and online components, capitalising on the relative strengths of each. Online material, with a strong emphasis on active engagement, is used to introduce students to the content before undertaking a more detailed reading of the key theoretical and research issues in the textbook. With this introduction to the material, lectures function as a "Review and Discussion" session rather than a didactic monologue. Outcomes of the mixed method suggest no adverse effects on student performance, and staff and students evaluate the new approach favourably. The mixed model approach to teaching large groups is one that might be adapted for a range of disciplines and content.

Introduction

Large group teaching is a reality for academics in a wide range of disciplines. Large lectures offer obvious economies of scale attractive to administrators. But it is not just administrators who appreciate the efficiencies of large groups. Instructors also acknowledge that large lectures help ensure consistency in the presentation of material and provide opportunities to conserve their time (Crull & Collins, 2004). Despite these putative advantages of large groups, they nevertheless present dilemmas for the staff that teach them. In a large group, where students may feel relatively anonymous, how can students best be engaged? How can lecturers working with large groups encourage active interaction? What kind of learning might we reasonably expect to take place in such a context?

Large group lectures have long been critiqued as problematic. Students comment that they often spend their time copying information, without understanding. However, devising a cost-efficient alternative has not been easy. Given reductions in funding to university departments and an increasing emphasis on economic rationalism, large group teaching appears to be an inevitable part of tertiary education. One of our challenges as educators is to develop pedagogical models that meet the needs of both students and staff engaged in large groupwork.

In this chapter, we describe the way we teach large groups (of between 150 to 350 students) in our first-year undergraduate psychology courses using a mixed method that combines online material with face-to-face (FTF) lectures and tutorials. In the late 1990s, we managed a group of content experts and Web designers and together we developed a new way of teaching our large first-year classes. The chapter examines the impetus for changing our traditional teaching methods and the factors underlying our decision to integrate online approaches. We also explore some of the difficulties we have encountered along the way and ways we have found to deal with the problems that have arisen. We begin with a description of the pedagogical theories that underpin our model.

Issues and Controversies: The Instructivist versus Constructivist Divide in Contemporary Academic Thought

The traditional two-hour "Sage on the Stage" lecture format has formed the basis of much of our teaching in the Division of Psychology at RMIT University, as it does in many universities around the world. The origins of the traditional lecture lie in the *instructivist approach*. Also referred to as direct instruction or explicit teaching, instructivism has been described as one-way communication from lecturer to student. The course content, typically specified through learning objectives, is determined by the teacher, who is in possession of this knowledge. At the heart of instructivism is a focus on the learning materials and their development, and on the role of the teacher in the learning process. Reflecting its behaviourist roots, learning objectives set by the instructor are seen as of paramount importance in guiding the student through the world. Students are rewarded (with grades or positive feedback) when they meet these objectives by responding in appropriate ways.

Instructivism, and transmission models of education in general, have been the target of considerable debate in education (e.g., Duffy & Kirkley, 2004; Ramsden, 1992). Instructivism has been criticized for focusing on the delivery of content at the expense of student processes. In contemporary pedagogy, instructivism has been almost entirely replaced with the rhetoric of *constructivism* and *situated cognition*. These related models of learning acknowledge the active role of the learner and the situated nature of "sense making." At the heart of constructivism and building on cognitivist principles is a focus on the learner as creator of his or her own knowledge system. Through interaction with their environment, which will include learning opportunities created by teachers, the student "constructs, investigates, and modifies his or her own model of the world in an iterative fashion" (Low, 2003, p. 6). Students entertain hypotheses about the world, test them, and then construct understandings and synthesize conceptual structures.

Despite the rhetoric that constructivist models have superseded instructivism, instructivist approaches persist in tertiary education. Research suggests that even in relatively small classes of between 15 to 40 students, taught by staff highly regarded for their teaching, students typically make few active contributions to the direction of the class, spending less than 3% of the time talking (Nunn, 1996). In addition, only one-quarter of the students in the class are involved in that interaction. Therefore, interaction may involve little more than answering specific questions or asking questions that are then answered by the teacher (Duffy & Kirkley, 2004). In small universities, participation rates are only a little higher. For example, Smith (1983) noted that in small American colleges, 14% of class time involves student talk.

How is this empirical picture of practice to be reconciled with the contemporary rhetoric of teaching and learning? The introduction of constructivist pedagogy has made considerable waves in the theoretical literature, but it appears to have had little impact on the way many academics teach. Koljatic (2000), for example, compared participation rates over a 15-year period to 1997 in North American universities and noted no change. Our own anecdotal evidence suggests that even when instructors support constructivist ideals, the implementation of these is often fraught and teachers frequently revert to more comfortable, instructivist techniques.

A Theoretical Solution: Combining Instructivism and Constructivism

In developing our model for teaching large groups, we were cognisant of the instructivist framework that already operated both within the teaching team and in the larger program into which we teach. Rather than seeking to completely replace that approach, we began

Table 1. The QAIT model of teaching and learning

Principle	Description
1. Quality	The degree to which information or skills are presented so that students can easily learn them.
2. Appropriateness	The degree to which the teacher makes sure that students are ready to learn a new lesson (that is, they have the necessary skills and knowledge to learn it) but have not already learned the lesson.
3. Incentive	The degree to which the teacher makes sure that students are motivated to work on instructional tasks and to learn the material being presented.
4. Time	The degree to which students are given enough time to learn the material being taught.

to explore the putative strengths of instructivism and examine ways we might integrate these with constructivist principles.

Robert Slavin (1995) developed a model of teaching and learning based on instructivist principles. In this model, known as the QAIT model, effective instruction is described as dependent on four components: quality, appropriateness, incentive, and time (see Table 1).

Quality of instruction includes the extent to which the content makes sense to the students. Instructional quality is related to clearly specified learning objectives, coordination of content and assessment, and informal tasks to check mastery of concepts (Slavin, 1995).

One of the most pressing dilemmas facing those who teach large groups is the diversity of prior knowledge and experience represented. Together with differences in learning preferences and rate, these issues impact on the *appropriateness* of the instruction. Teaching "to the lowest common denominator" is generally frowned upon, but in reality it is often difficult to find a pace of learning appropriate for all students in a group. Slavin (1995) notes that each of the common strategies used to deal with issues of appropriateness, such as grouping students or individualised instruction, has associated limitations.

Incentive refers to the students' motivation to study the material. "If students want to know something, they will be more likely to exert the necessary effort to learn it" (Slavin, 1995, p. 5). Research has suggested that motivation is enhanced by quality and appropriateness of instruction (Slavin, 1995).

Although learning takes *time*, increases in time spent teaching are not necessarily associated with enhanced learning. Time is comprised not just of allocated time (i.e., the time scheduled by the lecturer for interaction with the students) but also engaged time (i.e., the time students spend on learning tasks). As a rough rule of thumb, we recommend that students spend double the contact hours in their preparation for a course. Although there is no clear relationship between allocated time and student achievement, positive relationships have been noted between engaged time and achievement (Slavin, 1995).

Table 2. Low's (2003) principles of good teaching and learning

1. Good learning is based on existing knowledge and experience.
2. Good learning is idiosyncratic.
3. Good learning is goal-oriented.
4. Good learning is social.
5. Good learning depends on self-awareness.
6. Good learning is active.

These four elements were fundamental to our thinking as the model developed. Also central was our understanding of the psychological concepts of learning and memory and the impact of e-learning contexts.

Low (2003) identifies six points which have emerged from research undertaken in the last decade or so of what makes for good e-learning (and learning in general), and which also reflects a mixture of pedagogical approaches and psychological schools of thought. Low's six principles (Table 2) underpin our own model of large group teaching and have shaped the approach we developed. Although Low's principles arise from a constructivist approach, they have much in common with the QAIT instructive model and offer a useful way to integrate the two approaches to teaching and learning.

First, Low (2003) suggests that learning is based on *existing knowledge and experience*. All students, regardless of their age and background, come with prior knowledge, and it is when new knowledge is integrated into and activates these existing systems of the learner that good learning is most likely to occur.

Second, learning is *idiosyncratic*. Each individual, and the knowledge, experience, and learning preferences they bring to the learning situation, is unique. Learning programmes must acknowledge this by permitting different paths through, and perspectives on, the curriculum. These two factors impact on Slavin's principle of appropriateness. As instructors, we must develop pedagogical models that can accommodate considerable diversity.

Third, Low (2003) argues that good learning is *goal-oriented*. Learners, especially adult learners, have specific objectives in mind when they approach their learning. As Slavin (2003) notes, students have varying motivations for study. These objectives typically relate to their functioning, activities, and problem-solving in real-world environments. While Low's emphasis is on the learner, also important are the objectives of the course, which, though typically established by the instructor, as Slavin (1995) notes, may also operate within a broader context of accrediting and professional bodies.

Fourth, learning, according to Low, is a *social activity*. Students construct and use knowledge in a social context. Increasingly, research supports the importance of social interaction in the teaching and learning experience. Learning communities that encour-age collaborative learning have a range of advantages including increased active engagement and participation of students, enhanced quality of education, increased retention, and a greater sense of responsibility for one's own learning as well as the learning of others (Harris, 2003; Tinto, 2000). This point overlaps with Slavin's principle of time. Learning is not, even in instructivist models, simply a matter of what transpires between instructor and student, but involves the students' active engagement with others, often outside class time.

Fifth, learning depends on *self-awareness*. Good learning facilitates a sense of responsibility for one's learning. Inherent in that is an appreciation not only of what and why one is learning, but how one learns. This meta-cognitive process, not explicitly alluded to by Slavin (1995), allows students to engage in self-reflective practices, exploring their own learning preferences.

Finally, Low (2003) argues that good learning is *active*. Good teaching encourages students to engage with material actively, processing information at deep rather than shallow levels, and apply it in ways that are meaningfully constructed by the student. It is now widely accepted that simply putting one's lecture notes online does not constitute good teaching practice (Kinney, 2001). Rather, online educators are encouraged to devise ways to encourage active interaction with material.

When well designed, online learning is associated with a range of benefits. These benefits have been widely discussed. They include enhanced accessibility for both students and staff, the potential to meet a range of learning styles through the use of video, audio, and other media, and increases in active learning (Lynch, 2002). On this final point, Lynch argues that the efficiency of online learning permits more time for active engagement with the material and enhanced opportunities for application. Therefore, e-learning holds the potential to address a range of issues identified as important for good learning by both instructivist and constructivist models.

The problems associated with online learning have been less articulated than the benefits, but these include the related issues of retention and motivation. High dropout rates have been noted across a range of e-learning courses, and considerable research has examined the reasons for low retention (Lynch, 2002). Frustration and lack of experience with technology are thought to account for some of the dropouts. As Little and Francis (2004) note, "students who have difficulty using the technology may find themselves spending more time learning how to use the technology, and less time actually accessing and understanding the content." In order to address these issues, student orientation courses can be used to increase student familiarity both with the technology and the process of learning in an online environment. When used, these courses have decreased dropout rates by as much as 50% (Lynch, 2002).

Motivation and isolation also impact on online learning. It has been noted that one of the motivations for attending FTF classes is meeting and interacting with other students (Ashby & Broughan, 2000). Constructivist approaches underscore the importance of social interaction in learning. But this interaction is not confined to the classroom. Harris (2004) notes the value that students place on the casual interactions that happen before and after FTF classes and chance meetings around campus. These interactions are important in developing relationships and building support networks. Although social interaction is possible online, meaningful interaction typically takes longer online than off-line (Walther, 1996), and even when opportunities are provided for discussion, such as threaded discussions and chat, uptake can be difficult to facilitate (Ashby & Broughan, 2002).

Combining FTF with online delivery offers instructors the chance to take the best of e-learning and avoid some of the disadvantages. Our own model for first-year courses is such a mixed model, using both online and FTF modalities. In addition, the model draws on both instructivist and constructivist principles. This mixed model reflects the needs and capabilities of teachers and students, as well as the historical context from which the particular learning situation has evolved.

The Practical Solution: Mixed Method Model for Large Group Teaching and Learning

Institutional Background

The two courses in our division which represented the fledgling use of online technologies for teaching and learning in the mid-1990s were developed by two separate teaching teams, for different purposes, and were more or less at opposite ends of the instructivist-constructivist continuum. One of these courses was entitled "Psychology and the Computer Science Interface" and broadly covered aspects of artificial intelligence, and individual and group (social and organisational) processes with respect to human interactions with computers. Enrolment in this course comprised largely computer science and engineering students, and the pedagogical approach was solidly instructivist. Content was literally delivered to students via largely textual materials, e-mailed for convenience and later developed into a (still largely text-based) Web site. Activities such as a gender-based Turing Test utilised newsgroup technology to allow students to interact with each other, the instructors, and any learning confederates.

The other course was entitled "The Psychology of Cyberspace" and aimed to develop understandings of the social construction of self and community by allowing students to assume identities and then interact over a semester period in a MOO environment. As such the processes in which the students engage, exploring and building the virtual space, developing relationships, and experimenting with self-presentations, become the content of the course. The course is modelled on constructivist ideals.

The implementation of both these courses (and of a committee to oversee and steer further online developments) in our own division preceded the subsequent development in the late 1990s of a faculty-wide, flexible delivery plan and "Flexible Delivery Leadership Group." The primary overt aims of the faculty plan were (1) to develop a more "student-centred" approach to teaching and learning throughout the faculty as part of a broader institutional initiative (although the exact definition and theoretical/empirical rationale for this approach was generally unstated and left for participant and non-participant academics to draw their own conclusions about), and (2) to enable the development of a more "flexible teaching and learning environment" (although again the exact nature and meaning of "flexible learning" was somewhat vaguely, if at all, defined). An implicit assumption of these new flexible teaching and learning environments was that they would in some way result in cost efficiencies for the university at large, and perhaps entail less FTF contact hours for academics at the coalface.

Thus, while staff were subsequently sufficiently engaged with and instructed in the use of the technologies such as BlackBoard and CourseInfo, which would allow these developments (whatever they might be) to occur and be delivered, the overall rationale for the new pedagogical ethos remained ambiguous and subject to wide and animated debate. University-enforced divisional funding to support academics in the development of flexible learning materials via time-release from other duties was preferentially tied to projects which entailed the use of technology, even though this was not formally part of the understandings of the term "flexible delivery" offered by faculties. Given the pedagogically diverse offerings of "flexible learning" already available in our own division, the lack of clear definition and rationale at higher organisational levels fueled debate between academic colleagues even further.

At least three distinct groups of academics emerged. The first was comprised largely of the "early starters" with respect to the use of technology in teaching. This group was genuinely enthused with the prospect for change and improvement that this might bring to existing models of teaching and learning. The second group comprised those who were perhaps less informed and interested in these developments but who, in the face of clear signals from the university that involvement in such activities would be increasingly related to rewards (including relief from FTF teaching, increased opportunity to work from a home environment, and promotional opportunity) were willing to approach and be led into new developments. The third group consisted of those who might best be described as the "old guard," and who for reasons generally inarticulate refused to be party to any change in teaching methods. Typically, these individuals adopted a policy of non-participation in such activities, which has led to some reasonable difficulties in the enrichment and subsequent implementation of those courses and programs requiring teams of academics working with a common purpose, such as our large group, first-year psychology courses.

Elements of the Mixed Method Model

We have used technology to enable students and staff to participate in a blended model which bridges instructivist and constructivist principles. The pedagogical model we have adopted is illustrated in Figure 1.

Students undertake a FTF orientation session, designed to familiarise them with the components of the course and the way they operate in a unified whole. Additionally, this information is embedded in the online material (Figure 2). Each of these elements and how they relate to our model of teaching and learning will now be discussed.

Online material: The online material is the starting point for each topic. Individual lecturers use the online material to provide their own overview and synthesis of the topic. This overview begins with learning objectives which are tested in multiple-choice tests

Figure 1. Current pedagogical model used for introductory psychology courses (LO, learning objective)

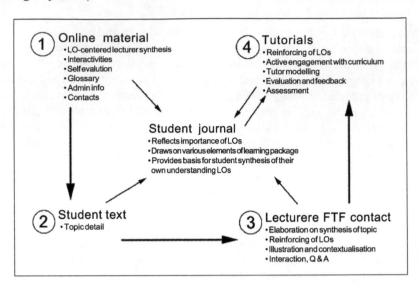

Figure 2. Interactive description of the course components

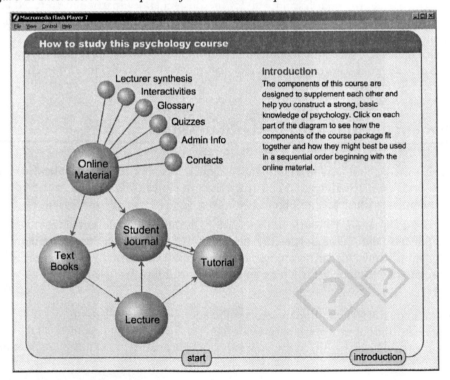

Figure 3. Example of interactive exercise

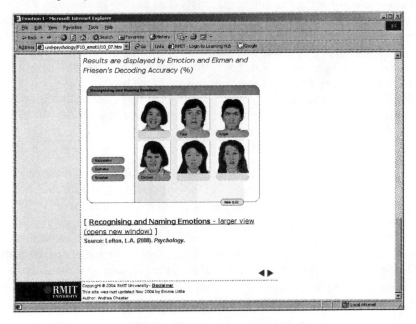

available both as a pre-test at the beginning of the module and a post-test at the end of the module. Lecturers, therefore, have the opportunity to structure material and contextualise the curriculum. These facets of the online material reflect Salvin's principle of *quality*.

Given the paucity of general psychology texts written by Australian academics for Australian students (and subsequent reliance on American texts) and the wide variety of student discipline cohorts that undertake studies in psychology, the appropriate contextualisation of curriculum by academics with well-developed understandings of the topic areas is a particularly salient issue.

In our initial version, large amounts of text were put online. Staff wrote as if they were creating an online textbook. The aim of the online material was not, however, to replace the textbook, as we already have a text that works well. Therefore, subsequent iterations have refined the text, reducing the time students spent passively reading and increasing active engagement by emphasising the constructivist principle of *interaction*. Each topic includes at least one activity, based on key research in the area as well as animated diagrams, videos, and a small number of Web links.[1]

An example of an interactive activity is provided in Figure 3. This interactivity is based on a classic study on the recognition of emotional expressions. Students identify emotional expressions and drag and drop appropriate emotional labels. When the exercise is complete, the students' responses are corrected and the data obtained by the cohort are collated and compared with that obtained by the original researchers.

The textbook: Having studied with the lecturer's own overview synthesis and structuring of the topic content via the online materials, and having begun their own journal process with respect to the learning objectives for the topic, students are advised to read relevant sections of the textbook next. The aim of this element of the learning package is to enable students to gain detailed information about the topic *before* attending the FTF lecture. It is emphasised to students that they should work through the online materials before reading the text so that their reading of the text will be more directed and focussed in relation to the learning objectives, and so that understandings developed will be within the conceptual and contextual framework recommended by the lecturer, as opposed to that provided by the text.

FTF lectures: Our initial trial-and-error implementation of the newly developed online materials was simply as an add-on to existing teaching elements, with no change to lecture format. The response from students to this implementation was mixed, with a major proportion of students indicating they would prefer not to have to use the online materials as they simply added to their workload. On the basis of this feedback, subsequent alteration of the lecture format, coupled with clear and explicit induction to the pedagogical rationale and teaching model, we were aiming for has led to better understanding and acceptance.

The most important change to the traditional form of delivery has been what occurs when the lecturer and students are together in the lecture theatre. One of the major outcomes of the new pedagogical model we adopted involved the facilitation of a higher quality interaction between lecturer and students during the time that would usually be occupied by a traditional instructivist extended monologue and note-taking session. We have halved our lecture time to one-hour each week and use the time as a "Review and Discussion," exploring key issues and addressing student questions.

We ask our students to prepare for the lecture by working through the online material for the week. There is nothing new about getting students to read a text or set of articles before coming to a lecture so that some prior knowledge and preparation may be assumed by the lecturer in their subsequent content delivery. However, our approach has been to formally and explicitly change the purpose and form of the interaction that occurs between lecturer and student in the lecture theatre. As previously stated, the purpose of the lecture is no longer to "transmit information" as such, but to provide an opportunity for the lecturer to engage students in an interaction which explores the essential concepts and learning objectives of the topic at a more advanced level and which permits students to participate in the generation of understandings.

As an example, in a session which relates to the topics of stress and anxiety, the lecturer may ask students to reflect upon any stressful experiences they may have had in the last week and then write a word or two about them in their journal. Responses are then volunteered from the class to be used as a basis for discussion of the various types of stress. Further class-elicited responses regarding perceptions of stressors and methods for improving resilience to stress provide an opportunity for students to contribute to the generation of knowledge in a group setting and to relate new understandings to their own experiences. With respect to Low's (2003) principles of good teaching and learning, these types of interactions therefore enable students to *bring their own knowledge and experience* to bear on the subject matter at hand, in a *social environment* where experiences can be shared and compared and with the instructor who is best qualified to *actively engage* students in high quality interactions regarding the curriculum.

The tutorials: There is a research methods component to the tutorial stream which typically occupies half of the two-hour block and which consists of students engaging with tutors to solve problems and test understandings of statistical and design concepts. Student evaluations are typically positive of these activities, and there was no change to the way this part of the tutorials was conducted. The other half of the tutorial time is devoted to curriculum topic-related review and activities, and we also felt that there was little need to alter this part of the tutorial program. However, some changes did occur in the types of activities planned by lecturers as a flow on from the altered interaction occurring in lectures insofar as, having had the opportunity to communicate directly and in a more extended way with the content expert in the lecture setting, it was felt that students could subsequently be expected to interact with each other from a higher starting level in tute sessions under the guidance and modelling of a tutor. This aspect of the model draws on Slavin's (1995) notion of appropriateness.

The journal: Students are given explicit advice on the setting up and use of their student journal at the first lecture. They are advised to prepare their loose-leafed journal for each forthcoming week by first using each of the learning objectives provided as a heading for a separate piece of A4 notepaper prior to beginning to study the online materials. Having examined these learning objectives and committed them to paper as headings, they are then advised to begin working through the overview, synthesis, interactivities, and tests provided online, and to make notes on any understandings they develop under each of these learning objective headings as appropriate. Subsequently, students read the relevant sections of the psychology text and/or other materials provided by the lecturer, and add any further information and understandings under relevant headings. The students bring this journal with them when they engage in the next element of the learning package, which is their interaction with the lecturer. Similar to the previous two elements, they include any additional or further understandings they develop during this session under the appropriate learning objective headings. Students bring their journal to the tutorials and these understandings are shared with the class, active engagement with curriculum occurs and, once again, any new understandings derived from this element of the teaching package are included in the journal. Finally, students are advised that once they have participated in all four elements of the teaching package that they should then, with reference to the information and understandings they have developed from these various elements, write their own synthesis of the information in the form of a response to each learning objective. This summary-synthesis (which may consist of 3 to 5 lines), and the extended notes which provide the basis for it, enable an efficient revision process for the end of semester exam.

The course consists of three FTF contact hours each week. The study-time weighting of non-contact components is not specified and the amount of time students spend on each aspect will be determined by factors including learning style, content of the module, and a range of individual variables.

Table 3. Student evaluation of mixed mode delivery (N = 122)

Online Material	Mean (maximum possible score of 10)
Readability of text on screen	8.4
Quality of images	8.2
Organisation	8.1
Clarity of language	8.1
Ease of navigation	8.0
Educational value of content	8.0
Usefulness of images	7.9

Evaluation of the Mixed Model

Our mixed-method model was designed to encourage a more active and conscious involvement of students in their learning process, both within the shortened "Review and Discussion" sessions with lecturers and in tutorials, as well as in their own individual study time. Quantitative data suggest we have had some success. Student performance, as indicated by end of semester multiple-choice exam marks, has not suffered since implementation of the online material. No significant decrease was noted in marks after the implementation of the mixed model. In addition, a significant correlation exists between the use of the online material and final grades, $r(125) = .42, p < .001$. No significant difference in the number of dropouts has been noted since the introduction of the mixed-method model.

In one area, the research methods component, grades were significantly enhanced, following the implementation of the mixed-method model, $t(186) = -4.2, p < .001$. This is an interesting finding because research methods are not taught online, but rather are primarily taught through a series of self-directed readings. How then might the mixed-method approach have influenced learning in this area? One possible explanation is that the mixed-method approach provides students with a structured way of learning more independently and thus has generalised to the research methods component. Tracking the impact of these less tangible, but important, outcomes of the method is one of our next tasks as we continue to evaluate the course.

Of particular interest is whether students use the components as we intended them to be used. Self-reports indicate that in one cohort of 122 students, 60% regularly accessed the online material prior to the lecture. Although this use by nearly two-thirds of the students is pleasing, there is still a sizable group with whom we need to work further.

Additional data suggest high levels of student satisfaction. Student evaluations are summarised in Table 3 and indicate generally high levels of satisfaction with their teaching and learning experiences, with mean scores of around 8 out of 10 on all aspects. Qualitative feedback suggests that students appreciate the flexibility in time and place that is afforded by the package. Comments such as the following are common: "I like the flexibility in studying this way." Therefore, the model appears to have enhanced the learning process in these first-year courses.

Interviews with staff suggest a range of benefits associated with the mixed model. Perceived advantages include a shorter lecture time, which encourages succinct communication of the key issues and enhanced student attention.

Only having an hour in which to communicate my ideas has really sharpened my teaching. I have to think carefully about what to focus on.

The model has also provided opportunities for both students and staff to reflect on the evolving teaching and learning process. As one staff member who was involved in both the development and delivery of the course commented:

Writing the online material and then teaching it has given me a chance to rethink what I do in my teaching, how I engage students and interact with them.

In addition, the multi-modal/multi-component style of delivery is perceived to cater to a wide range of teaching and learning preferences.

From the students' perspective, limitations typically involve technical constraints (such as difficulty playing some interactivities) and access issues. Online experience and confidence can impact on students' use of the online components, as can access to the Internet. Not all students flourish in this course, and it may be that some students prefer to be passive learners or fail to understand the intention of the new teaching and learning strategy. The integration of a more thorough orientation session to familiarise students with the online components of the course is part of our approach to address these issues. Hopefully, this strategy will also increase the number of students who work through the online material prior to the lecture.

Evaluations of the initial implementation conducted to determine how students were using the online component revealed that the majority (up to 70% in one cohort) were printing the materials and then reading the print version. Reasons for doing so related to difficulties reading information on the screen and the cost of Internet connections. Our most recent revisions to the online material have involved reducing the content and increasing interaction, encouraging students to engage with the material online. We have also produced a CD-ROM version of the material available to all students at low cost.

Although the mixed-method model caters to a range of preferred styles in both teachers and learners, we have learned that an explicit, agreed framework is required so that staff are not working at cross-purposes. To this end, both students and staff need to be clearly and universally apprised of the methods of teaching and learning to be utilised in a course, as well as how each component functions within the broader pedagogical model.

Developing a major resource, like the online material described, takes considerable time, commitment to purpose and ideal, and several iterations. These were flagship courses and received preferential resourcing, however, the success of the project also was dependent on the enthusiasm and additional time of the staff involved. Projects need to build in time for revision. There is a need therefore for appropriate administrative, economic, and cultural structures within which these types of developments can occur: Staff cannot be expected to undertake these developments in addition to current loads or without the support, collaboration, and encouragement of colleagues.

Academics need to work as part of a team for fruitful and efficient developments to occur. The team should include reference groups of various stakeholders (staff, students, institution), professional multimedia developers working closely with content experts, all within in a context of strong team leadership and clear goals.

References

Ashby, R., & Broughan, C. (2002). Factors affecting students' use of virtual learning environments. *Psychology Learning and Teaching, 2,* 140-141.

Crull, S.R., & Collins, S.M. (2004). Adapting traditions: Teaching research methods in a large class setting. *Teaching Sociology, 32*(2), 206-213.

Duffy, T.M., & Kirkley, J.R. (2004). Learning theory and pedagogy applied in distance learning: The case of Cardean University. In T.M. Duffy & J.R. Kirkley (Eds.), *Learned-centered theory and practice in distance education: Cases from higher education* (pp. 107-141). NJ: Lawrence Erlbaum.

Harris, L. (2003). *Turning space into place: A community of online learners seek mutual support in a familiar environment of their own making.* Proceedings of the ASCILITE conference. Retrieved January 20, 2005, from www.ascilite.org.au/conferences/adelaide03/docs/pdf/215.pdf

Jolliffe, A., Ritter, J., & Stevens, D. (2001). *The online learning handbook: Developing and using Web-based learning.* London: Kogan Page.

Kinney, N.E. (2001). A guide to design and testing in online psychology courses. *Psychology Teaching and Learning, 4,* 103-125.

Koljatic, M. (2000). *A longitudinal assessment of college student perceptions of good practices in undergraduate education.* Unpublished doctoral dissertation, Indiana University.

Little, E., & Francis, A. (2004, in press). Teaching introductory psychology through flexible delivery: A case study. *Psychology Learning and Teaching.*

Low, C. (2003). Educational psychology and the nature of e-learning. *Training Journal,* January, 4-7.

Lynch, M.M. (2002). *The online educator: A guide to creating the virtual classroom.* London: Routledge.

Nicols, D. (1998). Using research on learning to improve teaching practices in higher education. In C. Rust (Ed.), *Improving student learning: Improving students as learners* (pp. 86-96). Oxford: Oxford Centre for Staff and Learning Development.

Nunn, C.E. (1996). Discussion in the college classroom. *Journal of Higher Education, 67,* 243-266.

Ramsden, M. (1992). *Learning to teach in higher education*. London: Routledge.

Slavin, R. (1995). A model of effective instruction. *The Educational Forum, 59,* 166-176. Retrieved March 18, 2005, from www.successforall.net/resource/research/modeleffect.htm

Smith, D.G. (1993). Instruction and outcomes in an undergraduate setting. In C.L. Ellner & C.P. Barnes (Eds.), *Studies in college teaching* (pp. 86-116). Lexington, MA: Heath.

Tinto, V. (2000). Learning better together: The impact of learning communities on student success in higher education. *Journal of Institutional Research, 9*(1), 48-53.

Walther, J.B. (1996). Computer-mediated communication: Impersonal, interpersonal, and hyperpersonal interaction. *Communication Research, 23,* 3-43.

Endnote

[1] Feedback from students after the first trial suggested that most Web links were not followed. Therefore, we edited the number, leaving only one or two per topic.

Chapter XII

Patchwork E-Dialogues in the Professional Development of New Teachers

Moira Hulme, University of Wolverhampton, UK

Julie Hughes, University of Wolverhampton, UK

Abstract

The encouragement of reflective writing within professional learning programmes is not new (Moon, 2003; Bolton, 2001; Winter, 1999). Electronic technologies, however, afford exciting opportunities to develop this practice to support participative and collaborative learning beyond barriers of time and place. This chapter explores the value of asynchronous dialogue in creating and sustaining communities of practice, with particular emphasis on the role of the e-mentor.

Introduction

In this chapter, we outline our commitment to and experiences of engaging in e-learning dialogue as teacher educators on an initial teacher education programme, PGCE (Post-graduate Certificate in Education), for the post-compulsory sector. Our approach to technology draws on social constructivist learning theory (Wenger, 1998) and is informed by critical, post-structuralist, and feminist epistemologies (Derrida, 1987; Deleuze & Guattari, 1987; Lather, 1991). Although we write here in relation to teacher education, we feel our commitment to person-centred practice development is equally applicable to other professional education and CPD settings within social work, nursing, and clinical education. In this chapter, we explain the importance of dialogue in professional learning, especially as a strategy in helping students make sense of de-contextualised propositional knowledge — the "language of abstraction" (Clandinin & Connolly, 1995). We emphasis the importance of "bringing the self" into discussions of professional practice and explain our choice of the "patchwork text" as a device for representing professional development (Winter, 2003). Technology lends itself particularly well to patchwork writing, and we describe the potential of VLEs (software products designed to support teaching and learning across the Internet) and Webfolios (electronic versions of portfolios) in supporting dialogue and reflection for developmental purposes (on course) and for presenting aspects of summative achievement (on completion). The challenges and issues involved in the changing roles of the tutor and student in e-dialogue are raised. In particular we discuss the role of the e-mentor in reducing learner dependency on "expert," external knowledge and in helping students construct their own understanding by framing and reframing the "dilemmas" of professional practice. As portfolio-building is becoming a routinised practice in personal and professional development planning, we conclude by reflecting on the importance of pedagogy in framing institutional approaches to Webfolio design.

Initial teacher education has been subject to intense and significant change in the last 10 years. In the compulsory sector, the Teacher Training Agency (TTA) developed an increasingly specific and prescriptive framework of national standards for qualified teacher status (QTS) between 1994 and 1998. In the post-compulsory sector, the Further Education National Training Organisation (FENTO) standards for learning and teaching were introduced in 2000, followed by a minimum core curriculum for literacy, language, and numeracy inclusion in 2003. Some writers have provided an optimistic reading of these changes as the advent of a "re-professionalised" teaching force (McCulloch, Helsby, & Knight, 2000), the welcome development of a "new professionalism" (Hargreaves, 1994), even a "transformative professionalism" (Sachs, 2003). Critics, however, suggest the standards (and the associated development of standardised pedagogies) represent "pedagogical deskilling" (Robertson, 1996). Reynolds (1999) argues, "Because of their specificity the standards, rather than providing insight into teaching, can be interpreted as an attempt to formularise classroom practice or to 'standardise' it in the narrowest sense" (p. 253).

One of the limitations of stripping down the craft skills involved in teaching and re-formulating practice in detailed lists of performance outcomes is a failure to encourage creative or flexible approaches (Furlong et al., 2000; Mahony & Hextall, 2000). Curriculum specifications, teaching standards, and assessment practices can be seen as abstract knowledge, de-contextualised and de-personalised. Clandinin and Connolly (1995) have lamented the ceaseless cascade of "official knowledge" pouring into schools and colleges: "There are no people, events, or things — only words cut off from their origins" (p.10). It is important that teacher educators help new teachers make sense of this "language of abstraction." One strategy is to blend the language of abstraction with the "language of story." Beginning teachers can be helped to make sense of propositional, non-temporal, generic knowledge through shared stories that are personal and contextual. Technology provides powerful tools that can support dialogue and collaboration, and in doing so, promote critically reflective practice across a community of peers (Brookfield, 1988; Schon, 1992).

The use of technology discussed here proceeds from a rejection of behaviourist notions of technologies as "drill and test" conditioning devices. The emerging literature on online learning foregrounds the social and communicative dimensions of learning (Laurillard, 2002; Salmon, 2000; Mason, 1998) and affords attention to the changing role of the tutor from the hierarchical relations of "subject expert" to the facilitator of person-centred teaching (Rogers, 1983). Our approach to professional learning is informed by Freire's (1970) rejection of the "banking concept" of learning. Our approach to mentoring and assessment seeks to accommodate the storying of professional growth conceived as a creative narrative of the process of "becoming." We feel that we are "becoming" e-mentors of new teachers in a "messy" and shifting space where "being in the swim" (Salmon, 2000) is at times a challenging, isolating, and highly rewarding activity.

Our commitment to "bringing teachers back in," as a central focus of professional learning, reflects a shift over the last 10 years in writing about professional knowledge and practice (Goodson, 1995, 2003). Chamberlayne, Bornat, and Wengraf (2000) have described this shift as a "subjective or cultural turn in which personal and social meanings as bases of action gain greater prominence" (p. 1). Issues of subjectivity and identity formation are brought to the fore. We employ De Lauretis' (1986) definition of subjectivity as "patterns by which experiential and emotional contexts, feelings, images, and memories are organised to form one's self-image, one's sense of self and others, and our possibilities of existence" (p. 5). As teacher educators this involves a reconfiguration of our role not simply in coaching learners in the technical skills of effective practice, but as "helping to bring the individual self into the school" (Chanfrault-Duchet, 2004, p. 279). This involves the displacement of functionalist constructions of "expertise" as a set of de-contextualised transferable skills, with a focus on the *active* construction of teacher knowledge and professional identity. Reflection is an important tool in this developmental journey.

Using Online Dialogue Journals to Develop Reflective Abilities

Reflective journal writing is an established technique in the professional education of teachers. Journaling can help beginning teachers make connections between specific, situated aspects of practice and general principles of professional knowledge. Thus, it has a potentially important role to play in countering the artificial separation of theory from practice. Dewey (1933) defined reflection as the "active, persistent, and careful consideration of any belief or supposed form of knowledge in the light of the grounds that support it and the further conclusions to which it tends" (p. 9). Being reflective involves postponing judgement, re-exploring firmly held beliefs, interrogating assumptions, and a readiness to embrace challenges to one's identity. The use of dialogue journals — written reflective exchanges between two or more people — originated in teacher education for schools in the 1980s (Moon, 2003). Research since then has in general been restricted to their use in teacher education for the compulsory sector and in teaching English as a foreign language (TEFL) and teaching English to speakers of other languages (TESOL). It is not a common practice in teacher education for the post compulsory sector, although it is adopted in many other professional vocational programmes such as nurse education (Bolton, 2001) and counselling.

The increasing availability of networked computers in the workplace and at home has extended opportunities for dialogue. There is an emerging body of research, reviewed by Becta (2004), that suggests that VLEs have value in supporting collaboration and dialogue within initial teacher education. Two main (and related) benefits are an increase in participation rates in discussions that are held online (Pilkington, Bennett, & Vaughan, 2000) and gains in confidence by participants (Selinger, 1997). Research by Tanner and Jones (2000) suggests that student teachers who might be reticent in face-to-face forums are more confident and participate at higher rates within online environments. In addition, research by Gibbs (1999) has indicated that students who engage in collaborative group work online show "higher levels of deep learning and significantly higher levels of strategic learning" (p. 221). Gibbs suggests that using VLEs in this way can promote "deeper conceptual understanding" (p. 221). A study of the use of FirstClass for communication purposes with PGCE students at the Open University by Kyriakidou (1999) found that online dialogue contributed to the professional development of students by facilitating reflective discussion. Similarly, Russell (2000) found that WebCT discussion with pre-service teachers significantly increased their level of reflection and preparedness to engage in routine self-study.

We have used online dialogue journals to support and sustain collaborative work among postgraduate students on supervised teaching practice in further education colleges in the West Midlands. Computer-mediated communication (CMC) was employed to overcome problems of spatial and temporal dislocation that are barriers to shared reflection and peer support during the practicum. Asynchronous dialogue helps to alleviate the sense of dislocation (from each other) and fragmentation (in terms of subject identity and curriculum studies) that can be experienced during lengthy periods of college-based placements. A virtual learning environment (VLE) afforded greater access to participants' writing and facilitated dialogue through reflective tasks supported by e-mentoring. The centrality of critical reflection and dialogue in this strategy reflects the Vygotskian notion that verbalisation is integral to the creative development of understanding and the development of more "inclusive" and "integrative" professional practice (Mezirow, 1991). The emphasis on collaborative ways of working is also an attempt to interrupt socialisation into occupational cultures characterised by fragmentation and a lack of trust. Many writers have discussed the need to break down "barriers to professionalism" (Kowalski, 1995) such as "privatism" in teaching (Hargreaves, 1994) and "balkanised cultures" (Fullan & Hargreaves, 1991, p. 52). By engaging in collaborative work in the pre-service stage, a greater commitment to collegiality may be fostered.

Collaborative Activities in the Formation of the Patchwork Text

A "patchwork text" is defined by Richard Winter (1999) as "a general name for written texts where the unifying structure is not simply a linear narrative but a series of loosely linked pieces illustrating a theme or gradually building up a set of perspectives" (p. 67). In addition to using a conventional VLE to support file sharing and discussion across a *whole group* of learners, we have experimented with an evolving Webfolio or e-portfolio as a *personal* record and instrument for professional development. Our use of an e-portfolio is designed to embrace and encourage a range of communicative styles and voices. It offers a radical departure from the bulky text-only versions of earlier "teaching files" that encouraged only the archiving of statements of evidence relating to the achievement of prescribed standards of competence. Significantly, we aim to go beyond simply offering "digitised versions of traditional assignments" (Oliver & Shaw, 2003, p. 64). The approach to portfolio building suggested here is sensitive to Knowles' (1998, p 23) critique of the "chain-like" sequencing of formal learning events. Rather than offering a "painting by numbers" script for assessment, the e-portfolio, used in this way, supports learners in fashioning or fabricating their *own* narrative of their personal and professional development — "mystory."

Moreover, the medium supports the inclusion of non-text patches. It offers additional tools for creativity and extends the range of possibilities for presenting students' achievements to different audiences. Multimedia offer opportunities for visual representations such as still photography, video, and graphics, which have traditionally been neglected by "disciplines of words" (Mead, 1995). This is particularly useful in representing aspects of practice that are difficult to capture in literary form. Digital photography can be used to support reflection. Images can be collated and used by groups to generate culture collages that interrogate organisational contexts and encourage beginning teachers to form indigenous readings of workplace culture. Images are effective elicitation tools. In this way, Banks (2001) argues, "photographs effectively exercise agency, causing people to do and think things they had forgotten, or to see things they had always known in a new way" (p. 95). We have used metaphoric imagery as a way of explicating the tacit knowledge that informs practice. Metaphors are not simply descriptive or decorative uses of language. The selection of images tells us something about the processes of sense making and meaning making. Metaphor selections represent acts of cognition and suggest the parameters or interpretative frameworks within which and through which individuals act. By using a variety of techniques, beginning teachers can construct a spiral narrative that reflects their struggle to make sense of the new roles and identities that they must negotiate. These might include writing a personal learning autobiography, the collective construction of culture collage, photo montage, photo essays, critical incident analysis, and the shared storying of experience.

Learner-Centredness:
Ownership and Sharing of Assets

An important dimension in the use of e-portfolios is the capacity to support and encourage self-direction. The communicative and collaborative functions of e-portfolio offer an informal, open learning space in which the learner makes the choices over form and content. The author selects which materials and discussions to share with members of a self-selected community of peers. "Asset sharing" is dynamic and relational rather than imposed and static. The sharing of assets is a communicative act in which the writers and asset sharers decide if their chosen community may view, comment, copy, or collaborate in their reflection. Within the community, dialogue is voluntary and grafted onto earlier assets.

For some members of the community this was a challenging and intrusive activity. Early asset sharing was coupled with ground rules set within face-to-face seminars and formative written feedback. The netiquette for asset sharing and dialogue was based upon this agreed communicative framework of respect and reciprocity. As e-mentors, we would argue that this blended approach to establishing reflective e-dialogues allows for early "online socialization" (Salmon, 2000), bridging the real and virtual dialogue spaces created within the PGCE. Establishing the role of the e-mentor and e-peer was an interesting early transitionary dialogue. All dialogue included here is as it appears within the internal assets; the emphasis is upon exchange and creating a safe and comfortable space using the technology rather than adhering to the rules governing academic literacies.

JH: How do you feel about me intruding in your digital learning space?

Is my e-voice the same or different to my gel pen voice?

Claire E: I don't feel like you are intruding but providing another form of contact (or safety net). It is good to know there is someone else at the end of the virtual tunnel who knows which track I am heading along!!! As for your e-voice, in this era of technology advancement, I still like to see the gel pen voice and keep a "real" contact.

Claire W: Julie, your e-voice does seem different to me — your sentences are a lot longer and it makes the comments sound more like a train of thought.

Elaine: It is almost like Internet chatrooms where you do not see the person at the other end of your cyber chat.

Jane: I'm fine with you sharing my digital learning space — it's dead handy in that I can access my work from anywhere and read your comments and not just from home on my work in box files! I think it's pretty much like having a conversation over e-mail or msn. I think that in general when something is written it can be understood differently than if someone had said something. People just have to be careful with what they write.

Elaine: I have no problem with you intruding into my digital space, although I always feel like Internet spies may be watching whenever I send anything via the Internet. Paranoid I know. Similarly to Jane's comment, this reminds me a lot of msn messenger, where I usually end up rambling.

Valentina: Hi. I don't mind you intruding my learning space, as Jane said it is like talking via e-mail or msn. I don't mind talking to people on pace, but I'm still not convinced about this e-portfolio. I find it so much easier on paper!!!!

It was important to recognise the students' existing transferable skills and literacies and to foreground their fears of the medium. The early e-portfolio exchanges mimicked traditional teacher-student turn taking models, and as e-mentors, we were keen for the knowledge construction to be discursive and unravelled by offering multiple points of departure.

From "Assessment Careers" to "Learning Careers": The Role of the E-Mentor

One of the issues that we are confronted with in our encouragement of dialogue journals is the perceived constraint of summative assessment (Ecclestone & Pryor, 2003). Does the requirement of assessment de-legitimate the author's voice? Here, we need to consider asymmetrical power relations and appreciate the act of writing as social practice. There are clear tensions between the development of perspectives that afford attention and significance to learner "voice" and the value of experiential and reflective learning, and assessment and accountability regimes based on performance to prescribed standards. Next, the following account by Tom takes us back to the dilemma we face in our work with students schooled to play the game of assessment. Students are often keen to re-engage in a long established game of cat and mouse with the "assessor." Success in their learning careers thus far may well have been premised on compliance with the teacher's game of "guess what's in my head," the Bakhtinian (1986) notion of "ventriloquation."

As far as I can imagine, the sharing of journals with a mentor and later one's STE group leads to a pressure to self-censor. One's own history becomes a field of omission and recreation, where feelings on the past are reconstructed to be palatable to others....In the interests of being seen to "develop," it is needed to maintain a "constructive" and perhaps "empathetic" view... The reflective journal — seen in a critical light — could be a way of reconstructing the past to make it seem as if things can be done by the teacher about circumstances we cannot really change, and eventually reconstructing the "teacher self" to take on personal responsibility for social, cultural, and political problems.

Tom's reading of reflective practice alludes not to empowerment but to subjugation, an imposition of a particular "regime of truth." The act of writing in a learning journal is seen as a "confessional" practice designed to form particular identities. Through the discourse of "evidence-based practice" and re-formed versions of "teacher professionalism," individuals are constructed as "modern" professionals, with an attendant set of preferred characteristics. In his journal entry, Tom shows us how a critical pedagogy might be subsumed within a modernisation agenda that is characterised by individualisation rather than collegiality, where compliance rather than creativity is valued. As students struggle to take on the "authoritative voice" of the tutor/course leader/programme ethos, the e-mentor's task is the persistent refusal to occupy entrenched positions and to act as critical friend and co-learner. Through such resistance the learner is denied the comfort zone of mimicry and the myth of ready-made solutions for each emergent dilemma.

Reflective practice entails an embracing of: uncertainty as to what you are doing and where you are going; confidence to search for something when we have no idea what it is; the letting go of the security blanket of needing answers. This kind of work leads to more searching questions, the opening of fascinating avenues to explore, but few secure answers. (Bolton, 2001, p. 15)

The role of the e-mentor is not to pass judgement and close avenues for debate, but to open these out through the use of reflective prompts and dialogue across the group. The online environment offers a secure and disembodied environment within which to assert, explore, question, and reformulate responses to professional practice scenarios. An important role of the e-mentor lies in sustaining the discussion, preventing premature closure, returning to explore incidents again from a different perspective; inviting the re-reading of incidents through an alternative lens. All the extracts presented here are snatches of text taken from dialogue between tutor and students. The following response is an attempt to encourage Karen to re-visit an assessment of a critical incident in which a discussion activity in an evening class of adult learners had escalated "out of control." Karen's reading of the event concluded with a series of questions exploring how she might re-assert her control over the situation by silencing contributions. In her writing, Karen confronts the feelings she has about "losing" the power struggle in "her" domain of the classroom. Through dialogue, an attempt is made to postpone an initial defensive reaction and step back to look again at the dynamics and assumptions involved in this encounter.

You don't really want to stop the students contributing, do you? How else might you phrase this question? What strategies can you use to balance a need to control the parameters of discussion and encourage active participation and engagement? What options are available to you? Your journal also addresses the issue of working with adult learners and how you feel about working with "peers." What issues does this raise for you? How are you working through this? What does this say about your developing teacher identity?

The following response to Sofiah is taken from a longer series of prompts encouraging a re-exploration of an incident where classroom management concerns culminated in an angry rebuke of "disengaged" learners. The journal provides a space to explore interpretations from other perspectives. Consideration of the learners' stories of these encounters is useful in making sense of incidents and learning from them. The questions try to encourage practical deliberation but also personal reflection.

Have you profiled these learners? What background information might be helpful here? Did these students interrupt with "inappropriate" comments or low level/ disruptive chatter among themselves? For what other reasons might students not participate in set tasks, other than "laziness"? Do these students always sit together and follow a settled pattern in classes? How can you avoid unprofitable anger taking over next time? Were you angry because you felt "undermined" or because the students disrupted others or because they risk "failure" in the exam? Looking back, how do you now feel about this incident? How have you made sense of it? What, if anything, would you now do differently?

From Tutor-Mediated Toward Community-Supported Learning

A dialogic approach to developing reflection and reflective writing is driven by a social and political responsibility to encourage all new teachers to enter their profession as *re*inscribers and *de*constructors of text. The shift of addressivity afforded by the e-portfolio supports multiple narration. Participatory narratives are progressively determined by and within the group. This suggests the building of a sustainable community independent of the academic e-mentor; a community which offers the possibility of sustained critique, support, and networking beyond the realms of their PGCE. The following example contains anonymous dialogue as the subject is sensitive but is increasingly common in the PCE sector.

1.   The groups were all very distressed and in some cases quite angry about the treatment they had received from the teacher and from the college itself, and wanted to take legal action. They have all paid for the course and some are relying on

passing for university entrance in September. I left at the end of the session feeling very pressured — the group were relying on me to get them through a years worth of work in eight weeks… The main thing I have had to take out of this whole mess is the need to draw professional boundaries for myself. I want to help as much as I can with any class, particularly classes that have been badly treated, but there is only so much available that I can give, and if I push myself too hard, then there is a danger all of my classes will suffer because of it. I am a bit disappointed by some of the attitudes I have encountered and the treatment this class have and are receiving, but I cannot get too involved while I have so much else going on, so I will just have to offer my best support in the time available.

2.   It's not fair that the curriculum manager should expect so much from you and put this kind of pressure on you into saying yes you would take over the class for extra lessons…I think it must have taken you a lot to say no to your manager, but you should take pride in your ability to have dealt with the situation so successfully and professionally. You can't and shouldn't feel pressured into doing something that you can't phsyically do, as much as you may want to. I think sometimes you just have to detach yourself from such situations and realise that you have done your best and it is now up to the college to sort the problem out.

3.   Thanks for the support — I think you are right, if there is one thing that upsets students it is uncertainty and being messed about.

4.   Firstly, congratulations on not bowing to the pressure of taking yet another group, they can be quite sneaky at the college with getting you to teach other classes.

5.   X's journal this week really highlights the difficulty of deciding where you draw the line regarding your responsibilities to your students, and X's comments seem to reflect a similar thing. I've found a similar thing in my own placement: There's always more that you can do for your students, and you really need to keep everything in perspective and make sure you prioritise in a way that suits your students AND you. Well done on standing up for yourself — you can't take responsibility for fitting a whole year's teaching into a few weeks!

6.   I think it was very brave of you to stand firm on this situation and you were right to do so. I think I would have backed down and took on the high workload and sunk in the process. Considering you were worried about your acertiveness, I think this shows how you have developed.

These exchanges between a "becoming" group of new teachers demonstrate a politicised knowingness of the "games" of further education. They did not look to the e-mentor as "expert" to guide and inform, but instead to each other for community support, reciprocity, and challenge. Student 1 does not disclose with ease within the classroom situation — hence, the references to growing assertiveness, yet the horizontal nomadic spaces offered within the e-portfolio allowed this student to narrate her reflective story in a highly self-aware manner. Student 4 speaks to and for the group as a collective drawing together or "weaving" the strands of the patchwork within pressing professional discourses (Salmon, 2000). This evidences the possibilities for a discursive space for resistance sustained by and through new technologies.

What Issues are Involved in Introducing E-Dialogue in Teacher Education?

Our engagement with technology in promoting dialogue has raised the following issues:

1. **Struggle to legitimate informal horizontal dialogue in professional education programmes:** The movement to "outcomes-based education" creates a pull toward valorising visible and measurable demonstrations of achieved competence. Informal learning is slippery and constant and does not deliver itself up to scrutiny and judgement easily. The development of self-knowledge and situated understanding, using the tools of dialogue and narrative, are not easily reducible to the convenience of "chunk and check" assessment.

2. **Input into the design of learning environments that will accommodate dialogical practice:** The dual cultures of technology and pedagogy need to be utilised fully in the design of learning environments capable of advancing the development of an online constructivist pedagogy. Communication, collaboration, and dialogue are essential features of e-portfolio design. Webfolios should not be conceived as repositories from which student assets might be harvested for summative assessment. A content-driven model undervalues the significant processes involved in the development of professional judgement.

3. **Resistance from strategic learners anxious to "play the game" of assessment:** The close and sustained conversations encouraged through sharing stories work against the considerable pressures to mimic the "authoritative voice" of the tutor as "expert." The absence of a compulsion to share diminishes the likelihood of inauthentic contributions to discussions. The capacity of learners to direct asset sharing is an important consideration in challenging students' long-held notions about "writing for assessment."

4. **Training needs of learners and mentors — technical and pedagogical:** Innovation within teaching and learning requires embedding through a process of backward mapping, rather than "rolling out" (or "over" colleagues and students). Technological literacy and a commitment/readiness to change require support and time, rather than hasty imposition. There are clear resourcing implications here. The history of curriculum reform is littered with short-term, top-down experiments that falter and fail with the withdrawal of the "pioneer" or "champion." Sustained exposure to the technology is necessary from induction. The fostering of a non-threatening and supportive community takes time. The regular and autonomous sharing of writing is likely to take a minimum of three months to establish.

5. **Equitable access to resources away from the university campus:** Technological tools, like any other learning resource, need to be assessed to ensure equitable access for all learners. Initial assessment of learners' needs should consider variations in the availability and speed of online access, as well as levels of competence and confidence in using tools without (and/or beyond initial) face-to-face support. It is important that technological "advances" do not further exacer-

bate the problems faced by learners who are already disadvantaged or excluded by traditional academic practices.

6. **Issues in tutors' online participation in (and assessment of) digital portfolios:** There is no denying the considerable demands placed on tutors who choose to engage in online mentoring. The requirement to fade from the discussion and enable learners to eventually support a self-sustaining online community is important. The tutor might aim to progressively recede to the less visible and less interventionist role of moderator and lurker. Not all tutors will feel comfortable with this re-positioning and may struggle to cede "authority," ownership, and control to the learner. Dialogue journals strengthen the relationship between tutor and learners. However, what may initially begin as mundane and superficial readings as writers "suss out"' the environment, can quickly become absorbing, fascinating, and exhausting to maintain.

7. **Interoperability of e-portfolio across platforms (on graduation):** Accreditation is one step in a teaching career, it is not an end in itself. Professional learning does not cease with the award of a formal teaching qualification. In designing platforms to support e-portfolio building, it is important to look to the future. Will the learner be able to continue to compile and/or showcase their journey, the ongoing story of their professional development? Will potential employers be able to access updated versions? How can the conversations be sustained in new contexts of practice as fresh challenges emerge?

Future Trends

VLEs have been available from the mid-1990s and can be used at a number of levels for a range of different purposes (O'Leary, 2002). The challenge facing educationists in the future is to move from the simple "content and support model" of VLE use (Mason, 1998) toward more "integrated" models that support interaction and collaboration. The former require only the archiving of course materials and the transmission of information to passive recipients. The latter requires much higher levels of learner participation as decision-maker and contributor. Learning environments informed by constructivist approaches need to offer open-ended, exploratory, authentic learning tasks that encourage meta-cognition and enhance student motivation. Unlike objectivist pedagogy that sees the learner as passive receptor of de-contextualised knowledge, constructivist approaches accentuate the knowers "construction" of reality as a purposive act. This extended version of VLE use is not simply about giving information but also coming to understand through collaboration and dialogue (Laurillard, 2001; Bohm, 1996). The use of dialogue journals is one strategy in this move from transmissionist to collaborative uses of information and learning technologies (ILT).

The use of Webfolios to record and support personal development is developing rapidly in post-compulsory education and within performance management structures in employment. The Dearing Report (DfEE, 1997) first recommended the use of progress files for recording transcripts of student achievement and as "a means by which students can monitor, build, and reflect upon their personal development." Since 2005, it is mandatory for all undergraduate students to be given an opportunity to engage in personal development planning (PDP) (Quality Assurance Agency, 2001). A systematic review of evidence by Gough et al. (2003) indicates that PDP has a positive effect on learning, attainment, and approaches to learning. PDP software packages are being piloted at a growing number of higher education institutions and include: LUSID (Liverpool University Student Interactive Database); RAPID (Recording Academic, Professional, and Individual Development) at Loughborough University; the "Matrix" of skills, abilities, and qualities at the University of East Anglia; e-PARS (Personal Academic Record System) at Nottingham University; the PESCA portfolio (Personal, Employment, Social, Career, and Academic) at Exeter University; "Keynote" at Nottingham Trent University; and "PebblePAD" at the University of Wolverhampton. The development of electronic portfolios is likely to be a growing market as higher education institutions meet the challenge of introducing PDP across all undergraduate programmes.

Portfolio building is becoming a formal requirement of representation and progression in teaching from the career entry stage through to headship. Portfolios were advocated by the Teacher Training Agency in 2003 with the introduction of the Career Entry and Development Profile. The Department for Education and Science (2001) directed all teachers in the compulsory sector to develop a professional portfolio as an integral part of the emerging performance management culture. Since the introduction of the upper pay scale in September 2000, 259,000 teachers have collated portfolio evidence to pass the threshold standards. The professionalisation of the workforce for the post-compulsory sector is anxiously pursuing this model. Professional development portfolios are now increasingly used to prepare for job interviews, threshold, or Advanced Skills Teacher (AST) applications, and performance review/appraisal meetings. There will be a growing demand for software packages that support the profiling of personal development and achievement from initial accreditation into employment within teaching and related occupational fields such as health and social care.

The availability of a greater range of technologies generally available among the student population also opens up new and exciting opportunities. In the past, educators have been constrained by the limits of commercial courseware authoring systems. A challenge for the future will be to harness the new technologies that are increasingly available in the public domain to support learning. Future developments are likely to include greater incorporation of mobile learning (i.e., hand-held devices, personal digital assistants, smart phones, podcasting) within blended learning. This is evidenced in students inclusion of artefacts in their Webfolios captured using camera phones or produced with alternative software (e.g., Flash produced photo essays). Such developments further extend the possibilities of using image and audio files as reflective prompts and portfolio assets.

Conclusion

In this chapter, we have considered the use of online dialogue within VLE and Webfolio environments to support the development of reflective abilities in beginning teachers.

Our approach is informed by a concern to place the teacher at the centre of professional development. We have used technology to support the "storying" of professional development and the sharing of stories, critical incidents, and personal narratives across a community of peers.

In our experience, online dialogue journals supported within VLE workgroup folders have many strengths. They can accommodate collaborative working — shared resources and dialogue — at a distance. Dispersed groups in workplace settings are able to stay in touch quickly and easily. A single posting can reach every group member. Access permissions can be used to create a secure and safe space for discussion. A transparent record of activity is developed through discussion threads that can be moderated. In addition, the asynchronous nature of communication allows time for learners to formulate considered responses. In considering this use of technology, however, it is also important to acknowledge the potential problems. Asynchronous communication may prove a barrier to the formation of group identity with learners who do not meet face-to-face. Online "talk" lacks the visual cues that support face-to-face communication, and this may prove an obstacle for some learners. The location of workgroup folders within a formal learning environment, hosted by the "assessing" institution, may distort communication. There are cost implications for learners in accessing online activities away from the university campus, and this may raise equity issues. It is also important to recognise that learners need to develop the skills and motivation to participate effectively in an online learning environment. Not all learners will elect to participate to the same extent. There is also the danger that more assertive online "voices" may stifle discussion and influence the contributions of others.

Many of these potential problems, however, can be managed by ensuring that initial activities are exploratory but tightly framed. It is important to offer strong support in the early stages of online socialisation (Salmon, 2000). Initial tasks need to be carefully scaffolded and adequate consideration given to the provision of induction activities to promote early engagement. Conducting a skills audit (including previous experience of computer-mediated communication (CMC) in formal and informal learning contexts) during the induction stage is useful in identifying the range of support needs and planning to meet these needs. Of critical importance is the role of the e-mentor in encouraging participation and promoting different forms of reflection — practical/ technical, personal, and critical — through the careful use of open questions. The e-mentor's task is to postpone judgement and premature closure and to encourage writers to re-explore practice scenarios through alternative lenses. Rather than providing the "authoritative voice" and acting as a relay device for "official" or "codified knowledge" (Bernstein, 1996), the e-mentor promotes communicative acts that help beginning teachers to reach their own understanding. Supporting dialogue and asset sharing through the communicative functions of e-portfolio has the additional advantage of affording enhanced levels of learner control and self-direction. Writers and asset sharers decide if their chosen community may view, comment, copy, or collaborate in their reflection. This shift in addressivity is fundamental to claims of student-centredness.

As portfolio building becomes a routinised practice in personal and professional development, it is important that pedagogical concerns and an appreciation of how adults learn inform institutional approaches to Webfolio design and usage. The discussion of patchwork e-dialogues presented here is premised on a model of participative, collaborative practice (Huberman, 1993). From this perspective, teachers are not reduced to "subjects" but remain central agents in their own development. We support Smyth and Shacklock's (1998) call for teachers to develop "indigenous, comprehensive theories of their teaching" (p. 27). The framing and reframing of problems through dialogue is integral to this process. From this perspective, digital technologies are seen as enabling technologies with the capacity to help learners develop self-knowledge and deeper conceptual understanding and to erode their sense of isolation in fragmented occupational cultures. By foregrounding the developmental purposes of professional portfolios, we can resist their co-option as digital archives, tools of "representational fabrication" (Ball, 2004; Clegg, 2004). The extent to which staff are able to exploit the communicative functions of new media in developing discursive activities will determine whether Webfolios become "cover stories" of the audit culture or powerful developmental tools in the future.

References

Bakhtin, M.M. (1986). *Speech genres and other late essays*. Austin: University of Texas Press.

Ball, S.J. (2004) Performativities and fabrications in the education economy. In S.J. Ball (Ed.), *The reader in sociology of education* (pp.143-155). London: Routledge Falmer.

Banks, M. (2001) *Visual methods in social research*. London: Sage.

Bernstein, B. (1996) *Pedagogy, symbolic control and identity. Theory, research, critique*. London: Taylor and Francis.

Bohm, D. (1996) *On dialogue*. London: Routledge.

Bolton, G. (2001). *Reflective practice: Writing and professional sevelopment*. London: Paul Chapman.

British Educational Communications and Technology Agency (2004). *What research says about virtual learning environments in teaching and learning* (2nd ed.). Retrieved July 12, 2005, from www.becta.org.uk/research/ictrn

Brookfield, S. (Ed.) (1988). *Training educators of adults*. London: Routledge.

Chamberlayne, P., Bornat, J., & Wengraf, T. (Eds.). (2000). *The turn to biographical methods in social science: Comparative issues and examples*. London: Routledge.

Chanfrault-Duchet, M.F (2004). In quest of teachers' professional identity: The life story as a methodological tool. In P. Chamberlayne, J. Bornat, & U. Apitzsch (Eds.), *Biographical methods and professional practice: An international perspective*. Bristol: Policy Press.

Clandinin, J., & Connelly, M. (Eds.). (1995). *Teachers' professional knowledge landscapes*. New York: Teacher College Press.

Clegg, S. (2004) Critical readings: Progress files and the production of the autonomous learner. *Teaching in Higher Education, 19*(3), 287-298.

De Lauretis, T. (1986). *Feminist studies/critical studies*. Bloomington: University of Indiana Press.

Deleuze, G., & Guattari, F. (1987). *A thousand plateaus*. London: Continuum.

Department for Education and Employment (1997). *Report of the National Committee of Inquiry into Higher Education (Dearing Report)*. London: The Stationery Office.

Department for Education and Science (2001). *Learning and teaching: A strategy for professional development*. DfES circular 0072/2001. London: The Stationery Office.

Derrida, J. (1987). Some questions and responses. In N. Fabb, et al. (Eds.), *The linguistics of writing: Arguments between language and literature* (pp. 252-264). Manchester: Manchester University Press.

Dewey, J. (1933). *How we think*. Buffalo, NY: Prometheus Books. (Original work published in 1910)

Ecclestone, K., & Pryor, J. (2003). 'Learner careers' or 'assessment careers'? The impact of assessment systems on learning. *British Educational Research Journal, 29*(4), 471-488.

Freire, P. (1970). *Pedagogy of the oppressed*. London: Penguin.

Fullan, M., & Hargreaves, A. (1991). *Understanding teacher development*. London: Cassell.

Furlong, J., Barton, L., Miles, S., Whiting, C., & Whitty, G. (2000). *Teacher education in transition*. Buckingham: Open University Press.

Gibbs, G.R. (1999). Learning how to learn using a virtual learning environment for philosophy. *Journal of Computer Assisted Learning, 15*, 221-231.

Goodson, I. (1995). *The making of curriculum: Collected essays* (2nd ed.). London: Falmer Press.

Goodson, I. (2003). *Professional knowledge, professional lives*. Maidenhead: Open University Press.

Gough, D.A., Kiwan, D., Sutcliffe, S., Simpson, D., & Houghton, N. (2003). *A systematic map and synthesis review of the effectiveness of personal development planning for improving student learning*. London: EPPI-Centre, Institute of Education.

Hargreaves, A. (1994). *Changing teachers, changing times: Teachers' work and culture in the postmodern age*. London: Cassell.

Huberman, M. (1993). *The lives of teachers*. New York: Teachers College Press, Columbia University.

Knowles, M.S., Holton, E.F., & Swanson, R.A. (1998). *The adult learner: The definitive classic in adult education and human resource development* (5th ed.). MA: Butterwirth-Heinemann.

Kowalski, T.J. (1995). Preparing teachers to be leaders: Barriers in the workplace. In M. O'Hair & S. Odell (Eds.), *Educating teachers for leadership and change* (pp. 243-257). Thousand Oaks, CA: Corwin.

Kyriakidou, M. (1999, September 2-5). *Electronic-conferencing: Promoting a collaborative community with learning opportunities for developing teachers*. British

Educational Research Association (BERA) annual conference, University of Sussex at Brighton. Retrieved July 31, 2005, from www.leeds.ac.uk/educol/documents/00001374.htm

Lather, P. (1991). *Getting smart. Feminist research and pedagogy with/in the postmodern.* London: Routledge.

Laurillard, D. (2002). *Rethinking university teaching* (2nd ed.). London: Routledge.

Mahony, P., & Hextall, I. (2000). *Reconstructing teaching: Standards, performance and accountability.* London: Routledge Falmer.

Mason, R. (1998). Models of online courses. *ALN Magazine, 2*(2). Article 5. Retrieved August 31, 2005, from *www.aln.org/publications/magazine/v2n2/mason.asp*

McCulloch, G., Helsby, G., & Knight, P. (2000). *The politics of professionalism.* London: Continuum.

Mead, M. (1995). Visual anthropology in a discipline of words. In P. Hockings (Ed.), *Principles of visual anthropology* (pp. 3-10). New York: Mouton de Gruyter.

Mezirow, J. (1991). *Transformative dimensions of adult learning.* San Francisco: Jossey Bass.

Moon, J.A. (2003). *Reflection in learning and professional development.* London: Kogan Page.

O'Leary, R. (2002) *Virtual learning environments.* Learning and Teaching Support Network Generic Centre/ ALT Guides, LTSN. Retrieved July 12, 2005, from www.bbk.ac.uk/tlt/resources/VLE.pdf

Oliver, M., & Shaw, G.P. (2003). Asynchronous discussion in support of medical education. *Journal of Asynchronous Learning Networks, 7*(1), 56-67.

Pilkington, R., Bennett, C., & Vaughan, S. (2000). An evaluation of computer mediated communication to support group discussion in continuing education. *Educational Technology & Society, 3*(3). Retrieved July 31, 2005, from http://ifets.ieee.org/periodical/vol_3_2000/d10.html

Quality Assurance Agency (2001). *Guidelines for higher education progress files* (online). Retrieved July 12, 2005, from www.qaa.ac.uk/academicinfrastructure/progressFiles/guidelines/progfile2001.asp

Reynolds, D. (1999). School effectiveness, school improvement and contemporary education policies. In J. Demaine (Ed.), *Education policy and contemporary politics.* London: Macmillan.

Robertson, S. (1996). Teachers' work, restructuring and post-Fordism: Constructing the new professionalism. In I.F. Goodson & A. Hargreaves (Eds.), *Teachers' professional lives* (pp. 28-55). London: Falmer Press.

Rogers, C. (1983). *Freedom to learn for the 1980s.* New York: Merrill-Wright.

Russell, T. (2000, April 24-28). *Using WebCT technology to foster self-study by teacher candidates after an early extended practicum.* Annual meeting of the American Educational Research Association (AERA), New Orleans. Retrieved July 12, 2005, from http://educ.queensu.ca/~ar/aera2000/russellt.pdf

Sachs, J. (2003). *The activist teaching profession*. Buckingham: Open University Press.

Salmon, G. (2000). *E-Moderating: The key to teaching and learning online*. London: Kogan Page.

Schon, D.A. (1987). *The reflective practitioner: How professionals think in action*. New York: Basic Books.

Selinger, M. (1997). Open learning, electronic communications and beginning teachers. *European Journal of Teacher Education, 20*(1), 71-84.

Smyth, J., & Shacklock, G. (1998). *Remaking teaching: Ideology, policy and practice*. London: Routledge.

Tanner, H., & Jones, S. (2000, September 7-10). *Using ICT to support interactive teaching and learning on a secondary mathematics PGCE course*. British Educational Research Association (BERA) annual conference, Cardiff University. Retrieved July 12, 2005, from www.leeds.ac.uk/educol/documents/00001628.htm

Wenger, E. (1998). *Communities of practice: Learning, meaning and identity*. Cambridge: Cambridge University Press.

Winter, R. (1999). *Professional experience & the investigative imagination: The art of reflective writing*. London: Routledge.

Winter, R. (2003) Contextualising the patchwork text: Addressing problems of coursework assessment in higher education. *Innovations in Education and Teaching International, 40*(2), 112-122.

Chapter XIII

Understanding Roles within Technology Supported Teaching and Learning:
Implications for Staff, Academic Units, and Institutions

Lori Lockyer, University of Wollongong, Australia

Sue Bennett, University of Wollongong, Australia

Abstract

This chapter provides a case study of a postgraduate course focused on network-based learning, which from its original design was based on constructivist learning principles. Over time, this course has evolved to incorporate increasing use of learning technology — particularly, synchronous and asynchronous communication tools. This evolution has led to a reappraisal and less emphasis on face-to-face class meetings. The course has also increased its student base through distance and offshore offerings. These shifts have translated into changes in the way the course is resourced in both human and infrastructure terms. The case uses Goodyear, Salmon, Spector, Steeples, and Tickner's (2001) roles and responsibilities of an online teacher to analyse the teaching team's perspective on the resource implications of a move to increased technology-facilitated teaching and learning for the teaching staff, the academic department, and the institution.

Introduction

Technology-supported learning in higher education is often considered hand-in-hand with changing pedagogical approaches and styles from instructive to more constructivist views of teaching and learning (Owston, 1997; Reeves & Reeves, 1997). This is understandable since the early adoption of online technologies coincided with general calls for higher education teaching to move from teacher-directed to learner-centred pedagogical approaches (Ramsden, 1992). Thus, in the literature of online teaching and learning, the changed role of the teacher is often discussed in terms of changing pedagogical style. In this context, moving online has been conceptualised as a change from traditional, teacher-directed, face-to-face classes to innovative, learner-centred online experiences (Herrington & Oliver, 2001).

This has made it somewhat difficult to determine which changes to practice occur because of changes in pedagogy and which occur because teaching and learning is now mediated by online technologies. Little is known about the changing role of the teacher when courses already based on constructivist learning principles are adapted to make use of (or greater use of) technology. In order to disentangle the issue of changing pedagogy and increasing technology use, it is necessary to explore what happens when a course underpinned by a constructivist approach evolves from primarily face-to-face to primarily online delivery. This analysis enables the authors to examine the characteristics of online teaching practice.

Background

As teaching and learning in higher education has increasingly moved from face-to-face classes to online interaction, teachers have been coming to terms with what this means for how they go about their work. From the outset of online education, observations have been made about how it has changed the environment for teachers and learners (Collis, 1996; Palloff & Pratt, 1999). Commentators, practitioners, and researchers have for some time been trying to identify the particular skills and competencies required by a good online teacher or facilitator (cf. Berge, 1995). More recently, Salmon (2000) has suggested that there are five characteristics demonstrated by effective e-moderators: understanding the online environment; technical proficiency with the software tools; skills to engage learners in online communication; content expertise to promote knowledge construction; and personality traits, like confidence and adaptability.

While Salmon's framework concentrates particularly on giving insights into the nature of online communication in the teaching and learning process, a more general model seeks to encompass a wider range of a teacher's roles and responsibilities (Goodyear et al., 2001). The responsibilities associated with each teaching role are summarised in Table 1.

This chapter uses the Goodyear et al. (2001) model as an analysis framework within a case study of a postgraduate course in educational technology — network-based learning (NBL) — which evolved from primarily face-to-face to primarily online delivery. Qualitative data collected by the teaching team from the introduction and subsequent implementations of the course (from 1999 through 2003) including course documentation, student work samples, and teacher observations and field notes were analysed using the *roles and responsibilities of the online teacher* framework to consider the impact of this shift online for teachers, academic departments, and institutions. The authors also draw conclusions about the implications of these for how online teachers work.

This chapter provides a case study of a postgraduate course that has made increasing use of a range of technology tools to support learning and which was originally designed with a constructivist underpinning. The evolution of this course has been in its primary delivery mechanisms with a greater use of online communication tools and a decreasing emphasis on face-to-face meetings. Over time, the course has also expanded its student base through new distance and offshore offerings. The focus of analysis for this case is on the implications of technology-supported teaching and learning for teaching staff, the academic unit, and the institution from the teacher's perspective.

Table 1. The roles and responsibilities of the online teacher

Role	Responsibilities
Process facilitator	Facilitates a range of online activities, mainly in a group or public setting, that are supportive of student learning.
Advisor/Counsellor	Works with learners on an individual or private basis, offering them advice or counselling to help them get the most out of their engagement in a course.
Assessor	Provides grades, feedback and validation of learners' work.
Researcher	Develops new knowledge of relevance to the content areas being taught.
Content facilitator	Facilitates the learners' growing understanding of course content.
Technologist	Makes technological choices that improve the environment available to learners.
Designer	Designs and plans effective online learning tasks, mainly prior to the course commencing.
Manager-administrator	Manages administrative processes such as learner registration, security, record keeping etc.

Adapting to Change: The Case of Network-Based Learning

Context within the Study Program

The *Information Technology in Education and Training* (ITET) program within the faculty of education at the University of Wollongong in Australia offers a range of postgraduate courses focusing on the use of technologies to facilitate learning in all educational sectors. Students represent a range of professional backgrounds including: school teachers and principals; adult educators from college, university, and corporate training settings; and instructional and e-learning designers.

Constructivist approaches to teaching and learning are the underpinning philosophy of the program and thus set the strategic direction for design and implementation. Each course is designed based on the identified learning outcomes and includes opportunity for students to:

*   acknowledge and build upon their prior knowledge and experience,
*   explore theory and make links between theory with practice (their own and others),
*   engage in authentic activities and assessment tasks,
*   choose and/or tailor assessment tasks to their professional context, and
*   engage in both self-directed and collaborative learning.

The basis of design for each course within the program can be defined using the learning design framework of learning tasks, resources, and supports (Oliver, 1999; Oliver & Herrington, 2001). A set of assessment *tasks* forms the focal point for each course, with non-assessable learning activities providing opportunities to support components (or sub-tasks) of the assessments. Pre-set readings, past student work, and student-identified curriculum materials form the *resource* set for each course. And a detailed week-by-week schedule *supports* the students by identifying: the specific topics to be covered; the readings timetable; class activities and foci; and assessment task due dates.

While online education was one of many topics explored through various courses within the ITET program, the teaching team decided that the international focus on and research developments within the area warranted a specific course to focus on network-based learning. The intended focus was the theoretical and practical issues of networking, the Internet, Web-based learning, and computer-mediated communications (CMC) in the primary, secondary, and tertiary educational sectors.

Network-Based Learning: Past and Present

The focus and broad content coverage of Network-Based Learning (NBL) remained largely consistent from its inception. The course was first offered in 1999 with face-to-face class meetings held on campus, for three hours, once per fortnight (that is, seven meetings in a 14-week academic session) in the faculty's dedicated multimedia computer teaching lab. Students engaged in individual and collaborative assessment tasks outside of class time. The course lecturer created a Web site (using hypermedia authoring software) that was hosted on a faculty-maintained server. There was some use of e-mail and a discussion forum tool for communication, but this was ad hoc and not integrated into the learning activities. In the main, the Web site was an adjunct to the supports and resources provided in class and its use by students was not a required element of the course.

Since the first implementation of the NBL course, the context for the ITET program changed. Developments and accessibility of learning technologies, the expanded research base for online learning, a more distributed student market (local, national, and off-shore), an institution-wide strategy toward flexible delivery, and subsequent centralisation of teaching and learning supports and systems have led to an increase in formal inclusion of online technologies to facilitate the program and decreased face-to-face class meetings.

By 2003, the NBL course was being implemented as a blended educational experience with no more than four campus-based meetings per session. Required and structured online learning activities became key points of contact for lecturers and students. These online activities and electronic resources and supports were created or organised by the course lecturer and made accessible within an institution-wide learning management system (LMS).

Figures 1 and 2 depict the sequential flow of the original, primarily face-to-face (F2F) experience (1999) and redesigned, primarily online interaction (2003) NBL learning

Figure 1. The original NBL learning design (1999), primarily face-to-face

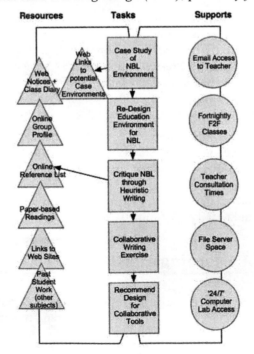

design. In these diagrams, the emerging area of learning designs provides the formalism with which to illustrate the NBL course (see Oliver, Harper, Hedberg, Wills, & Agostinho, 2002) with resources represented as triangles, tasks as squares, and supports as circles. Vertical arrows in the central column indicate the sequence from one task to the next. An arrow from a resource to a task indicates that the resource provides specific support for that task, while an arrow from a task to a resource indicates that the resource is generated from student activity. Resources and supports without arrows indicate more general elements available throughout the course.

Implications of the Shift to Online

A comparison of learning tasks, resources, and supports provides an initial picture of the impact of the shift to online delivery.

By 2003, the assessment tasks for NBL had evolved to take advantage of the online environment, although they were still based on similar learning strategies. The main changes were as follows:

- The initial task in 1999 required the students to select a network-based learning environment and develop a case study describing it. In the 2003 redesign this task was moved to the end of the course, and the first task became an analysis of NBL

Figure 2. The revised NBL learning design (2003), primarily online interaction

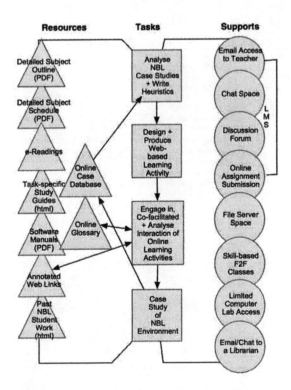

Table 2. Role/responsibility — DESIGN

	Face-to-Face	Online
Teacher	Develop a coherent design for the course. Select appropriate strategies for learners. Create sequence of individual and collaborative activities, organised around timetabled classes.	Develop a coherent design for the course. Select appropriate strategies for learners. Create sequence of individual and collaborative activities. Integrate/adapt activities to suit functionality of CMC tools. Design tools to work with LMS to facilitate learning activities (e.g., case database).
Academic Unit	Primarily left to the individual teacher beyond initial review and approval of new or revised course proposals (i.e., descriptions and objectives).	Initial review/approval of revisions as for face-to-face course. Funding and support for technology-based teaching innovation.
Institution	Primarily left to individual teacher beyond initial review and approval of new or revised course proposals (i.e., descriptions and objectives).	Initial review/approval of revisions as for face-to-face course. Central educational development and interactive resources unit provides increased support for instructional design, LMS skill development and technology-based content and tool creation. Develop tools to work with LMS to facilitate learning activities (e.g., case database).

Table 3. Role/responsibility — RESEARCH

	Face-to-Face	Online
Teacher	Focus on improving face-to-face presentation and facilitation skills. Evaluate effectiveness of course through analysis of student performance, student queries and personal reflection. Locate resources needed for discipline teaching. Request teaching survey to be conducted during class. Contribute to scholarship of teaching in specific discipline depending on particular staff interests.	Focus on improving online presentation and facilitation skills. Evaluate effectiveness of course through analysis of student performance, student queries and personal reflection. Locate resources needed for discipline teaching. Request teaching survey to be conducted at distance. Contribute to scholarship of teaching in specific discipline depending on particular staff interests, and in online pedagogy. Research design and efficacy of tools to support online delivery of constructivist pedagogy. Research student leaning outcomes associated with online delivery.
Academic Unit	Promote scholarship of teaching within discipline.	Promote scholarship of teaching within discipline and research/scholarship in online teaching in higher education.
Institution	Provide central process for teaching surveys conducted on campus. Promote scholarship of teaching within discipline.	Develop process for online or mail out of teaching surveys. Promote scholarship of teaching within discipline and research/scholarship in online teaching in higher education.

Table 4. Role/responsibility — PROCESS FACILITATION

	Face-to-Face	Online
Teacher	Interact with students face-to-face in class setting and provide opportunities for communication between students. Provide advice and feedback to group during class. Send group emails to make announcements between meetings.	Use CMC tools for specific learning activities with and between students. Use CMC tools for general discussion, advice, and announcements.
Academic Unit	Provide dedicated computer teaching laboratory for technology-focused teaching program.	Program-specific computer teaching laboratory can be made more widely available to other teaching programs. Provide support to staff/students from other programs that may not have same level of technology skills as technology-related program staff/students. Recognise workload for online teaching and allow flexible working hours for staff teaching online.
Institution	Provide infrastructure and tools to support the few courses using CMC tools.	Provide infrastructure, software and backup procedures for institution-wide implementation of online learning (LMS).

Table 5. Role/responsibility — ADVICE

	Face-to-Face	Online
Teacher	Provide individual consultation during class meetings, or in office at set times or by appointment. Use phone and email contact as an adjunct.	Provide individual consultation by email. Ensure class-based issues raised though individual consultation are communicated to whole group by email. Use phone contact as an adjunct. Direct enrolment, program and course related issues to appropriate personnel.
Academic Unit	Provide enrolment and program-related advice and procedures through a range of staff, including administrative officers, program coordinator, and teaching staff.	Provide enrolment and program-related advice and procedures through a range of staff, including administrative officers, program coordinator, and teaching staff. Recognise that teaching staff may not need to be physically present on campus to provide student consultation.
Institution	Provide bibliographic instruction and reference services to student in library.	Provide online support for bibliographic and references services (e.g., e-mail a librarian; chat to a librarian; online tutorials and guides).

Table 6. Role/responsibility — ASSESSMENT

	Face-to-Face	**Online**
Teacher	Annotate printed assignments and prepare feedback sheets for non-text assignments. Collect assignments on paper or disk in person and return during class. Provide feedback to group during class. Use marking guides and rubrics.	Annotate electronic assignments and prepare feedback sheets for non-text assignments. Collect and return assignments through learning management system and via FTP server. Provide feedback to group via CMC. Use marking guides and rubrics.
Academic Unit	Provide on-campus assessment collection and return procedures.	Reduced need for established on-campus assessment collection and return procedures.
Institution	Provide system for central recording of final marks.	Provide system for central recording of final marks. Provide secure assignment submission guidelines/procedures.

Table 7. Role/responsibility — CONTENT FACILITATION

	Face-to-Face	**Online**
Teacher	Prepare workshops sessions. Prepare print materials (handouts, course outlines, list of Web links) and some electronic materials (eg. simple Web site). Check availability of appropriate library resources. Request recommended texts be placed in reserve section in library. Ensure availability of recommended texts in bookshop.	Prepare electronic materials for course Web site. Link to additional resources available on the Web. Check availability of electronic resources through library databases. Provide texts/articles to be converted to e-readings.
Academic Unit	Provide Web server to host some online content at discretion of individual teachers.	Provide Web server to host specific content (e.g., case database).
Institution	Provide print-based library collection including procedures for course-specific reserve collection.	Establish centralised repository/content management procedures (e.g., e-readings – process for submission, processing, copyright management of text-based resources).

Table 8. Role/responsibility — TECHNOLOGY

	Face-to-Face	Online
Teacher	Develop skills to create course resources and using presentation technologies. Develop skills in using office productivity tools.	Develop skills to create and integrate electronic course resources. Develop skills in using office productivity tools. Develop skills in using LMS.
Academic Unit	Provide FTP server for student file storage/back up. Purchase software for computer teaching laboratory.	Provide FTP server for (some) assignment submission.
Institution	Provide presentation technology in some teaching rooms. Provide support and training for staff to use technology.	Provide Internet access/wireless network throughout campus. Provide digital video recording technology in teaching rooms with online delivery mechanism. Establish and maintain LMS software and review periodically. Provide support and training for staff to use technology.

Table 9. Role/responsibility — MANAGEMENT/ADMINISTRATION

	Face-to-Face	Online
Teacher	Develop course documentation. Maintain class rolls and marking records in spreadsheet and enter results into student administration reporting package at end of teaching sessions. Maintain an archive of electronic assignments. Manage teaching team through face-to-face meetings and email contact. Liaise with other units (library, student administration).	Develop course documentation. Maintain class rolls and marking records in spreadsheet or LMS and enter results into student administration reporting package at end of teaching sessions. Maintain an archive of electronic assignments. Manage of teaching team through email contact and face-to-face meetings where possible. Liaise with other units (resource design and development, IT services, library, student administration). Direct enquiries as teacher becomes 'first port of call' for all student issues.
Academic Unit	Manage student after-hours security access to teaching laboratories. Manage access to online content.	Manage access to specific online content hosted by unit.
Institution	Administer face-to-face/paper-based student enrolment procedures. Provide student email accounts (used at a minimal level).	Use online enrolment system given increased numbers of students studying at a distance. Provide student email accounts (used heavily). Maintain student authentication procedures for LMS access. Develop online security systems for changing/loss of passwords. Enforce Internet quota policy and procedures for non-course based downloads.

environments in which past student case studies were provided as source material for heuristic, "rule of thumb" (Hoban, Heider, & Stoner, 1980), writing. The aim of the revised task was for learners to develop generalisations about network-based learning based on multiple real-life examples. The final task in the 2003 course still required students to develop a case study, but this became a more analytical task, incorporating the critiquing nature of the 1999 heuristic writing task.

- In 1999, the second task required students to prepare a written report describing a conceptual redesign for an NBL environment. By 2003, this had become a construction task for which students designed and developed a prototype Web-based learning activity. This activity was made possible by the availability of appropriate authoring tools.

- By 2003, the collaborative journal article writing task and the design recommendations task that followed had been replaced by a task that required students to engage in, co-facilitate, and analyse a number of online class interactions. This change is indicative of the change in the way the subject was delivered, with students becoming more involved in learning activities online, which in turn offered opportunities for students to act as facilitators, participants, and observers in online interactions.

Comparing the resourcing and support for these tasks reveals the implications of the shift online for teaching staff, the academic unit, and the institution. The similarities and differences can be analysed using the Goodyear et al. (2001) roles and responsibilities of an online teacher as a framework. Tables 2 through 9 summarise the responsibilities for the teacher in the face-to-face and the online modes of NBL and extends these to consider the roles of the academic unit and the institution. (Note: In doing this, it must be remembered that the NBL course, although initially face-to-face, did include technology-related components within its first implementations.)

Conclusion

The focus of this chapter was to analyse the implications for teachers, the academic unit, and the institution when technology becomes integral rather than adjunct to an academic course underpinned by a constructivist approach to learning. A comparison of the responsibilities arising in the face-to-face and online contexts in the previous section reveals that while many are relevant to both, a shift to online learning brings with it new responsibilities for the teacher and new requirements at the unit and institutional levels.

For the teacher, the implications for increasing the technology support within this course were less about changing pedagogy and more about finding effective ways to facilitate the teaching and learning process. In essence, this changes the pattern of work for delivery of a course (Bennett & Lockyer, 2004). More time is spent preparing the tools and curriculum materials prior to the teaching session. These resources must provide general guidance for students based on what the teacher anticipates they will need, with some opportunity to adapt and add to these as the course progresses. This differs markedly from the face-to-face setting in which the teacher would normally tailor resources to the student cohort though verbal discussions. Interestingly, online students come to expect that they will see the entire course instructions and resources laid out for them in the first week.

The demands for technical and practical skill development are amplified for the teacher of an online course. When a course is primarily delivered face-to-face, technology plays a supporting role, but with online delivery there is a technology skill, use, and time demand implication for everything that the teacher does. For example, assessment of student work changes from providing handwritten comments on a printed assignment collected and returned in class to downloading the submission, printing the work (as per preference), preparing feedback in electronic form or annotating the file, and returning feedback via an LMS or e-mail. At the institutional level, systems must be consistent across all disciplines and practices must be codified. Thus, there may be difficulties in tailoring to specific needs of staff or students, or to differences in the nature of assignments.

Communicating with students as a class or as individuals becomes spread throughout the teaching week rather than being limited to scheduled class time or consultation hours. Written communication must be precise to minimise opportunities for misunderstanding, and teachers must ensure that course-related issues communicated to individual students are also disseminated to the whole group.

Students studying at a distance or visiting campus infrequently also tend to direct all, not just course-related, inquiries to the teacher. The teacher becomes the "first port-of-call" for questions related to enrolment procedures, program academic advice, and technical and administrative difficulties. The teacher, in turn, is required to direct students to the appropriate academic unit or institutional source to resolve their issues or mediate on the student's behalf. This tends to make the other staff members within the academic unit more removed from the student experience.

The case of network-based learning exemplifies some attempts to move toward repositories for resource materials initiated by both the teaching team (e.g., program-based curriculum materials) and the institution (e.g., e-readings service). These activities are occurring more widely, with more global projects aimed at developing clearinghouses of curriculum materials (or learning object repositories) and the development of content management tools that integrate with learning management systems. However, within programs, academic units, and institutions, there remain questions about the breath to which these can be implemented and the consistency with which they are used by the teaching staff institution-wide. These questions are exacerbated at the global level in terms of the practicality of using learning object repositories.

The NBL case also demonstrates the teaching team's significant effort to develop technology tools (such as the case database) that would support constructivist approaches to learning within the online environment. While many learning management systems have tools to support both content delivery and teacher/student interaction, many are teacher-directed or managed. The now extensive experiences of teachers working with and around learning management systems could guide improvements in the functionality of the in-built tools, a move needed in order to facilitate the kinds of student learning experiences many teachers wish to implement.

While this discussion has been based on a case study of a particular situation, readers may find the experience of NBL relevant to their own teaching and learning context. Although initially focused on the perspective of the teacher, the Goodyear et al. (2001) framework of process facilitation; advice and counsel; assessment; research; content facilitation; technology design; and, management and administration provides a useful model for identifying the implications in terms of teaching and learning responsibilities from the perspective of student, teacher, academic unit, and institution.

At an individual teacher level, an analysis underpinned by this model can provide guidance or expectations for engagement in online teaching and learning. At a broader academic unit or institutional level, use of this model may provide direction for the establishment of more effective policies and practices to facilitate technology-supported learning across teaching program.

Increased integration of technology within academic programs may not have to mean a change in pedagogical approaches, particularly if those programs are already drawn upon strategies that are accepted to foster high quality learning. However, the practical and technological implications for facilitating those teaching and learning strategies adds layers of complexity to the roles and responsibilities for all involved in the process. This case, and the issues it raises, highlights a need for consistency. At the institutional level, consistency in implementation means that appropriate facilities and supports can be provided effectively, which can help to streamline teachers' work and enhance students' learning experience.

The case of NBL provides a concrete qualitative indication of the implications of implementing significant levels of technology-supported teaching and learning. A continuing practical question relates to the quantitative costs of such an exercise, particularly at the institutional level. While seemingly a daunting question to answer, it also needs to be considered in light of its aim or purpose. This needs to be considered with respect to the outcome of the activity, particularly in terms of expanding the reach of education and/or the realisation of student learning outcomes.

References

Bennett, S., & Lockyer, L. (2004). Becoming an online teacher: Adapting to a changed environment for teaching and learning in higher education. *Educational Media International, 41*(3), 231-244.

Berge, Z. (1995). The role of the online instructor/facilitator. *Educational Technology, 35*(1), 22-30.

Collis, B. (1996). *Tele-learning in a digital world: The future of distance learning.* London: International Thomson Publishing.

Goodyear, P., Salmon, G., Spector, J., Steeples, C., & Tickner, S. (2001). Competencies for online teaching: A special report. *Educational Technology Research and Development, 49*(1), 65-72.

Herrington, J., & Oliver, R. (2001). *Online learning: Professional development for the changing role of the lecturer.* Paper presented at the Moving Online Conference II, Gold Coast, Queensland, Australia. Lismore, NSW: Southern Cross University. Available online at www.scu.edu.au/scools/sawd/monconf/MOC2_papers.html

Hoban, D.J., Heider, M., & Stoner, J. (1980). Further consideration of heuristic guidelines for multiple institution instructional development projects. *Journal of Instructional Development, 4*(2), 2-9.

Oliver, R. (1999). Exploring strategies for on-line teaching and learning. *Distance Education, 20*(2), 240-254.

Oliver, R., Harper, B., Hedberg, J., Wills, S., & Agostinho, S. (2002). Formalising the description of learning designs. In A. Goody, J. Herrington, & M. Northcote (Eds.), *Quality conversations: Research and development in higher education* (Vol. 25, pp. 496-504). Jamison, ACT: HERDSA.

Oliver, R., & Herrington, J. (2001). *Teaching and learning online: A beginner's guide to e-learning and e-teaching in higher education.* Western Australia: Edith Cowan University.

Owston, R.D. (1997). The World Wide Web: A technology to enhance teaching and learning? *Educational Researcher, 26*(2), 27-33.

Paloff, R.H., & Pratt, K. (1999). *Building learning communities in cyberspace: Effective strategies for the on-line classroom.* San Francisco: Jossey-Bass.

Ramsden, P. (1992). *Learning to teach in higher education.* London: Routledge.

Reeves, T.C., & Reeves, P.M. (1997). Effective dimensions of interactive learning on the World Wide Web. In B.H. Khan (Ed.), *Web-based instruction* (pp. 59-66). Englewood Cliffs, NJ: Educational Technology Publications.

Salmon, G. (2000). *E-moderating: The key to teaching and learning online.* London: Kogan Page.

Chapter XIV

The Role of the Online Instructor as a Guide on the Side

Margaret Mazzolini, Swinburne University of Technology, Australia

Sarah Maddison, Swinburne University of Technology, Australia

Abstract

We present research results and advice on the role of the online instructor in relation to a particular example of technology-supported learning and teaching — the use of asynchronous discussion forums. Pedagogical issues and studies discussed here are based on six years of designing, coordinating, and teaching into Swinburne Astronomy Online (SAO), an online international program. We discuss some implementation issues associated with the use of asynchronous forums and the induction of instructors, plus the role of the online instructor as a "guide on the side." As an example of issues involved in maintaining a constructive online learning environment, we discuss strategies used to accommodate students with varying degrees of prior learning. We also summarise results of our research on student-instructor interactions, plus feedback on students' and instructors' perceptions of the online experience. The results of this research are used to inform the induction and mentoring of instructors in SAO.

Introduction

Designing and implementing a completely online program from the ground up presents both rewards and considerable challenges to anyone with an interest in curriculum design, in general, and online education, in particular. The use of online communications represents a key enabling technological tool for the delivery of online education. The case study discussed in this chapter is set within the context of designing, developing, and running an international online program featuring asynchronous discussion forums as a central part of the learning and teaching process. Our analysis of factors that influence the success of online delivery supported by asynchronous forum discussions is informed by both our research and practice.

The authors are the designer and original coordinator (MM) and the current coordinator (SM) of Swinburne Astronomy Online (SAO)[1], a fully online master's program in astronomy. At the stage when SAO was first designed and implemented as a pilot scheme in 1999, there was little if any conventional wisdom, anecdotal or otherwise, about how to run international online programs. The whole project provided an opportunity for creative curriculum design, as well as the usual number of false starts while attempting to establish what did and did not work in the SAO context.

After the success of the pilot scheme, SAO launched a master's degree in 2000, and student numbers have since grown from 50 to about 250 per semester. The student cohort is allocated into approximately 10 instructor moderated discussion groups. SAO students are typically articulate, enthusiastic adult students (average age mid 40s) who are residents from more than 30 countries and share a passion for astronomy, but generally lack any prior experience of learning online. Their backgrounds and educational experiences vary greatly, ranging from PhDs in chemistry, degrees in engineering, medicine, science, and humanities, right through to those who have not studied for over 30 years but are keen amateur astronomers.

In the first part of this chapter, we discuss the role of asynchronous discussions in SAO as a case study in online delivery. We identify the challenges posed by the need to provide online induction of new instructors, manage the volume of forum discussions, and handle widely varying levels of student expertise. We also outline strategies that we implemented in SAO in response to these issues. In latter sections of the chapter, we outline some of the results from our evaluative research studies based on the SAO database of discussion forum postings and survey responses of students and instructors. We discuss the often counter-intuitive conclusions suggested by this research about ways in which instructors and students interact in asynchronous online discussion forums, and we suggest implications for the induction and professional development of instructors.

The Role of Asynchronous Discussions in SAO: A Case Study

As the whole spectrum from online-supported to fully online-delivered programs becomes more commonplace, increasing numbers of instructors and program coordinators across many discipline areas are now at least tentatively dipping their toes into the communications aspects of online delivery. In common with any new educational technology, online education will endure or fail on the basis of whether it initiates new and useful approaches to learning and teaching. Too many educational technology developments in the past have offered alluringly high-tech or apparently cheap ways of delivering existing approaches to teaching, but have failed in the long run to make any significant pedagogical impact. To quote Alexander and Blight:

> ... promised revolutions in education will only be realised when qualitatively different learning experiences are afforded through the application of information and communication technologies, rather than the provision of 're-packaged' learning experiences which have only the appearance of being 'up-to-date'. (1996)

While it can be argued that online delivery systems are still largely being used as convenient tools to allow students to download course material (shifting the cost of printing from institution to student in the process), it is clear that one of the "killer applications" of online delivery so far has been the growing use of online communications, in the form of e-mail, synchronous chat and instant messaging systems, asynchronous discussion forums, blogs, Webcam systems, and so on. Online communication modes were initially limited by bandwidth considerations, but high bandwidth Internet is now a reality in many western countries. However, just as asynchronous communication via text messaging technology (SMS and now MMS) is proving to be remarkably resilient in the face of synchronous mobile communications, asynchronous discussion forums are still prevalent in online education. In synchronous online discussions of any size, our experience has been that discussion threads (topics) can quickly become entangled, making life difficult for both instructors and students. In contrast, in asynchronous forum discussions, each thread is organised under its own heading, which is an extremely important consideration in SAO forums which can involve 30 or so active contributors. While synchronous communications may prove to be more effective in supporting the social side of student interactions, asynchronous forums will be seen to be better at dealing with the "academic" aspects of online programs (Motteram, 2001).

SAO communications have always taken place through asynchronous discussion forums by necessity, as both the students and instructors are resident across the world's time zones and tend to be busy people. Discussion threads build up as geographically separated students come online in their particular time zones, and relationships are established between students who have never met or visited each other's countries but who share a passion for astronomy. In SAO, it has become evident that the advantages of asynchronous communications extend beyond the time zone issue, providing students and instructors with opportunities to research and reflect upon current discussion topics before they post answers to each other's questions (Laurillard, 1996), an aspect commonly assumed to assist non-native English speakers in particular (Asano, 1999; Biesenbach-Lucas, 2003; Mazzolini & Maddison, 2004; Murphy & Collins, 1997). As one of the first SAO students commented, "It's more like the classic Greek form of tuition, with the course tutors and students sitting round a forum discussing the subject."

Teaching via online asynchronous discussion forums can prove to be a very rewarding experience, but it must be conceded that it can also present a significant pedagogical challenge to instructors who are used to the immediate visual and audio feedback of face-to-face delivery (Collins & Berge, 1997; Schrum & Berge, 1997; Markel, 2001; Schrum & Hong, 2002). Communicating with the quiet, non-participating students "down the back of the online class" can present a special challenge when the only means by which instructor-student contact can occur is via forum postings and e-mails (Benfield, 2002). Normally outgoing instructors may find online teaching somewhat frustrating when body language and verbal clues count for nothing and personality can only be expressed via the written word. In contrast, less outgoing instructors may welcome the opportunity to take time to craft their responses to students' postings and find that they are able to take on roles online that they would not normally assume in face-to-face teaching (Paloff & Pratt, 1999; Levitch & Milheim, 2003).

Depending on the way online programs are set up and also on the natural inclinations of the instructor involved, the instructor's role in asynchronous discussion forums can vary from being the "sage on the stage," to the "guide on the side" or even "the ghost in the wings" (Benfield, 2002; Mazzolini & Maddison, 2003; Thomas, 2001). In SAO, instructors have been encouraged to follow a broadly Socratic "guide on the side" approach when participating in online discussion forums (MacKnight, 2000). The motivation for this approach is overtly constructivist in nature, in that it assumes that student knowledge and preconceptions can be drawn out through asynchronous student-student and instructor-student interaction involving the asking and answering of questions, and that misconceptions can be made explicit and resolved through online dialogue in ways not available in purely paper-based distance education (Anderson, 2002; Gold, 2001; Markel, 2001; Berge, 1995; Schrum & Hong, 2002).

Implementing an online program for mainly local students and instructors can be challenging. Once both students and instructors are located around the world, an even higher level of coordination and planning is required, together with a clear focus on learning outcomes and a sensitivity to social contexts. Added to this, the background astronomical knowledge of SAO students varies from the complete novice to more advanced students who have taken courses and been reading astronomy texts for years. This can make discussion forum participation somewhat intimidating for those new to astronomy, and while SAO instructors are encouraged to play a relatively low-key part in most discussions, the role of the instructor is crucial in ensuring that all students have opportunities to participate effectively.

Managing Discussion Forum Participation into an Online Program

Previous experience of the program designer as an online student had underlined the importance of three basic, but key, issues to the success of online forums as learning environments: the induction of new instructors; challenges of managing the volume of postings; and issues involved in handling a wide range of background expertise of students.

Introducing New Instructors to Online Teaching

After the success of the 1999 pilot scheme, more instructors located in several countries were employed to teach the growing numbers of SAO students. The experience of the first SAO instructors was shared informally among new appointees via e-mail, and new instructors were encouraged to monitor forums conducted by more experienced instructors. Originally, the coordinator reminded instructors of requirements and deadlines via an e-mail mailing list, but this was soon supplemented with a (password protected) instructors' Web site.

As the size of SAO has grown, more than 30 instructors have taught in the program at various times. Due to competing commitments, external instructors come and go, so recruiting and training new instructors is a constant task. Many external instructors are young, enthusiastic astronomy researchers with little or no prior teaching experience. While a lack of teaching experience is never ideal, these instructors are open minded about trying new teaching approaches online, and their enthusiasm and astronomy expertise are definite pluses. The fact that SAO instructors act as "guides on the side" and students aim to answer each other's questions in the first instance makes it relatively easy for instructors to find their feet.

The induction of new SAO instructors has yet to become as formalized as is the case in large-scale organizations like the Open University (Salmon, 2000). Induction usually takes place via phone and e-mail contact combined with access to the greatly expanded instructors' Web site, and involves providing instructions on how the program works and what is expected of instructors, plus tips on how to run discussion forums effectively and how to deal with challenging students. New instructors are given access to discussion forum archives for a previous semester's class so that they can learn by example. Information gained from our research on how to run discussion forums effectively is also fed back to the instructors, as is summary feedback from university student surveys. Before the semester officially begins, SAO has an introductory "Week 0" in which instructors and students post introductions and familiarise themselves with the online learning environment. This week is quite important in building a sense of community (and even friendships) in the forums, especially the introductory classes that host students new to SAO. Instructors are asked to post their own biography and personally welcome each student, making them feel part of the class.

When inducting new instructors, one of the main points stressed is the need to maintain a consistent presence in the forums (Benfield, 2002). The students need to know that the instructors are out there, even if when not answering questions, so SAO instructors are encouraged to send some sort of posting to the forums every 3 days at a minimum in order that students will know that their instructors are still monitoring the forums. If instructors go "missing in action," the students start e-mailing the coordinator with complaints, whereas if they are forewarned that instructors will be off-line for a few days, then there is no problem as the students generally understand that their instructors are busy and teaching is just one of their many duties. However, instructors who fail to contribute to forum discussions for extended periods are a nightmare for the coordinator, resulting in a barrage of e-mails from disgruntled students. These instructors usually get poor student feedback at the end of the semester and may not be re-hired.

Another important aspect of instructor induction involves discussing how to deal with "challenging" students and conflicts within the forums. While conflicts between individual SAO students are rarely a problem due to the wide variety of background knowledge, each forum is likely to contain both novice and relatively expert students as we shall discuss. This can result in discussions being dominated by a vocal minority, while others are left feeling intimidated or downright annoyed. Such situations need to be quickly identified and averted before they become a problem, with delicate handling via private e-mail so as not to offend or stifle enthusiasm. While it may not be possible to accommodate all student sensitivities, we do try to make the forums as open and supportive as possible.

Throughout the semester, new instructors are monitored by the coordinator and online teaching panel meetings are held where new and experienced instructors can discuss any teaching issues as they arise. Online meetings between the coordinator and individual instructors are held at the end of the semester to gain their feedback and discuss any problems and possible improvements to their teaching.

Managing the Volume of Forum Discussions

Discussion forums that become unmanageably large can act as a strong disincentive to student participation. This is particularly so where bandwidth is limited, but also where clumsy interfaces (too often provided with commercial learning systems) require students to click laboriously through threads in order to follow discussions. SAO was designed to keep the number of postings in any one forum manageable by restricting the number of participants per forum, opening forums for limited amounts of time, and keeping postings on-topic.

In SAO, students are divided into groups containing up to approximately 30 students per instructor, and each group has its own set of discussion forums. The forums are broken up into seven two-week blocks throughout the semester, and students are required to post at least one question or "extension comment" about course material covered in each two-week period, and also answer at least one question posed by someone else per forum. Students clarify their understanding of concepts and further develop their science communication skills by answering each other's questions, often in considerable depth.

SAO students are only required to make a minimum of two forum postings in every two-week period, but many post significantly more often than that. On average, students make more than four postings per two-week discussion forum (Mazzolini & Maddison, 2003a). The total number of postings per forum mostly stays at a manageable level of just over 100, although forums containing 200 postings or more can occur early in each semester. Forums this large can represent a significant load to busy students and instructors trying valiantly to keep track of discussion threads.

One reason for overly the large number of postings can be the temptation for overenthu-siastic novice students to discuss every new astronomy press release, rather than keep on-topic. While off-topic postings can be interesting and other students may well join in, they can tend to "swamp" on-topic postings. Rather than squash students' enthu-siasm if and when they are tempted to stray off topic, SAO instructors are advised to direct them gently away from these course-specific forums to a set of non-assessment general interest "SAO community forums" set up for this purpose. In the SAO community forums, enthusiasts can discuss any astronomy topic they choose with fellow students from across the entire SAO program. SAO also follows the practice of providing a community forum where students are encouraged to discuss both positive and negative aspects of their SAO learning experience (Salmon, 2000), though students can also e-mail feedback directly to the coordinator.

SAO forum sizes are usually kept to a maximum of 30 to help limit the number of postings. Actual sizes have varied overall from 14 to 41 students per forum (the larger limit occurring when two smaller forums led by the same instructor elected to merge). In Mazzolini and Maddison (2003a), we observed that differing forum sizes had little effect on participation rates, though there was some indication that threads were longer in larger forums, and that instructors in the smallest forums posted more often and initiated more threads than usual. It is difficult for instructors to gauge the progress of their students if the latter fail to post many questions or comments. Anecdotal experience suggests that SAO forums with less than around 20 students place heavy demands on instructors because they feel the need to work hard at maintaining the conversations by initiating new threads and extending existing ones. At the other extreme, when the SAO class size is much over 30 or even 25 for advanced units, quieter students who may be having problems may become "lost in the noise" if instructors (and students!) are struggling to keep up with excessive numbers of postings.

While restricting forum sizes can aid instructors and students by limiting the number of forum postings, as overall students numbers have grown it has also become increasingly important to set up effective communication strategies to avoid the "death by e-mail" syndrome for the coordinator. Because e-mail is a relatively immediate form of commu-nication, students frequently expect a rapid (or even instant!) response to all e-mail queries. The administrator of an online program can also be inundated with student e-mails. While on-campus students understand that offices are open during set hours and that queues must be joined and appointments need to be made, online students can appear to be unaware of world time zones and the fact that we might be asleep while they have a burning question! "E-mail impatience" needs to be managed so that students do not unnecessarily burden the administrator.

The SAO coordinator takes a proactive approach by e-mailing all students and instruc-tors with weekly reminders of deadlines, changes to the forums, administration updates, and other upcoming events. These e-mails are also posted on an archival forum so that students (and instructors) have access to a complete set. In this way, the coordinator can divert students who tend to ask questions already covered in previous weekly updates to the archive. Students are also encouraged to turn to their instructors as the first point of contact.

Handling Black Belts and White Belts

Many SAO participants identify as novices with little background in astronomy and are quite nervous about revealing supposed ignorance online, however, others who have read about astronomy for years sometimes regard their first forums as an opportunity to unleash years of enthusiasm and acquired knowledge by providing lengthy answers to questions as soon as they are posted. Left unchecked, this can overwhelm and even mislead novice students who need time to research and compose answers to posted questions, especially if it means that only the more difficult questions stay unanswered for any length of time. Handling this can be quite a challenge for new instructors and becomes even more of an issue if overly confident students tend to dominate discussions but are not necessarily accurate in their postings.

In SAO, we were keen to develop an approach that assisted novice students to find the time and opportunity to answer questions, while not completely dampening the enthusiasm of their more knowledgeable or confident classmates. In order to avoid typecasting students by labels they might regard as pejorative, we "borrowed" terms from martial arts that we hoped might amuse rather than insult our students, by referring to them as "black belts" and "white belts." When students first join SAO, they are directed to a Web page which contains advice on how to post to discussion forums, including the following:

People enter this course with all sorts of prior knowledge in astronomy. Some of you are in the 'black belt' league (you know who you are!) because of other courses you have attended, the wide range of informal reading you have carried out in astronomy, or your amateur astronomy expertise. Others of us (the 'white belters') are discovering many of these exciting new concepts for the first time in this course.

The format of the newsgroup discussions requires everyone, every two weeks, to post at least one question or comment about the current coursework, and attempt to answer at least one question posed by someone else. Our experience is that this can generate a supportive environment where black belters and white belters (and everyone in between) can help each other. It is important, however, that the black belters don't jump in and answer all the questions immediately, otherwise others may feel intimidated. If you fall in the black belt category, please use the first week to post some good questions and comments, and then maybe wait until later in the second week to step in and clear up the tricky outstanding questions. If anyone is consistently having difficulty finding questions they can answer, they should e-mail their instructor and discuss the problem.

Students' reactions to strategies we have used to handle this issue are best discussed in the context of responses received to an e-mail survey carried out in 2002. Survey responses were received from 85 students (a 37% response rate) to a range of questions concerning student and instructor participation. Specifically, 10 students mentioned black belt/white belt issues when responding to invitations to "comment on styles of instructor participation most useful for teaching and learning, and why" (Maddison & Mazzolini, 2005). Responses received included comments on the challenge of keeping up with the overeager black belts who quickly replied to many of the posted questions:

When you have two or three people in the class that do this, then you are left with little to work with and are less prominent to the instructor and probably get less marks for the ones you can post. You do caution for the black belters to not jump in too quickly, perhaps you could caution that they not answer so many and do not have to answer *every* day.

When we wanted to remind overly enthusiastic students to delay posting answers to every question in sight, we would post a friendly message to "all black belts," with follow-up private e-mails from instructors asking individuals who persistently attempted to dominate discussions not to answer questions until the second week of each forum. Most novice students seemed to feel good about being labeled as white belts, judging by the number who self-identified themselves in this way, and responded that strategies used by instructors were helpful:

The black belt reminders were helpful as were [the instructor's] posting of a few questions, at least early in the semester, for white belters to get started on. Also, the reminders that we should consider answering a question even if someone has already provided some response to it.

However, it was clear from responses to the 2002 survey that overly extensive postings by black belts still intimidated some students. At face value, this may be no worse that the situation often met in face-to-face tutorial classes, where confident students can tend to "take over" discussions leaving others reluctant to contribute (Metts, 2005). SAO students are required to post regularly, and this can act as a positive incentive to quiet students to get engaged. One female participant commented:

Despite being an absolute minority in the class, I don't really feel that gender issues swayed my level of participation really in the newsgroups, I was still quite vocal. Of course, had I not been in an online newsgroup situation but in an actual classroom, I feel quite sure I would have been drowned out by the male black belters, but this is really due to the fact that as a novice I needed time to really research and prepare my answers to discussion questions, not the result of a gender issue.

Teachers can intervene in face-to-face classes by taking over-enthusiastic students aside to discuss their contribution style, however, online instructors face the challenge of judging how best to intervene via the printed word only, without unduly offending or discouraging enthusiastic students in the process. Proactive strategies include setting up ground rules from the start (such as the black belts information provided at the start of each SAO semester), and heading off problems of students dominating discussions as they arise in the initial forums. This has implications for the induction and mentoring of new instructors, and also for the need for coordinators to monitor teaching and provide advice quickly to instructors if a forum looks like it is being unduly dominated by a few students.

Educational Research vs. Conventional Wisdom: What is Really Happening in Online Forms?

SAO was designed to build on students' prior understanding and special interests, with encouragement to students to work together to construct their learning through online discussions, and instructors were advised to step in to guide only as needed. For all online instructors, a particular challenge lies in working out how much and in what ways to intervene in students' discussions in order to aid learning. In this constructivist paradigm, effective interventions should occur without the need for instructors to dominate the discussions. The authors' research interests have been focussed on studying ways in which online instructors and students interact, and, in particular, looking for indicators that might assist program coordinators to judge the "health" of online discussion forums.

As forum discussions are a key feature, SAO has provided an excellent case study with which to make comparative studies of student and instructor forum participation. While online discussions offer excellent opportunities for evaluative research because class interactions are automatically recorded, the predictive power of many studies published are quite limited due to small class sizes. In contrast, the large number of SAO postings and survey responses provide a valuable resource for the study of instructor and student interactions. Typically 250 students are enrolled in 10 forums at any time under the same overall guidelines, and each semester students make of the order of 7,000 discussion forum postings and 100 responses to university evaluation surveys about their SAO experience.

Over the last few years, the authors have (with ethics permission) carried out research into ways in which teaching and learning take place in SAO. This research has been based on extensive archives of over 40,000 postings to nearly 400 SAO discussion forums, plus in excess of 500 university evaluation survey responses collected over six consecutive semesters together with targeted surveys of instructors and students. In particular, we have used these archives to conduct two large studies on student and instructor interactions in forums (Mazzolini & Maddison, 2003, 2005). We investigated whether student participation rates, lengths of discussion threads, and student perceptions concerning their learning are influenced by the frequency, timing, and nature of instructors' postings. We also gathered qualitative survey responses on these aspects of forum participation from instructors and students. The results of this research are summarised and have been used to improve the support and advice provided to new SAO instructors.

The Instructor as Sage, Guide, or Ghost

The role of the instructor in discussion forums plays a key part in many forms of online education. Without face-to-face feedback, it can be difficult for both instructors and coordinators to judge when their students' learning is being effectively supported. A key issue for the SAO coordination team in the early days of the program was whether an instructor who posts often is a "good" instructor. Or, taking a pragmatic approach, are coordinators justified in stepping in if they notice that an instructor is posting quite infrequently?

Opinions on this issue are divided in the literature. Frequent instructor participation is often assumed to encourage student participation. To quote Kearsley (2000):

One factor that strongly affects the amount of student interaction and participation is the level of instructor involvement. If the instructor regularly posts messages in the discussion forum or provides comments to students via e-mail, this increases student involvement and participation in a course. So a cardinal rule of good online teaching is that the instructor must participate a lot to get students to do likewise.

In contrast, some authors suggest that instructor participation may be overdone:

However, the instructor needs to maintain a balance between too little and too much participation. Because the learning community is a critical feature of the online course, the instructor need not respond to every student post but instead should determine the appropriate time to jump in, make a comment, ask another question, or redirect the discussion. Too much participation by the instructor can have the effect of reducing the amount of interaction among the students and create an unnecessary degree of reliance on the teacher. (Paloff & Pratt, 2001)

This quote by Paloff and Pratt (2001) sets the theme for our investigations of instructor and student interactions in SAO forums. Casual observation had suggested that instructors who posted frequently would encourage greater participation by students, but as reported in Mazzolini and Maddison (2003, 2005), we found that the volume of student and instructor postings in forums did not necessarily indicate how well the forums were going. Instead, we found that the more instructors posted, the fewer postings students made and the shorter were the discussion threads on average. We also expected that by making the effort to initiate new postings, instructors would encourage their students to post more often. Again, our results were counter-intuitive; we found that, on average, SAO instructors who attempted to increase the amount of discussion by initiating new postings did not succeed. Forums with fewer student postings and shorter discussion threads than most are not necessarily deficient as learning environments — it may be that frequent instructor intervention makes discussions more efficient. However, if online coordinators judge forums intuitively by the number of postings, then they are likely to encourage their instructors to post frequently and to start new discussion threads in order to encourage students to participate. Our research into SAO forum interactions suggests that this strategy is likely to be ineffective.

We also looked at student responses to university evaluation surveys over the same six semesters to see if students of "ghosts in the wings" instructors rated their learning experiences any differently to those whose instructors took more prominent places in "centre stage." We found a small but significant correlation suggesting that students perceived instructors who posted often as displaying greater enthusiasm and expertise as compared to instructors who posted infrequently. However, when it came to overall satisfaction with their learning experience, SAO students were generally very satisfied, rating the program highly independently of how often their instructors participated in forum discussions.

From the point of view of program coordination, there is a balance to be achieved between advising instructors to hold back so as not to stifle student participation and encouraging instructors to share their expertise in the subject of discussion. We can speculate on reasons behind these observed correlations: For example, if we consider the negative correlation observed between student and instructor posting rates, it may be that students do not feel the need to post often if they observe that their instructors are posting frequently and answering outstanding questions in the process (i.e., if they take their instructor's word as final). Alternatively, instructors may feel the need to post frequently if their forums appear to have "gone quiet," and that may happen for reasons unrelated to the instructor. More work clearly needs to be done before claims of cause and effect can be made reliably.

We also looked for correlations between student posting rates and whether our instructors posted mainly during or at the end of forums (Mazzolini & Maddison, 2005). In SAO, the timing of instructor postings matters — instructor postings made during forums mainly act to "guide" discussions, whereas postings at the end of forums primarily have a "wrap up" function, answering unresolved questions and closing off discussion threads. When we analysed instructor postings, we found that on average instructors posted approximately half their postings during each forum and half at the end. Those instructors who posted the majority of their postings at the end of forums scored particularly high for enthusiasm and expertise on university evaluation surveys, but as these were also the instructors who tended to post the most overall, this was not surprising.

Student contributions to SAO forums were always intended to be dominated by questions and answers, but it is not easy to tell from a casual inspection just how much the instructors have contributed in terms of asking initial and follow-up questions, and whether this is even necessary. It is also possible that contributions by articulate, enthusiastic adult students will maintain a momentum of their own, almost independent of the way in which instructors participate. To investigate this, we also classified instructor postings according to whether they started new discussion threads, posted answers to student questions, and/or posted follow-up questions in existing discussion threads. We found that the overwhelming majority of instructor postings were answers to student questions, and rarely did instructors ask follow-up questions or start new discussion threads. When we looked for correlations between styles of instructor postings and university evaluation survey responses, we saw very little effect with the exception that students did seem to regard instructors who answered many questions as more enthusiastic, and, as one would expect, students reacted negatively when instructors mainly posted "housekeeping" postings rather than engaging actively in the discussions.

Instructor and Student Perceptions of the Online Learning Experience

We have already discussed whether SAO instructors' posting patterns revealed any correlations with student posting patterns and responses to university evaluation surveys. To gain more direct feedback, in 2002 as discussed earlier, we surveyed 215 students (to which 37% responded) and also 20 instructors (to which 85% responded) about a number of aspects of forum participation and sought their opinions on whether frequent instructor postings influenced student-posting patterns. Students indicated that they appreciated frequent instructor postings, although a very small number suggested that instructors hold off answering students' questions for anything from a few days to a week to give students a chance to provide answers first.

Some of the survey results disagreed with our analysis of postings discussed earlier. For example, all but one of the instructors surveyed believed that frequent postings by instructors either did not affect, or even increased, the level of student discussion. General university survey results indicated that instructors who posted more often at the end of forums were rated more highly on enthusiasm and expertise, but in our targeted 2002 survey, students indicated that they preferred it when instructors post mostly during forums.

In contrast, instructors were roughly evenly split on the question of whether they mainly posted during or at the end of forums, in agreement with the posting patterns we reported on earlier. One of the most experienced SAO instructors commented:

I see two roles for the instructor: (a) during the two-week period, to monitor the discussion, correct any significant misconceptions, trigger discussion, and steer the discussion in an appropriate direction. All this is best achieved with a fairly light touch. The aim is to stimulate a good discussion, get students to answer each other's questions as far as possible, but correct any answers which may be misleading. (b) At the end of the two-week period, answer any remaining unanswered questions, or finish off and tidy up any extended discussions.

Some instructors suggested that posting at the end of discussion forums may not be effective:

I find that it is most useful to post my contributions (both questions and answers) during each two-week forum. That way I know my contributions will be looked at. I find that it is hard to get students to look back at previous two-week periods in any detail. Most students always want to move onto the next topic and some struggle to keep up with even that.

In the 2002 survey, approximately one-third of the student respondents indicated that they appreciated it when instructors ask questions in forums, and some also explicitly mentioned follow-up or subsidiary questions. Comments included:

I like when an instructor adds questions to expand the discussion without finishing the prior one. It leaves it open for people to consider. It can be helpful when an instructor posts questions as often it is difficult to come up with a question that is appropriate to the topic.

The majority of instructors surveyed indicated that they often asked follow-up questions in order to continue existing discussion threads or start new ones. Instructors also indicated that they also believed (correctly) that students were likely to appreciate this strategy. Several instructors commented on the effectiveness of this "Socratic approach," for example:

I definitely like to 'answer' questions with questions, or at least give hints as to how the answer might be found by further research/thought. This often invokes a response — often a simple hint is all that's needed to get them on the right track.

Instructors were asked to comment on what styles of instructor participation they regarded as the most effective for teaching and learning .Their responses were broadly in agreement with the "guide on the side" philosophy of the SAO program, for example: *I have found the most effective style is one where the instructor's participation is not markedly different from that of a student, except that the instructor tends to know more of the answers. So just like the students, I pose speculative questions, give partial answers which raise more questions, or point colleagues to an interesting WWW site.*

However, in our statistical analysis of forum postings, we found that the overwhelming majority of instructor postings were answers to student questions, and that instructor postings that included questions constituted only a very small proportion of the total.

Conclusion

In this chapter, we have discussed a range of issues related to the design, development, and coordination of an international online program in which asynchronous discussion forums play a key role in the learning and teaching environment. In particular, we have shared our experience on aspects of the implementation of asynchronous forums, the induction of new online instructors, and dealing with challenging students.

Our research has shown that trying to judge the "health" of discussion forums by the rate of student participation and the length of discussion threads alone can be misleading and that student-instructor interactions can be more complex that conventional wisdom may suggest. In these studies, we found that the ways in which instructors posted to forums correlated with students' forum participation in unexpected ways. Instructors' perceptions of their teaching online did not necessarily agree with our analysis of posting rates, and the rate of student participation and the length of discussion threads were not necessarily good ways to judge the quality of learning taking place. It seems that intuition is not necessarily a reliable guide to the success of online forums, therefore, this is an area where evaluative research can make an invaluable contribution.

We believe that continued student satisfaction with the SAO discussion forums, despite growth in the size of the program, is largely due to limiting the size of individual forums plus supporting the role of the instructor as the "guide on the side," thereby allowing students to take a more central role in their own learning. For all its challenges, from the perspective of an instructor who is interested in guiding rather than directing student learning, online education can be a remarkably engaging and rewarding experience.

References

Alexander, S., & Blight, D. (1996). *Technology in international Education. Executive Summary of IDP commissioned research.* Retrieved April 3, 2005, from www.iml.uts.edu.au/about/staff/alexander/idpexsum.html

Anderson, A.C. (2002). Just because it's online doesn't mean it's learner-centred! *ENC Focus, 9*(1). Retrieved April 3, 2005, from www.enc.org/features/focus/archive/pd/

Asano, Y. (1999). *Virtual recitation: Advantages and disadvantages.* TCC '99: Fourth Annual TCC Online Conference. Retrieved August 7, 2005, from http://makahiki.kcc.hawaii.edu/tcc/tcon99/papers/asano.html

Benfield, G. (2002). *Designing and managing effective online discussions. OCSLD earning and Teaching Briefing Papers Series.* Retrieved August 16, 2005, from www.brookes.ac.uk/services/ocsd/2_learntch/briefing_papers/online_discussions.pdf

Berge, Z. (1995). Facilitating computer conferencing: Recommendations from the field. *Educational Technology, 35*(1), 22-30.

Biesenbach-Lucas, S. (2003). Asynchronous discussion groups in teacher training classes: Perceptions of native and non-native students. *Journal of Asynchronous Networks, 7*(3), 24-33.

Ciano, L. (2003). *Special considerations when teaching non-native English in an online environment.* TCC Online Conference 2003. Retrieved April 3, 2005, from http://makahiki.kcc.hawaii.edu/tcc/2003/conference/presentations/ciano.html

Collins, M., & Berge, Z. (1997, March). *Moderating online electronic discussion groups.* Paper presented at the American Educational Research Association. Chicago. Retrieved April 3, 2005, from www.emoderators.com/moderators/sur_aera97.html

Gold, S. (2001). A constructivist approach to online training for online teachers. *Journal of Asynchronous Learning Networks, 5*(1), 35-57.

Ishikawa, L. (2002). *Intercultural aspects of CMC. Dmst 4503 Seminar in Internet Communication.* Retrieved April 3, 2005, from www.du.edu/~jrutenbe/4503/intercultural.htm

Kearsley, G. (2000). *Learning and teaching in cyberspace.* Belmont, CA: Wadsworth.

Laurillard, D. (1996). *The changing university. Instructional Technology Forum.* Retrieved August 16, 2005, from http://itech1.coe.uga.edu/itforum/paper13/paper13.html

Levitch, S., & Milheim, W. (2003). Transitioning instructor skills to the virtual classroom. *Educational Technology, 42*(2), 42-46.

MacKnight, C. (2000). Teaching critical thinking through online discussions. *Educause Quarterly, 4,* 38-41.

Maddison, S., & Mazzolini, M. (2005). *Blackbelts versus whitebelts - Dealing with online students from a wide range of academic backgrounds.* Submitted for publication.

Markel, S. (2001). Technology and education online discussion forums: It's in the response. *Online Journal of Distance Learning Administration, 4*(2). Retrieved April 3, 2005, from www.westga.edu/~distance/ojdla/summer42/markel42.html

Mazzolini, M. (2002). The use of online discussion forums as a learning and teaching tool in astronomy. *Publications of the Astronomical Society of Australia, 19*(4), 448-454.

Mazzolini, M., & Maddison, S. (2003). Sage, guide or ghost? The effect of instructor intervention on student participation in online discussion forums. *Computers & Education, 40*(3), 237-253.

Mazzolini, M., & Maddison, S. (2003a). Widening the circle: Managing discussion forums in a growing online program. In G. Crisp, D. Thiele, I. Scholten, S. Barker, & J. Baron (Eds.), *Interact, integrate, impact: Proceedings of the 20th Annual Conference of the Australasian Society for Computers in Learning in Tertiary Education, ASCILITE 2003* (pp. 322-331). University of Adelaide, Australia.

Mazzolini, M., & Maddison, S. (2004). Education without frontiers? International participation in an online astronomy program. In R. Atkinson, C. McBeath, D. Jonas-Dwyer, & R. Philips (Eds.), Beyond the comfort zone, (pp. 6-6-615). *Proceedings of the 21st Annual Conference of the Australasian Society for Computers in*

Learning in Tertiary Education, University of Western Australia, Perth.

Mazzolini, M., & Maddison, S. (2005). When to jump in: The role of the instructor in online discussion forums. Accepted for publication in *Computers & Education.*

McIsaac, M.S. (2002). Online learning from an international perspective. *Education Media International, 39*(1), 17-21.

Metts, S. (2005). *Suggestions for classroom discussion.* Retrieved July 24, 2005, from www.cat.ilstu.edu/teaching_tips/handouts/classdis.shtml

Morse, K. (2003). Does one size fit all? Exploring asynchronous learning in a multicultural environment. *Journal of Asynchronous Learning Networks, 7*(1). Retrieved April 3, 2005, from www.sloan-c.org/publications/jaln/v7n1/v7n1_morse.asp

Motteram, G. (2001). The role of synchronous communication in fully distance education. *Australian Journal of Educational Technology, 17*(2), 131-149.

Murphy K.L., & Collins M.P. (1997). Communications conventions in instructional electronic chats. *First Monday, 2*(11). Retrieved August 7, 2005, from http://firstmonday.dk/issues/issue2_11/murphy/index.html

Northover, M. (2002). Online discussion boards – Friend or foe? In A. Williamson, C. Gunn, A. Young, & T. Clear (Eds.), *Winds of change in the sea of learning: Proceedings of the 19th Annual Conference of the Australasian Society for Computers in Learning in Tertiary Education, ASCILITE 2002* (pp. 477-484). UNITEC Institute of Technology, Auckland, New Zealand.

Paloff, R.M., & Pratt, K. (1999). *Building learning communities in cyberspace – Effective strategies for the online classroom.* San Francisco: Jossey-Bass.

Paloff, R.M., & Pratt, K. (2001). *Lessons from the cyberspace classroom – The realities of online teaching.* San Francisco: Jossey-Bass.

Pan, C.C., Tsai, M.H., Tsai, P.Y., Tao, Y., & Cornell, R. (2003). Technology's impact: Symbiotic or asymbiotic impact on differing cultures? *Educational Media International, 40*(3-4), 319-330.

Salmon, G. (2000). *E-Moderating: The key to teaching and learning online.* London: Kogan-Page.

Schrum, L., & Berge, Z. (1997). Creating student interaction within the educational experience— A challenge for online teachers. *Canadian Journal of Educational Communication, 26*(3), 133-144.

Schrum, L., & Hong, S. (2002). Dimensions and strategies for online success: Voices from experienced educators. *Journal of Asynchronous Learning Networks, 6*(1), 57-67.

Thomas, C. (2001). *On line or face-to-face: Which is the better way to 'talk'?* Retrieved April 4, 2005, from http://iiswinprd03.petersons.com/distancelearning/code/articles/distancelearnface7.asp

Tu, C.H. (2001). How Chinese perceive social presence: An examination of interaction in online learning environment. *Education Media International, 38*(1), 45-60.

Tylee, J. (year unknown). *Cultural issues and the online environment.* Retrieved April 3, 2005, from www.csu.edu.au/division/celt/resources/cultural_issues.pdf

Endnote

[1]   www.astronomy.swin.edu.au/sao

Section III:

Technological Issues

Chapter XV

Online Learning Activities in Second Year Environmental Geography

Sally Priest, University of Southampton, UK

Karen Fill, University of Southampton, UK

Abstract

This chapter discusses the design, technical development, delivery, and evaluation of two online learning activities in environmental geography. A "blended" approach was adopted in order to best integrate the new materials within the existing unit. The primary aim of these online activities was to provide students with opportunities to develop and demonstrate valuable practical skills, while increasing their understanding of environmental management. A purpose-built system was created in order to overcome initial technological challenges. The online activities have already been delivered successfully to a large number of students over two academic years. Evaluation and staff reflection highlight the benefits and limitations of the new activities, and the chapter concludes with recommendations for others wishing to adopt a similar approach.

Introduction

In the academic year 2003-2004, staff in the School of Geography at the University of Southampton created two online learning activities for students on a level two unit entitled *Physical Geography in Environmental Management.* The activities introduced the concepts of managing and querying environmental data, using and developing environmental indicators, analysis, reflection, and decision support. As they worked through the learning activities, the students had access to a wide range of Web-based resources plus repurposed data from the Environment Agency's River Habitat Survey (Environment Agency, 1998). Their responses to both formative and summative assessments were captured online. Some elements were computer assessed and others marked by the unit tutors. The staff and students were all campus based. These online activities complemented lectures and other face-to-face sessions on a unit that has been taught, in one guise or another, for 20 years at the University of Southampton.

This chapter describes the development and implementation of these online learning activities in terms of the pedagogic opportunities and technical challenges encountered and overcome. It reviews the learning outcomes achieved by the students and discusses their evaluation of the resources. Tutors' reflections on the impact of this innovation are included. The chapter concludes with recommendations, both specific to this unit and for those working in the wider field of technology-supported learning.

The innovations and evaluation were undertaken under the auspices of the *Digital Libraries in Support of Innovative Approaches to Learning and Teaching in Geography* project (DialogPLUS, 2004).

Background

Overview of the Unit as Traditionally Taught

Physical Geography in Environmental Management is primarily lecture based; however, the unit is pioneering in many respects. Since its inception, it has been a test-bed for new pedagogic approaches within the School of Geography. The unit is taken by postgraduates and undergraduates, as well as geography specialists and non-geographers. This varied mix of students makes it ideally suited for evolving new and innovative approaches. Indeed, the unit was an early adopter of the MicroCosm® open hypermedia system (Clark, Ball, & Sadler, 1995); the first in the School to use PowerPoint and subsequently Web-based resources; and the School's own virtual learning environment (VLE) was initially developed to house its resources.

The associated practical elements have developed from paper-based, via early computer techniques to support learning, to the first stages of Web-enabled education. Early attempts at e-learning focussed primarily on the delivery of resources across the Web and the use of simple computer models, rather than engaging students with any meaningful interaction, other than choice of options and parameters for modeling. The opportunity, within the DialogPLUS project, to address this perceived need for engagement, coupled with increasing numbers of students, provided the impetus for further change.

The Pedagogic Approach

A learning environment is a place where people can draw upon resources to make sense out of things and construct meaningful solutions to problems. (Wilson, 1996, p. 3)

For more than 20 years, tutors on this unit have adopted a constructivist perspective, progressively evolving an approach that embeds learning in "realistic and relevant contexts" (Honebein, 1996, p. 11). Practical elements give the students opportunities to learn in different ways, developing a variety of skills. The previous practicals involved electronic resources developed in MicroCosm® (see www.vmsi-microcosm.com). Advances in technology, primarily Web-based delivery, offered the potential for more experiential student learning, without a major change of rationale. This remains the activity-based enhancement of student learning in an alternative environment to lectures.

The mix of traditional lectures and online activities employed on the unit for the last two academic years conforms to the emerging 21st century paradigm (Kerres & de Witt, 2003) of "blended learning." Oliver (2004) is critical of this term, arguing that it is either inconsistent or redundant (p. 6) and that, because it originates from the world of corporate training, its use in higher education is somehow belittling (p. 7). However, increasingly lecturers are employing a mix of traditional (off-line) and online approaches and they and their students seem comfortable with the term and the approach. Indeed, Childs (2004) found students enthusiastic about blended learning, which they understood to mean a combination of listening to lectures, finding and using Web-based resources, and interacting with particular software to solve problems.

It is certainly crucial to specify and address clear learning outcomes, to ensure that there are opportunities for learners to engage with core concepts, and to provide what Weller, Pegler, and Mason (2003) refer to as an "overarching narrative" that directs and frames interaction with resources and constructive learning. These have been guiding principles in the creation of the online learning activities reported here. Within an activity, the students find a mix of media — text, image, and data — and of task types — assimilative, analytic, communicative, and reflective (Laurillard, 2002). This mix is intended to address the needs of different learning preferences and to engage all students in tasks that facilitate their individual construction of meaning.

In order to integrate the online elements fully within the overall approach to teaching and learning, the rest of the unit was examined and other aspects were redeveloped. For example, lecture content was modified to ensure that the role and purpose of the online activities blended appropriately with the more established elements. The timing of online activities and associated assessment was also addressed, as this is crucial to learning (Perkin, 1999). It was important that the students were not overloaded and had sufficient time to concentrate on the set tasks. Therefore, the online activities were introduced quite early within the unit so that they did not impinge on the later coursework essay, or on examination preparation. Modification to the unit involved a slight overall reduction in content to facilitate independent work and in-depth study of the remaining topics.

Technical Challenges

System Requirements

The technical environment was one of a number of different challenges addressed when developing the e-learning activities. The University of Southampton's preferred VLE is Blackboard™. However, this was unsuitable for the proposed online activities for a number of reasons. The pedagogic rationale behind the integration and adoption of these new online elements was the interactivity afforded by modern technology and the possibilities for introducing students to new and interesting datasets. The then current version of Blackboard™ did not offer the level of interactivity required to achieve the desired learning outcomes, it did not permit the students to enter "free" answers for automatic marking, and feedback options were restricted to "immediate" or "not at all". Therefore, it was decided to author the material independently of the established VLE, and to create content within dynamic Web pages authored in PHP (see www.php.net).

Despite the bespoke system overcoming many of the constraints of the Blackboard™ VLE, a number of outstanding issues remained. It was intended that these e-learning elements formed part of the summative assessment for the unit. This necessitated system recognition of student users, storage of online submissions, and recording of individual marks. This was achieved by using password protected log-ins and an underlying student database.

Although formative elements of the online activities were computer assessed, the summative components were marked by tutors. Thus, it was also important that submissions could be viewed and marked easily, and feedback entered. This was facilitated by the creation of a password protected tutor interface which allowed access to individual student entries. Although there are plans to implement electronic feedback, in the first instance the tutor screens were also designed to be printed out and handed back to the students.

Access to Datasets

A primary reason for developing the e-learning practicals was to allow students to gain firsthand experience of using data in a similar manner to a professional environmental manager. The chosen dataset was the River Habitat Survey (RHS) with entries for more than 14,000 UK river sites collected, authenticated, and managed by the Environment Agency, who kindly permitted us to extract and reconfigure data for educational purposes. For ease of online access, the reconfigured dataset was mounted within dynamic Web pages. The technical design was complicated by the need for students to perform queries on the data in much the same way as if it were in the original database. Although time consuming and challenging, the repurposing of the RHS dataset significantly enhanced the students' experience, as they had the opportunity to manipulate real data. An unexpected result is that the repurposed RHS data Web pages have been suitable for use within other geography teaching at Southampton.

Web Design

There was initial debate about whether the Web pages should look different from those already authored for the School of Geography, or whether consistency was important for the students. A further complication was that these online activities were some of the first outputs of DialogPLUS, so it was important to highlight digital library aspects and consider any design implications that might impact more widely on that project.

After consultation with a number of people (i.e., educationalists, Web developers, geography tutors) about these design implications, it was deemed most important that the Web pages were identifiable to the students and seamless with those already being used within the School of Geography's undergraduate Web site. These had already addressed accessibility issues (see www.w3.org/WAI/), and consistency would reassure students that the online activities were endorsed by the School of Geography and build trust in what, to many, was a new learning experience (Graham, 1999; Carter, 2002).

In order to address these issues and as a way of separating content, tasks, and external resources, the main body of the screen was split into three areas: navigation, content, and digital library (see the example in Figure 1). From a pedagogic viewpoint, this layout reinforced the content of the task for students by placing it in the centre of the screen. The digital library resources held separately on the right then offered opportunities for wider learning and/or access to data to complete specific tasks. Incorporating all this via links within the main content might have overloaded the students and diverted them from following the narrative explaining the tasks and rationale.

The Online Learning Activities

To assist the students, the structure of both activities was kept the same. Each had an *introduction, aims and learning outcomes, practical content,* and sections describing *expectations* and *assessment criteria.* This consistency was important as the majority of students had little experience with online learning. The potential nervousness of an inexperienced user group, plus that of the development team about how the system would perform, prompted the decision to hold associated "clinic" sessions which students were encouraged to attend if they had any problems or queries. These were timetabled in a university computer lab and staffed by a tutor and/or a postgraduate teaching assistant. Students could undertake the activities during these sessions as well as in their own time.

Figure 1. Example of the layout and design of the Web pages

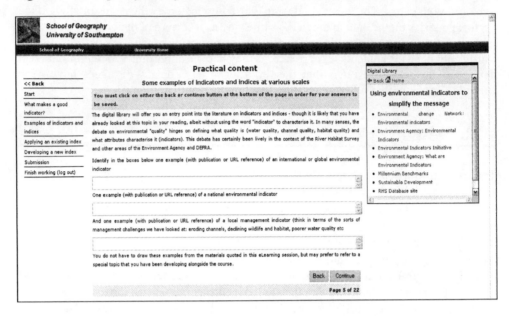

Access to an activity was available at all times from campus or personal computers, so support was also offered via an online discussion board. The tutor monitored this regularly and responded swiftly to queries. This is discussed in more detail below.

Learning Outcomes

In order to ensure that core concepts were established, specific learning outcomes for the online activities were decided at the outset and informed the design of both content and learning environment (see Figure 2). These emphasise the importance, use, and interpretation of data in environmental management. They also provide the basis for examining the success of these learning activities below.

Practical Content

This section explores in more depth the different components of the online activities and their importance and role within student learning. The content of the activities was designed around a narrative to guide students through the use of resources and from task to task (see Figures 3 and 4).

Figure 2. Example of learning outcomes

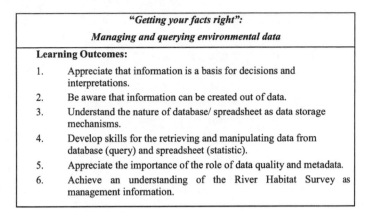

"*Getting your facts right*":
Managing and querying environmental data
Learning Outcomes:
1. Appreciate that information is a basis for decisions and interpretations.
2. Be aware that information can be created out of data.
3. Understand the nature of database/ spreadsheet as data storage mechanisms.
4. Develop skills for the retrieving and manipulating data from database (query) and spreadsheet (statistic).
5. Appreciate the importance of the role of data quality and metadata.
6. Achieve an understanding of the River Habitat Survey as management information.

Figure 3. Introduction and first tasks in an online activity

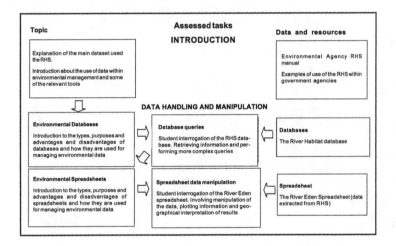

The complete list of tasks and associated skills for the first activity is shown in Figure 5. Some tasks were formative, however all ultimately contributed to the assessed elements.

While these online activities are mainly linear (Plowman, 1996), it is appreciated that not all students learn best in this manner (Honey & Mumford, 1992). Some flexibility is possible as resources can be visited and tasks completed in any order. Significant aspects are the external resources, which include papers in academic journals, external governmental Web sites, and Environmental Agency reports. This variety of sources was intended to encourage students to read broadly and gain experience of interpreting

Figure 4. Assessed elements of an online activity

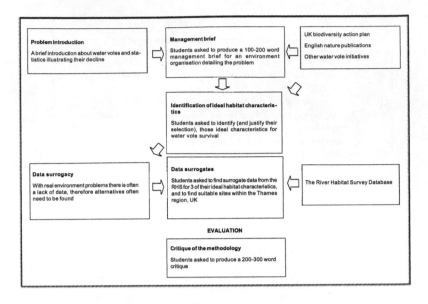

Figure 5. Indicative list of tasks performed in Online Activity 1

Task performed	Associated skill demonstrated
▪ Read explanatory text online	Research/interpretation
▪ View/read background resources	Research/interpretation/critical analysis
▪ Practice querying the database	Practical (data handling and manipulation)
▪ Use query to find answers to questions	Practical and interpretation
▪ Enter answers online	*Completion of assessed activity*
▪ Read explanatory text online	Research/interpretation
▪ View spreadsheet extract	Practical (data handling and manipulation)
▪ View map	Practical (data handling and manipulation)
▪ Explore spreadsheet	Practical (data handling and manipulation)
▪ Sort spreadsheet data	Practical (data handling and manipulation)
▪ Calculate and enter answers online	Practical and interpretation
▪ Plot & interpret graphs	Practical and interpretation
▪ Enter values read off the graphs	*Completion of assessed activity*
▪ Read explanatory text online	Research/interpretation
▪ Research/ reflect on a specified problem using external resources	Research/interpretation/critical analysis
▪ Write a 300 word management brief (in online box)	Interpretation/critical analysis/ability to summarise/ clear expression
▪ List 5 factors & assess their significance using a drop down list.	Interpretation of data and resources/ environmental decision-making/ writing and justification skills
▪ Use database to identify 3 attributes that will act as surrogates for the previous attributes	Practical querying skills/ data interpretation/ decision-making
▪ Enter 3 attributes, their RHS categories & reason for choosing them, site refs.	Writing and justification skills
▪ Use database to identify sites.	
▪ Enter list of suitable sites	Practical (data handling and manipulation)
▪ Write a 500 word critique of methodology/techniques used (in online box)	*Completion of assessed activity* Interpretation/critical analysis/writing and summarising skills
▪ Submit work online	*Completion of assessed activity*

the different data types that underpin environmental management decisions. However, linking to external resources creates a maintenance issue, as availability depends upon stability on the host site.

Assessment Rationale

Consistent with the pedagogic motivations for implementing these activities and adding different learning experiences to the unit, the assessed elements also aimed to broaden the measures of student attainment. The online activities could have been purely formative, but in our experience, it can be very difficult to motivate students to complete optional exercises. To reinforce the importance of practical environmental decision-making, some components of the online activities had to be summatively assessed. Other assessments on the unit are more "traditional," including a 2,000-word essay-style report investigating a management problem and an unseen written examination.

In the first year, it was decided that the online activities would only comprise 10% of the overall assessment. This was felt sufficient to induce students to complete the tasks, in addition to any intrinsic motivation (Biggs, 2003). It was also conservative enough to provide a "factor of safety" if the technology failed. Although the system had been tested and seemed robust, it was impossible to test for large numbers of concurrent users, a situation likely to arise with 130 to 150 students on the unit. Therefore, it was considered inappropriate to place too great a weighting on the system that they were effectively "testing" for the first time. If one or both of the online activities did irretrievably fail, the situation could be resolved much more easily if only 5 to 10% of overall assessment was affected. This low weighting did cause some problems related to levels of study time and assessment, however, it was warranted to shield the students from potential technological problems. Following the success in the first year, the weighting was increased to 25%. Student feedback in year two appeared to endorse this allocation, with 75% of those who returned an evaluation form (n=56) agreeing that the maximum mark of 12.5% for each assessed online activity was fair.

The assessed tasks were a mixture of short answers and longer questions. The shorter ones enabled students to demonstrate that they could perform queries and find specific information. The longer ones, which involved entering written answers, aimed to assess whether students had understood the process of decision-making and all the problems involved. The majority of the shorter answer components were marked automatically. This assisted the speed, validity, and impartiality of marking and permitted feedback to the students at an earlier stage than would otherwise be possible, while also reducing tutor workload on a very popular unit.

Technological limitations are related to computer marking of written answers. Indeed, since the questions aimed to test the students' ability to make and justify sound environmental decisions, there is much ambiguity related to a "correct" answer. Therefore, although it was possible to develop a broad mark scheme from which to grade students' work, a great deal of judgement was still required to assess whether answers were appropriate. Certainly, some student answers were surprising in their level of ingenuity and thoughtfulness, and automated marking on these more innovative or subjective topics would entail a great deal of moderation. It is therefore likely that this component of the assessment will continue to be marked in the traditional way.

There were also system constraints. The boxes designed to hold student answers only permitted textual content. Although it would have been possible to develop them to hold images or graphs, it was felt that the time taken to do this would be counterproductive. Students were asked to produce graphs in a spreadsheet, thus practising these valuable skills. However, the most important learning outcome was not to produce attractive charts, but rather to interpret relationships in the data thus portrayed. Therefore, a detailed text-based description of the relationships between the data, and the significance of them, demonstrated to the marker not only that a student had undertaken the activity, but that they had also understood the results.

Students' Use of the Online Learning Activities

Students were observed doing the online activities during the timetabled clinics. Although no technical problems occurred, there was some dissatisfaction voiced with respect to the linear navigation (Next/Back only). As explained, tutors felt it was desirable to lead the learners logically through the activities, but many students wanted to be able to look ahead, jump back, or dip in and out of the resources. To facilitate this, a menu or tabbed navigation could easily be provided in the future.

Most students worked quietly as individuals, but it was noticeable that some worked in groups of three or four, discussing the resources and possible answers to the formative questions. While this usefully develops team skills required in their future working lives, the underlying approach was cognitive, rather than social and constructivist, and the tutors felt that such collaboration posed challenges for differentiating between students and (importantly) correctly rewarding individual effort and performance. This raises a number of important points about validating and assessing online coursework. Students seemed engaged and were overheard discussing key concepts, such as "bank erosion," reassuring each other about data selections and analysis. Many students made hand-written notes as they looked at the Web-based resources; under the current conditions in university labs, users cannot bookmark Web pages to return to later. This may change over the next few years with a proposed learning portal and greater customisation. Some kept several resource windows open (minimised) as they paged through the online activity, consulting them from time to time. Some students used MS Word to compose text answers, others typed directly into the Web form boxes. The embedded discussion forums were mainly used by a small number of students to pose questions to the tutor. This is discussed in this chapter's section on staff perspectives.

Evaluation

Student Evaluation of the Resources

In the second year of implementation, students were asked to complete a questionnaire about the online learning activities. Completed forms were received from 56 (43%) of the 130 students who took the unit. Although a moderate sample, their responses were particularly positive with respect to description of content and learning objectives; the inclusion of required tools to access and manipulate online resources; the embedded mechanisms for information and support; the appropriateness of assessments; and, most encouragingly, the contribution of these activities to improving their knowledge and skills. The most negative response was the suggestion that they might prefer to be assessed by essays rather than online activities, suggesting general acceptance of the assessment components of the online activities. Only six students commented that the time estimation for completing the activities was too short. This was a marked improvement over the previous year, when the majority of negative comments were concerned with the length of time taken to complete the activities.

Twenty-six respondents contributed qualitative comments. Typical general comments indicated that this was an interesting new experience but not particularly enjoyable. Negative comments were about computer failures and limited navigation. Overall, both quantitative and qualitative feedback indicated strong endorsement of the online activities' contribution to improving skills.

On the scored questions, there were no significantly different responses from male and female students. The eight post-graduate respondents were significantly ($p<0.0001$) more positive than the undergraduates about the ease of using the activities and the contribution that another, non-assessed, online activity had made to their submitted work.

Achieved Learning Outcomes

Students generally performed the set tasks well and attainment was high, the average grade being 72%, with a range of marks between 50 and 94%. In most cases, the results of the online activities illustrate that the learning outcomes were met. The majority of students correctly demonstrated that they had gained data manipulation and retrieval skills. They were then able to use them within other areas of the unit. Other written coursework, in particular, has revealed an increased understanding of the difficulties of making environmental decisions and how they can be overcome.

There is also anecdotal evidence to suggest that the computerised elements have contributed to other areas of student learning. Students completed these elements prior to starting their final year dissertation. A number chose to use some of the data and ideas within their dissertation and also on other units in their degree programme.

Staff Perspectives

This section draws on both formal and informal student feedback and staff reflections over the two years of development and implementation.

Development Challenges

None of the technical challenges proved insurmountable. After a handful of minor teething problems, the dynamic Web page system has been extremely robust and has run, with slight content changes, for two academic sessions. The interactive elements are central to the student learning and have justified the design and creation of the mode of delivery. Many of the generic elements, such as the student login system and the tutor reporting structure, have been repurposed for other online activities on other units.

The development of content was stressful and time consuming, not only initially but also closer to delivery. However, time spent establishing unambiguous learning outcomes and tasks that allow students to achieve them were clearly important to our success. The upfront effort was also consolidated in the second year, and the subsequent delivery was therefore less demanding.

Implementation of the Online Activities

The role of the tutor in online learning activities is both similar and different to that in more traditional teaching and learning (Bennett & Marsh, 2001). In practice, balancing the level of support was tricky; too much assistance might be counterproductive to student learning, but too little might be worse. Two support mechanisms were implemented: a discussion forum and the clinics described. The forum allowed students to submit queries at any time, enabled the tutor and/or other students to reply, and everyone to see the contributions. It had been hoped that students would discuss higher order ideas, in addition to asking specific questions. In year one, this did not happen and the forum was only used by a small number of students to pose questions to the tutor. In the second year, while postings were still mainly questions rather than discussion, students did volunteer answers to each other.

Similarly, the clinics did not always work as anticipated (i.e., that students would come to ask questions arising from work they had already done online). Rather, they chose to use them to do the work, raising queries dynamically. They also discussed things with each other at these times which obviated the need for the online forum.

Physical Geography in Environmental Management attracts large numbers of students, between 120 and 150 each year. Therefore, adding elements to the unit always raises issues of tutor workload, particularly with regards to marking. Computer-based practicals are not new on this unit, so although development time and resources were required, implementing "blended learning" was not onerous, and there was no significant increase in marking and administration. The computerised marking of some tasks did not reduce tutor effort significantly. Short textual answers still involved human marking, and where automatic marking was used, it required a thoughtful approach and substantial development time.

Student Attitudes to E-Learning

Many of the students seemed initially nervous about completing and submitting work online. System stability and mechanisms for saving work concerned many. This eased after successful submission of the first activity. Another uncertainty related to their actual ability to complete the work, with some students concerned that they did not have sufficient computer skills. Most of these anxieties disappeared following encouragement to start the online activities, with the reassurance that the "clinics" and discussion forum could be used for support if needed.

A handful of students still struggled a little with the more practical elements of the tasks and became quite upset and annoyed about having to do them. This was tackled by working with these students and reinforcing the teaching and learning rationale. Explaining that they stood to gain important practical skills and would use them again in the future did seem to have a positive affect. Despite initial misgivings about working and submitting online, most students did well. Confidence gained from the first activity was apparent when observing their work on the second. Attendance at clinics was reduced and students appeared to be much more comfortable with the whole concept of online learning.

There is no denying that assessment is important to students. Feedback about the timing of the unit assessment has been mixed. Informal student comments indicated that some students did not appreciate that there were a number of smaller pieces of work and felt as though they were constantly working, rather than having periods where little was being undertaken. Some felt more under pressure and overworked. The majority, however, were positive about the spread assignments and being able to complete part of the overall assessment earlier in the unit. Most also welcomed the alternative means of assessment. Many find examinations very stressful and do not work best under these conditions. They enjoyed being challenged by new material and seemed to engage with the practical nature of the activities. This reinforces the rationale for broadening assessment options and challenging the students in different ways.

Students also liked receiving their marks relatively soon after the submission deadlines. Activity one scripts were returned within two weeks, prior to activity two. Students seemed to appreciate this effort and were keen both to know their marks and to read the comments. They seemed to gain confidence from this feedback on their progress on the unit.

Some students perceived, wrongly, that work completed and submitted online did not warrant the same academic standards as more conventional assignments. For example, there was inappropriate referencing and poor English in textual answers. Following this discovery when marking activity one, tutors reinforced the need to demonstrate academic skills. This was less of a problem in the second year, as requirements were made clear upfront.

School Recommendations and Feedback

The School of Geography was very supportive of the use of new technology and the introduction of new methods of teaching. Staff were consulted about the online learning activities and, when asked for feedback, were honest, open and gave their time freely. For example, the mix of short answer questions and longer text-based questions meant that students who spent time and effort were rewarded with high marks for successfully completing the exercises. The average of 72% suggested that students did well on these types of assessment but raised a question. Objective, computerised marking can result in higher marks than some human markers might award, an issue debated at school level. Some staff expressed concern that both the tasks performed and the automated marking reduced the ability to distinguish between students.

The main purpose of the assessment was to ascertain whether students understood the role of data within environmental management and that they could take on the role of a manager and make justifiable environmental decisions. Marks were given if students were able to perform a particular task and demonstrate a certain skill. There was very little scope for differentiation, they had either gained the skill or not. Only in the more judgemental elements, was it possible to differentiate and these were human-marked.

Perceived Enhancement of the Student Experience

Overall, the development of these activities has enhanced the learning experience and provided an added dimension to the unit. Students have encountered some of the difficulties, conflicts, and frustrations involved when making decisions with limited data. In achieving the learning outcomes, they have gained relevant practical skills, and it has afforded those who struggle with traditional essays and examinations increased opportunities to do well.

Students need to be enthused and engaged with materials in order to promote effective learning (Laurillard, 2002). Our online activities have successfully done this. As well as investigating the River Habitat Survey data, students have benefited from reading the linked resources, such as professional or government reports that they might not have previously accessed. Coupled with more academic journal articles, exposure to these alternative sources of information helps to provide a more solid grounding in the subject.

Race (1996) states that feedback on progression is one of the four prerequisites for successful learning. The timing and relevance of student feedback is essential for student improvement (Laurillard, 2002; Mutch, 2003). This was certainly true, with both students and tutors benefiting from the early opportunity to gauge progress. Staff were reassured that students were beginning to grasp some of the key issues in environmental management, while students gained the essential encouragement that they were on the correct track (Lisewski & Settle, 1996) and could continue to progress.

Recommendations

After two years of developing, implementing, supporting, and evaluating these online learning activities, the resulting recommendations fall into four categories related to technology, content, staff, and students.

Technology Related

Technology-supported teaching and learning can enhance student experience and attainment, particularly online activities that permit engagement with real data as students investigate and apply concepts introduced in off-line teaching sessions. This is the type of blended learning the authors of this chapter recommend for campus-based students in higher education. It also addresses the disadvantages of earlier computer-assisted courseware described by Spellman (2000, p. 74) which simulated "reality."

It is important to work within system constraints, as well as trying to push the boundaries. This implies being aware of limitations, as well as the benefits and opportunities, recognising the need for technical support, and planning for it in terms of availability, deadlines, and possible costs. It is essential to remain flexible, particularly early on, in order to deal with any unexpected technical issues.

Systems should be tested where possible for ease of use by the intended learners. Consistency with institutional or departmental learning environment serves to reassure. Seamless integration of online resources to support, but not impinge on the learning, is vital. Therefore, an uncomplicated Web design, checked for accessibility, is advocated.

To minimise risks from technological failure, start with low weighting for online assessments. For small-scale implementations, it is not always possible to engage in the full risk analysis and management recommended by Zakrzewski and Steven (2000), but it is vital to have contingency plans in the event of system malfunction (Harwood, 2005) and not to react in an ad hoc manner.

Content Related

There was a tendency to produce, or link to, more content than was truly required, resulting in tasks that took much longer than anticipated, or even occurred in testing. Recommendations here include careful selection of further resources that students might be directed to and early testing by both staff and students. The repurposing of datasets can be difficult and time consuming, but, once completed, the format may serve to support many different learning activities.

Careful consideration should be given to the type of activities developed. There were a number of other options explored that proved unworkable because of the high level of interactivity required and associated technological development to make them worthwhile for students. It is vital to align content and learning outcomes. As Honebein suggested, "interpretation of the goals and subsequent translation into learning activities is the real art in the design of constructivist learning environments" (1996, p. 18).

Staff Related

When developing activities of this nature, ensure that other teaching staff understand the role and also the limitations of the technology involved. Regardless of how nervous staff are, during the early stages of implementing innovative learning activities, it is important not to pass this on to the students. Try to instil confidence and offer thoughtful support. Both staff and students should have a grasp on why the activities are being done online.

Staff should be aware of the time and resources required to design, implement, and maintain interactive online activities. The costs versus the benefits need to be carefully considered. In this case, the upfront effort was justified due to the large number of students on the unit and the skills and understanding that the tasks developed.

Student Related

Students can become very agitated about online assessments. Explain the rationale for using the technology and offer both online and face-to-face support. Formative assessments allow them to become familiar with the format and requirements and may lead to better summative results (Pattinson, 2004). Guidelines on the time expected to be spent on online activities should be reviewed, based on actual experience, and students advised to consult tutors if they are taking considerably longer. If students report that something is not working, do not always assume that the technology has failed. It is important to check student understanding of the subject, the task at hand, and their sequence of actions.

Campus-based students may not make much use of online discussion boards, unless there is real value in doing so. Marking forum contributions can distort the process. It is recommended that tutors monitor online discussion carefully, reply swiftly to queries, and praise student contributions that contribute to the learning of others.

Conclusion

This chapter has outlined the development, implementation, and evaluation of two online learning activities in geography. Despite initial technological problems and constraints, both staff and students have benefited from their development. The activities have provided students with the opportunity to experience some of the real difficulties and conflicts of professional environmental managers, while also developing practical skills. Staff have benefited from the opportunity to incorporate new and interesting data, ideas, and concepts into the existing unit, while gaining from the ability of the system to undertake some of the administrative and marking duties. The recommendations presented here provide both ideas and words of caution to those wishing to blend online activities with traditional teaching and learning on their units.

Acknowledgments

Thanks are due to UK's Joint Information Systems Committee and USA's National Science Foundation for funding and supporting the DialogPLUS project; and UK's Environment Agency for permitting the use of the River Habitat Survey dataset.

References

Bennett, S., & Marsh, D. (2001). Are we expecting online tutors to run before they can walk? *Innovations in Education and Teaching International, 39*(1), 14-20.

Biggs, J. (2003). *Teaching for quality learning at university* (2nd ed.). Bury St Edmunds, UK: The Society for Research into Higher Education and the Open University Press.

Carter, J. (2002). A framework for the development of multimedia systems for use in engineering education. *Computers & Education, 39*, 111-128.

Childs, M. (2004). Is there an e-pedagogy of resource-and-problem based learning? Using digital resources in three case studies. *Interactions, 8*(2). Retrieved March 30, 2005, from www2.warwick.ac.uk/services/cap/resources/interactions/archive/issue24/childs/

Clark, M.J., Ball, J.H., & Sadler, J.D. (1995). Multimedia delivery of coastal zone management training. *Innovations in Education and Training International, 32*(3), 229-238.

DialogPLUS (2004). DialogPlus: Digital libraries in support of innovative approaches to learning and teaching in geography. *Proceedings of the Fourth ACM/IEEE-CS Joint Conference on Digital Libraries (JCDL 2004).*

Environment Agency. (1998). *River Habitat Quality: The physical characteristics of rivers and streams in the UK and the Isle of Man.* (RHS Report No. 2). Bristol, UK: Environment Agency.

Graham, L. (1999). *The principles of interactive design.* Devon: Delmar Publishing.

Harwood, I.A. (2005). When summative computer-aided assessments go wrong: Disaster recovery after a major failure. *British Journal of Educational Technology, 36, Special issue on Thwarted Innovation in e-Learning.*

Honebein, P. (1996). Seven goals for the design of constructivist learning environments. In B. Wilson (Ed.), *Constructivist learning environments* (pp. 17-24). NJ: Educational Technology Publications.

Honey, P. & Mumford, A. (1992). *The manual of learning styles* (3rd ed.). Maidenhead: Peter Honey.

Kerres, M., & de Witt, C. (2003). A didactical framework for the design of blended learning arrangements. *Journal of Educational Media, 28*(2-3), 101-113.

Laurillard, D. (2002). *Rethinking university teaching: A framework for the effective use of educational technology* (2nd ed.). London: RoutledgeFalmer.

Lisewski, B. & Settle, C. (1996). Integrating multimedia resource-based learning into the curriculum. In S. Brown & B. Smith (Eds.), *Resource-based learning* (pp.109-119). London: Kogan Page.

Mutch, A. (2003). Exploring the practice of feedback to students. *Active Learning in Higher Education, 4*(1), 24-38.

Oliver, M. (2004). *Against the term blended learning. OU Knowledge Network.* Retrieved March 30, 2005, from http://kn.open.ac.uk/public/document.cfm?docid=5053

Pattinson, S. (2004). *The use of CAA for formative and summative assessment – Student views and outcomes.* Paper presented at the CAA Conference. Retrieved March 22, 2005, from www.caaconference.com/

Perkin, M. (1999). Validating formative and summative assessment. In S. Brown, J. Bull, & P. Race (Eds.), *Computer-assisted assessment in higher education* (pp. 29-37). London: Kogan Page.

Plowman, L. (1996). Narrative, linearity and interactivity: Making sense of interactive multimedia. *British Journal of Educational Technology, 27*(2), 92-105.

Race, P. (1996). Helping students to learn from resources. In S. Brown & B. Smith (Eds.), *Resource-based learning* (pp. 22-37). London: Kogan.

Spellman, G. (2000). Evaluation of CAL in higher education geography. *Journal of Computer Assisted Learning, 16,* 72-82.

Weller, M., Pegler, C., & Mason, R. (2003). *Working with learning objects— Some pedagogical suggestions.* Paper presented at the Association for Learning Technology conference. Retrieved March 4, 2005, from http://iet.open.ac.uk/pp/m.j.weller/pub/altc.doc

Wilson, B.G. (Ed.). (1996). *Constructivist learning environments: Case studies in instructional design.* Englewood Cliffs, NJ: Educational Technology Publications, Inc.

Zakrzewski, S., & Steven, C. (2000). A model for computer-based assessment: The Catherine Wheel principle. *Assessment & Evaluation in Higher Education, 25*(2) 201-215.

Chapter XVI

Lessons in Implementing a Learning Management System in a University:
The Academic User Perspective

Fiona Darroch, University of Southern Queensland, Australia

Mark Toleman, University of Southern Queensland, Australia

Abstract

This chapter examines the implementation of two learning management systems (LMS) in a university environment. Within the context of a case study and from the perspective of academic users, there is a review of the technological and organizational challenges that arise. There is an in-depth analysis of the implementation in terms of what went well and what should be done differently (i.e., lessons learned). Along with the macro-environmental factors that influence the global e-learning space, the related pedagogical issues, learning models, and technological toolsets are also explored. The authors hope that the experiences chronicled in the case study may act as a lesson to others contemplating such a project of the many technical and organizational issues that need to be addressed, with an emphasis on understanding the importance of the viewpoint of academic users.

Introduction

The phenomenon known as online education (also known as e-learning) is an emerging educational model that is touted as having a significant and rapidly growing future, predicted to exceed $US20 billion by 2005 (Turban, Aronson, & Liang, 2005). Managing the technical, infrastructural, cultural, and organizational issues is crucial to the effective deployment of online learning environments. In order to harness the full power of such an environment, it is especially important to ensure that the process is effective from the academic user perspective. The macro environmental factors such as technical, social, governmental, organizational, and pedagogical that shape the online education environment are wide ranging and frequently interconnected, resulting in an emerging picture that is complex and extremely dynamic. The Internet and associated technologies simultaneously present opportunities and challenges for institutions operating in the global higher education economy, thus requiring an innovative organizational response to maximize competitive advantage.

The mission of this chapter is to provide a clear understanding, from an academic user perspective, of the main issues associated with implementing a learning management system (LMS) into the online education environment. Two compelling reasons drive the significance of the lessons arising from a case study such as this: first, the continued significant level of financial investment in information systems implementation projects; and second, the continuing track record of problems associated with project implementations, especially concerning systems meeting user requirements. The academic user group is at the nexus of the technology and its deployment, and thus plays a critical role in the overall success of the online education experience. Hence, wisdom should be harvested from such situations and made available to others contemplating such projects.

This chapter explores the implementation of an LMS in an online education environment in an Australian university. In this context, online education means an open and distributed learning environment that uses pedagogical tools, enabled by Internet and e-technologies, to support the teaching, learning, and knowledge building processes through meaningful action and interaction (Dabbagh & Bannan-Ritland, 2005). LMS are specialized, integrated software toolsets, developed specifically for the support of online course delivery (Sturgess & Nouwens, 2004). Examples include WebCT Vista, Blackboard, Lotus Notes Learning Space, Moodle, PlaceWare Virtual Classroom, First Class (Turban et al., 2005) and Webfuse (Jones, Lynch, & Jamieson, 2003). These packages have a suite of integrated functionality to support a wide range of requirements for online education including: discussion boards, e-mail, assignment submission, assessment tools, virtual classrooms, lecture notes, presentations, and resource materials (Turban et al., 2005). The rest of this chapter is structured as follows. The next section reviews the macro environmental factors that shape the online education environment. This is followed by an examination of the case study context, and then a discussion of the online educational model and the pedagogy of online education. The main sections of the chapter follow which cover the technological toolset and an examination of the lessons arising from an LMS implementation. The final sections cover recommendations, future trends, and conclusions.

Macro Environmental Factors Affecting Online Education

Organizations such as universities involved in online education in the 21st century are subject to a wide range of macro environmental influences that individually and collectively shape their operational space. These influences may act as drivers or constraints (or both), and manifest themselves in concepts such as technological advance, globalization and internationalization, socioeconomic and cultural changes and influences, strategic management and competitive advantage, innovation, outsourcing, government policy, and human resource issues. The emerging environment is one of volatility and constant change.

The force of change wrought by technological advances such as the Internet and related technologies has shaped the environment for organizations involved in online education. Organizations in such an environment need to be "fast, flexible, and fluid," a far cry from the generally accepted, stolid nature of universities (Taylor, 2001). The two most significant technological enablers have been the global connectivity of networks offered by the Internet and the universal browser protocol of the World Wide Web (WWW) (Dabbagh & Bannan-Ritland, 2005). This is in addition to the rich array of other technological tools discussed in more detail later in this chapter.

The ever declining cost of access to information communication technologies (such as videoconferencing) as well as computer processing (30% per annum) means that 1 billion people now have access to the Internet, and this has a positive influence on online education (Taylor, 2000; Turban et al., 2005). The move from print-based to Internet-based delivery results in a change from a proportional cost model to a fixed cost model, wherein extra students bring no additional cost (Taylor, 2000).

Globalization has a profound influence on online education through the "awareness of the globe as a single environment" (Dabbagh & Bannan-Ritland, 2005), as well as notions of a global economy and global citizenship (Vickers & McClellan, 2004). Online education is facilitated by the accompanying time-space compression, and the increasing connectedness of communities and places (Singh, 2004). The underlying, persistent theme with globalization is that it demands a dynamic, fluid response.

Some claim that offering a program internationally has positive impacts such as a tendency toward the inclusion of global and multicultural topics (Vickers & McClellan, 2004) and encouraging the understanding of the varied cultures involved (Verma, Kochan, & Lansbury, 1995). Online education is an especially important initiative to the emerging economies of the world, offering opportunities where there are changed expectations regarding access to education (Turban et al., 2005). Others claim that globalization of education may have a negative impact as it is dominated by the western world-view, based on materialism, hedonism, and consumerism (Jackson, 2003), since it is fundamentally an initiative of rich, developed countries (Hicks, 2003). This trend has the potential to become a form of neo-colonialism (Haigh, 2003). The global lifelong learning economy is fertile ground for institutions involved in online education (Taylor, 2001).

Socioeconomic and cultural changes have had a facilitating impact on online education. Student profiles have changed whereby studies may be completed in more flexible, non-traditional ways which cater for travel, family, and work commitments (Turban et al., 2005; Leskes, 2004). Alternate avenues of university entry have further diversified the student profile (Postle, Taylor, Taylor, & Clarke, 1999). This has led to changed student expectations toward a more customer-oriented focus (Swannell & Taylor, 1999), demanding flexible delivery, value for money, life-long learning, and continuing professional education (Postle et al., 1999). The online environment highlights the importance of independent learning skills (Holley, 2002). Cultural factors such as a person's race, gender, and cultural heritage all impact an individual's approach to learning (Carnell & Askew, 1998).

Strategic management and competitive advantage issues play an important role in shaping the online education environment, as they have been associated with a move away from "public good," toward an exported service industry, the end result of which is the commodification of higher education (Haigh, 2003). Singh (2004) raises the related concern that market forces rather than altruism drive the production of knowledge. Technology that underpins competitive advantage must be astutely managed (Chanaron & Jolly, 1999). The increased opportunity for theft and manipulation of copyrighted materials in the online environment is another management challenge (Oravec, 2003).

Innovation is a related concept to competitive advantage and strategic decision making. In online education an advanced technology per se will not offer a competitive advantage since it is likely to be available to competitors (Zhuang, 1995) but relies on how strategically it is implemented in its content and delivery (Morgan, 2001). Many industry leaders such as Peter Drucker and Oracle's Larry Ellison consider that the current model of traditional, campus-based university education is outmoded, and that the future of all university education will be greatly impacted along the lines of the emerging fifth generation online education model (Oravec, 2003).

Outsourcing is a related aspect of competitive advantage and strategic capability that must be considered. IT outsourcing is commonplace, but suffers high rates of customer dissatisfaction (Al-Hakim, 2004). Value-enhancing activities which are the basis of differentiation are lost when they are outsourced (Johnson & Scholes, 2002). An example of outsourcing is the provision of the online education platform such as that offered by NextEd (*NextEd*, 2004). Management of the external contracts requires different managerial competencies to that of in-house production, and considerable problems have arisen in this area (Johnson & Scholes, 2002).

A range of human resource issues influence the online education environment and necessitate new management approaches. The trend toward ever larger student cohorts and mounting levels of student cheating has resulted in much increased work pressures for faculty (Pain & Le Heron, 2003). Staff expectations about workloads and their distribution, as well as their perception of student independence are also at issue (Holley, 2002). Online delivery may result in increased workloads and moves workload upfront in the course delivery schedule (Froese, Zhu, & Bhat, 2000).

Government policy may act as a driver for online education, as seen in the Clinton Administration's policies of the 1990s, which focused on making computer and network technology an enabler for American education (Vedantham & Breeden, 1995). On the other hand, economic rationalism, whereby governments are reducing funding to institutions and moving toward a more market-driven, user-pays approach, places significant constraints on institutions operating in that environment (Swannell & Taylor, 1999).

Background to the Case Study

The case study is set in a regional, Australian public university. There are approximately 26,000 students in total, 20,000 (77%) distance education students, and 8,300 (32%) international students. Originating as a college of advanced education 32 years ago, the university has a long history of distance education, initially, nationally, and more recently, internationally. The extension from the traditional correspondence, print-based distance education into an online environment was seen as a natural expansion path and was the chosen direction of senior management of the previous administration (Taylor & Swannell, 2000). The case study university has won several prestigious international awards in the distance and e-learning environment. Most recently, the new vice chancellor has set a policy directive to badge the university's vision as being Australia's leading "transnational" educator, in which the management of the online education environment will play a pivotal role. Hence, the contextual emphasis in this case study is on the deployment of an LMS in a predominantly distance education university environment where the user community is the academic staff.

The case reviews the implementation of two LMS (WebCT Vista and Blackboard) within the mentioned university setting. The framework of enquiry was in the form of recorded, semi-structured, in-depth interviews with academic users. The interviews were based on a guideline which was designed to explore the major issues raised in contemporary published research literature, particularly that which informed the mentioned macro environmental factors. This approach enabled the development of a deeper understanding of the issues as they emerged and suited the exploratory nature of this research (Zikmund, 2003). Occasional brief statements from interviewees (placed in double quotes) have been included in order to convey meaning as accurately as possible.

The interviewees were chosen according to Creswell's (1998, p. 62) purposeful sampling technique. The aim was to explore the academic user perspective as broadly and inclusively as possible, and reach saturation on major issues, while maintaining a diversity of perspective. Thus, all interviewees had extensive experience with one or both LMS and were proactive, interested users, some with specialist skills in online pedagogy. Importantly, all recommendations contained herein arose directly from the interviewees, based on their experiences.

There are several key areas that relate to the technological issues that impact staff using LMS in a university environment. Before examining the main issues arising from the implementation and use of an LMS, it is necessary to review the online education model, consider the related pedagogical issues, and also to describe the toolsets available in such environments.

The Online Educational Model

Online education evolved from earlier educational models such as distance education, computer-based/computer-assisted training, and the traditional classroom model. A forerunner to online education is distance education, wherein delivery was outside of the traditional classroom (same time, same place, face-to-face paradigm), and was mainly concerned with addressing geographical isolation from university campuses and was initially aimed at adults who had work or family responsibilities (Dabbagh & Bannan-Ritland, 2005; Volery & Lord, 2000). Traditional distance learning models based on correspondence and print materials have been in existence for more than a century and tend to be a form of directed learning with varying degrees of student independence (Dabbagh & Bannan-Ritland, 2005). The traditional classroom-based, face-to-face situation and classic computer-assisted instruction are also both forms of the directed learning approach (Dabbagh & Bannan-Ritland, 2005). The characteristics of such environments are that they are a linear, basics-first, teacher-centred approach, occurring in real-time and with stable information sources (Dabbagh & Bannan-Ritland, 2005).

Technological progress has been one of the main enablers that has seen the online model extend beyond the preceding generations to what Taylor (2001) calls the emerging fifth generation, namely the "intelligent flexible learning model." This model is characterized by highly sophisticated and integrated use of Internet technologies, as well as the potential to deliver vastly improved cost-effective economies of scale (Taylor, 2001). Online education environments tend to offer anytime-anywhere flexibility, operate where control is decentralized, with dynamic, unbounded information sources, and are based on ever-evolving technologies (Dabbagh & Bannan-Ritland, 2005). Furthermore, technologies facilitate online education to encompass the concept of learning as a "social process," something not catered for in the traditional distance education paradigm (Dabbagh & Bannan-Ritland, 2005). Online, distributed learning incorporates a wide range of digital technologies, access to course materials, the concepts of self-learning, and interaction and collaborative work between students and academics (Volery & Lord, 2000).

Clearly the challenges of fulfilling this emergent "intelligent flexible learning model" are substantial. One of the main findings from the case study was that while some of the intent had been fulfilled, there were significant shortcomings and unanimous agreement that it "could be a whole lot better." The case study university offers three modes of study, viz. face-to-face, external distance (print and electronic resources), and fully online. A subject may be offered in any or all of these modes, which results in a variety of learning models in operation. Moreover, autonomy by academic course leaders over course structure and delivery, as well as a deficiency of audit/quality control processes further defrays standardization. Overall this has resulted in the lack of a clearly defined and articulated vision of the model of online education.

It was felt that the model in the case study was more like an online distribution of traditional-type course materials rather than a flexible, online teaching one: "We've taken the independent learner focus, print-based mode and plonked it on the Internet." This situation has been attributed to the lack of processes to ensure a high level of model fulfilment; inadequate training in and excessive resource requirements for full online development; little incentive for academics to invest in such activities; and suboptimal support structures which stymie the dissemination of innovative approaches. The overall finding was that there is a dissonance between senior management's well publicised vision of online education, and the resultant situation as it has been operationalized. It is important to further understand the integral role that pedagogy plays in the online education model.

The Pedagogy of Online Education

Pedagogical issues are core to the online education environment. The opportunity for group interaction via Web-based learning environments requires a new approach to pedagogy which has transformed distance education, culminating in the last decade in new models of open, flexible, distributed learning environments (Dabbagh & Bannan-Ritland, 2005). It has been suggested that the lack of social interaction (among students and instructors) in the prior distance education models (and the attendant problems of isolation and alienation that increase attrition) may be ameliorated by the application of telecommunications technology (Dabbagh & Bannan-Ritland, 2005). This assertion was supported in the case study with an academic reporting that "online communication forums improve the student-teacher relationship out of sight, better than distance access/interaction, and faster response."

Online discussion forums can emulate the face-to-face experience of the classroom situation (Turban et al., 2005). The case study findings follow. Asynchronous communication via discussion groups and e-mail is a cheaper, more convenient option than voice messages. Asynchronous communication is comparable to the classroom in facilitating learning communities under a social constructivist paradigm, but less effective in supporting relationship growth (through lack of body language). It was also found that the asynchronous media can be more inclusive because it allows everyone (not just the fastest and loudest) to contribute, as well as facilitating a more considered response due to the delay. Furthermore, such media offer greater equality among students, since respondents are not judged on gender, looks, voice, or verbal language competency.

Yet, it is widely reported that the promised revolution in pedagogy via the new technologies has not been fully realized, because faculty are not yet sufficiently skilled nor are adequate resources available to fully deliver on the earlier claims (Zemsky & Massy, 2004). In fact, the most common experience has been for the success of LMS and PowerPoint software that focus more on online distribution of traditional-type course materials rather than on online teaching (Zemsky & Massy, 2004). The case study findings are that despite efforts by specialized instructional designers and academic innovators to try to make online courses more pedagogically sound, the impact is neither widespread nor uniform. This is partly because academics are not necessarily trained in teaching/pedagogy. Thus, the case study situation affirms that full advantage has not been taken of the potential for a more interactive, flexible model that harvests the power of the Internet communication tools.

The Technological Toolset

The technological toolset plays a crucially important role in the online education environment. The following tools are some of the many different forms of enabling applications for online education. Digital tools include those that allow access to CD-ROM and DVD formats (Dabbagh & Bannan-Ritland, 2005). Web-based tools include hypertext and hypermedia, Web-authoring tools such as Dreamweaver and FrontPage. Group communication tools facilitate the electronic exchange of ideas and information between related groups of users. They include e-mail, discussion groups, list servers, and chat rooms. Audio and video tools include those that allow access to audio files, audio conferencing, video files, streaming video, and video conferencing. Graphics tools allow users to develop electronic drawings particularly for incorporation in other software. Group support systems tools include those that support a range of collaborative functionality such as brainstorming and voting (Turban et al., 2005).

Many of the collaborative packages, such as Lotus Notes, NetMeeting, Interwise, and Groove, developed for the general market also facilitate online education, (Turban et al., 2005). However, Allan and Lawless (2003) note that such interdependence may cause students stress.

Another consideration of these tools is whether they are synchronous or asynchronous in nature (Dabbagh & Bannan-Ritland, 2005). Synchronous tools such as chat rooms depend on immediate communicative responses from participants. Asynchronous tools such as e-mail do not necessarily require an immediate response, and therefore place less time-related demands on participants.

The case study environment incorporates many of these technologies. In determining the strengths and weaknesses of the toolsets, it is important to explore three key aspects: whether the technologies available are fully utilized; whether they perform to expectation; and whether there are other technologies that would be desirable to harness in order to give substance to the fifth generation environment (Taylor, 2001).

Are the Available Technologies Fully Utilized?

The findings from the case study were that asynchronous tools, especially discussion groups and e-mail, were considered the most useful. Synchronous tools such as chat rooms were sometimes considered too hard to manage in terms of content structure, potential numbers of participants, and varying global time zones. It was also felt that the time commitment from both the academic and student perspectives was excessive when considering the likely value of the learning outcomes, thus representing a poor return on time invested. Another category of less-utilized tools includes online submission of assessments, interactive assessments, learning aids, and online quizzes.

Factors that were cited as affecting the adoption of these technologies included inadequate training, restricted time and resources available to understand the application, and access to information. Experience from the case study suggests that adoption should be evolutionary to avert information overload. Eroded trust in the support for and performance of the technologies has resulted in an overly cautious embrace of many of the features available, which was evidenced in the troublesome case of online submission of assignments. This was compounded by concern that it would become an integral part of an academic's role to be up-to-date in the technology, as well as unwittingly becoming a default technology support provider for students.

Do the Technologies Perform to Expectation?

While there were some aspects of the technologies that performed well, a number of problems were identified, along with failure to make the technology seamless for the academic users. Furthermore, it was often difficult to distinguish between the many potential failure factors such as hardware reliability and availability, software performance, power supply, technical support, and management decision-making. This was evidenced in a range of technologies including the online assignment submission system, chat room log, computer managed assessment, and the backup facility.

The case study exposed serious concerns from academics over inadequate problem management processes, workflows, and turnaround times for fixes for technological problems. Academics becoming involved in their students' system problems emerged as an adjunct problem. This was exacerbated by a lack of integration of support areas and long lead times for problem resolution. This resulted in academics either constraining their use of the system or finding workarounds. For example, to overcome slow material uploads with WebCT, some academics develop Web material with an alternate product, load it onto another server, and link it to WebCT. It is also faster for students who then bookmark the site directly, thus avoiding the WebCT interface.

Are there Other Technologies that are Desirable?

Research into online education environments suggests that the choices and decisions about the combination of technologies, pedagogical models, and instructional designs are important to the success of online delivery. In the case study, a small group of pioneering innovators has identified and trialled a number of products worthy of further consideration. Some of these may be an alternative to current products, while others may offer additional functionality. An example of an alternative product is Web Crossing (*Web Crossing*, 2005) which offers a suite of integrated functionality including discussion groups and bulletin boards, newsgroups and mailing lists, e-mail, calendar services, real-time chats, live events, and full Web application programming features. Features that distinguish it from the current WebCT platform are its much-needed editing facilities and its range of alternative user access paths (viz. via interface, nntp newsgroup reader, or e-mail) which assist students operating in low-end networks, as well as a capacity for more personalized interactions.

Open source products are another group that are becoming increasingly important to consider. One of the potential advantages of open source is the avoidance of forced upgrade schedule problems (Sturgess & Nouwens, 2004). An example of an open source product is Moodle (*Moodle*, 2005), an alternative LMS which has received very favourable reviews by a number of academic users in the case study. An open source simulated conference package, OpenConf (*OpenConf*, 2005), has also been successfully trailed.

Other technologies trialed in the case study include: Breeze (an integrated audio and PowerPoint application) (*Macromedia Breeze*, 2005) which also offers the capability to develop interactive Web sites and learning objects, as well as host online meetings and classes; and Dreamweaver (*Macromedia Dreamweaver*, 2005), a Web authoring tool.

These additional packages extend the online experience in many ways including enhancing the social presence and personal interactions. When planning to implement an LMS and associated support technologies, there are several key issues that must be considered.

Lessons Learned Implementing as LMS

Post-implementation reviews of software projects present the opportunity to learn from that experience and apply it to future projects. These lessons cover what went well and what could have been better.

What Went Well?

There were a number of aspects considered by the academic users to have gone well during the LMS implementations. In the Blackboard implementation, the support was described by the interviewees as well coordinated, very supportive of both academic and student users, and effective in dealing with technical problems. That student support was well catered for was an additional benefit as it averted the problem of academics becoming an inappropriate, quasi support network. The Blackboard environment was adapted to suit users, and functionality was changed in response to early user requests, which resulted in most aspects of the technologies performing well.

Interviewees reported that one of the highlights of the WebCT implementation was the effective introductory training. Another positive was the strong culture of teamwork that developed among academic users who (mainly out of necessity) supported one another in the early stages of the implementation. Academics felt that the increased opportunity for participation in higher education arising from online education is well suited to the changed circumstances, expectations, and roles of students. Furthermore, they reported that it fostered a positive student-teacher relationship, thus increasing motivation to use the system.

What Could Have Been Better?

On the other hand, there were many aspects of the implementations that were cited as being problematic including the management of the implementation and support processes and structures, system functionality and technical performance, training, and the online model.

In contrast to the Blackboard experience, the management of the WebCT implementation was ill-prepared, wherein users felt that the system was "foisted" on them. Decisions were made with little consultation and academics were left to "cop the flack." These problems were exacerbated by an unrealistic implementation schedule for the preparation of courses being offered online. Problem management processes and support structures for WebCT were under-resourced and lacked coordination. Problems emerged in both the WebCT and Blackboard environments with the adoption of overly restrictive and inflexible content management policies and administratively onerous update processes. These policies resulted in pedagogical issues being ignored. Various organizational and change management issues such as increased and changed workloads also had a negative impact.

As the LMS is the core component of online education environments, the functionality of such systems is of crucial importance. Users expressed their disappointment at the loss of functionality when moving from the prior in-house developed system. There was a perceived reduction in competitive advantage through the adoption of a commercial off-the-shelf package. Amendments to restrict functionality in WebCT reduced its flexibility, and concerns were raised concerning the up-to-date nature of the installed version. Ironically, customizations to Blackboard (to meet user requirements) had severely compromised future upgrade paths. It was felt that academics were not adequately consulted regarding functionality and flexibility. In the case of WebCT, these difficulties were compounded by serious performance and usability problems when the system initially went live.

Despite successful early training in WebCT, there was a need for advanced courses to realize the benefits of a more mature environment, as well as a need for tailored, context-sensitive training courses. Confusion and frustration associated with the model of online education arose in the case study experience because of the influence of its history as a correspondence-based distance education provider, which has "blinkered our view," "taking our baggage with us, instead of being fresh and creative." Online courses are often developed on the basis of the existing distance mode materials, rather than from the ground up in an online form. Furthermore, the model is deemed to be lacking in pedagogical considerations, standards, and quality assurance processes. It is felt that the views of users, particularly innovators, are not being effectively supported and this is compromising the online education outcome.

Recommendations

Recommendations arising from the case study fall into four categories: organizational; the online education model; pedagogy; and the technical environment.

First, the choice of an LMS must take account of many factors and seek to address the requirements of all stakeholders, including academic users. Hence, it is recommended that users are widely consulted and listened to in respect of their needs for a system that provides flexible functionality and a user-friendly and intuitive interface. In determining the best option, an open source LMS (such as Moodle) should be considered as a development base, as it offers advantages in terms of avoiding upgrade path problems, and furthermore, presents an organization with the opportunity to have a system with a unique look and feel that can lead to a competitive advantage.

The process of reviewing the problems and controversies associated with the implementation phase in the case study gave rise to a number of recommendations. Users considered it critical to adequately resource the technical environment in terms of hardware and support. Core systems such as LMS require a stable, predictable, documented environment with an expectation of 24/7 uptime. This, in turn, demands that acceptable contingency and backup plans are in place for the operation of the LMS and associated systems. Another related recommendation is the need for a seamless coordination of the various technical and functional support areas and that academics do not become involved in support roles. There is also a requirement for an effective problem/change management mechanism that will garner user support, empower users by ensuring strong user representation in decision-making, and provide meaningful feedback. The resolution process should include an in-depth assessment to identify, report, and address the source of the problem. It is recommended that staged implementations and/or pilots be adopted so that the impact of problems may be limited. This would also facilitate the early identification of inappropriate or poorly performing technologies.

Second, it is clear that the model adopted for online education is a critical consideration. The most important recommendation here is that the model should be reviewed, clarified, and agreed with all stakeholders, and the outcome effectively articulated ensuring that academic users are appraised of the benefits. In the development and ongoing evolution of the model, exemplars should be identified as a guide for others. Innovators and pioneers must be allowed the flexibility, scope, and support to experiment and explore more creative options and push the boundaries in a reflective, no-blame environment. Adoption of the Microsoft dictum of "eat our own dog food" is recommended through the use of online education for internal professional development courses, to aid understanding of the user perspective. Agreed standards, benchmarks, and quality assurance processes should be developed to support the chosen online model. Consideration should be given to supplementary materials (non-interactive components on CDROM) to address the varying standards of technical facilities experienced by the global student cohort which may affect download speeds.

Third, pedagogical considerations of the online environment should be reviewed and incorporated into the model along with appropriate training. A learning and teaching group should be established to provide expert advice on appropriate pedagogical considerations that reflect the e-learning environment, free of baggage from any prior, outmoded models such as the correspondence model. Furthermore, flexible processes should be developed to support the online environment that accommodate academic freedom and facilitate content management without excessive controls over users.

Lastly, the technical environment is crucial. Aside from the core LMS, additional specialized packages that offer supplementary functionality are very important. Such packages extend the online experience in many ways including enhancing both the social presence and personal interactions. It is recommended that open source products be considered for additional supplementary functionality.

Future Trends

Online education is an emerging force in the global education environment. Because technology plays such a pivotal role in this area, it is assured that there will be a constant rate of change. The constant advances in the technological toolset as well as in networks, infrastructure, and bandwidth mean that the applications that depend on them are constantly improving.

Aside from changing technologies, there are three other important issues to examine in terms of future trends. First, there is a trend toward a global, life-long learning economy which means that the environment will become progressively more market-driven wherein the organization's success will depend on the customer's (student's) view of value, quality, and product suitability (Taylor & Swannell, 2000). Second, it is important to be cognizant of the emerging and future models of online education, an example of which is the "intelligent flexible learning model" which emphasizes the use of high-end Internet technologies (Taylor, 2001). Third, consideration must be given to the adoption of open source software tools and applications, as they are becoming an important and credible alternative. There are increasing numbers of such systems available, and consistent with trends in other open source areas, this is set to increase.

Conclusion

Many challenges in the online education environment are brought on by organizational, cultural, and technical factors. These must be addressed in order to ensure an optimal outcome. Taking account of the academic user perspective in the management of this environment is critical. This chapter addresses a wide ranging audience including educators and academics alike, with a balance of theory and practice via a case study supported by contemporary online education research. It identifies major issues that organizations must consider in the selection, implementation, and use of an LMS. This is backed by a comprehensive array of in-depth recommendations that relate to all the main issues discussed.

The macro environmental influences that shape this environment are wide ranging and often interconnected resulting in complex situations and include technology, social, governmental, organizational, and pedagogical factors. The online education environment has simultaneously presented universities with rich opportunities and major challenges. It has been shown that this complex, changing environment demands that organizations respond in a highly flexible and adaptable manner in order to take advantage of the opportunities.

There are major issues that should be given serious consideration. A clear vision of the model of online education is essential, as this is the basis upon which the technologies are layered. The views of users, particularly innovators, must be supported to ensure that the operational manifestation of online education is as rewarding as possible. Well coordinated and resourced support processes and procedures for problem management are crucial. The most important considerations regarding the deployment of online education technologies in terms of enriching the experience of academic users are user friendliness, intuitiveness, appropriate support structures, training, and functional richness.

While, the implementation of LMS have many characteristics in common with the broad range of software projects, there are several distinguishing aspects that require a more specific understanding. Hence, the knowledge and insights distilled from this case study will facilitate others to benefit by the wisdom and lessons learned that have arisen from this experience.

References

Al-Hakim, L. (2004, July 4-6). *Criticality of failure factors affecting information technology outsourcing*. Paper presented at the International Business Information Management Conference, Amman, Jordan.

Allan, J., & Lawless, N. (2003). Stress caused by on-line collaboration in e-learning: A developing model. *Education and Training, 45*(8/9), 564-572.

Carnell, E., & Askew, S. (1998). *Transforming learning: Individual and global change*. London: Cassell.

Chanaron, J.J., & Jolly, D. (1999). Technological management: Expanding the perspective of management of technology. *Management Decision, 37*(8), 613-620.

Creswell, J.W. (1998). *Qualitative inquiry and research design: Choosing among five traditions*. London: Sage Publications.

Dabbagh, N., & Bannan-Ritland, B. (2005). *Online learning: Concepts, strategies, and application*. NJ: Pearson.

Froese, T., Zhu, D., & Bhat, S. (2000). WWW courseware in applied science: Cases and lessons. *Computer Applications in Engineering Education, 9*(2), 63-77.

Haigh, M. (2003). Internationalising the university curriculum: A response to M.G. Jackson. *Journal of Geography in Higher Education, 27*(3), 331-340.

Hicks, D. (2003). Thirty years of global education: A reminder of key principles and precedents. *Educational Review, 55*(3), 265-276.

Holley, D. (2002). Which room is the virtual seminar in please? *Education and Training, 44*(3), 112-121.

Jackson, M.G. (2003). Internationalising the university curriculum. *Journal of Geography in Higher Education, 27*(3), 325-330.

Johnson, G., & Scholes, K. (2002). *Exploring corporate strategy* (6th ed.). Harlow, Essex: Pearson Education.

Jones, D., Lynch, T., & Jamieson, K. (2003, June 24-27). *Emergent development of Web-based education*. Paper presented at the Informing Science & Information Technology Education Joint Conference, Pori, Finland.

Leskes, A. (2004). Greater expectations and learning in the new globally engaged academy. *Peer Review, 6*(2), 4-8.

Macromedia Breeze. (2005). Retrieved July 25, 2005, from www.macromedia.com/software/breeze/?promoid=BIRL

Macromedia Dreamweaver. (2005). Retrieved July 25, 2005, from www.macromedia.com/software/dreamweaver/

Moodle. (2005). Retrieved July 25, 2005, from http://moodle.org/

Morgan, G. (2001). Thirteen 'must ask' questions about e-learning products and services. *The Learning Organization, 8*(5), 203-210.

NextEd. (2004). Retrieved July 25, 2005, from www.nexted.com/

OpenConf. (2005). Retrieved July 25, 2005, from www.zakongroup.com/technology/openconf.shtml>

Oravec, J.A. (2003). Some influences of on-line distance learning on U.S. higher education. *Journal of Further and Higher Education, 27*(1), 89-103.

Pain, D., & Le Heron, J. (2003). WebCT and online assessment: The best thing since SOAP? *Educational Technology & Society, 6*(2), 62-71.

Postle, G., Taylor, J.C., Taylor, J., & Clarke, J. (1999, July 7-10). *Flexible delivery and inclusivity: Pedagogical and logistical perspectives*. Paper presented at the 8th European Access Network Convention, Malta.

Singh, P. (2004). Globalization and education. *Educational Theory, 54*(1), 103-116.

Sturgess, P., & Nouwens, F. (2004). Evaluation of online learning management systems. *Turkish Online Journal of Distance Education, 5*(3).

Swannell, P., & Taylor, J.C. (1999). *It was the best of times, it was the worst of times*. Niece, France.

Taylor, J.C. (2000). Coach education in the 21st century: Challenges and opportunities. *The Sport Educator, 12*(1), 11-16.

Taylor, J.C. (2001). *5th generation distance education* (No. 40): DETYA. Retrieved from www.detya.gov.au/archive/highered/hes/hes40/hes40.pdf

Taylor, J.C., & Swannell, P. (2000). USQ: An e-university in an e-world. *International Review of Research in Open and Distance Learning, 1*(2).

Turban, E., Aronson, J.E., & Liang, T.P. (2005). *Decision support systems and intelligent systems* (7th ed.). Upper Saddle River, NJ: Prentice Hall.

Vedantham, A., & Breeden, L. (1995). Networking for K-12 education: The federal perspective. *Internet Research: Electronic Networking Applications and Policy, 5*(1), 29-39.

Verma, A., Kochan, T., & Lansbury, R. (1995). Employment relations in an era of global markets. In A. Verma, T. Kochan, & R. Lansbury (Eds.), *Employment relations in the growing Asian economies* (pp. 1-26). London: Routledge.

Vickers, L.A., & McClellan, G. (2004). Bringing the World to North Dakota. *Peer Review, 6*(2), 22-25.

Volery, T., & Lord, D. (2000). Critical success factors in online education. *International Journal of Educational Management, 14*(5), 216-223.

Web Crossing. (2005). Retrieved July 24, 2005, from www.webcrossing.com/Home/

Zemsky, R., & Massy, W.F. (2004). *Thwarted innovation: What happened to e-learning and why.* University of Pennsylvania.

Zhuang, L. (1995). Bridging the gap between technology and business strategy: A pilot study on the innovation process. *Management Decision, 33*(8), 13-21.

Zikmund, W.G. (2003). *Business research methods* (7th ed.). Mason, Ohio: Thomson Learning.

Chapter XVII

Learning through Chat:
University of the Arts London Case Studies in Online Learning in Art, Design and Communication

David Rowsell, University of the Arts London, UK

Tim Jackson, University of the Arts London, UK

Abstract

Synchronous computer conferencing, or "chat," is an effective and versatile tool of online learning, providing users with opportunities for real-time communication. Chat can be used for a variety of educational purposes, including academic seminars, student tutorials, recruitment interviews, and student presentations. In this chapter, we argue that through practice, in a socially open learning environment, chat is a focused learning activity, providing a forum where identities emerge and activity is at its greatest. We demonstrate the diverse and growing uses of chat through reference to examples from the chat archives of online distance courses at the University of the Arts London. We contextualise chat within a social learning framework and provide an analytical framework drawn from conversational analysis in order to examine the issues associated with chat in practice and how practice is improved through specific methodologies, new protocols, and inventive application.

Introduction

This chapter aims to examine, analyse, and evaluate the use and practice of synchronous computer-mediated conferencing (SCMC), or "chat," through reference to online courses running at the University of the Arts London (UAL). UAL offers a variety of courses under its specialism in art, design, and communication.

The application of chat, particularly in online distance learning, stems from its value in helping build online communities, imparting a sense of a social learning space to an online course, and engendering a feeling of immediacy in peer and tutor interactions.

Our conception of teaching is of practices that support and promote learning through peer-to-peer interactions and through activities that are socially important (Lave & Wenger, 1991; Vygotsky, 1978). In an online environment, chat systems are one of the most important online tools responsible for achieving high levels of social interaction.

The technical simplicity of chat environments imparts flexibility, promoting its use for a range of learning and teaching purposes. According to the intended objectives for a chat session, different protocols of use may apply and different techniques or modes of chat may need to be developed. For example, we have employed chat for free-flowing discussions, highly structured student presentations, tutorials, and candidate interviews. Each re-purposing of the technology has led us to develop appropriate learning and teaching practices.

Chat provides regular opportunities for live meetings in the virtual learning environment, (VLE) and regular meetings keep students motivated. In this respect, chat is an important component in building an online learning community. It is inclusive and democratic, allowing all participants to contribute as meaningful social actors in the learning space.

Chat as a social technology of communication is usefully construed within the framework of conversational analysis (CA). CA illuminates the processes and structures of conversation and is capable of providing insights into behaviour in the chat room. By understanding something of normal conversational structures, we begin to understand some of the problems associated with using chat.

Whilst chat systems are technologically simple, they are extremely flexible and adaptable in use. Their flexibility allows all participants in a session to contribute equally in shaping the forms of communication as well as the content. As participants become more confident, they are able to help determine the manner and use of chat sessions. In this way, chat practice continues to grow, incorporating an expanding range of valuable uses.

The Place of Chat in Building an Online Learning Community

In order to build a successful online social space, the VLE must be perceived by all participants as an active and busy place (Garrison, 1995). Leaving a course inactive for any length of time will certainly demotivate students.

Explicit patterns of learning activities and interaction, covering the working week, help reassure students that they will meet a tutor and their peers when they go online at specific times (Rowsell & Jackson, 2004; Salmon, 2002). This is certainly true for chat sessions, which work best when timetabled. Chat sessions are scheduled once a week for each module on each course. More than one session might occasionally be required, but session timetabling nevertheless remains rigorous.

Allowing students communication spaces of their own is also important. For example, we create a "club" discussion board for student use and we ensure that they have access to private chat rooms whenever they wish. Students like to use chat to organise meetings, problem solve with help from their peers, and engage in group work and social activities. They will often prefer chat meetings to e-mail as group decisions can be made much more quickly in a chat room than through e-mail.

In order to become a successful member of the online learning community, students need to develop and project an online personality (Palloff & Pratt, 1999). The ability to do this emerges when the learner is able to create a visualisation of their peers and can deal with emotions through text. In chat, the successful participant is able to construct an internal dialogue on the basis of the text message stream alone. This requires imagination and skill but has the advantage of evoking a sense of presence that participants inhabit an important virtual learning space (Cherny, 1999).

Palloff and Pratt (1999) warn us that encouraging a social online space may not necessarily lead to an online learning space; learning needs to be overlaid on social needs. The role of the tutor is essential in this, guiding students and aiding them through structured activity is paramount if the online community is to progress and become an online learning community.

Chat and Conversational Analysis

By comparison with face-to-face conversation, chat appears impoverished (Ten Have, 1989). Intonation, gaze, and body language are absent in chat. Nevertheless, chat still tends to follow the familiar structures and forms of conversation. That is, aside from the content of a chat session, familiar conversational structures are observable. For example, sequencing of participant contributions in a chat session tends to follow the recognisable patterns of face-to-face conversational interaction. Therefore, speakers in chat may take the floor or yield the floor, and the rules under which exchanges are managed are much the same in a chat session as they would be in a face-to-face conversation.

An ethnomethodological approach to conversation treats it as governed by socially generated rules evolved through practice with the aim of solving communication problems. Exchanges are regularised and structured in anticipated ways (Bilmes, 1986). Therefore, conversation is considered a socially cooperative activity where participants aid each other in determining and creating meanings (Nofsinger, 1991; Atkinson & Heritage, 1984; Grice, 1975).

For the practiced conversationalist, there is a technology of conversation that proves instrumentally useful in ensuring that the transmission and reception of information is reliably accomplished (Sacks, 1992; Sacks, Schegloff, & Jefferson, 1974). Conversational analysis, through the examination of real conversations, has helped reveal the workings of the technology of conversation. Perhaps the most important aspect of this conversational technology is how conversation is structured and regularised through what Sacks termed the "management of a conversational turn" (Sacks, Schegloff, & Jefferson, 1974).

That participants take turns to speak in a conversation is familiar from experience. What may not be so evident is how the mechanisms of turn-taking work. It might be thought that participants simply wait for a gap or break in the flow of conversation, but in general, pauses are very short and can be ambiguous, perhaps indicating either a moment of thought, taking a breath, or the end of a contribution.

A turn, in a conversation, might consist of a participant contributing anything from a single word to a lengthy construction composed of many sentences. Sacks identifies a number of means by which participants assign responsibilities in a conversation and manage turn-taking (Sacks, 1992). For example, the current speaker might select another speaker, usually by naming them. Importantly, conversational contributions tend to occur in what are termed "adjacency pairs," and this pairing structure is of primary importance in helping participants determine turn-taking or who speaks next.

The most common form of an adjacency pair is when a speaker asks a question, inviting another speaker to respond with an answer. The two parts of an adjacency pair have a conditional relevance to one another, so that given one part of a pair the nature of a corresponding part is generally predictable. Alongside question and answer, some further adjacency pairs include: request and offer; request and denial; invitation and acceptance. Although there may be insertions between the first and second part of an adjacency pair, in general, we expect a speaker to cease speaking once they have uttered the first part of a pair and we expect another to take up speaking with the second part of the pair.

Adjacency pairs frequently occur in complex relationships and combinations. A speaker might, for example, sequence two or more adjacency pairs or they may insert one pair into another. The structure of an adjacency pair provides the points at which speakers take their turns to speak, where the imperative passes from one speaker to another. Technically, these switches between speakers are known as "transition relevance places" (TRPs). Participants are presented with choices at TRPs, in as much as they may decide to follow a norm or not.

If a conversation is managed effectively, then participants often respond with contributions that indicate the agreed and shared understandings captured in the conversation. For example, a participant might summarise what has been said (a "formulation") or finish a speaker's sentence (a "collaborative completion"). When things go awry, participants might attempt to "repair" the conversational break. Or a participant who senses that the conversation is about to break down might change what they are about to say (a "revision").

The intricacies of turn-taking do not represent a purely formal aspect of conversation; the complexity of conversational form is driven by the needs of speakers to be understood and to achieve specific goals through the means of conversation.

Problematic Exchanges in Chat

In applying CA to chat, we immediately see that one of the most common problems in a chat session is making sense of the turn-taking structure in the evolving chat record. TRPs can sometimes be difficult to identify, particularly for novice participants (Winiecki, 2003; Herring, 1999; Werry, 1996).

In most chat systems, text appears only once a participant has finished typing and has hit their return key. Participants in these kinds of environments may have no feedback on what is happening outside of the visible text. Therefore, messages may arrive out of order or contributions might be interrupted (if they are broken up into chunks). On other occasions, a delay in the sequence of messages occurs, leaving everyone waiting and wondering about the next contribution. A lengthy contribution by one participant may therefore be misinterpreted as the end of a topic or sequence of pairs by another participant.

Once sent, a chat contribution will appear almost immediately on the screens of all participants. The illusion is of writing (and speaking) in real-time. However, because of the linear ordering of contributions through the chat software, there is no guarantee about where, in the message stream, any particular contribution will appear. Two messages sent at the same time will be selected for preference by the software and ordered accordingly. This obviously takes no account of the meaning of messages, the relationships between pairs of contributions, or the intentions of speakers.

In a fast-moving chat session, precise timing of contributions may well be called for if a participant is not to miss their turn. By missing a turn, overlaps are likely to occur where intended adjacency pairs become separated by remarks from other participants. In an educational context, where it is preferable to have clear objectives for a chat session, some management of participants' contributions is usually necessary, requiring specific chat management skills from those who are hosting the session.

Simple chat environments offer little help in overcoming these problems of overlapping contributions and topic decay. More complex chat software systems such as ICQ and Ytalk offer each participant a window (field) where their contributions are placed. In this way, participants have an overview of what others are doing at any one time. This kind of feedback enables better timing of contributions by participants as well as providing additional information about topic contributions. However, a disadvantage of these systems is the limit they put on the number of participants in a session. Each participant needs a separate window and all windows need to be displayed at once, so limits on the numbers of participants are decided according to available screen (or browser) space.

Chat Management through Formal Moderation

The greater the number of participants in a chat session, the greater the potential for overlaps and topic drift, leading to misunderstandings and confusions. On occasion, a

Figure 1. Formal moderation of chat

[1]	< ED > so anyone what difficulties did you find with online group work?#
[2]	< TP > ?
[3]	< TH > !
[4]	< ED > TP, TH go ahead#
[5]	< TP > this online group or another course?#
[6]	< ED > this course#
[7]	< TP > !
[8]	< TH > i think i did not understand the task for this week –
[9]	< TH > i have no online documents to share so far as i never taught online#
[10]	< ED > TP?#
[11]	< TP > problem = no group! Lol#
[12]	< ED > ok TH... yes TP that is the biggest prob of all#
[13]	< JW > !
[14]	< TH > !
[15]	< ED > JW?#
[16]	< JW > there wasn't much activity on our discussion board#
[17]	< ED > TH?#
[18]	< TH > i think there are not many participants in my group –
[19]	< TH > who actually take the course –
[20]	< TH > i agree with JW#

more formal kind of moderation may be required from the tutor. Formal moderation is a way of determining how and when participants make contributions and enforcing an orderly turn-taking structure when none has naturally arisen.

Formally moderated chat sessions employ specific markers to enable the participants to manage turn-taking. Markers may be used to encode a participant's intention to ask a question, make a statement, continue a contribution, or finish a contribution. For example, the following single-keystroke code could be used:

- **Question request:** "?" (question mark)
- **Contribution request:** "!" (exclamation mark)
- **Continuation** (contribution is submitted in chunks): " - " (dash)
- **End of a contribution:** "#" (hash)

The conventional meaning and use of the exclamation mark is explicitly avoided within chat sessions. This is in recognition of the potential for misinterpreting emphasis or emotional meaning that can arise in the absence of other communication cues. Figure 1 shows part of a moderated chat session demonstrating the use of these codes.

Such formally moderated chat may help order a session, but for many participants it can feel restrictive and frustrating. Immediacy of response is often lost and participants may find themselves waiting too long before they can make their contribution. While waiting, they may find they want to change their contribution and there is then a tendency to over-edit their contributions. Under these conditions, the thoughts of participants become more private than in a free-flowing chat session. This is less desirable from a learning perspective.

Chat Management in Practice

Planning a Chat Session

No matter how chat is used for learning and teaching, a session will generally need some structuring in order to maintain topics, avoid confusion, and regularise participant turn-taking.

Different interpretations of chat contributions may lead to sessions veering suddenly off topic; the larger the number of participants, the more likely this is to happen. Smaller groups of between four to eight participants are probably the easiest to manage for the more unstructured sessions where conversation flows freely and where contributions from all participants are most likely.

An original focus of a chat session topic can easily broaden according to the various interpretations and viewpoints of the students. This diversity of response is to be encouraged as integral to the learning experience. However, the tutor should anticipate diversity and plan for possible clusters of responses in order to facilitate a smooth and free-flowing session. Such session planning is aided through the use of mind-maps. In a mind-map, ideas radiate from a central focus to provide a holistic picture of a situation. Ideas can represent the potential areas of response that students or participants are likely to generate given the chat session topic. The benefits of doing this include the retention of focus of the chat session topic even when numerous threads develop. Therefore, a tutor is able to respond quickly to the diversity of points raised because they have anticipated these through their planning. Prompting with questions can also lead participants into previously identified regions of the mind-map should the discussion begin to fall off.

A tutor may then lead a chat session just as easily as they do in a face-to-face seminar or tutorial. This can be achieved without necessarily reverting to the formal moderation methods discussed earlier, particularly when participants have progressed beyond the chat novice stage.

Usually a tutor will take the lead in a session and begin to organise participants and their responses through forms of addressivity, bringing in named students or posing questions to the group as a whole. Tutors may also summarise or refer to earlier learning sessions or learning materials. Their role in leading is to ensure that a session fulfils its learning objectives and in this they have a meta-conversational role, being both inside the conversation as an ordinary participant and outside in a directorial sense as they attempt to steer the course of the conversation in as natural a way as possible toward explicit goals.

Session Summary

As with face-to-face teaching, the tutor hosting the chat will often complete a learning session with a summary or formulation of what has been discussed and an indication of what students need to do next. It is evident from Figure 2 that the tutor's summary has been influenced by students' contributions during the course of the session. It is also clear that a student was able to gain clarification of a specific point that would arguably have gone unnoticed had the summary not been made. While summarising is commonly used in face-to-face teaching, its value and implementation are greatly enhanced in chat.

Figure 2. Tutor's session summary

[1]	< Tutor > couple of quick points –
[2]	< Tutor > you have done some good work here –
[3]	< Tutor > this is a key skill for anyone in buying –
[4]	< Tutor > you need to know instinctively how to assess a competitor –
[5]	< Tutor > and what they're doing –
[6]	< Tutor > new lines - poor / best sellers etc –
[7]	< Tutor > always keep an eye out for promotions - they can really hit sales
[8]	< EH > how often would buyers visit other stores then?
[9]	< Tutor > daily
[10]	< Tutor > or at least someone from the department will –
[11]	< Tutor > mostly over lunch –
[12]	< EH > i see. didn't realise it would be every day!
[13]	< Tutor > the competition is so great - short term promotions –
[14]	< Tutor > sudden promotions –
[15]	< Tutor > all of which can shift customers into a competitor's store –
[16]	< Tutor > ok?
[17]	< PS > ok
[18]	< Tutor > I have posted next weeks final learning activity –
[19]	< Tutor > and will post feedback for last week before I go on Sunday –
[20]	< Tutor > ok?
[21]	< EH > ok thanks
[22]	< PS > ok, have a good trip and thanks for a great session again#
[23]	< Tutor > have a good weekend

There is a particular strength in online learning methods that encourages regular discussion, by contrast with instructional courses that depend on participants interacting with software.

Tutor formulations, or summaries, represent a common practice in learning contexts. Formulations represent another way of stepping back from the flow of a conversation to see what is going on and are part of the tutor's directorial methods.

Student Presentations in Chat

An effective method of structuring a chat session, affording a manageable interaction amongst participants, follows the model of student presentations in face-to-face teaching.

In advance, students are asked to research a topic and present their findings during the chat session. In the illustrated example (Figure 3), students were asked to break their posts into chunks so that the flow of the presentation was not greatly interrupted by long pauses while a lengthy sentence was typed. This practice also enables observers more time to digest information or the substance of contributions as they emerge.

Figure 3. Student presentation in chat

[1]	< Tutor > ok EL that's excellent
[2]	< AS > shall I go next?
[3]	< Tutor > a really thorough review
[4]	< Tutor > yes pls AS
[5]	< AS > I looked at O
[6]	< AS > This is a high street up market fashion retailer
[7]	< AS > as well as having concessions
[8]	< AS > within department stores
[9]	< AS > it sells womens wear as well as accessories
[10]	< AS > and more recently underwear
[11] to [25] continuous dialogue	
[26]	< AS > coats were from 90 - £150 (faux fur)
[27]	< AS > promotion was advertised
[28]	< AS > in heat magazine 15% off with voucher
[29]	< AS > garments were displayed with a boutique feel
[30]	< Tutor> ok AS - once again an excellent review
[31]	< Tutor > have to stop it there
[32]	< AS > bags, jewellery were in a separate part of the store
[33]	< Tutor > to give PN a go
[34]	< Tutor > seeing the time
[35]	< Tutor > thanks AS

Each student in the cited example had about 10 or 15 minutes to present and about four students presented during an hour chat session. The subject of the student presentations was a review of a high street fashion retailer in the period just before Christmas. Each student chose a retailer and researched them by visiting appropriate stores. They were then asked to provide an overview of their subject's store layout and display, together with an account of prices and offers.

In this session, the controlling factor was the time allowed for each student to present their review and not the number or volume of posts made. However, in the time available, each student managed between 20 and 30 posts with an average line length of seven or eight words. The informal messaging requirements of chat, in terms of sentence structure, grammar, and spelling, means that the student is less concerned with writing correct sentences than they are with conveying as much content as possible in the time available. Presentations under these conditions have a compressed character but are usually concise and rich in relevant detail. Any gaps in students' work or their understanding show up very clearly in chat of this kind. The example illustrates diversity in the use of chat and clearly demonstrates its potential use in assessments including *viva voces*.

Assembly

Because chat happens in real-time, scheduling sessions is important. These need to be timetabled for participants sometimes in different time zones and on different continents. Exactly when to use synchronous as opposed to asynchronous communication is, for us, a matter of integration into weekly schedules. The pattern of learning and teaching defined through a weekly schedule automatically promotes synchronous activity at specific points in the week.

Usually, chat sessions are timetabled to last for an hour, with five- or ten-minute assembly periods that begin before the hour. Half-hour or even 20-minute chat sessions have been used for tutorials and assessment, but the specification of an assembly period remains.

Having an assembly period allows time for all participants to find their way to the chat room and engage in social exchanges before the session begins. It is important for the chat facilitator to state clearly when the session is beginning, in order to draw a line under these assembly discussions. If this policy is adopted in the first chat session, participants quickly learn to accept it and chat sessions can begin immediately to make effective use of the time available.

Just as chat sessions begin with an assembly period, they finish with a signing off period. Signing off usually happens as soon as the tutor signals the session completed. Signing off differs from assembly in that it tends to take less time and contains fewer social exchanges, although this may be the time when participants confirm arrangements made earlier in the session or when a student directs a last question to a tutor.

Evidence of Self-Directed Learning

Students quickly adopt the routines and protocols of behaviour appropriate to chat sessions. Figure 4 shows a weekly chat session on a short (seven-week) course that occurred in week five of the course. On this occasion, the tutor was unavoidably absent for the first 50 minutes of an hour-long session, arriving with only 10 minutes remaining. On arriving, the tutor found that not only were all students present but that they had engaged in a learning session without the tutor. This was possible because the topic for discussion had been posted in advance (as part of their weekly learning activities) and students routinely experienced a significant amount of learning from discussions with their peers. In this case, the session was intended as a discussion following up on student activity that involved researching fashion representation in retail outlets.

One of the most interesting aspects of this chat session is the fact that the students started to focus on the learning topic themselves at 12:04, which is approximately when the session would have begun had the tutor been available. By the time the tutor arrived, the students had been chatting on topic for almost an hour. It is important to note that these students had only known each other for five weeks and the course was not at post-graduate level, where one might have expected a more self-directed approach to learning. Students were able to work cooperatively despite only a short association as a cohort of students.

Developing the Learning Value of Chat

At UAL we have used chat for interviews, student presentations, conducting staff meetings, and blended learning. New uses for chat continually emerge or suggest themselves as a result of teaching practice. Some of these developments have been prompted and helped by technological innovations. For example, we have extended text-based chat environments through the addition of video and audio tools.

Our use of video and chat has been extensive, widening our experience and practice but also extending our understanding of the mechanisms and problems associated with all forms of online synchronous communication. One drawback of audiovisual chat, for example, is that archives are not so readily scanned. It is much easier to read through an hour's worth of text chat archives than it is to scan an hour's worth of video.

Developments in the formats of text-based chat are likely in the near future. Changes in the technology and display of chat are unlikely to solve all of the problems of turn-taking and topic overlap we experience with basic chat rooms, but there are possible improvements that are worth experimenting with. For example, systems exist that have indicators showing when participants are typing, allowing better anticipation and timing of contributions.

Redesigning the layout of chat contributions may also be advantageous. The current organisation of chat as a linear stack of postings is a legacy from early designs for data exchange systems (Shankar et al., 2000). To date, however, the popularity and usefulness

Figure 4. Students start and continue a session in the tutor's absence

	NM has entered. [11:59:43 AM]
[1]	< DF > Hi NM
[2]	< LT > hi everyone
[3]	< DF> Hi LT
	SK has entered. [12:00:03 PM]
[4]	< NM > hi everyone
[5]	< WK > hi
[6]	< SK > Hi all
	MR has entered. [12:01:02 PM]
[7]	< DF > Hello
[8]	< MR > Hi everyone
[9]	< DF > MR - how was the show?
[10]	< MR > Could not make it - unfortunately
[11]	< SK > Thats a pity you missed out MR
[12]	< MR > I would love to have gone but just could not get my schedule organised to let me attend
[13]	< DF > NM - have you found out anymore about the New Look scheme? are you thinking of applying?
[14]	< NM > yes definitely, I need to get some experience more than anything so am currently looking into that and then I am going to apply next year as the springboard is every autumn
[15]	< NM> have you decided anymore on what further courses you want to take?
[16]	< DF > they do a 3 day course on visual merch and space planning that i'd love to do, but i'm not sure whats next for me
[17]	< DF > what did you all think of this week?
[18]	< WK > it was fun for me
[19]	< SK > Sounds interesting DK. Are you more interested in merchandising than buying, or are you just building experience?
[20]	< LT > this week was fun but found it hard to get time to go window shopping
[21]	< DF > SK - I have a lot of experience in visual merchandising and really enjoy it but im keen to learn more about buying. Its something id like to do in the future
[22]	< MR > I must admit to getting sleepy going through all the collections as a lot of them are really quite similar after a while
[23]	< DF > i know what you mean
[24]	< WK > i agree

Figure 4. continued

[25]	< DF > I wasnt sure what to write this week. I think I was reading too much into it and making it harder than it had to be
[26]	< SK > This week was really good, but got a little caught up at work, still have to add to the discussion board
[27]	< DF > I do too. Ive written it, just need to post it on
[28]	< SK > I did the same DK, got lost in all the research, and need to cut it all down to core facts
[29]	< NM > DK- i was the same as you, i wasn't too sure what to do but just looked at it simply and then wrote what i thought, i also loved it as it gave me the excuse to go shopping
[30]	< DF > MR - when buyers come to you do they sometimes ask you to source a copy of particular designers products
[31]	< MR > No. By the time I talk to the designers they have worked up a storyboard with all sorts of pictures and designs on it to give the mood.
[32]	< DF > do you think that it is better for the high street to imitate designers or to use their own creativity?
[33]	< WK > little bit of both...i think
[34]	< MR > I agree - the designers should be at the cutting edge of things and the high street has to work with those concepts and then make them cheaper and wearable
[35]	< DF > whats it like in the US? is there a lot of imitation on the high street?
[36]	< WK > not imitating, but they should go to similar direction
[37]	< NM > definately, they need to imitate the designers in order to sell fashionable clothes but ading their own individuality to the designs will set them apart from the other high street stores
Tutor has entered. [12:54:26 PM]	

of chat in learning contexts is evidence of the adaptability and inventiveness of users. There is a value in designing simple systems and whatever technologies and software we move to in the future, flexibility in use will remain a key priority.

Conclusion

A central benefit of chat as a tool of learning and teaching is that it provides a means of conducting real-time multiple user communication. This is an attractive feature when considered against the learning benefits afforded by the instant dialogue norm of a face-to-face course.

Synchronous communication presents opportunities for mirroring those elements of face-to-face learning that cannot be implemented by asynchronous tools such as e-mail and discussion boards. However, chat does more than this in that it opens up the learning environment as a social space, a place where all participants can contribute to the manner and direction of their education. This social space can be used for directed learning but also for organisational, administrative, and personal purposes.

Conversational analysis helps provide a framework of understanding for practice, and within this framework it is possible to see how we might begin to solve many of the communication and coordination problems that accompany chat practice. CA suggests means by which chat sessions can be managed and directed to learning and teaching ends. In practice, as with all teaching, managing a chat session and contributing accurately are acquired skills that continue to develop with experience.

Many of the problems first encountered in chat rooms are quickly reduced through good session planning and skilled hosting, making inventive use of the minimal tools a chat room supplies. Good chat practice begins with the overall planning of learning activities and the identification of learning outcomes. From this beginning, a tutor can direct a chat session in unobtrusive ways without the need for strict and formal moderation. In the informal chat room, students become much more active contributors and better learners.

The educational needs for the student in a chat room are much the same as they are for the face-to-face student in the seminar room. In the online environment, however, explicit structures have to be supplied to ensure that student needs are satisfied. Interaction does not happen as a matter of course, there must always be good learning and teaching reasons for using chat, and activity needs to be normalised within the educational context, ensuring that chat sessions work to accepted objectives, aims, and outcomes.

Chat is best used as a planned activity, directed through learning activities embedded within patterned and scheduled learning tasks. At the same time, chat remains a flexible tool, capable of being turned to a range of purposes and circumstances. For example, chat can be adjusted to differences in group size, activity objectives, and learning outcomes.

For the online student, a chat room becomes both a social space and a learning space. As students grow in confidence, they learn to project themselves emotionally into this differentiated environment. The chat room then becomes the locus of maximum direct activity in the learning environment, serving to motivate students because of its guarantee of interaction with others. The continuous and live discourse evident in chat facilitates a deeper and more effective learning experience, and the immediacy of responses to students helps sustain creative and critical thought, providing clarification for student questions and an impetus for discoveries and consolidations. This places the chat room at the centre of the online student's learning.

References

Atkinson, J.M., & Heritage, J. (Eds.). (1984). *Structures of social action: Studies in conversation analysis.* Cambridge: Cambridge University Press

Bilmes, J. (1986). *Discourse and behaviour.* New York/London: Plenum.

Cherny, L. (1999). *Conversation and community: Chat in a virtual world.* Stanford: CSLI Publications.

Grice, H.P. (1975). Logic and conversation. In P. Cole & J.L. Morgan(Eds.), *Syntax and semantics: Vol III. Speech acts.* New York: Seminar Press.

Herring, S. (1999). Interactional coherence in CMC. *Journal of Computer-Mediated Communication, 4*(4).

Lave, J., & Wenger, E. (1991). *Situated learning: Legitimate peripheral participation.* Cambridge: Cambridge University Press.

Nofsinger, R.E. (1991). *Everyday conversation.* Newbury Park: Sage.

Palloff, R., & Pratt, K. (1999). Defining and redefining community. In *Building learning communities in cyberspace: Effective strategies for the online classroom.* San Francisco: Jossey-Bass.

Rowsell, D., & Jackson, T. (2004). Online learning in art, design and communication: An explanation of the use of weekly activity schedules. In A. Davies (Ed.), *Enhancing curricula: Towards the scholarship of teaching in art, design and communication in higher education.* London: Centre for Learning in Teaching in Art and Design.

Sacks, H. (1992). *Lectures on conversation* (2 volumes). G. Jefferson (Ed.). Oxford: Basil Blackwell.

Sacks, H., Schegloff, E., & Jefferson, G. (1974). A simplest systematics for the organization of turn-taking in conversation. *Language, 50*(4), 696-735.

Salmon, G. (2002). *Etivities: The key to active online learning.* London: Kogan Page.

Shankar, T.R., VanKleek, M., Vicente, A., & Smith, B.K. (2000). Fugue: A computer mediated conversational system that supports turn negotiation. *Proceedings of the 33rd Hawaii International Conference on System Sciences.*

Ten Have, P. (1989). Text analysis programs: An exploration of CA at the PC. *Human/ Computer Interaction, The 1st International Conference on Understanding Language Use in Everyday Life.* University of Calgary.

Ten Have, P. (1999). *Doing conversation analysis: A practical guide. Introducing qualitative methods.* London: Sage.

Vygotsky, L. (1978). *Mind in society.* London: Harvard University Press.

Werry, C. (1996). Linguistic and interactional features of Internet relay chat. In S. Herring (Ed.), *Computer-mediated communication: Linguistic, social and cross-cultural perspectives* (pp. 47-63).

Winiecki, D.J. (2003). Reconstructing learning: Talking-interaction in the online, asynchronous classroom. In M. Moore & B. Anderson (Eds.), *Handbook of distance education.* Hillsdale, NJ: Lawrence Erlbaum.

Chapter XVIII

From SYnthia to Calma to Sybil:
Developing Strategies for Interactive Learning in Music

Michael Clarke, University of Huddersfield, UK

Abstract

This chapter describes the development of software for teaching music and music technology at the University of Huddersfield in three projects spanning the last 14 years. The importance of engaging music students with sound itself and the potential of technology to facilitate this is a key feature of all three projects. The value of developing software that is adaptable and extensible is explained. The lessons that have been learnt in the development of these projects are described, and the chapter ends with a provocative vision for the future.

Introduction

Over the last 14 years research in learning technology has been a strong feature in music at the University of Huddersfield. Three different software packages (*SYnthia*, *Calma*, and *Sybil*) have been developed, and although they do not all cover the same aspects of music, each successive package has built on the lessons learned from the previous software. Initially, each of the packages grew out of our own teaching situation at Huddersfield and challenges we faced, but the issues and the solutions we have proposed have proved of wider interest, nationally and internationally. All three programs have been awarded European Academic Software Awards (in Heidelberg in 1994, in Rotterdam in 2000, and in Le Locle/Neuchâtel in 2004, respectively). A key goal of all three packages has been to give students the opportunity to engage with music as sound not just as text on the page, and for this engagement to be interactive.

The chapter charts the development of this work, compares the approaches of the different programs, and describes the lessons we have learnt. It investigates the general issues raised by these developments and explores their potential for wider application. It ends with a vision for the future.

Background

Huddersfield is one of the largest music departments in the UK. It has long had a reputation for combining theoretical and historical "academic" study of music with a practical engagement with the practice of music through composition and performance. It also has had a long involvement with music technology, initially just as a component of the music degree, but also, more recently, in specialised music technology degrees. Some of these degrees are run in conjunction with electrical engineering, and students come from a variety of backgrounds. Two of the software packages described here were designed particularly with a view to making technology more accessible to students from an arts background, to facilitate the teaching of students with a range of different academic experience, and to encourage a creative approach to the use of technology in music.

All three packages aim to engage students with sound. Simply reading a book or attending a lecture can lead to study that is remote from the sound that is the key element in the discipline. Lecturers may play musical examples and written texts may direct students to scores or CDs, but for many students this is not as stimulating as experiencing the music for themselves, especially engaging with it interactively.

Of course much commercial software does exist for music. This is especially the case for the sub-discipline of music technology. However, little, if any of this, provides the sort of learning experience we have been seeking to create. Most music technology software is designed for the production of music and not for teaching the underlying principles. Indeed, some of this software encourages a trial-and-error approach, with little opportunity for the user to develop a better understanding of how and why things work. This can sometimes produce good results, creatively speaking, but for a degree course, we believe our goal should be to deepen students' understanding and to provide them with the skills and knowledge to develop and adapt as the technology advances. The challenge is how to devise a curriculum that will help students to develop technical understanding and to do so in a way that is seen as creatively relevant and stimulating.

More generally in music there is again much commercially produced software. This ranges from excellent notational packages (e.g., Finale or Sibelius) to pedagogic software for aural training (e.g., Auralia) or the teaching of basic theory (e.g., Musition). These latter types of programs generally take a rather mechanical approach, using "drill" exercises to practice skills and test knowledge, mimicking and automating the way these topics have often been taught in the past. Such software does have a place, but our aims were different, perhaps complementary. We wanted to use technology to bring students closer to real musical experience, not distance them from it in exercises that are remote from everyday musical experience.

The following sections will give an overview of the features of each program in turn. This will be followed by a discussion of general issues raised by these developments.

The Software

SYnthia

The Problem

SYnthia (Synthesis Instruction Aid) was developed to help with a particular problem we faced in teaching music technology to music students: Such students, usually from a primarily artistic background, often had the potential to make excellent use of technology in their creative work but faced an initial barrier in developing the skills to work with such equipment. Although some took to this easily and quickly, many found working with technology off-putting. This is still an issue today but was even more so in the early 1990s, before digital technology was such a significant part of everyday life (in the form of mobile phones, MP3 players, home computers, etc.). We also wanted to enable students to develop a deep understanding of how the technology worked so that their creative interaction with it could be idiomatic and their creative invention originate from the nature of the technology they were using. We wanted to make the technology as accessible as possible to all, and we believed that it was not necessarily always just those who most quickly took to the medium who might make good creative use of it in the longer term (Clarke & Hunter, 1995).

The research underlying the production of *SYnthia* was also related to a broader investigation of the state of teaching of electro-acoustic music in the UK at the time. A survey was conducted and the results analysed and published (Smith & Clarke, 1993). The survey dealt with issues of curriculum design, teaching methods, the technology used, funding levels, class sizes, and the role of electro-acoustic music within the broader music curriculum. The outcome of the survey informed our thinking in the development of *SYnthia*.

Figure 1. Screen shots from SYnthia

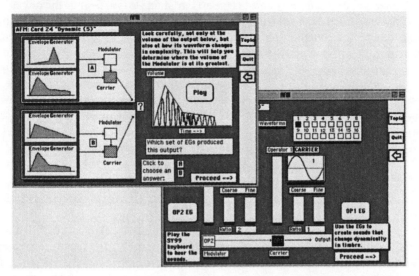

The Solution

The key strategy in responding to all these issues was to use computer technology to provide an environment in which students could learn the theory of music technology alongside opportunities to hear sound examples and experiment aurally with the ideas presented to them through interactive exercises. In this way, we hoped to bring the theory alive, make it relevant to the students' musical aspirations, and, at least in the more advanced exercises, make a link between theory and creative work.

To do this, we needed to create a package that was able to generate sounds and for it to be possible to manipulate these sounds using on-screen controls. We also needed to be able to run the package on affordable machines, so that it could be used on multiple workstations. In the early 1990s, only expensive specialist computers could generate and manipulate complex sounds in real-time. Therefore, we had to look for another solution. This was to use the computer to control an external synthesiser which generated the sounds. For the sound generation, we chose the Yamaha SY99 (hence, the capitalised "SY" in *SYnthia*), then one of the most versatile and sophisticated machines on the market. The software was written for a Macintosh computer using HyperCard and with HyperMIDI to handle the sending of messages to the synthesiser. Text and diagrams were provided on screen together with various mouse-activated controls to trigger sound examples and control parameters of the sounds interactively. The screen design and range of controls was very limited by today's standards, but we found it was possible to produce a program that functioned effectively. One of the most difficult programming tasks was the development of a graphic interface for controlling sound envelopes.

SYnthia was structured hierarchically into four modules, each comprising a number of topics themselves divided into pages. (HyperCard made this aspect of the development straightforward.) These ranged from pages primarily consisting of text (although as far as possible, we tried to avoid too much text on a single page) to pages for interactive experimentation with sound. For the most part, pages fall somewhere between these extremes, and few pages do not involve some element of aural engagement. Figure 1 shows two screen shots from *SYnthia*. They combine text and graphics to explain theoretical issues with interactive on-screen controls that enable students to experiment with the ideas for themselves in the domain of sound. These screen shots also give some indication of the navigation methods. Buttons are provided to proceed to the next page, to return to the previous page, to quit, or to move up one level in the structure.

Review

In most respects, *SYnthia* proved highly successful. To a large extent, it fulfilled the goal of providing students with a link between theory and sound, and gave them an interactive environment in which to experiment. It significantly improved their knowledge of synthesis techniques and their creative application. It was in use at Huddersfield for almost 10 years before becoming obsolete through changes in technology, such as new operating systems, and being replaced by *Sybil*. It was distributed by ASK in Karlsruhe and was used as far afield as New Zealand. Some of the limitations of the program were the result of technical limitations at the time. The fact that the program needed a specific combination of a Macintosh computer and a Yamaha SY99 synthesiser restricted the range of people able to use it. The use of a commercial synthesiser limited the range of techniques we could teach to those provided by the manufacturer. The interface and interactivity also were limited by the technology. We ran short of time in the development schedule to fully implement the direct link between study and creativity as fully as we would have liked. Ideally, we would have programmed a full editor for the SY99 as a final component of the package, enabling students to save sounds they created during their theoretical study, manipulate them further, and then use them in their own compositions. Although a start was made on this, it was too big a task to complete in the one year of the main project development. This did not make such links between study and creativity impossible, but it was not as intuitive for the students as we would have liked.

Despite its limitations, some more obvious today than they were 10 years ago, we remain proud of the program and believe it served a useful role at Huddersfield and elsewhere. It also provided us with invaluable experience for our later projects.

Calma

The Problem

Calma (Computer Assisted Learning for Musical Awareness) grew out of work by Professor George Pratt at Huddersfield. He was concerned that aural training within

Figure 2. Screenshot of the Calma articulation exercise

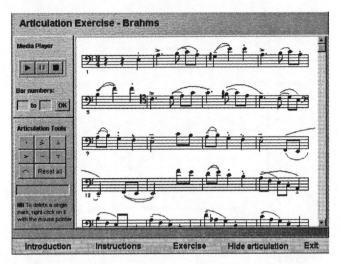

music curricula was too remote for the real everyday experience of musicians and from the needs of students. Traditionally, aural was often taught as musical dictation, a member of staff playing, for example, a Bach chorale on the piano and the students being required to notate what they heard. Quite often, little real teaching took place; the format was simply repeated in the hope that students would improve. In reality, students usually fell into one of two camps: those who had perfect pitch and could often get excellent results anyway; and those who struggled and continued to do so in the absence of any real help. Furthermore, this training was too narrow and neglected to develop many aspects aural sensitivity demanded of musicians in real life. For example, the emphasis was almost always on pitch and rhythm, as they could be fitted onto the striated lattice-work of traditional musical notation with much less attention being given to issues such as phrasing, timbral quality, rubato, or pitch inflection.

Professor Pratt had already developed an alternative approach to this area of the curriculum which he renamed "musical awareness." His book (Pratt, 1998) outlines this approach and gives practical guidance on how to implement it. The aim of *Calma* was to enhance certain aspects of this approach through the use of computer technology. It was not intended as a replacement for the many other important aspects of musical awareness (e.g., interaction between students playing together and listening intently to one another) but as an addition. As already noted, other software existed for aural training. These packages very much followed the traditional dictation approach, of some value, but on their own were too narrow and artificial.

The Solution

The project evolved over time and the end result was two interrelated approaches. Initially the idea was to produce a finite set of musical awareness exercises, each focusing

Figure 3. Outline of the Calma structure (from the Calma Handbook)

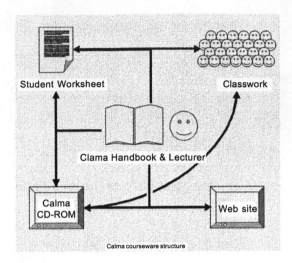

on particular aspects of aural development and complementing those which did not use a computer. Later, we decided we wanted to produce a more flexible, extensible package which would allow other lecturers to adapt material or develop their own exercises. This resulted in the creation of an "editor" for the development of teaching materials. This was an important change of approach and is discussed in more general terms later in this chapter.

An example of the specific exercises is the articulation exercise (Figure 2). This exercise enables students to listen to real-life performances of three different compositions and annotate the score provided on screen to show the articulation used by the performer as they had perceived it. The student then compares their annotation with one we provided (in red as opposed to blue for the student's annotation). A key feature is the use of real performances on the real instruments (facilitated by the kind collaboration of Hyperion), unlike most traditional aural training which reduced everything to a piano rendition. The focus on articulation and phrasing draws the students' attention to a vital aspect of musical experience frequently ignored by more traditional approaches. The use of the computer enables students to work at their own pace, hearing the passages complete or in part as often as necessary to develop confidence.

A vital part of *Calma* is that it did not view the computer-based work in isolation. The integration of aural training into the real activities of student musicians meant that such exercises were linked to other activities. In this case, for example, students working with the articulation exercises are also encouraged to work together in small groups playing musical passages to each other, experimenting with and discussing the options for articulation in the music they play. Figure 3, from the *Calma Handbook*, was an attempt to show the general structure within which the computer exercises might be incorporated:

Figure 4. The Calma player/editor

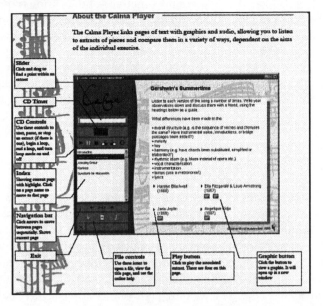

The lecturer uses the *Calma Handbook* as a guide to using the *Calma* exercises on the CD-ROM. These exercises may be supplemented by additional material on the Web site, and lecturers may prepare their own material to contribute to the site. The lecturer works with the students (individually or in small groups) in using the exercises and associated worksheets within the larger context of classwork. As will be discussed at greater length, an important lesson we learnt in developing *Calma* was to respect the limitations of computer technology as well as being enthusiastic about what it could achieve. We came to realise the importance of allowing flexibility in the exercises we were creating. The curriculum might evolve necessitating changes, or different staff may wish to incorporate alternative exercises or change the text. This led us away from creating specific exercises toward producing an "editor" (which would enable staff to easily create their own materials) and a "player" (which students could use to do the exercises). Once again, the emphasis was on real musical experience. So the *Calma* editor enabled precise extracts to be played from a CD placed in the CD drive of the computer. In this way, copyright issues were bypassed. No sound was copied, the computer simply acted as a sophisticated CD player, able to produce precisely selected examples at the click of a mouse. Students simply had to get the appropriate CD from the music department library for use with the exercise. Alternatively, if copyright could be negotiated, or if staff made their own recordings, compilation CDs could be made for use with an exercise.

Therefore, devising an exercise involved assembling a combination of text, diagrams, or pictures or score extracts if desired (again, copyright permitting) together with buttons to trigger the playback of selected passages from the music. The editor was designed to make this process as simple as possible, and documentation was produced to facilitate this process. The *Calma* team produced a series of sample exercises to illustrate some of the possibilities. Figure 4 shows one of these. This is taken from the *Calma Handbook* and the screen shot is annotated to explain the functions of the various controls. In this exercise, the student is given the opportunity to compare different realisations of George Gershwin's *Summertime*. The student is encouraged to engage with the sounds themselves and answer questions relating to what is heard. Staff may, for example, choose to have students complete worksheets individually prior to a class discussion, or to have small groups of students work together in consultation. Flexibility is the key. We tried to provide tools that could be used differently in varied contexts and to suit different teaching styles.

Review

Calma has proven successful in extending the scope of computer-based teaching materials related to the development of students' aural skills and providing them with a more integrated and musical approach to this study. It has been taken up and used at other institutions; for example, at Leeds University Dr. Rachel Cowgill has incorporated it into a first year musicology course. As this illustrates, the flexibility built into the editor/player approach means that it in fact has wider use than simply for aural training. In fact, this is a positive advantage because it encourages the integration of aural skills into other areas of the curriculum rather than isolating them artificially. Funding for the project was extended by the University of Huddersfield to explore the use of this approach in other disciplines altogether where the combination of text, graphics, and audio was important. The program was expanded to incorporate video clips in much the same way as audio. The *Calma* team worked with staff from a number of disciplines (marketing, textiles, careers guidance, cultural studies, and physiotherapy), helping them to develop teaching materials using the *Calma* editor. A major new development for us in *Calma* was the idea of producing a tool to enable others to easily produce teaching and learning materials rather than authoring a fixed course ourselves.

Despite its success in many respects, *Calma* has alerted us to a number of problems. Unlike the other two packages, the area of the curriculum for which *Calma* was developed was not one in which staff routinely use software. In some cases, it has proved more difficult to persuade staff to take advantage of the technology, adapt their teaching strategies, and become involved in developing materials for *Calma*. Personnel changes also made this more difficult and is clearly another factor that needs to be considered in any such development.

Sustainability has been another issue. *Calma* was the only one of our programs where the actual coding of the program was undertaken entirely by someone on a short-term contract. Future maintenance and development will therefore be difficult. Where the staff involved in the development of a program are those teaching the subject on a permanent basis, their hands-on knowledge of the inner workings of a program makes such maintenance much easier. The issue will be revisited later in the chapter.

Sybil

The Problem

Sybil, in part, grew out of a need to replace *SYnthia,* which was becoming obsolete. However, it is a completely new program with many significant differences. In part, these are because our courses, the students, and student needs have changed. Also, it is because technology (and with it music technology) has advanced very rapidly in the 10 years between the two programs, opening up new possibilities for pedagogic software and also changing expectations. Students themselves now have a generally higher level of experience and confidence in using technology, and many have their own computers at home. Furthermore, our own thinking on the design of such software has developed through the experience of producing the two earlier packages and a result of the experience of seeing them in operation. *Sybil* also incorporates some features of *Calma,* in particular, its extensibility and its use of CD playback. Therefore, *Sybil* can be seen as a culmination of our research in this field to date.

The essential problem for *Sybil* to solve was similar to that when we started *SYnthia.* We wanted to link the technical and the creative, and we wanted to make the technology widely accessible to students whatever their previous technical experience. However, our courses had now expanded to include music technology degrees, some of them in collaboration with engineering and drawing in students from more technical backgrounds as well as those from more traditional musical backgrounds. Thus, the problem was now bidirectional: not only did we need to make technology accessible to the musicians, we also needed to help the technically oriented explore the creative aspects of the technology.

Initial work toward *Sybil* took the form of a project named *SYnthia II.* This project examined the potential for generating the sounds within the computer and investigated issues relating to interface design (Padden, Clarke, Dix, & Kirby, 1996). Although much useful research was done in this project which later informed the development of *Sybil,* we discovered the technology at that time was still not capable of achieving what we wanted, except on specialist research machines, and the development of a full replacement program was postponed.

The Solution

The combination of faster computers and the development of sophisticated audio programming languages eventually meant that the project to replace *SYnthia* was feasible. A key feature was the generation of the sound, not by an external synthesiser, but by the computer itself. This made for a much more compact package and, since the synthesis was in software, it permitted much greater flexibility in the choice of algorithms and how they were presented. We chose Macintosh once again as our main platform since this is what we are most familiar with and has a large following in the computer music world (but the program is largely portable, see Figure 5). Max/MSP was chosen as the audio programming language. It is powerful and flexible and is increasingly used by a wide

Figure 5. Live display of the signal and spectrum in Sybil

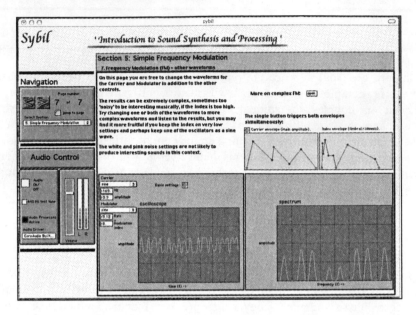

range of people from researchers to performers to composers of various styles of music. It has the further advantage of providing a basis on which to build a good user interface. Unlike *SYnthia*, there is also the possibility of providing a live visual display of the signal and the spectrum of the sound being generated. In this way the theoretical can be reinforced by both visual and aural feedback. Figure 5 shows a screenshot from *Sybil*. Text is accompanied by sound, generated in real-time, which can be played and adjusted experimentally as it is heard. The student is learning about a particular form of synthesis, and can both hear and see the effect of changing the parameters. The visual feedback shows both the shape of the waveform (on the left of Figure 5) and its spectral content (to the right of Figure 5) displayed. As the parameters are adjusted, the display changes in real-time with the sound itself. The aural and visual feedback greatly enhances the student's understanding and memory of the theoretical issues. This is particularly useful in complex examples where the relationship between a particular parameter and its effect on the spectrum of the sound is more difficult to grasp intuitively.

Max/MSP made programming of many aspects of *Sybil* much easier than had been the case with *SYnthia*. A particular stumbling block initially, however, was that Max/MSP was not designed primarily with the sort of hierarchical structuring of content that had been easy with HyperCard: Max/MSP is mainly intended for audio performance not for pedagogic presentation of materials. Therefore, a significant amount of effort was needed to program a means of navigation through successive sections and pages.

Max/MSP makes both extensibility and portability relatively easy. Max/MSP is available for both Max OS9 and OSX, and for Windows XP. For the most part, software developed on one platform can be easily ported to the other. Once the software is written, it can be compiled as either a standalone (in which case the application created runs without any additional software) or as a collective (in which it must be run with the freely available RunTime version of Max/MSP). This means that students who have their own machines can run the software without any additional cost or needing to own Max/MSP themselves. If the source code is made available, *Sybil* can also be easily adapted or extended by anyone with knowledge of programming in Max/MSP. Given the large and growing number of Max/MSP users internationally in the computer music community, the development of teaching materials can be shared by many people. Drawing on the experience of *Calma,* the aim with *Sybil* from the start was to make not just a number of modules but a toolkit to enable others to extend the range of materials. Our aim is to work toward the development of an international shared library of *Sybil* modules. Initial responses following presentations in autumn 2004 at IRCAM in Paris and at the International Computer Music Conference in Miami (Clarke, Watkins, Adkins, & Bokowiec, 2004) are encouraging, with a wide range of people declaring an interest in taking part in this project.

The flexibility of *Sybil* is further increased by the fact that Max/MSP is itself extensible. Although MSP is already very comprehensive in its range of synthesis and processing algorithms (and frequently updated to take account of new developments), if an algorithm is required that is not currently available, it can be added by anyone able to program in C. I have done this myself in collaboration with Xavier Rodet of IRCAM for *FOF* and *FOG* synthesis (for more on these formant-based approaches to synthesis see Clarke & Rodet, 2003). This made possible the production of a *Sybil* module for teaching this complex and rather specialist form of synthesis.

Since the basic concept of *Sybil* is to provide a structured set of materials for interaction with sound, clearly its use is not restricted to the teaching of sound synthesis and processing. For example, it may well also have use in areas such as music psychology and acoustics. Recently, it has been used in the development of an interactive aural analysis of one of the standard works in the computer music repertoire: Jonathan Harvey's *Mortuos Plango, Vivos Voco*, (Clarke, 2006). For this purpose the *Sybil* browser was extended to incorporate a CD player option. As with *Calma,* this is simply an elaborate CD player capable of playing precise moments in the work at the click of a mouse.

Review

It is only relatively recently that *Sybil* has been completed and is too early to try and judge its success. However, we very much believe that this software, drawing on previous experience and taking advantage of new technological developments, is a major advance on our earlier work. Many of the restrictions we faced in the past have now disappeared. Certainly, the reception of the program where it has been demonstrated — in Britain, Switzerland, France, and the USA — has been very positive, and music technologists from different continents have registered an interest in using existing *Sybil* modules and in helping create a shared international library of *Sybil* modules. A Web site to facilitate this is currently under construction. Student reaction in trials of the prototype was very positive and produced a number of helpful suggestions for improvements. Even science-based students who had covered much of the more basic technical material previously commented that this approach enabled them to deepen their understanding. Currently, two modules are in their first year of use at Huddersfield: *A Basic Introduction to Sound Synthesis and Processing* and *An Introduction to FOF Synthesis.*

In the case of *Sybil,* we also have managed to resolve one of the weaknesses of *SYnthia* — the relationship between theoretical study and the student's own creative work. In our department, as in many others now, Max/MSP itself forms part of the curriculum. In the first two years, students take modules in learning to program in Max/MSP; in their final year, students undertake creative work using this software. This means that there is a direct link between *Sybil* and the students' creative work. We can make the source code for *Sybil* available for them, and they can adapt it for their creative work using the techniques and sounds they have worked with in *Sybil* and expanding them into their own work. A further possible implication of the students themselves studying the programming language in which their tuition materials are written is that they could themselves undertake projects to develop further *Sybil* modules.

A current limitation is that the XP version of Max/MSP (a relatively recent development) does not currently support CD playback. This means that the analysis module and any similar developments requiring CD playback are only available on Macintosh. *Sybil* is also of course dependent on the continuing availability of Max/MSP, but this does not seem likely to be a problem in the foreseeable future.

Overall, we believe the positive aspects of *Sybil* far outweigh the few minor drawbacks, and we are not aware of any other software that provides this level of instruction about theoretical issues combined with interactive experience leading to creative work.

More generally, it is perhaps worth noting that none of our software packages emphasises student assessment. Some software developments make automated assessment in one form or another (e.g., multiple choice questions) a major feature. Our primary goal has always been to develop a stimulating environment for learning and other means of formal assessment have seemed more appropriate for the most part. Clearly, many situations exist where testing can be carried out efficiently and appropriately by computer. Certainly in music, however, much of what is most important cannot be assessed in an automated fashion (creativity, imagination, interpretive sensibility). As previously mentioned, we have tried to recognise where learning technology has something valuable and distinctive to contribute, but also to realise the boundaries of its usefulness.

Strategies for Future Development

From our past experience, we have learnt the value of technology in the teaching of music and music technology. Most positively, the demands music places on the technology, which until recently seemed to stretch it to its limits and beyond, are now no longer such a problem. A threshold seems to have been crossed, and whilst more computer power is always welcome, the current situation no longer impedes useful developments. Issues of affordability and portability have also improved greatly.

How best to take advantage of this new potential? Our experience has taught us a number of lessons. We believe the relationship between the development of software and its users, staff, and students is a crucial issue. The traditional model is that of the expert programmer developing software for the client, the end-user. Such a model also exists in relation to the development of software for music. The programmer writes code and the musician composes using the tools that have been provided. In music technology, however, there is a need for a more creative, integrated approach, and it is toward this that we educate our students. If musicians become skilled in the technological side, and if the "technologists" become experienced in musical issues, a deeper level of creative integration ensues, and this is more likely to lead to imaginative and idiomatic work. The creativity originates within the medium itself and is not simply something "added on" once the technical work is complete.

Our experience indicates that much the same vision is needed in learning technology; the best results have come where technology and pedagogy have interacted at a deep level. Such an approach impacts on a whole range of issues. Staff needs to develop an understanding of the technological medium to the extent where they can think imaginatively about its use in an idiomatic way. They can be inventive and creative in thinking about how the technology can be used in a way that draws on knowledge of how the technical system works; there can be a genuine interaction between pedagogic and technical imaginative invention.

This type of interaction is relatively easy in a subject area like music technology where many staff are involved not only in using computers but in programming. In the future perhaps all academic staff should become programmers. This might seem too radical a proposal, but then technology has already advanced much further into academic life than in the past: Word processing and Internet use, for example, are now taken for granted. An intermediary position, especially in subjects where the technological demands are less, is for software to be developed that enables staff to input content without the need for lower level programming skills. *Calma* is one example of such software, while PowerPoint is another. Conversely, perhaps more learning technologists need to be subject specialists (in the way that there are subject specialist librarians) with a deep understanding of the subject.

Such developments would not only result in a greater level of creativity in program development, they also would help resolve the problems discussed earlier relating to software maintenance and ownership (and, therefore, willingness to utilise the packages). This also relates to the style of package that is produced. We have moved from producing completed, closed programs to open-ended extensible projects. This has obvious advantages for adaptability and revision. But it also marks a change in relationship between "product" and "user." This relationship becomes an interactive one in which the user contributes to the ongoing development of the package. With *Sybil,* we are intending to use the Internet as a means for staff in different institutions to exchange materials created in *Sybil*. The user, therefore, becomes part of the development team; traditional distinctions between developer and end-user are blurred.

We mentioned in relation to *Sybil* that students were learning the programming language in which their teaching materials were created. This was a coincidental development related to the subject area. But imagine this extended to students more generally (and perhaps as with staff, computer programming in the future will become part of general literacy?). If this were to be the case, once again the boundary between producer and user, between developer and student might be blurred. Students would not only use the software but would adapt and extend it themselves. This is perhaps an extension of the idea of students giving seminars in a more traditional environment. This may seem a distant prospect, but in music technology at Huddersfield, this is already beginning to happen, though yet to be formalised.[i] And, of course, in terms of simply exchanging textual information, this is already happening on a large scale via the Web.

This vision may appear to represent a complete capitulation to technology. We would see it rather as the full creative involvement of technology in teaching. The importance of integration of technology into the broader context of teaching and the recognition of the limitations of technology were discussed (see section on *Calma*). In music, it is very clear that technology has its limits. The human interaction of people (students or staff *and* students) performing music to each other and responding to what they hear can never be replaced by technology. It is important that technology is used where it has something to offer, and that we should be imaginative in looking for new possibilities, but that it should also be recognised where a different solution is needed. The technological should not be kept separate, at arms length, from other teaching media. The different approaches need to be blended into a coherent package. At present, there is a sense in which sometimes technology is too "special," therefore, either put on a pedestal or in a ghetto. It needs to become, and indeed in some cases already is becoming, an everyday tool, like a pen and paper, to be used as appropriate alongside other methods.

But the vision described is about more than simply using technology. It is about the breaking down of barriers between the providers of materials and their users. Combined with the Internet, this could result in teaching and learning becoming an international exchange. The main issues and problems then, as with the Internet more generally, become issues of quality control, plagiarism, and the sheer quantity of materials. Strategies and technical solutions for the management of this type of situation are increasingly important issues for further research.

Conclusion

The discussions in this chapter have centred on music. The key issue here has been the integration of theoretical learning with experience of the sound itself and the opportunity for the student to manipulate sound interactively. The generation of sound or playback of sound from CD, the live display of the audio signal and its spectral content graphically make this a highly technical area in which to develop software. Music is a highly technological subject and always has been (consider, for example, the design of the violin), and some of the issues raised may not be so critical in other disciplines. Not all subjects perhaps will confront such difficult challenges. However, similar problems are faced by a range of subjects, including many of the sciences, in which the linking of theoretical abstractions with practical examples is important for learning. Some of the issues discussed here are of particular relevance to such subjects; others have more general application. Our research and practical experience in music have led us to the following conclusions:

1. Theory is best learnt in a context where the student can directly relate such ideas to experience of its practical implications and can interact creatively with these.

2. The traditional programmer/staff/student divide is too rigid, and the best results come where these boundaries become flexible.

3. Just as important as developing the software itself is developing a curriculum in which the software can be fully integrated. The software must be designed to facilitate integration.

4. The limitations of technology need to be recognised, and technical solutions should not be forced where an alternative is better.

5. Technological developments should not be dominated by issues of automated assessment or seen exclusively, or even primarily, as a time/cost-saving device. Such a narrow view of technology is not likely to make the most of its potential and may in the long run be detrimental to its standing.

6. To make the most of technology, more staff and students need to become increasingly computer literate and able to take part in software development with a deeper understanding of the medium.

Continuing developments in computer technology, the increasing use and ownership of computers by staff and students, and the developing experience of people working in this field, make this a time for optimism about the future of learning technology. We need to remain responsive to the new opportunities these developments offer. Our expectations and our presumptions will no doubt continue to be challenged by new opportunities. However, the most crucial thing will continue to be the focus on teaching and learning and how technology can serve this goal. This is why the integration of technical skills and subject-specific knowledge is so important: Only then can the full potential of the technology be harnessed in a way that is appropriate and idiomatic for the subject.

Acknowledgments

With grateful thanks to all those who have taken part in the three projects, especially to Dr James Saunders for his helpful suggestions for this text. The three packages were developed by different teams at different times: *SYnthia* (1992-4) by Michael Clarke and Stuart Hunter; *Calma* (1996-2001) co-directed by Michael Clarke and George Pratt with Julia Bowder, Michael Pengelly and James Saunders; and *Sybil* (2002-4) by Michael Clarke, Ashley Watkins, Mathew Adkins and Mark Bokowiec. The *Calma* project was funded by an FDTL award and extended with funding from the University of Huddersfield. For further information on the software see: www.hud.ac.uk/mh/music/calma/calma.html and www.hud.ac.uk/mh/music/sybil/sybil.html

References

Clarke, J.M. (2006). Jonathan Harvey's *Mortuos Plango, Vivos Voco*. In M. Simoni (Ed.), *Analytical methods of electroacoustic music*. New York: Routledge.

Clarke, J.M., & Hunter, S. (1995). Educating the next generation: Integrating technological skills with artistic creativity in computer music courses in higher education. *Musicus, 4*, 47-52.

Clarke, J.M., & Rodet, X. (2003). Real-time FOF and FOG synthesis in MSP and its integration with PSOLA. *Proceedings of the International Computer Music Conference* (pp. 287-290). San Francisco: International Computer Music Association.

Clarke, J.M., Watkins, A., Adkins, M., & Bokowiec, M.A. (2004). Sybil: Synthesis by interactive learning. *Proceedings of the International Computer Music Conference* (pp. 354-357). San Francisco: International Computer Music Association.

Padden, M.S., Clarke, J.M., Dix, A.J., & Kirby, M.A.R. (1996). Towards SYnthia II: An assessment of design strategies for computer assisted learning of sound synthesis. *Proceedings of the International Computer Music Conference* (pp. 214-215). San Francisco: International Computer Music Association.

Pratt, G. (1998). *Aural awareness: Principles and practice*. Oxford: Oxford University Press. (First published by Open University Press, 1990)

Smith, G., & Clarke, J.M. (1993). Electroacoustic music in higher education. *British Journal of Music Education, 10*(2), 85-90.

Endnote

[i]   Students working in MSP at Huddersfield are developing their own materials which could well be incorporated into *Sybil* eventually, and one of the team involved in producing *Sybil*, Ashley Watkins, was a student on work placement.

Chapter XIX

Lecturing by Streamed Digital Video:
Blood, Sweat, Tears and Success

Chris Smith, University of Central Lancashire, UK

Abstract

Streamed video is being increasingly introduced into higher education, allowing remote students to participate synchronously or asynchronously. This chapter reports the outcomes arising from three uses of asynchronously streamed video in undergraduate psychology modules. Student feedback and estimation of the impact of using streamed video on examination performance were obtained. The feedback was sufficiently positive, and, with reservations, the impact on examination performance was sufficiently apparent for it to be concluded that streamed video offers tangible benefits for the student learning experience and may improve learning performance. Tutors have a flexible, accessible, and productive means of incorporating moving images into learning resources, and institutions may need less teaching accommodation. In this chapter, after an introductory section, the background to the project is described and the project is outlined in terms of the issues, controversies, problems, solutions, and recommendations related to it. Finally, future trends are considered.

Introduction

Although it is not hard to agree with the view taken in the Joint Information Systems Council report on "Effective Practice with e-learning" that "e-learning is fundamentally about learning and not about technology" (HEFCE JISC report, 2004, p. 9), a more considered view must be that e-learning is technology-dependent and is really about the interaction between the learner, the learning process, and the technology. This chapter adopts this approach, focusing on examples of evaluative studies of the use and effects of streamed video on learning and teaching.

Broadband technology is increasing more quickly in terms of availability, uptake, and speed than any other comparable new technology. With it comes widespread access to video content. The BBC, for example, is already putting video content on the Web, and pilot schemes are already operating for on-demand entertainment services via video streamed down broadband connections.

Before broadband, video could only be sent across networks or the Internet in small chunks, because of the density of video data. Accordingly, streaming was developed as a means of hiding the joins between files to give the impression of continuous video. Nevertheless, streaming video across a network or the Internet is still a relatively new technique, which is not widespread and is only now beginning to attract attention in the HE community. The use of streamed digital video as a teaching and learning resource is rapidly becoming an attractive option for many educators; it is an innovation which expands the range of learning resources available to students by moving away from static text-and-graphic resources toward a video-rich learning environment.

So, what is streamed video? And what are its educational uses? "Streaming" is a technique whereby information is provided by a Web server in a "just in time" format to a user requesting a large file. Rather than downloading an entire audio or video file and then playing the file, streaming sends a portion of the file and begins playing the file, while continuing to send successive portions of the file. As a method for delivery of instruction, the process that incorporates streaming video includes:

- Presentation of material via lecture and visual presentation materials
- "Capturing" the presentation (both audio and video) typically on videotape
- Converting the audio and video to digital formats that are capable of being streamed
- Storing these files on an appropriate server
- Files are streamed to a student when requested by a Web browser

The instructor can lecture and present materials using the same media as in a traditional classroom (e.g., chalk, overheads, video tapes, computer-generated images, demonstrations). All aspects of the presentation are captured on video and audio. To some extent, providing instruction via streaming video is a re-creation of the classroom experience in an online delivery format.

Interaction between students and the instructor, however, is significantly different than in a synchronous delivery mode (e.g., traditional classroom or two-way interactive video). Students do not have real-time interaction opportunities with the instructor.

Interaction happens at a later face-to-face meeting, through e-mail, phone calls, or some combination of techniques.

However, a distinction needs to be made between synchronous and asynchronous transmission of streamed video. The former refers to, for example, sending a lecture live by streamed video to students at another location – something which was formerly achievable only by closed-circuit television (which required viewers to be present in a specified location, or, at best, one of a few locations). The obvious practical advantages of streamed video in terms of access are that a lecture can reach any PC on a network, which, given access rights to the network, could mean any PC anywhere. However, synchronous transmission is a convenience with no obvious pedagogical advantages, and, in any case, lectures are widely considered to be an ineffective teaching technique. They lack interactivity and — unless they are recorded — students must take notes at a pace and with a clarity which captures the meaning of what is being said. Even recorded lectures are linear in terms of access for the student, who has no control over the proceedings and is forced to be a passive learner.

Asynchronous transmission, however, offers significant advantages for students and staff. For students, the advantages include:

• The lecture is available at any time via the Internet or the university network.

• Students have control over when, wher,e and how they watch the lecture — "how" meaning that they control the sequence, duration, and repetition of the video clips which make up the lecture. Learner control allows the student to adopt their preferred mode of learning at their preferred time and in their preferred location.

• Students also have control over access to any supplementary materials which accompany the lecture, such as graphics, text, references, and Internet links.

These points correlate positively with students' attitudes to distance learning (Green et al., 2003) and to learning styles (Katz, 2002; Dewar & Whittington, 2000; Smith & Whiteley, 2003).

In addition, this environment is richer. It can offer images, interactivity, and integration with other resources. It can integrate, *inter alia*, still and moving images, live or recorded lectures, locally produced video, Web resources, and synchronous and asynchronous communication tools. Thus, streamed video allows remote access to lectures and, when integrated into a multimedia package, creates a rich, accessible, interactive, and controllable teaching resource.

As such, streamed video makes a major contribution to e-learning by contributing to the criteria for effective practice in learning generally, as identified by JISC (2004); namely, the practice should:

• Engage learners in the learning process.

• Encourage independent learning skills.

• Develop learners' skills and knowledge.

• Motivate further learning.

Effective learning is likely to occur given:

- the right resources
- the right mode (or blend of modes) for delivery

In this chapter, it is argued — with evidence — that streamed video is an important resource for effective learning, especially when blended with other modes to create a rich, flexible package. The chapter focuses on asynchronous transmission and on the pedagogical issues of teaching using streamed video. Three examples of such uses are described as are outcomes from attempts to evaluate their impact on student behaviour and learning. Future trends and the issues they raise are also discussed.

Background

Streamed video is already widely used at a few universities. For example, the University of Cincinnati offers six complete courses and over 400 individual items of instructional material events via videostreaming (2005). For this university, videostreaming is successfully replacing the classroom and is drawing the wider learning community and the university closer together. At the University of Western Australia, videostreaming has given access more than 6,000 students access to more than 1,800 recordings of lectures (2005). Approximately 50,000 hits have been recorded to date — 60% of which came from off campus. The University of Sydney is also using streamed video to deliver lectures both synchronously and asynchronously by digital video taping — streamed video by another name (White, Sartore, Cartwright, & Curthoys, 2004). However, in these examples streamed video is mostly being used for transmitting unenhanced recordings of live lectures.

No evaluation of the uses of streamed video has been reported in the cases described, other than usage figures. The emphasis has been on producing a resources library and improving access to teaching materials without considering or attempting to assess the pedagogical effects. However, at the University of Southampton, streaming video has been used to support the learning of first-year student nurses in three applications in a life sciences module, as one of many innovations designed to increase the range of resources and support available to students (Green et al., 2003; Bracher, Collier, Ottewill, & Shepard (2005). A total of 656 students used online directed-learning sessions that incorporated streamed video. Just more than half of the students actually viewed the video streams. Their feedback showed that 32% found access easy, 59% enjoyed using the resources, and 25% were very confident that they learned from the video streams. Different types of video were used and embedded in diverse ways, but the results were consistent across the three applications.

These results suggest that streamed video can contribute useful resources to support learning by student nurses. However, for a variety of reasons, streamed video did not appeal or was not adequately accessible to all students, and when the results are viewed from another angle (i.e., in terms of what students did *not* report) the results showed that

68% of the students did not find access easy, 41% did not enjoy using the resources, and 75% were not confident that they learned from them. This is hardly a ringing endorsement for streamed video use.

Issues, Controversies and Problems in the Use of Streamed Video

Technological Issues

Capacity has been the main technological issue. Streamed digital video is information-rich. When we first used it asynchronously, we were limited to short clips which students had to select individually. However, these constraints disappeared with improvements in the compression and transmission of files, so that a file could be as long as was needed to cover a topic within the lecture. Thus, there are now no major technological limitations of using streamed video across a network or the Internet.

Pedagogical Issues

As was mentioned, a lecture which is sent live by streamed video (synchronous transmission) to students at a remote location offers nothing extra in pedagogical terms compared to a live face-to-face lecture or a televised lecture. On the other hand, when the opportunities offered by asynchronous transmission are fully exploited, it can offer significant advantages for students and staff.

For students, the major advantages can be that:

- The lecture is available at any time via the Internet or the university network.

- Students have control over when, where, and how they watch the lecture — "how" meaning that they control the sequence, duration, and repetition of the video clips which make up the lecture. Learner control allows the student to adopt their preferred mode of learning at their preferred time and in their preferred location.

- The content of the lecture can be supplemented by the addition of graphics, text, references, Internet links, and self-assessment questions.

These points have all been found to correlate positively with students' attitudes to distance learning and to learning styles.

For staff, the major advantages are:

- A lecture can usually be easily edited, updated, and amended, because it consists of many short clips of video and many small files to provide the supplementary text, graphics, and so forth.

- Staff workload is reduced, at least in terms of timetabled commitments and of time spent delivering lectures.
- Lecture content can be more easily controlled and delivered, thereby producing a more complete learning experience for students.
- Using streamed video reduces the level of demand on scarce teaching resources such as large lecture theatres.
- Distance learning, off-campus, and multi-site courses are facilitated.

There are few disadvantages associated with streamed video, but arguably:
- The student experience becomes more remote, impersonal, and less "connected."
- Enhancing streamed video lectures is time consuming.
- Preparation is likely to require technical support.
- The effectiveness of the medium for learning has not been fully researched or evaluated.

Practical Issues

Preparation is the major practical issue with the use of streamed video. Software now exists to aid the production of materials for streaming, but it remains a complex task. A widely expressed axiom is that one hour of online material takes 10 hours to prepare. As in other areas, however, the learning experience is a rapid one, but in the case studies outlined next, we acknowledge that our technical support played a major role in the production of the materials and in providing the learning experience for us.

A minor practical issue is that of access. Students without remote access or who have to pay for their online connection time may be reluctant to access online teaching materials. However, the growing use of broadband and in many institutions the introduction of network terminals in halls of residence or the provision of laptops mean that this problem is a diminishing one.

Problems

A major problem for all areas of learning technology is evaluation. As far as can be ascertained from their Web sites, the University of Cincinnati seems to have adopted videostreaming without prior evaluation, while the University of Western Australia simply records the number of hits on its Web site.

The School of Psychology at the University of Sydney has adopted a more systematic approach to evaluating the effectiveness of streamed video — comparing streamed video with both live face-to-face lectures and live video-conferenced lectures. Both live modes were perceived as being significantly more satisfactory, but the opportunity to rewind the video was a valued option of streamed video. Student examination and coursework performance were not measured, nor are any views of staff reported.

Although the study reported here describes three uses of streamed video — each of which was evaluated as far as possible, and each of which addresses the issues and problems outlined earlier — most of what follows is about one of those uses, namely a streamed video lecture on creative thinking.

Solutions and Recommendations

This study is a fuller evaluation of the use of streamed video for teaching and learning than has been reported elsewhere. The study attempts to evaluate what was done from three angles:

1. Staff experience in creating and using streamed video within psychology modules
2. Student experience of using streamed video materials
3. Effects of learning from streamed video materials on student performance

Staff Experiences of Creating and Using Video Streamed Materials

The author of this chapter has used streamed video in teaching for several years, beginning as part of a wider, internally-funded teaching and learning project for which approximately £,2000 was allocated for staff hours within the Department of Psychology and £500 for staff hours in the Learning Development Unit (LDU). Approximately 50% of this funding was for the project described here, and little of this money and time was spent on preparation of learning materials, which would not have occurred anyway.

As part of the wider project, a lecture on the psychology of creative behaviour was chosen as suitable for videostreaming. The lecture is part of a second year cognitive psychology module, which is a compulsory module for BSc. psychology students and other students wishing to obtain eligibility for membership of the British Psychological Society. The module regularly attracts more than 150 students and, if current recruitment patterns continue, will attract over 200 in future.

The first step was to edit the existing lecture notes for the lecture into about 20 short pieces, each of which had a heading. The 20 "soundbites" were then recorded in the LDU — using as many takes as necessary. A text summary of each video clip was also prepared and added below the clip, in order to both summarise the point being made in the clip and to enable anyone without hearing, speakers, headphones, or a soundcard to make sense of the clip.

Preparing the material was not lengthy; it took about 90 minutes to film 40 minutes of video. Note that the lecture lasts slightly less than the standard 50 minutes, presumably because:

1. It includes no unnecessary verbiage, set-up time, or other non-essential activities.
2. The pace of delivery was faster because students can view each clip as many times as they wish and the lecturer does not need to adopt note-taking pace.

Thus, videostreaming lectures gives staff a choice between including more material than conventional lectures or giving shorter lectures, or a combination of both.

The video clips were assembled into a package with an introductory page, navigation aids, and the text summary of each clip at the bottom. The screen was split into two with the left half containing the video of the lecture and the right half available for the full text or any other material. A pause button allowed notes to be taken at leisure from the screen.

The final version was then uploaded to the university video server and links were set up from within the module Web site, which contains other essential material for the module and which students had already accessed for various purposes.

The lecture was revised the following year. Preparation and video recordinging took 90 minutes. Supporting materials were prepared by Learning Development Unit (LDU), which, in the view of the author, transform the original videostreamed lecture — providing as much breadth and depth as students could possibly use. The revision consisted of:

- providing a much more transparent navigation structure.
- embedding the streamed video into a narrative by enhancing the textual and graphical support and incorporating hot links to related Web sites. Thus, students were able to explore the topic much more easily and thoroughly if they chose to.

From the author's point of view, this updating was straightforward and not particularly time-consuming, but the creation, collation, and editing of the supporting materials by the LDU was a major undertaking by specialists. They are easy to update, but have to be updated frequently as Web sites disappear and new ones are created.

This part of the project was unfunded, but was achieved quickly and easily from the expertise acquired from developing the original version and by using that version as a template. Thus, in effect, no additional cost implications were involved in the revision, even though it was quite substantial. This would not necessarily be the case in all institutions. A second, smaller revision was undertaken the following year, consisting of expanding the front page and adding a set of self-assessment questions.

Two colleagues, encouraged by the author's work, decided to introduce streamed video into their teaching by:

1. preparing videostreamed material as an introduction to a seminar topic in the cognitive psychology module.

2. adding videostreamed material to introductions to sections of an existing online version of a topic on a third level module — to outline the aims, objectives, and outcomes.

Their feedback raised the following salient points about their experience of introducing streamed video:

- For the colleague who prepared the seminar introduction, the exercise brought home the value for students of having access to and control over the materials — including access to materials not available in the library. The preparation took longer than a standard lecture and was a useful exercise in appreciating the differences between a standard mode of delivery (where, for example, ad libbing and adding extra points are possible) and the carefully structured and supported videostreamed material.

- The colleague who embedded an introduction to each major section of an online lecture felt this prepared the students for fuller use of the existing interactive materials. It was a useful exercise for her in learning about the need to direct students and to guide them in benefiting more from the material. Preparation and video recording took 90 minutes.

The Student Experience of Using Streamed Video

Thus, three items of videostreamed material were prepared for use in part with the aims of:

- evaluating as fully as possible the student experiences of videostreaming.
- assessing whether using streamed video materials affects student performance.

Data were gathered from questions on module evaluation questionnaires (MEQs) for each module, other questionnaires, examination performance, or a combination of these.

The results for the seminar introduction consisted of no more than a small amount of positive MEQ feedback. For the videoed introduction to sections within an online topic, the feedback was not specific about the use of streamed video, but the online topic itself was very well received with:

- 22 students "very satisfied"
- 10 students "satisfied"
- 1 student "very dissatisfied"
- A frequent comment was that the freedom to access the material at any time was greatly valued.

Student feedback on the original version of the creative thinking lecture was positive, as recorded by responses to a question on the MEQ. However, this feedback was obtained from relatively few students, some of whom may have watched, rather than used the lecture. For the revised versions of the lecture, a feedback questionnaire was used in addition to the questions on the MEQ.

There was sufficient feedback to draw the clear conclusions:

- Satisfaction levels rose from 52% to 69%.
- There was much positive feedback from the questionnaire and from open-ended comments to the effect that:
  - the material was very easy to use, useful, and easy to learn from.
  - users felt that they learned a lot from it.
  - the best features were accessibility, the links, the text, the comprehensiveness, and the opportunity to determine the pace.

• There were many positive comments and requests for more such online lectures. There were also many negative comments. Some were about technical problems, some about specific issues, and some simply expressed a general preference for traditional lectures.

Effects of Learning from Streamed Video Materials on Student Performance

For the seminar introduction, no measures of performance were available. For the introductions to sections within an existing online version of a topic on a third-level module, the examination scores revealed a statistically significant difference between the mean scores for question on the topic containing the streamed video (58.63%) and a compulsory question (53.17%). The mean of 58.63% was the highest for any question, and the question was the most popular. Further statistical comparisons between this question and other questions were not possible because of small numbers (students were required to answer only three questions). It should also be noted that the statistically significant result is a comparison of two different questions, either of which may have been intrinsically harder or easier than the other.

For the creative thinking lecture, there was clear data for student performance from questions on an MCQ paper. The results were:

• For the original version, the mean scores for MCQs related to the lecture were 43.4% and 70.8%, while the mean for the paper was 67.4%.

• For the initial use of revised version, scores for related MCQs were 70.7% and 86.8%, while the paper mean was 54.0%.

• For the second revised version, scores for related MCQs were 61.3% and 74.3%, while the paper mean was 58.3%.

More detailed statistical analysis is precluded because the questions on the paper are changed each time it is used and because within each usage the questions cannot be matched for difficulty. Nevertheless, the figures must be regarded as encouraging and strongly suggest that students have learned more from the streamed video lecture.

Future Trends

Continuing and Extending Our Use of Streamed Video

We are continuing to use streamed video and are extending our use of it — at least by responding to the feedback we have received and seeking thereby to improve the learning experience for students.

- We are exploring the provision of more interactivity as a priority, by linking a message board in an MLE to the videostreamed lectures.

- We also are seeking to evaluate the use of streamed video in greater breadth and depth. In the case of the creativity module, we have introduced self-assessment questions and are obtaining feedback about these. We expect that these questions will be widely used, because they resemble the multiple-choice questions which form part of the examination.

- We intend to acquire more extensive usage data, including having the results of answering the self-assessment questions submitted automatically to a database each time a student attempts them. This would allow us to amend the questions by omitting those which are too easy or too difficult, but would also be a guide to those parts of the lecture, if any, which students find difficult.

- We are seeking to obtain better feedback from students and perhaps identifying case study examples of good practice in its use.

- From the staff perspective, we are seeking, in particular, to reduce preparation time by building on the experience gained to date.

Many aspects of this first substantial use of streamed video can be improved upon. It has been a learning experience for all concerned, but a worthwhile one, which we wish to build on. We remain committed to the need to evaluate the impact of technology on learning and, in this case, to evaluating the effectiveness of learning from streamed video in any valid way.

Short-Term General Trends in the Use of Streamed Video

The technology now seems to work well and streamed video is effective pedagogically. The main general short-term trend is likely to be that streamed video is used more widely and that further uses for it are identified — without adversely disrupting the balance in delivery modes, which provides a full learning experience for students.

The Long-Term Role of Streamed Video

In the longer term, streamed video is likely to become an integral component of online teaching — to the extent that students will likely encounter online lecture-like materials with streamed video and may find it difficult to imagine such materials, while staff, too, will find it progressively easier to produce and update their streamed video materials.

There are two major long-term trends in the use of learning technology for students:

1. increased availability of and access to information

2. greater freedom for students to control their own learning

This leads to a potential end point for the evolutionary, developmental process, which is leading inexorably toward a transparent interface between the learner, the learning process, and the developer. When this end point is reached, the student will be able to access their course material from anywhere at any time and to control it fully. So, for example, a student may use a tablet PC (for taking notes) to watch a streamed video lecture at whatever hour of the day of night they choose, replaying any point within the lecture as many times as they need to, accessing Web sites, video clips, self-assessment questions, and any other provision in what amounts to a complete learning package.

There are, of course, many other aspects to the student learning experience which students would not experience if streamed video via broadband were used exclusively. It is not suggested here that it should be; in particular, continued face-to-face (F2F) contact is regarded as essential. However, it is suggested that learning is enhanced and the learning experience is not diminished by the scenario which has just been described. This scenario is not an unrealistic or distant possibility, given the rapidly increasing availability of broadband (and the rapidly increasing bandwidth available within it). In our institution, network access is available in all student residences, remote access to the network is available from anywhere, and some of the videostreamed materials are themselves available on publicly accessible Web sites.

But what does all this imply for staff? There are four major implications for staff:

1. Easier ways must be found to produce materials of the types which include streamed video.

2. Training to use appropriate software or technology must be available for academic staff.

3. Preparation time will be greatly and rapidly reduced by the effects of easier production and training.

4. Within the foreseeable future, many staff will give far fewer, if any, F2F lectures. This is not to say, however, that the benefits of streamed video lectures are the same for all subject areas or topics — or that staff preferences should be ignored. It is to say, however, that demonstrable benefits for student learning, access to that learning, and for institutions should not be ignored either.

This last point is, perhaps, the most controversial. It sees an end to the group lecture — and with it the need to have large areas of a campus devoted to teaching space. The infrastructure and administration of lecturing to large groups will diminish accordingly.

Conclusion

Many points and much food for thought have arisen from the work described in this chapter. They are listed below in no particular order:

*   The uses we have made of streamed video show that it has a range of uses within the curriculum.

- It is technically feasible and reliable.
- It can replace traditional lectures.
- It can supplement topics delivered online.
- It is difficult and time consuming to do from scratch, but it becomes much easier, given development, technical support, and practice.
- Initially, there are cost implications for staff development, but these diminish rapidly.
- Production of videostreamed materials will continue to become easier as software, training, good practice, and familiarity with the medium are further developed.
- Streaming video will become an integral part of student learning and staff teaching.
- In teaching terms, much has been learned which will facilitate future use of videostreaming and also impact indirectly on other teaching modes of delivery.
- So far, student feedback is almost entirely positive and is usually very positive.
- The availability of what is effectively a rewindable hard copy of a lecture must generally aid student learning.

Many aspects of this first substantial use of streamed video can be improved upon. It has been a learning experience for all concerned, but a worthwhile one, which we wish to build on.

The technology now seems to work well, and the main need is to introduce streamed video more widely and to identify further uses of it — without disrupting adversely the balance in delivery modes, which provides a full learning experience for students. For example, providing more interactivity is a priority, for example, by linking a message board in an MLE to the videostreamed lectures — rather than making staff available when lectures were streamed to a remote site, as was done in Sydney[3].

We also would seek to evaluate the use of streamed video in greater breadth and depth. For example, we would seek to obtain better feedback from students and perhaps would identify case study examples of good practice in its use. We would continue to assess the effectiveness of learning from streamed video.

Many points and much food for thought have arisen from this ongoing project. The project has already shown that streamed video has a range of uses within the curriculum: It is technically feasible and reliable; it can replace traditional lectures; it can supplement topics delivered online; it was not unduly difficult or time consuming to create, given development and technical support; student feedback has been generally positive; and there is an indication that learning is facilitated.

Finally, on a purely personal note as a lecturer with decades of experience, I would like to add that learning technology, generally and streamed video, in particular, have removed the routine from lecturing and have made me feel that students are learning much more effectively from my attempts to teach them.

References

Bracher, M., Collier, R., Ottewill, R., & Shepard, K. (2005). Accessing and engaging with video streams for educational purposes: Experiences, issues and concerns. *ALT-J: Research in Learning Technology, 13*(2), 139-150.

Dewar, T., & Whittington, D. (2000). Online learners and their learning strategies. *Educational Computing Research, 23*(4), 385-403.

Green, S.M., Voegeli, D., Harrison, M., Phillips, J., Knowles, J., Weaver, M., et al. (2003). Evaluating the use of streaming video to support student learning in a first-year life sciences course for student nurses. *Nurse Education Today, 23*(4), 255-261.

HEFCE JISC report (2004). *Effective practice with e-learning.*

Katz, Y.J. (2002). Attitudes affecting college students' preferences for distance learning. *Journal of Computer Assisted Learning, 18*(1), 2-9.

Smith, C.D., & Whiteley, H.E. (2003, July). Distance learning and learning styles: Bridging the gap. In *Proceedings of the 3rd International Conference on Technology in Teaching/Learning in Higher Education* (pp. 279-284). Heidelberg, Germany.

University of Cincinnati (2005). *Case study example of streamed video lectures from the University of Cincinnati.* Retrieved April 4, 2005, from www.microsoft.com/windows/windowsmedia/archives/casestudies/univcincinnati/default.asp

University of Western Australia (2005). *Reports of using streamed video.* Retrieved April 4, 2005, from http://ilectures.uwa.edu.au/ilectures~uwa.htm

White, W., Sartore, J.G., Cartwright, A., & Curthoys, I. (2004, April). *Digital videotaping (DVT): An evaluation of an innovative mode for lecture delivery for teaching psychology.* Paper presented at PLAT2004 (Psychology of Teaching and Learning) Conference, Strathclyde University, UK.

About the Authors

John O'Donoghue's background covers a wide range of educational experiences, initially teaching in a social priority area school, moving later to post graduate lecturing, advising and consultancy for both initial teaching training and education departments, and more recently a within a National ICT Research Unit. He has held the position of chair and president of the Association for Learning Technology (ALT) and has hosted a previous conference. John has held honorary research fellowships at universities both in the UK and abroad. He now holds a visiting research fellowship at the University of Wollongong, Australia. John is currently a senior learning and teaching fellow at the Centre of Excellence in Learning and Teaching at the University of Wolverhampton where he has a responsibility for advising and developing technology supported learning for staff and students. This embraces all the academic and pedagogical aspects of networked learning technologies. He has acted as a consultant in a number of peripheral projects which utilize the Internet and the Web as a means of communication, his specialist area being its use as a medium for student/ pupil services and delivery, learning, teaching, and management. John continues to write and publish extensively on the use and exploitation of the information in IT. He sits on a number of review, editorial, and program committees.

* * *

Sue Bennett is a senior lecturer in the Faculty of Education and deputy director of the Centre for Research in Interactive Learning Environments. She teaches within the information technology in education and training program and is the coordinator of international initiatives within this area. Sue has extensive experience in the design, development, and evaluation of multimedia and online instructional materials developed for both university and commercial clients. Her ICT in education research has particular foci on case-based learning strategies and the integration of learning objects within learning designs by K-12 and tertiary teachers.

Paul Brett is the University of Wolverhampton's (UK) coordinator of e-learning and responsible for the implementation of the institution's e-learning strategy. He is also the current chair of the UK HeLF which represents the interests of UK HEIs Heads of e-Learning. He has previously taught in Venezuela and in Dubai. His publications and PhD research focused on the learning benefits of the use of multimedia.

Kin Fai Cheng is a research assistant in the Centre for Learning Enhancement And Research at The Chinese University of Hong Kong. He has a background in psychology and has been working on a number of Web-based education development and evaluation projects. His main duty in the Centre is to facilitate practical aspects of the various projects and ensure smooth operations.

Andrea Chester is a lecturer in psychology at RMIT University, Australia, where she teaches a range of undergraduate psychology courses in social and counselling psychology. She has been developing, presenting, and evaluating online courses for more than 10 years and has an interest in the pedagogical issues surrounding online learning and teaching. Her research has focused on the use of technology for educational and therapeutic use.

Michael Clarke is a composer and developer of software for music. His compositions have been performed in many countries, and he has won international awards for both his music and software. Since 1987, he has been director of the Electroacoustic Music Studios at the University of Huddersfield, UK, where he is now professor of music.

John Cowan has been engaged in educational innovation for 40 years. Originally a structural engineer and designer, when he entered academia he tried to find ways to improve education in his discipline. He harnessed the potential of independence in learning — in respect of pace, approach, content, and assessment. He was appointed to the first UK chair in engineering education, and then moved on to the Open University, first as Scottish director and then as professor of learning development. On his retirement, his degree in social sciences qualified him to join a social sciences course team in designing a new degree, and then in teaching on it, online, until 2003. He is still actively engaged as a consultant and teacher, in contexts where blended learning is a strong feature.

Fiona Darroch is a lecturer in information systems at the University of Southern Queensland (Australia). Her computing career has been spent mainly in industry in the areas of project management, business analysis, and applications development; with a move to academia two years ago. She is currently pursuing a research master's degree.

Particular areas of research interest include the academic-practitioner relationship divide and research relevance; extreme project management; agile system development methodologies; analysis and design methods, and online learning environments. Teaching responsibilities include systems analysis and design, project management, and database design.

Alison Davies is research projects officer in the learning development unit (LDU) at the University of Birmingham (UK) and is responsible for working with and advising LDU project leaders on the design and implementation of evaluation procedures. She is also responsible for disseminating project results within the university and to the wider academic community. Recent research includes blended approaches to learning in physiotherapy, and using problem-based approaches to build student learning communities to encourage peer and independent learning. In addition to supporting LDU project evaluations, Alison has recently been involved with the JISC-funded e-spaces project "How Learning Spaces Are Influencing the Design of Physical Learning Spaces in the Post-16 Sector," and has received a teaching support fellowship to investigate staff and student views and experiences of plagiarism across the University of Birmingham.

Roisin Donnelly has been working for the past six years in the Learning and Teaching Centre in the Dublin Institute of Technology (Republic of Ireland), where she has been involved in designing and delivering continuous professional development opportunities (both short courses and accredited programs) for academic staff in e-learning, and continues to deliver e-learning pedagogy workshops and consultations as part of the Institute's e-learning training program. She has a range of publications to date reflecting her teaching and research interests, including e-learning pedagogy, design, tutoring and evaluation, blended learning, and using the WWW for research. She is continuing her research in higher education through an EdD. Her research specialism is e-learning pedagogy.

Gloria Maria Dunlop has 20 years experience lecturing in higher education with a particular interest in adult and continuing education for healthcare professionals. As a UK registered podiatrist, she has worked closely with a range of healthcare professional in the education sector and in the Scottish National Health Service to develop flexible and accessible distance learning courses that can contribute to lifelong learning and continuing professional development for allied healthcare professionals and nurses. She has a particular interest and five years experience in teaching and designing e-learning opportunities for healthcare professionals using WebCT and has acted as advisor and consultant to the Scottish Executive Health Department and NHS Education for Scotland.

Karen Fill has a BSc in computer and management sciences and an MSc in information systems. She has worked in commercial organizations as a systems analyst and designer. From 1989 to 1994, she was a part-time lecturer in business information systems on a range of undergraduate and management programs at the University of Portsmouth Business School. In 2001, she joined the Centre for Learning & Teaching at the University of

Southampton as a researcher, contributing particularly to projects on the innovative use of technology to support teaching and learning. She has been working on the DialogPLUS project since November 2003.

Andrew Francis lectures in general and biological psychology, coordinates the master of technology in science communication and e-learning at RMIT University, and is actively involved in the development and evaluation of fresh pedagogical models and multimedia for the teaching of psychology. Major projects he has led include the development of an interactive multimedia textbook for the teaching of biological psychology, and of a fully online first-year psychology course in collaboration with Open University Australia and the Australian Broadcasting Corporation.

Julie Hughes is principal lecturer in teaching and learning in the School of Education, University of Wolverhampton. Julie works in teacher education for the post-compulsory sector supporting new teachers and their mentors and in the recently established University CeTL. Julie's teaching and research interests include the development of reflective practices, literacies, and communities using dialogue journals and techniques. Julie's recent work is fascinated with the possibilities of harnessing technology to support the education of critically aware and engaged practitioners. Julie and her student groups are extensively involved with the embedding of the University of Wolverhampton's ePortfolio, pebblePAD as a teaching and learning tool.

Moira Hulme is principal lecturer within the school of education, University of Wolverhampton. She leads the learning technology and pedagogic research cluster at the university and was recently seconded to the Wolverhampton Centre for Excellence in Teaching and Learning (CeTL) as research and innovation coordinator. Previously, Moira was research fellow, Institute of Education, University of Warwick, and lecturer in education, Keele University. In addition to learning technology, her main areas of research interest are education policy, teacher education, and professionalism.

Tim Jackson is a principal lecturer at the London College of Fashion. Tim has developed and works on a number of online courses at the college including a full-time FdA in fashion marketing and a short course in fashion buying, which are run using Blackboard. He has co-published and presented on aspects e-learning at conferences with David Rowsell.

Pat Jefferies is a principal lecturer and university teacher fellow within De Montfort University, Bedford. After spending 9 years in the faculty of computing sciences & engineering, she transferred into the school of education where she is currently chair of the faculty learning & teaching committee as well as being course leader for the PGCE 14-19 provision in applied ICT, applied business, and applied leisure & tourism. Pat's particular research interests are in "blended" learning approaches within a campus-based HE environment. As such, she has been an invited guest speaker at several other universities, has been part of a JISC funded project team, and has gained a wide range of refereed publications.

Martin Jenkins is academic manager of the Centre for Active Learning (CeAL) at the University of Gloucestershire. CeAL will be conducting pedagogic research into active learning, and Martin has a particular interest in the role of learning technology. Prior to this, he was head of learning technology support at the University, responsible for centrally supported e-learning developments. Martin has been actively involved in staff development and student skills support since the late 1980s, as a chartered librarian and latterly as a learning technologist. In 2004, he was awarded a national teaching fellowship.

Christina Keing is a computer officer in the Information Technology Services Centre of The Chinese University of Hong Kong, where she specializes in providing effective IT solutions to enhance teaching, learning, administrative workflow, and knowledge preservation. She planned and implemented the online learning platform for the university and has been involved in major projects in related to e-learning. She has also taught part-time in the advanced postgraduate diploma in education program.

Paul Lam is a research assistant professor in the Centre for Learning Enhancement And Research at The Chinese University of Hong Kong. He has extensive experience in English language teaching at the school-level, and this education experience has been applied in several education development projects in Hong Kong universities. Paul's current focus is on the design, development, and evaluation of Web-assisted teaching and learning.

Lori Lockyer is a senior lecturer in the information technology in education and training program within the faculty of education; head of the School of Medicine's division of educational development; and director of the Digital Media Centre. She has been designing for and teaching within technology-supported learning environments for more than eight years. Lori's research focuses on the use of information and communication technologies in K-12 education; within professional education; and for health education and heath service initiatives. She is particularly interested in technology-supported collaborative learning.

Sarah Maddison is computational astrophysicist at the Centre for Astrophysics & Supercomputing, Swinburne University, Australia. She has a BSc (Hons) in mathematics and a Ph.D. in computational astrophysics, and has held postdoctoral fellowships in the United States and France. Her main astronomical interests are in star and planet formation. As coordinator of Swinburne Astronomy Online, Sarah also conducts educational research to better understand how to enhance the online learning experience for her students. She is particularly interested in the online interaction between instructors and students, as well the effects of gender, primary language, and background experience on students' online learning experience.

Margaret Mazzolini is both deputy head of higher education and director of curriculum development at Swinburne University of Technology in Melbourne, Australia. She manages the curriculum framework project, a curriculum renewal process across all undergraduate programs in Swinburne's Higher Education division. Margaret holds both an honors degree and a PhD in theoretical physics, together with a master's in online education, and has considerable experience in curriculum development at both tertiary and secondary level. Her main educational research interests are currently in the implementation of active learning techniques and the development of appropriate assessment techniques in the online environment. She is especially interested in evaluating the effectiveness of ways in which instructors and students interact through asynchronous online communications.

Colin McCaig, Research Fellow at the Centre for Research and Evaluation at Sheffield Hallam University, graduated as a mature student from the University of Huddersfield (BA Hons 1st class historical and political studies) in 1994 and took a master's in political economy at the University of Sheffield in 1995. He then began doctoral research into the politics of education, submitting *Preparing for Government: Educational Policymaking in the Labour Party* to the University of Sheffield in 1999. He has subsequently developed research interests in further and higher education policy issues, particularly with regard to e-learning and pedagogy, widening participation reform of the post-16 qualification structure.

Carmel McNaught is professor of learning enhancement in the Centre for Learning Enhancement And Research at The Chinese University of Hong Kong. Carmel has had more than 30 years experience in teaching and research in higher education, and has had appointments in eight universities in Australasia and southern Africa, working in the discipline areas of chemistry, science education, second language learning, e-learning, and higher education curriculum and policy matters. Current research interests include evaluation of innovation in higher education, strategies for embedding learning support into the curriculum, and understanding the broader implementation of the use of technology in higher education. She has contributed to more than 220 academic publications.

Sue Morón-García is interested in the way in which technology is used to support teaching and learning, the effect on the teaching and learning facilitated and on those expected to adopt it! This, and the way in which technology use was affected by academics' approach to teaching, formed the basis of her doctoral research at the Institute of Educational Technology, UK Open University. She is currently based in the Engineering Centre for Excellence in Teaching and Learning at Loughborough University and recently worked on a Joint Information Systems Committee project exploring the potential of digital content repositories to facilitate the sharing of teaching and learning materials.

Barbara Newland is a head of educational development services at Bournemouth University with responsibility for developing and implementing the University's e-learning strategy. Prior to this, Barbara was the learning technology team leader at Durham University. Barbara has more than 12 years experience supporting the effective use of e-learning, and in 2005, she was awarded a National Teaching Fellowship. Barbara's current research interests include evaluating the impact and accessibility of virtual learning environments on learning and teaching, and the effective use of personal development planning.

Ciara O'Farrell is an academic developer in the Centre of Academic Practice and Student Learning Trinity College, Dublin, assisting the college in developing a strong and integrated framework for supporting best academic practice and the highest quality of student learning. Ciara holds a PhD in English from University College Dublin, and her most recent publication is a critical biography of Abbey Theatre playwright Louis D'Alton, published by Four Courts Press. Her current educational research and teaching interests focus on writing skills, portfolios, assessment, academic mentoring, and postgraduate research supervision.

Susi Peacock works as a learning technologist with responsibility for the implementation of distance and networked learning across the University College. Her main role is to facilitate staff learning and understanding of flexible learning. Her research interests include change management, learning in and through different contexts, plagiarism, and student learning of clinical skills. She has been involved in external projects including the ELICIT project, JISCinfoNet, and the ISLE project. She is editor of ALT-N and a reviewer for *Nurse Education in Practice*. She teaches "Network Technologies in the Learning Environment" on the MSc in professional education.

Sally Priest completed both her BSc and her PhD at the school of geography at the University of Southampton. Sally's doctoral research examined flood management and responses to flood risk in both the UK and Australia. As well as continuing to research flooding and other areas of environmental management, Sally is employed by the DialogPLUS initiative as a teaching fellow within the School of Geography to design, develop, and embed digital and online resources within undergraduate geographical teaching.

Neil Ringan is the head of eLaB at the University of Bolton where he is responsible for implementing the institutional e-learning strategy and supporting academic departments and staff. Prior to this, he was director of the Learning Innovation Centre at the University of Huddersfield. Neil has been involved in the use of technology-based approaches to learning and teaching since the mid-1980s, initially to support his role as a lecturer in chemistry. He has held a number of roles in educational development, supporting colleagues in areas including peer observation of teaching, portfolio development, assessment, and curriculum design as well as e-learning.

David Rowsell is the senior research fellow based in the IT Research and Development Unit (ITRDU) at the University of the Arts, London. David has been instrumental in the development and teaching of a number of online courses as well as coordinating the implementation of the University's virtual learning environment. David has research interests in e-learning, tools for learning in art and design, and alternative interface technologies. He has published in the areas of aesthetics, art and design theory, the use of digital learning materials, the use of virtual learning environments, and the design of online learning.

Roy Seden is currently quality enhancement manager at Derby University, responsible for implementing both the university learning, teaching, and assessment strategy and the continuing professional development framework. Throughout his career, he has been involved in a wide range of learning and teaching projects funded by the HEFCE (TLTP, FDTL), the HEA/ILTHE and the EC (Lingua, Petra), normally with a strong e-learning component, has served on a number of external committees relating to excellence awards, external examining, and the built environment, and has supported a number of successful national teacher fellow award winners. He has also gained a wide range of published and presented refereed research activities and has fulfilled four PhD supervision and examination roles.

Chris Smith is in the department of psychology at the University of Central Lancashire in Preston, UK, where he is joint director of the learning and literacy research unit. In addition, he is project director for a major project on learning styles, funded by the Higher Education Funding Council for England. His research interests include dyslexia, literacy development in children, the effects of technology on teaching and learning, and individual differences between learners. He is also involved in evaluating of the impact of public sector projects such as Sure Start across north west England.

Kelly Smith is the head of the Technology Enhanced Enterprise Education (TE3) project based in the learning development unit at the University of Birmingham. TE3 provides funding to develop and enhance enterprise education through the use of learning technologies in the 12 partner universities and university colleges of the Mercia Institute of Enterprise. Resources developed with TE3 funds are shared across partners. The latter aspect of TE3 has led to Kelly's involvement with a regional JISC pilot project for distributed e-learning based at University College Worcester investigating electronic repository use. Kelly has worked in higher education for 9 years, first as a lecturer in psychology specializing in teaching statistics and research methods and researching into visual cognition. Kelly then moved into medical education at the University of Birmingham and the University of Oxford, working with subject experts to create and evaluate e-learning resources and advising on best educational practice.

Maria Smith graduated from the University of Sheffield, BA Hons sociology, and is now a research fellow in the Centre for Research and Evaluation at Sheffield Hallam University. Her research interests include inequality, the gender pay gap, and the experience of working and studying within higher education. She runs the diversity and equality research at Sheffield Hallam University, the staff experience survey and is also a member of the Race Equality Academic Policy Development Group. In addition, she is interested in the digital divide and inequitable access to information learning technology in further education for female and less academically inclined learners.

Mark Toleman is an associate professor of information systems at the University of Southern Queensland where he has supervised postgraduate students and taught undergraduate and postgraduate computing subjects to engineers, scientists, and business students for nearly 20 years. He has a PhD in computer science from the University of Queensland and has published more than 80 articles in books, refereed journals, and refereed conference proceedings. He is director of the Electronic Business Advisory and Research Centre (e-BARC) and deputy chair of the University of Southern Queensland's Academic Board. Mark is also a member of the Association for Information Systems, Computer-Human Interaction Special Interest of the Human Factors and Ergonomics Society of Australia, and the International Federation for Information Processing Working Group 13.1.

Index

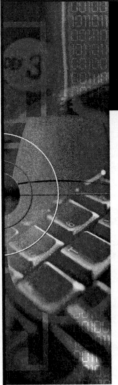